Immortal

The Biography of George Best

DUNCAN HAMILTON

D1324965

WINDMILL BOOKS

Published by Windmill Books 2014

4 6 8 10 9 7 5

Copyright © Duncan Hamilton 2013

Duncan Hamilton has asserted his right under the
Copyright, Designs and Patents Act, 1988, to be identified
as the author of this work.

First published in Great Britain in 2013 by Century

Windmill Books
The Random House Group Limited
20 Vauxhall Bridge Road, London SW1V 2SA

Addresses for companies within The Random House Group Limited can
be found at: www.randomhouse.co.uk/offices.htm

The Random House Group Limited Reg. No. 954009

www.randomhouse.co.uk

A CIP catalogue record for this book
is available from the British Library

ISBN 9780099558583

Typeset in Minion by Palimpsest Books Production Ltd,
Falkirk, Stirlingshire

Printed and bound by Clays Ltd, St Ives PLC

MIX
Paper from
responsible sources
FSC® C018179

Penguin Random House is committed to a sustainable
future for our business, our readers and our planet.
This book is made from Forest Stewardship
Council® certified paper.

To those who saw George Best play.
To those who wish they'd seen him play.
To Belfast. Thanks for your boy.

Contents

Foreword
What Piece of Work is a Man

3 December 2005, Belfast

His coffin, resting on a metal bier, was placed alongside his father's armchair in the L-shaped living room. Private prayers were said over him. He'd spent his childhood in this house and he had always been drawn back here, finding it unchanged. The house represented the only fixed point in his life.

The room was modest but neatly furnished. There were lilac-washed walls, a pale grey carpet and a darker grey sofa, a circular dining table, a rectangular rug of variegated reds spread in front of a wooden, Adams-style fireplace. The brass of its grate gleamed after vigorous polishing. A teak cabinet displayed a few of his schoolboy medals and trophies – miniature cups and wooden shields – and also his full inter-national caps, which he'd given, long ago, to his parents. His two-foot-high, framed photograph – a black and white portrait taken at his professional zenith in 1968 – hung in the corner above the television set. The camera had caught him beautifully – debonair, virile-looking and physically perfect.

Each of the Indian-red brick terraces in Burren Way, his wee street on the Cregagh Estate in East Belfast, looked almost identical when you walked past them: a picture window, a low, trim privet hedge and a creosoted picket gate leading to a concrete path. But the front garden of this house – number 16 – was a shrine to him. It was proof of how one life is capable of touching so many others; and also of the force of his presence in those lives. In the eight days since his death, people he'd never met, names he'd never known, had come like pilgrims on a mission to offer condolences and convey their grief and say thank you for who he had been and what he had done. The emotional connection each demonstrated towards him was visceral and profoundly felt, as though he'd been a member of their family.

There were old men with sad, creased faces, who had followed him in his prime. There were awed boys, born three decades or more after that prime began, who had only heard anecdotes of his mastery from their fathers and grandfathers. There were elderly women, who once had wanted to dote on him like a son. There were the daughters of the 1960s – with grown-up children and also grandchildren of their own nowadays – who, as teenagers, had written love letters to him and pleaded to be his girlfriend. There were young girls clutching a carnation in each hand for him – one red, the other white.

The clipped square of lawn was smothered in hand-delivered garlands, wreaths and heaped sprays of cellophane-wrapped floral tributes. There were football scarves and shirts, too. The crimson silk of his club, Manchester United, and the emerald of his country, Northern Ireland, stood out amid the shock of colours belonging to other teams, among them Celtic and Glasgow Rangers, Arsenal and Spurs, Everton and Liverpool, Linfield and Glentoran. The shirts intertwined as though a truce had been struck between rivals, suspending long-established territorial feuds and putting aside tribal loyalties solely for his sake. Attached to them were scribbled notes and poems on heart-shaped cards, the messages written in Biro or felt tip, the words smudged and stained during a week of frost and sleet and rain. One declared he'd made the world 'a better place'. Another promised that his 'legend' would 'go on'. A third shared Pelé's assessment of him as 'The Greatest Footballer' and an honorary Brazilian. Those who brought them lingered awhile afterwards and looked around them, as if trying to picture him there long ago.

He'd been a football-obsessed lad whose shoes constantly fell apart because he couldn't stop kicking a ball; who slept with that ball next to pinned-up posters from *Charles Buchan's Football Monthly* in the back box-room; and who always preferred to turn right after leaving the house because that way led him to the corner-shop wall, against which he thumped shots in umpteen hours of practice, and also to three and a quarter acres of scruffy greenery, where pretend cup finals were played with sweaters and coats for goalposts. He ran there in his first pair of boots because he liked the sound the studs made against the paving slabs. Every goal he scored was recorded on the leather, written in Blanco with the end of a matchstick. He sold, gave away or misplaced a lot of medals and memorabilia; but he always kept those boots, a reminder of the child he had once been.

He'd pushed the *Belfast Telegraph* through neighbours' letterboxes for a few shillings a week to supplement his pocket money. He'd shred his father's copy after it was read, cutting out the match reports and stories and then fastidiously gluing them into a scrapbook, the thick, rough pages becoming ragged through constant turning. His father took scissors to that newspaper, too. He saved some of the articles it subsequently printed about his son, putting his loose library in one of the bottom drawers of the same living-room cabinet where the trophies were shown off. The *Telegraph* clippings, foxed, dust-dry and stiff at the edges with age, tell his early story: the waif who went across the water at 15; the teenager of supreme talent who transfixed and bewitched whoever saw him. The memorial edition of the *Telegraph* produced described him as his country's 'most famous son' and the splash head-line – big, white capitals on a lamp-black background – read:

GOD BLESS YOU

On a wintry Saturday some of the foulest elements Mother Nature could muster were in collaboration, as if conspiring together to make sure Belfast was dressed appropriately in mourning for him. There was low, mottled cloud, which refused to break, above a thin fog that rested on the low peaks of the grassy hills in the middle distance, and a strong wind blew rain across the high-rise tenements and the blue-tiled roofs of the back-to-backs. The pouring rain gave a black glaze to the morning. The stacked clouds cast everything in a diffuse half-light. The whip of the wind bowed the leafless tops of spindly trees into semi-arches.

Those lining the sodden streets to pay their respects fought against the damp and the shivering cold. Umbrellas were put up. Caps and hats and hoods were put on. Some had camped overnight. Others arrived with the dawn. There were 5,000 huddled on the pavements connecting Burren Way to North Bank. There were tens of thousands more – 20 to 30 deep in places – on the Cregagh Road, the Upper Knockbreda Road, the Upper Newtownards Road and the Knock Road. There were 17,000 more, walking through the tall, urn-topped pillars of Stormont's iron gates and trampling between the red-twigged limes and over the manicured rise of its grounds to queue beside the Royal Mile of Prince of Wales Avenue, a plumb-straight strip of tarmac that led to 60 wide steps and the symmetrical Georgian splendour of the Parliament building with its carved pediment and balcony and six Ionic columns of white Portland Stone. Hymns and hallelujah eulogies awaited him inside the Central Hall, where the tallow gleam of chandeliers illuminated the gold and walnut-coloured marble.

In a country blighted by the segregation of The Troubles, he had been a unifying presence. Irrespective of where you prayed on Sunday, you were proud of him; and prouder still to say he was your countryman because he had brought some small relief from the barbed wire and the barricades and the checkpoints. He was resolutely non-political. Sectarianism and discrimination were alien and abhorrent to him. He had never asked – and never cared – whether you were Catholic or Protestant. So every flag in the city was at half-mast; and everywhere there was a feeling of wrenching loss and regret, tears blinked back or wiped away, and a palpable sense that his death – at only 59 years old – had meaning.

The mourners had a need to celebrate and to explain his magnetic appeal to one another, each preaching to the already converted. Stories were swapped between strangers, who found companionship and comfort in nostalgic conversation. No matter that it was almost 31 years since he'd last appeared in the pre-Premiership First Division. The matches discussed were recalled on the basis of what he contributed to them. What memory preserved of him was so luminous – as though he was floodlit – that everyone else faded into silhouette. Team-mates, such as Denis Law and Bobby Charlton, existed purely to pass the ball to him. The opposition was there only so he could torment them.

On the genealogic map of British football, in which the aristocracy is determined through talent and performance, the blue-bloods are prolific goalscorers such as Dixie Dean and Tommy Lawton, wing wizards like Tom Finney and Stanley Matthews and his own dashing contemporaries, among them Bobby Moore and Jimmy Greaves. But no footballer imposed himself so completely on to the romantic imagination as he had done. No footballer was so emblematic – and probably never will be again – of the era during which he flourished. And, as though able to override the rules of physics to find infinite space in a finite range, no footballer had so joyously enlivened the senses. To witness some of the wondrous things he could do was sometimes to disbelieve the evidence of your own eyes.

The capsule description of him was 'genius' – a statement which is accurate but also inadequate. For its definition in the *Shorter Oxford English Dictionary* – 'extraordinary, imaginative, creative or inventive' – doesn't come close to reflecting his mesmerising individualism or his singular approach. The term anyway has been devalued through repetition, undeservedly anointing players who alongside him seemed averagely modest.

Genius?

He was much more than that. For five years, from the beginning of 1966 to the end of 1970, he was comprehensively better than the rest – the most accomplished player on God's earth.

The lucky ones, who had seen him from the cramped terraces of Old Trafford and Windsor Park, boasted of the fact and sympathised with those who, through the unfortunate circumstance of not being born soon enough, were deprived of the privilege and had only glimpsed him second-hand on grainy monochrome or early colour film.

They spoke of a variety of treasured goals scored from near-impossible angles or spun out of the least promising thread – dinks as gentle as a caress and shots of rippling power. They spoke reverentially of skills that were supernatural and which stirred the spirit: gloriously precocious, labyrinthine runs that began on the half-way line and increased in pace the further he travelled. They spoke of poise and balletic balance, classified as being otherworldly. They spoke also of a fabulous tensile strength that enabled his willowy body to survive challenges that, if committed outside the marked perimeter of a football field, would have counted as common assault or grievous bodily harm. He was the complete player: sublimely two-footed, willing to tackle like a roughhouse centre-half, unafraid of competing in the air and the possessor of superb peripheral vision, which allowed him to see the scene ahead panoramically.

Oh, he was a cheeky bugger, too.

He approached each game as if it was a new adventure and he strutted through it, his demeanour and posture conveying the superiority he saw no need to hide or deny. Showmanship and improvisation were the tenets of his faith and he liked what he always called 'party pieces'. He'd beckon a defender towards him with both hands, like the matador taunting the bull to charge, and then pirouette past him with sinewy athleticism. He'd whip off one of his boots, gripping it in his hand, before pushing a pass away in his stockinged feet, a piece of tomfoolery designed to crush his opponent psychologically. In one game – bored and irritable – he'd peeled off his shirt and spun it provocatively above his head, like a cowboy's lasso. Having invited friends to a game, which was meandering dully, he decided to put his embossed, if unconventional, seal on the whole afternoon. Accepting a throw from the goalkeeper, he took it to the touchline, below which his guests occupied prime seats in the stand. He waved at them before standing on the ball, waiting to be tackled. A trio of defenders converged on him simultaneously. What followed was cleverer than a conjuring trick. He smartly struck three consecutive wall passes off their legs, lifted the ball over them and ran around to regain it. He then turned, the ball still under his control, and gave his friends a bow. The escapologist was free.

He'd beat a man twice – even when it wasn't necessary – because doing so came naturally to him and also for the sheer delight he took in it. After scoring, he usually acknowledged the feat with nothing more than a raised hand, as if to do anything overly ostentatious risked detracting from the glory of the goal itself. He was able to keep possession almost as long as he wished or willed it. He did all this on pitches that were broken and pulverised, and in front of crowds who were corralled like cattle beneath the corrugated iron of ramshackle-looking stands.

He was one of the most prominent figures of the 1960s – embedded into it and seminally significant in shaping its look and culture and mood. Here was a footballer treated like a pop icon and a pin-up, a fashion model and a sex symbol, always seductively charismatic. He represented the allure of youth, the radicalism of new styles and breezy, libertine attitudes – a working-class bachelor in a working-class sport, worshipped especially by anyone who made a living from the grease of everyday labour. It was the perfect conjunction of a personality to a period. He lived out the fantasies of others. In play-grounds and on parks every schoolboy of the 60s and early 70s visu-alised himself as him. In offices and on factory floors every man envied him because every woman adored him. Some women went to football matches *only* because he played in them. You'd hear them scream whenever he got the ball. Photographers complained he was too nippy for them. He slid in and then out of focus too quickly. Striving to take the definitive image of him in action always proved frustrating. The most successful pictures were posed and studio-lit. He was Hollywood-gorgeous and superbly groomed – a coiffured fringe and long sideburns, broodingly dark eyes, the line of the cheeks and jaw exquisitely sculptured, a cleft in his chin. If anyone could be said to be over-endowed with beauty, it was him. He was so brightly different from any other man in a room that in his company the merely good-looking seemed ordinarily plain.

Those wanting fame – a dubious privilege anyway – can waste half a lifetime or more in a futile hunt for it. Fame came to him instantly; he didn't have to go searching for it. This, moreover, was true fame; not the sort of here-today, gone-tomorrow popularity or spurious tabloid or TV celebrity – the 15 minutes Warhol once predicted for all of us. His fame was attained through his unique abilities and it endured because of them, too. Even those with no interest in football recognised him. He appeared on the front of music magazines and beneath the mastheads of women's weeklies and the Sunday supplements. He was hired to sell breakfast cereal and chewing gum, after-shave and hairspray, clothes and sunglasses. There were posters and greetings cards, stickers and jigsaws, pennants and colouring books, which became collector's items. He could sign a thousand autographs a day and smile for twice as many photographs. At one stage he received up to 10,500 letters a week. He broke into the gossip columns, the coverage tipping into voyeurism and prurience, and the most frivolous or trivial aspects of his world were written about, commented upon and analysed.

Being fêted also meant being pursued. 'If I could change one thing, just once in a while, it would be my face,' he'd said. He could go nowhere, and do nothing, anonymously. And whatever he did was always someone else's business. His degree of super-stardom – intense and suffocating – made him a fugitive and foreshortened his career because he couldn't cope with its perpetual demands. A combination of naïvety, innocence and ignorance meant that no one saw that his social whirl was actually a maelstrom in which, miserably trapped, release was impossible. The damage was done before anyone properly realised what was happening to him or how bad things would get in the future.

The conundrum for him was that football came easily; life, less so. The strain of being who he was – and living up to preconceptions – left him at various stages afraid, confused, angry, profligate and paranoid. What he eventually went through as a consequence was a nervous breakdown.

'What piece of work is a man,' wrote Shakespeare. In his case it was especially true. For he was not one man but several. That fact was reflected in his obituaries, which alluded to his sensitive and enigmatic nature and the contradictions within him. He worked hard to conceal himself from inquisitors, revealing only what he wanted them to know. The rest was shut up, locked away, out of reach even to those closest to him. To some he was a maze with an unreachable centre. In the paradigm of the knotted-up, troubled artist others detected a depressive and repressive streak, a poet's tendency towards introspection and melancholia, and a well of loneliness, too. It was occasionally traceable in a pained glance when few were looking.

The ostensible extrovert was really an introvert underneath. The apparently brazen self-confidence was a front. Here was someone who could be as insecure as an infant. He was flashy on the field, craving big crowds, yet withdrawn off it, glad to be with a minuscule group of friends he trusted or in self-imposed solitary confinement. He was ultra-competitive to an almost compulsive, excessively fixated degree and yet he abandoned his career before attaining his peak because finishing second disturbed him so much and coming third or lower was intolerable. He recoiled from showdowns of any sort – initially agreeing with any advice or instruction given to him to avoid arguments – and yet he vexed and tested the patience of his managers and agents by saying one thing and then intractably doing the opposite, which made confrontation with them inevitable. He was scared of rejection and yet he set himself challenges like dares – off and on the pitch – in which he risked experiencing it.

Sometimes he acted as if he was all physical talent and no intellect. It wasn't the case. His IQ was close to 150 – high enough to qualify for membership of Mensa. He duelled with the cryptic crossword compilers of The Times and the Daily Telegraph. He trawled encyclopaedias endlessly for scraps of recondite information to make him unbeatable in general knowledge quizzes. One vignette shows something of a personality that was near monomaniacal in the need to come out on top. Once, after a debate during lunch in The Ivy restaurant over the source of the Niger, he vanished for almost an hour before reappearing with a textbook in his hand. He'd taken a taxi to his London flat to retrieve it from the shelf. He wanted to have the final, I-told-you-so word in the argument, which he couldn't bear to lose. He painted more than adequately, too – still lives and abstracts in watercolour and oil from his cherished Daler Rowney box and easel.

He'd developed a bookish habit, and what he chose revealed an investigative mind. His favourite author was Oscar Wilde and time and again he read and re-read a slim hardback of his collected wit and wisdom until he could quote from it verbatim. Among the very last books he read – annotating or folding back the pages – were *Man's Search for Meaning*, Viktor Frankl's experiences as a concentration camp survivor of Auschwitz and elsewhere, and the Dalai Lama's *Ancient World, Modern World*. The most poignant title, which he kept close by, was the fourth edition of what is commonly called 'The Big Book': *Alcoholics' Anonymous: The Story of How Many Thousands of Men and Women Have Recovered from Alcoholism.*

A familiar three-line verse explains why his final four decades became a chaotic soap opera performed in daily episodes in the public domain, where it ceased to belong to him alone.

> First, a man takes a drink
> Then the drink takes a drink
> And then the drink takes the man

The drink had taken him. 'When you take your first drink no one knows where it will lead,' he'd said. This led him into miscreancy and all sorts of stupidities. Shortly before he died he appeared in a television documentary. He was rheumy-eyed, and dishevelled-looking in a blue-striped shirt and shorts, a New York Yankees baseball cap askew on his head, a pair of gold-rimmed spectacles sliding down his nose. He moved with the slowest circumspection and the punctuations in the interview he gave were weary sighs or exhausted pauses. 'At seven in the morning I am gasping for a drink,' he admitted. When death came its causes were listed as pneumonia and septicaemia, multiple organ failure, gastrointestinal bleeding and immunosuppression. Each was as a consequence of drinking.

Alcohol robbed him of all he had, stealing things one by one: his football gifts and his fantastic stamina, his looks and his last breaths. The prodigious amount he drank, and continued to drink, was inexplicable only to those who don't understand that alcohol is a poisonous drug for the alcoholic; and that alcoholism is a clinical illness.

We're not as ignorant about it as we used to be when he began exhibiting its symptoms. Society is more sympathetic and understanding towards alcoholics and their noonday and midnight demon. We don't think of them – as so many did of him – as irresponsible and worthless recidivists who don't care about their self-destruction or are too selfish or ignorant to say no to a drink. We've tempered our language, too, generally expunging those street slang synonyms – such as alchy and wino, swillpot and soak, lush and souse – that sound as if the alcoholic is being completely dismissed as a human being and deserves to be summed up by a wisecracking insult. The problem drinker isn't regularly played for cheap belly laughs any more in television comedies. We've become too aware of the wreckage alcoholism leaves behind to ridicule those who wrestle with it; and we've come to understand the reasons why people drink.

In the beginning he drank to combat shyness. He then drank to alleviate the pressure of all the clamouring attention he got. He later drank to assuage the isolation and separateness that attention paradoxically brought him. As the fortunes of the one club that meant everything to him began changing for the worse, he drank because of clinical depression. And, in the end, he drank to forget. Nothing could ever deter him from drinking; at least not for long. Not several public, hands-up concessions that he needed help. Not counselling or any pharmaceutical remedies, which included sewing anti-abuse tablets into his stomach. Not the death of his mother from alcohol-related illnesses.

Not two marriages; nor the divorces that ended them. Not the birth of his son. Not embarrassing himself on early-evening, live television. Not bankruptcy or prison. Not the obligation to auction off some of the medals and statuettes and honours he'd won. Not cirrhosis and a liver transplant. Not the scorn and fury aroused at the sight of him drinking again shortly after it. Not even the knowledge that he couldn't live much longer. To survive so long had been a kind of success, he'd said.

It is a human proclivity to find a culprit for every major setback. Some think they are never responsible for their own misfortunes. He accepted instead the hurt his drinking had inflicted on others – especially those he had loved and who had loved him in return – and he apologised for it. It's said only whoever makes the voyage can truly speak about it. When he described the convulsing course of his own, he readily conceded that he'd helped lick the labels that were stuck to him. He didn't complain. He didn't resort to how-wronged-I've-been, pious self-pity. He blamed no one but himself for his upsets and execrable mistakes. He saw the 60s like a party that had been unable to start without him. Life is never long enough for anyone. But he was grateful for what he'd had; what he called the 'three to six lifetimes' joyously packed into his landmark seasons. The years he'd had delivered all he'd ever asked for – and much extra besides. Old age seemed to him like a shipwreck anyway. He didn't want to be elderly, and he never saw himself becoming so, which is partly why he lived the way he did. Death didn't scare him.

In his dwindling days he'd allowed a photograph to be published in the *News of the World*. The bright lights of a hospital ward showed the details of his ravaged face; every crack and fissure had his autobiography written on it. By then he'd been bed-ridden for nearly two months, his system slowly collapsing. He'd complained of flu-like symptoms and then contracted a severe lung infection, which spread to his kidneys. His flesh melted away. He dropped from 12 stone to scarcely six. He looked ten years older than the date on his birth certificate. His breathing was shallow, like a baby's in its cot. His complexion was a dirty yellow. His lips were drawn down and his eyes, which stared into the lens, were pitted and dewy, the sockets rimmed red. His beard was white-grey and his thinning hair, swept back, revealed a high, heavily lined forehead. He was propped on plumped up pillows in London's Cromwell Hospital, swathed in plastic tubes and pipes. Already, he was being kept alive by the softly whirling machinery around him, his organs weakening beneath their cage of bone. He'd taken so much medication that none was suitable for transplant. There was a catheter attached to his neck, the veins as prominent as the patterns in marble. Another tube was inserted into his nasal passage. Red-black marks indicated bleeding into the skin. The photograph of his diseased body was his way of dissuading others from allowing a dependency on drink to claim them, too. 'Don't Die Like Me' was the instruction alongside it. He was unable to articulate the plea because, heavily sedated, he could barely speak.

He'd been condemned and meanly vilified for his reliance on alcohol. His story was presented as a morality play about what happens if you sin against your abundant gift and allow it to wither and waste. No compassion – or at least not much – was extended to him as his health degenerated.

Only as he lay dying was he reappraised properly; and what death brought was rehabilitation. His flaws and fallibilities were forgiven, his compulsion to drink comprehended at last. There was a belated appreciation that alcoholics don't want to be alcoholics; and that, like him, the alcoholic is a participant in their own self-harm and destruction essentially because of an addictive personality rather than through arrogance or wanton selfishness. He was seen as a victim rather than a villain.

The fascination and fertile hold his career had on those who'd seen its absolute pomp was also strong enough to obliterate the final, harrowing images of debilitating illness from the mind. He'd thought of himself as ageless – 'I still think I'm twenty-five,' he said at 55 – and this is how he appeared to everyone who lined the route of his cortège. The mourners saw him during his years of plenty. His face was unscored. His hair was luxuriant. His diminutive figure was zigzagging down the wing.

They remembered the frisson of anticipation he generated before a game and the pleasure he gave during it. They remembered his art as incarnational and inspirational. They remembered him foremost as the most extraordinary footballer, a man with a ball rather than a bottle, whose like hadn't been seen before – or since – and also as someone who transcended his sport.

The funeral he was given – akin to a state ceremonial – reflected the profound impact he had made. There was the thrum of helicopter rotors. There were outriders in fluorescent bibs, the headlight of each motorcycle burning through the murk. There was the coffin draped in the emerald flag with huge sprays of lilies and carnations on top of it – and more flowers thrown under-arm from the kerbside, dispatched as tenderly as a blown kiss and sliding across the waxed bonnet of the hearse. There were scarves, also thrown, that become tangled in the wipers. There was applause – hard and spontaneous, its echo heard around the city. There were huge screens showing clips of his goals. There was the unmistakable lilt of his voice replayed through loudspeakers.

And then there was silence, broken only by a lone, kilted piper's lament, the notes gliding across the wet air.

This is how George Best came home. This is how Belfast said goodbye to its boy.

PART ONE

Making Saturday Different from Before

1

To Those We Love at Home

He was a stocky, hardy-looking figure with hunched shoulders and he saw no need to be sartorially elegant; for he worked outdoors and his wardrobe never mattered to him. Clothes didn't maketh this man.

He almost always dressed the same way: a woollen coat with wide lapels, a chequered sports jacket and a pair of dark nylon trousers in winter; grey flannels, a shabby V-neck sweater and an open-necked white shirt in summer. His concession to formality was a sober tie with a penny piece Windsor knot. His craggy face was distinguished by the prominent grooves that spread either side of thin lips. Bristly, closely cropped white hair receded almost to the crown, revealing the age lines on his forehead. His dark eyes were hooded by thick brows in need of trimming. He smoked constantly. Nicotine stained his fingers and gave him a hacking cough. But everyone who had a voice in Northern Irish football recognised Bob Bishop – or 'The Bishop' as he was affectionately called – and Sherlock Holmes could have deduced his profession in a nanosecond. What gave him away were the smears of white touchline lime on his black shoes, and the newspaper, always folded to the sports pages, poking out of his slanted pocket.

No one – not even Bishop himself – was able to calculate the number of matches he'd seen or the mileage he'd clocked up criss-crossing the country. He didn't drive and couldn't have afforded a car anyway. So he walked to games or relied on buses, trains and – on special occasions only – taxis. But, through strategic planning and the cadging of lifts, he'd catch as many as three or four matches in a day; and he worked six days a week for Manchester United, seldom taking a holiday. Even on Sundays, after reading the previous night's sports editions again and checking the reports in that morning's newspapers, he would saunter off to watch boys kicking a ball around on the street or a patch of parkland. 'You never know where or when you might come across someone precious,' he'd say, comparing his job as a scout to a prospector's hopeful searching for gold.

United instructed its scouts to stay away from professional, semi-professional and senior amateur games. The stipulation from Old Trafford was: 'Find a thirteen, fourteen or fifteen-year-old boy – and then let our coaches do the rest.' Bishop covered the far corners of Northern Ireland for United – from schools and youth club competitions to Boys' Brigade matches and the amateur leagues. Regularly he got soaked. He froze in the bitter cold. Standing on the sidelines of communal or council pitches that offered no cover, he was blown about by vicious gales. It was unglamorous, frustrating and frequently futile work. It was also done out of devotion to the game rather than for financial gain. United recruited Bishop, born as the 20th century began, in 1950 and paid him £2 per week, plus travel expenses and a paltry meal allowance of two shillings. The club installed and settled the monthly rental of a black Bakelite telephone with a rotary dial. Bishop was a riveter in Belfast's shipyards, where the screech of cutting metal, the clank of hammers and the thump of machinery left him partially deaf. 'You had to shout sometimes to make him hear you,' said one of his friends. He managed a shipyard side and organised teams based around Boyland Youth Club, close to where he lived in a terraced house on Bloomdale Street in the east of the city. Boyland played as many as five or six sides over a weekend. Boys would crowd into the club on a Friday night waiting for Bishop to write his selections on a row of rectangular chalkboards, which were raised and lowered on chains from the ceiling. If a boy had been picked, but hadn't turned up to find out, Bishop would rub off his name with a cloth. It could take the absentee a month and a half to reclaim his place.

In 1960 Bishop was promoted to his role as United's head scout in Northern Ireland, following the death of his predecessor. United were especially impressed with two aspects of him. One was personal. He was a decent, principled fellow who wouldn't back-slide or shirk. He was punctual and reliable. As a confirmed bachelor – he lived with his sister who didn't like football – Bishop was only ever going to be wed to the game. His other interests were a blue budgerigar, which he allowed to fly around the living room and sit on his shoulder as he read, and black and white collie dogs. Another attraction for United was practical. He already had a web of contacts in the palm-sized black book in which he jotted down his observations on players. Bishop had never played professionally – nor had he come close to doing so – but he knew a potential pro as soon as he saw one and quickly vindicated United's faith in him. He'd already sent them Jackie Scott, an outside-forward who was given his First Division debut, aged 19, in 1952 and would go on to make two World Cup appearances for Northern Ireland during the 1958 finals in Sweden.

Football consumed Bishop's every waking hour. From the next, modest game, wherever it took place, might feasibly emerge tomorrow's star and he dare not miss him. To emphasise his commitment, he turned his weekend bolthole into a training camp. Well before the Second World War, Bishop's preference for clean, country air had taken him to Helen's Bay on the north coast of County Down. For five shillings a week he took over the tenancy of a ramshackle, one-room cottage from three men, each of them blind, who had grown weary of the rustic life. Bishop called it 'The Manse'. Its walls were rough stone. The nearest public transport was a mile away, partly reached along a cart-track. There was no electricity, which meant this rural idyll – Bishop's escape from the noise of the shipyards – was lit by oil-lamps. Water was drawn from a nearby well. He kept warm by chopping wood and tossing it on to a blackened, open fire over which a bulbous cooking pot also boiled and spat. Compensation for the loss of home comforts was the solitude the place provided. Here he thought and read and drank strong tea the colour of riding boots.

The cottage was still rudimentary when he began taking promising footballers there for coaching. Bishop moved in bunk beds and persuaded a local farmer to allow him to use one of his fields, which he christened 'Wembley Stadium'. Those who went there played beach football, bathed in the sea and gathered sticks and pieces of drift to burn. The cottage gave Bishop an edge in the competitive world in which he found himself. Most of the youngsters came from some of the roughest areas of Belfast and were raised within working-class families that were either hard-scrabble poor or hovering on or below the poverty line. Some had never seen the sea before Bishop introduced them to it. For them a trip to Helen's Bay – though less than ten miles from Belfast – counted as a far-away exotic holiday; even if, as so often happened, some had to sleep on the dusty floor either because of overcrowding or because one of Bishop's dogs decided to claim a bed and refused to budge from it.

He was taciturn – proving the adage that men of few words are the best men – and could be an uncompromisingly stiff and ruthless task-master. 'Get up,' he'd say to any player he thought had crumpled too easily in a tackle. 'If your leg is broken, you'll fall down again.' Though Bishop looked gruff, and could speak gruffly, he was kind-hearted and generous. He'd provide kit and boots and avuncular advice, seeking out and offering solace to those trialists who heard United say 'Thank you for coming and goodbye.' Bishop, a Protestant who didn't discriminate against Catholics, also won over parents who saw integrity in his plain-speaking.

He had a gift for spotting the gifted. Other scouts tried to find out where he was going, or where he'd just been. Communication between them during some of the low-grade games Bishop attended comprised nods or glances. No one wanted to give anything away. Bishop would be studied to see if that inscrutable poker face revealed which players interested him. Outwardly Bishop betrayed no emotion. Inwardly he was logging everything in front of him, filing it mentally into plus and minus columns. It seldom took him long to decide whether someone was good enough for United. Bishop knew if a player possessed what he always referred to enigmatically as 'It'. He regularly tried kidology on his competitors, over-praising a player who in reality he didn't rate and under-praising his genuine target.

Bishop's talent was an ability to see what his rivals couldn't. He looked at the boy and saw him as a man – the player he *would* become once his faults were eradicated.

On this basis he identified George Best.

Elaborate myths grew around George Best. The first is that Bob Bishop was oblivious to his existence before being browbeaten into arranging a trial game specifically on his behalf. It is nonsense. If *anyone* kicked a ball in Belfast, Bishop knew about him. The second is the eight-word wire he's said to have sent to Matt Busby: 'I think I have found you a genius.' Those who knew Bishop are sceptical, saying he would never have composed such a presumptuously bold telegram; he didn't show off or grandstand like that. Nor did he deal with Busby directly anyway. Bishop, a stickler for procedure and protocol, filed all his reports to Old Trafford's chief scout, Joe Armstrong. To go directly to Busby would have undermined his boss.

What's true – a fact that seems preposterous to us now – is that a queue of Bishop's competitors checked out Best at Cregagh Boys Club and concluded he was too puny to be taken on. Northern Ireland's schoolboy selectors didn't rate him either. He was 5ft 3in tall. He weighed 7st 7lb. His ribs and vertebrae poked prominently from sallow skin. His arms and legs were as thin as bamboo. Best felt ashamed of his physique. In gym classes he was given dispensation to wear a vest, enabling him to hide his skeletal appearance. He thought of his body as 'a disaster area' and added: 'There was more fat on a chip.' So the scouts conspicuously came and went again – from Glentoran, one of the clubs Best then supported, and also from Wolverhampton Wanderers, another he favoured because of the vivid gold of their shirts. 'There was always someone from the Irish and big English clubs at the games,' said Best, thinking of Spurs and Chelsea and also of Burnley, who were the League champions of 1960. Even Manchester City passed on the chance to snap up Best before the neighbours did.

He was a matchstick boy, who looked as if he would break easily – until someone gave him a ball. His domination of games for Cregagh, where he set up goals and scored them, was transparent.

Cregagh changed in a storeroom below a house. There was one rotting wooden door and no windows. The seating was uneven grey planks from which splinters regularly spiked someone on the thigh or the backside. Nails were driven into the concrete wall and used as clothes hooks. The pitch was soft and rutted, and Best said that a metal pail of cold water was available to 'take off the top layer of muck' after matches. It didn't matter. 'As we went off to our own games we imagined we were living the life of the big-time stars,' he added. The team was coached by Hugh 'Bud' McFarlane, a thinnish, balding man who, like Bishop, found a life-long bride in football. At Glentoran, he graduated from fourth to second team trainer and had boundless faith in Best. He badgered scouts to watch him. He wrote to clubs extolling his virtues. He told everyone that Best would grow and prosper. McFarlane's message was: forget what he looks like and concentrate on what he does. Best said fondly of him: 'He never stopped telling me that, despite my size, I'd make the grade one day.' Bishop heard McFarlane consistently lament his lack of success in converting the sceptics and so knew there was no urgency in signing him.

Best's Cregagh Boys Club versus Bishop's Boyland Youth Club in April 1961 wasn't a marquee match. The primary purpose of staging it was to fill what would otherwise have been a blank day for both of them. The secondary one was to allow Bishop to see Best, still three weeks short of his 15th birthday, take on opponents who were nearly 18. Best neither knew Bishop nor had an inkling of what he did. To Best he was only another old gent in a coat and cap. He claimed two goals on a clear, chilly afternoon. The second of them saw him cut in from wide on the left, swerve around three challenges and play a one-two before a low, angled shot grazed the post on its way in. Best could never remember whether Cregagh had won 4–1 or 4–2. He did recall, however, that McFarlane was uncommonly cheerful about it afterwards. In his team talk to Boyland, Bishop had spoken about the 'wee lad up front' and given explicit orders not to be charitable, a free invitation to use force to constrain him. 'No one was quick enough to get close to him in the first half,' said Bishop. 'In the second he jumped over most of the tackles.'

Bishop knew the supplementary questions Manchester United would ask him about Best. Busby was devoted to hearth and home. Filial ties were paramount to him and he wanted them to be similarly paramount for his players. Busby, via Armstrong, would expect to be told a lot of the things that Dickens took pages to explain about David Copperfield – his background and character as well as his parents' attitudes and lifestyle. Did he come from a close-knit and supportive family? Were the Bests hard-working and clean-living? Was his upbringing stable?

Busby would ask because he believed good parenting raised good players. 'If a boy's brought up properly, you only have to teach him about football,' he'd say. Bishop gathered the intelligence he needed from McFarlane and liked what he heard. The father, Dickie, was then 42 and worked as an iron-turner in the shipyards. He'd played amateur football, predominantly as a left-back, until he was 37 and hadn't been afraid to use his studs. The sporting gene, however, belonged to his mother, Ann, nearing 40. She was lady-like, sweetly polite, pristinely attired and still attractively raven-haired and dark-eyed; Best, unquestionably, inherited his looks from her. She'd been a hockey player of international promise, a standard that she would have attained if Hitler hadn't rearranged the fixture list, the war years wiping out the early blossom of her career. She'd done an assortment of work – from packing cigarettes and ice-cream to selling fish and chips. She was a disciplined and assiduous worker, who expected the same of her children. The couple met at a dance in 1939 and married in 1945. George was born in May 1946. He had two sisters: Carol, born in 1947, and Barbara, born in 1952 (another three siblings would subsequently follow – twin sisters, Julie and Grace, in 1963, and a brother, Ian, in 1966). The Bests were Free Presbyterian church-goers, friendly and conscientious, and the neighbourhood thought well of them. The home, scrupulously swept and polished, reflected the Bests' pride in themselves and Ann's industry as a housewife. The front step – a matter of pride among matriarchs – was washed down, scrubbed and then scrubbed again. The net curtains were snow white. The wooden floor had a mirror sheen achieved through elbow grease. When Ann wasn't at work, she was working at home – baking pies or apple tarts – or sewing and knitting, the soft, quick click-click of the needles heard around the house.

Best was named after his maternal grandfather, George Withers, who had his own pew in church and was the spiritual head of the family. Because of him Best went to Sunday school regularly, sometimes attending both morning and evening services. The man Best called 'my first hero' was silver-haired and wore dark spectacles. Best thought he was 'worldly in his own way' and radiated 'a special presence' whenever he entered a room.

Bishop also learned about Best as a promising academic pupil. He'd passed his 11-plus examination and earned a scholarship to the rugby-playing Grosvenor High School. On his first day – and during his first lesson, too – Best misunderstood the procedure during an alphabetical roll call of new pupils, wrongly believing the gowned master already knew he was sitting at his desk. After failing to respond to his name, he found the teacher looming angrily over him. 'He came down with a great whack on top of the desk and gave out an even louder cry of "Best" that terrified me,' he said. 'When I meekly announced myself he bawled me out for not having a tongue in my head.' Being humiliated, like the village idiot, was the beginning of a tormenting, bitter period for Best. Each term was akin to purgatory for him. He said his negative feelings towards the institution and the staff 'became almost pathological'. He felt out of place and friendless because, he added, 'none of my pals from the estate had gone there'. Best feigned sickness, buying packets of wine gums and only sucking the red sweets until his throat looked scarlet-sore and he could pretend to have tonsillitis. A doctor, believing the crude ruse, had Best's tonsils removed. His half-term reports were depressing, concluding either tacitly or explicitly that he 'must try harder'. But Best didn't want to try harder. He wanted to go to the local secondary modern, Lisnasharragh. 'They played football and it was close to home,' he said. His parents relented, seeing no sense in prolonging his misery.

In Dickie and Ann, Bishop saw a husband and wife prepared to put themselves second. The father tended not to watch his son play for Cregagh only because he didn't want to unsettle him. The mother made Oxo and cut oranges into slices for the half-time refreshments. She took her turn to wash the team's green jerseys, scrubbing the thick material by hand and then reaching for the ribbed washboard. Bishop was able to put another tick against Best's name because of his polite demeanour. He'd been taught manners and to show respect towards his elders and betters. Bishop likened him to 'Little Lord Fauntleroy'. He had one more piece of homework to do. Wanting to see whether Best could mix socially, and needing to get to know him better, Bishop invited his prodigy to the Helen's Bay cottage. 'We talked football constantly . . . until about three o'clock in the morning,' said Best. 'It was as though we were being groomed into the ways of Bob's own football thinking.' Bishop insisted on a pre-breakfast run for his footballers; Best thought it would be a half a mile jog-trot. At dawn, hearing the farmers' cockerels crow, he was roused for an exhausting cross-country chase that seemed like a marathon to him. He never forgot how Bishop 'ran us until we nearly dropped', and how the exertion left him 'sore and stiff' and limping. Bishop had seen enough. Within 48 hours, he filled in a preliminary signing-on form for Best, which he folded and tucked into the inside of his jacket pocket. 'I went to his house,' he said 'but he wasn't there. It was pitch dark outside. I could hear a ball being kicked somewhere, so I followed the noise.' Bishop found Best and walked him back to Burren Way, where the contract was agreed unhesitatingly. He then gave him his standard speech: 'I've got you to Old Trafford,' he said. 'But I can't keep you there.'

A plaque hung on the wall of the Bests' living room, its verse homily apt for its fortune-seeker.

> *However far we wander*
> *Wherever we may roam*
> *Our thoughts will be turned*
> *To those we love at home*

The sentiment contained in the final two lines was about to resonate with Best like never before.

There are two ways of assessing what George Best endured to get to Old Trafford and the way in which he was treated on his arrival. Neither is complimentary about Manchester United, the club emerging as either insensitive or bone-headed and also entirely responsible for one of the most famous false starts to a footballer's career.

As the crow flies, less than 250 miles separates Belfast from Manchester. To Best, who had never been further than Bangor, the town four miles to the east of Bob Bishop's cottage, the place seemed as remote as the moon. 'And I could see the moon from my bedroom window,' he said. He thought of himself then as 'shy but not stupid' and 'streetwise'. But, emphasising his innocence, Best could never summon the courage to protest if a shopkeeper gave him the incorrect change and he didn't like talking to strangers. He'd been sheltered in Burren Way. His mother had prepared most holidays and high days before – cutting sandwiches, polishing shoes, washing and flattening his hair – and he had always relished the excursions, as if he and the family were embarking on an epic voyage of exploration. He felt differently about going to Manchester. He was unable to rest or sleep. Apprehension made him nervously hyperactive. He checked and rechecked his bag – a blue-grey leather case on which he'd ostentatiously written his name in sweeping calligraphy. The letters were four inches high, the *G* and *B* painted in red and gold.

United had sent an overnight ticket for a bunk bed on the *Ulster Prince*, the single-funnel ferry that carried the black and red colours of shipowners Burns and Laird and sailed almost nowhere except along the route between Belfast and Liverpool and back again. Best saw the ship as an 'iron monster'.

One of Bishop's Boyland Boys, Eric McMordie, travelled with him.

Neither of them had worn long trousers before. Each mother had bought a pair especially for her son; Best's made his legs itch. Also from East Belfast, McMordie had four brothers and five sisters. His mother had lost at least three other children during childbirth or infancy. McMordie scarcely remembered his father, a bus driver. He had died when McMordie was only three years old. He and Best had faced one another in a school match, aged 11, and again during club games between Cregagh and McMordie's Orangefield. 'Everyone knew how talented he was,' he said of Best. He wasn't surprised to discover the two of them were journeying together. Well before Best had whipped Boyland on his own, Bishop told McMordie of 'a great little player from Cregagh' who had 'such special skills'.

Best never knew whether United wanted to test his and McMordie's initiative or simply didn't understand the disorientating trauma of leaving home. If it was the former, Best and McMordie failed. If – more likely – it was the latter, United let them down abysmally, a dereliction of the club's duty of care. Watching the *Ulster Prince* slip anchor and draw away from port, the boat crowded with holidaymakers waving enthusiastically from the rail, Ann Best felt such inconsolable sorrow that she never again accompanied her son anywhere if it meant saying a long goodbye to him. That evening she and Dickie wept together. On the boat Best and McMordie spoke about football and family and not much else. 'We hid in our cabins until dinner was called,' said McMordie. 'There was more food on the buffet than we'd ever seen in our lives. We didn't know what to do. We ate quickly and then went to hide again.'

The Bests assumed a United official would collect him at Liverpool docks. So did Best. Instead, he and McMordie found themselves next morning heaving their luggage to Lime Street railway station and anxiously scanning the departures board for the next Manchester train. 'I had a morbid fear of getting lost,' said Best, describing himself and

McMordie as 'very confused little boys' who 'didn't even have a clear idea of where we were going'. The taxi driver in Manchester responded to Best's request to be driven to Old Trafford by taking them to the cricket ground. It was, after all, the middle of the cricket season; and Lancashire were at home to Middlesex. So far, so bad. And worse followed.

In photographs Joe Armstrong has a slightly wizened and gnomic look about him; Busby called him the 'great little ferret'. He's white-haired, only 5ft 4in tall and nearing 70. His jackets look at least one half-size too big for him. Armstrong would eventually become 'Uncle Joe' to Best. His first impressions, however, weren't favourable. Armstrong rebuked him for failing to wait for the taxi he claimed United had booked for them. That he did so in only a mildly irritable way made no difference to Best. 'Meeting him reminded me of my first dreadful day at grammar school . . . I felt as though I'd been given a real scolding,' he said. Armstrong so cowed Best that, timorously, he sat down to a full English breakfast – despite the fact he'd eaten one only three hours earlier. 'I didn't have the guts to say anything,' he said.

Since the early 19th century – when the club that would eventually become Manchester United was still called Newton Heath – acres of Manchester had been emerald. More than 10 per cent of its population in the 1841 census was recorded as Irish-born. In the coming decade, following the Great Famine, the figure rose to 15 per cent. The past was no consolation to Best. The city of rain-slick streets and amber-lit windows largely remained as the writer and self-styled traveller J. B. Priestley described it in his book *English Journey* almost a quarter of a century earlier. Priestley had noted its 'little old houses and narrow streets'. He wrote of its 'rows of huge black warehouses', the public buildings that were 'big solid impressive fellows' and also of the smudge of towns clustered around it, beneath the dingy glare of the North West's skies. He thought Manchester's architecture was purposefully built to withstand foul weather. Manchester to Best meant the Ship Canal, which he'd never seen; the Hallé Orchestra, which he'd never heard; Lowry's Salford industrial landscapes, the figures in them thinner than him. The sights and the size of the city frightened him. He was overwhelmed. Everything passed in a bewildering blur. Nothing he did seemed right. Nothing he said was understood. His Irish accent was so pronounced he had to repeat sentences several times with an exaggerated slowness to be understood; he could have been speaking in tongues. Best wished Bishop had travelled with him as an interpreter.

The only thing that reminded Best vaguely of Burren Way were his digs – a three-bedroom terraced house in a cul-de-sac called Aycliffe Avenue in Chorlton-cum-Hardy. Number 9 had a grey slate roof and three rectangular front windows, one of them diamond-leaded. The brick work was mottled red and orange, and a ledge of flat concrete hooded and darkened the front door. A privet hedge divided the garden from the pavement. Inside the centre-piece of the living room was a light-brown, tiled fireplace above which a wide, Art Deco-shaped mirror hung on the wall. His landlady was delicate and bird-like. Her short, fair hair was tightly bunched into a perm and a pair of spectacles, the frames fanning into upward points at the corners, sat on her thin, ever-smiling face. Her name was Mary Fullaway. She looked at Best, dressed in his drainpipe pants and winkle-picker shoes, and thought he 'didn't look big enough for those long trousers'. She'd later admit: 'I said to myself, you'll never make a footballer . . . you're too small . . . I wanted to cook him a big meal.' Best sensed her thoughts. 'I've a feeling she was thinking of reporting United to the local branch of the Cruelty to Children organisation for sending us to her,' he said.

Best was filled with self-doubt and paralysed by fear. The youth team players were dauntingly well-developed and muscular, and Best saw himself as a 'raggle-taggle scrubbler' in comparison. Weary, feeling manifestly inferior and horribly homesick, he desolately kicked a ball about in training, trying to pretend it mattered and he cared. He began to feel the welcome had been deliberately lukewarm and low-key, as if United meant to intimidate him. The security of a printing apprenticeship in Belfast – his father had arranged it before United's offer – now had an allure Best had never recognised before. He'd go home, learn to set and ink type and play in the Irish leagues and talk in pubs of how he'd once taken his boots to Old Trafford. He dismissed his chances of making it in the First Division as 'zero'.

The training session could not end quickly enough for him. He sought refuge in the spare bedroom at Mrs Fullaway's; Best and McMordie even took the unnecessary precaution of locking themselves in. 'We didn't say much to one another for most of the day,' said McMordie. 'We were terribly scared without being able to confess it to one another. Only when we were by ourselves could I bring myself to tell George I didn't like it. I was going home. I missed my mother and my brothers and sisters. I didn't want to stay in Manchester. George said nothing. He looked at me and we turned out the light and lay in our beds.' Afraid of being left behind alone, Best told McMordie next morning: 'I'm coming with you.' McMordie said he was 'shocked', adding: 'I'd assumed George would stay. Then he told me he couldn't be there on his own.'

Best didn't want to tell United about the decision himself. So McMordie, only four months older, acted as spokesman after Armstrong arrived on the doorstep of Aycliffe Avenue to escort them to Old Trafford. 'Mrs Fullaway realised we weren't settling,' added McMordie. 'She told the club.' Armstrong asked: 'Is everything all right?' and McMordie has always recalled his own reply: 'No, we want to go back on the next boat.' He says now: 'I think it was the biggest shock of old Joe's life.' Armstrong tried to dissuade them; Best nonetheless thought he still harboured resentment against him because of the missed taxi 24 hours earlier. He couldn't look Armstrong in the eye.

Armstrong thought he was dealing with mild stage fright rather than full-scale dread and disillusionment. Since he could think of nothing else to say to them, Best and McMordie were taken to the Ship Canal, where United's first team trained. Armstrong believed an introduction to fellow Irishman Harry Gregg would convince them to think again. Sometimes the most honourable intentions lead to bad consequences. Gregg was 6ft and seemed wider than a coalhouse door to Best. Standing in front of him, he looked like Gulliver trapped in Brobdingnag. Given Gregg's roots and his history, Best was meeting someone he regarded as 'a living legend', which in normal circumstances ought to have counted as a red letter day for him. 'He was the player we all worshipped in Belfast,' he said. 'But I felt more uneasy than ever when I met him. It made me think: What was I doing there? What could I say to him?'

When Armstrong asked Best and McMordie whether an audience with Gregg had made them reconsider, the two of them, immovable on the matter, shook their heads at him. Armstrong shook his own at such intransigence and accepted defeat, reluctantly. 'He made us feel pathetic and, looking back, I suppose we were,' said Best who, after returning to Aycliffe Avenue to collect his belongings, also heard Mrs Fullaway announce she was 'baffled' at the news. He'd spent less than 36 hours in Manchester.

He ran back to the *Ulster Prince*, regarding it as a lifeboat that had come to his rescue.

After a night's contemplation, the term 'homesick' seemed to be a weakly inadequate excuse for quitting. It implied a lack of fibre and toughness. He thought of the sacrifices his parents had made on his behalf. He also thought about facing his friends and the neighbours. What could he tell them? He felt guilty, and also on the edge of tears. 'I was cheating my mum and dad,' he said.

Dickie and Ann Best didn't have a telephone. There was no way of alerting his parents either to his departure from Manchester or his imminent arrival in Belfast. He didn't know how to send a telegram or where to send it from. He'd rehearsed what to say to them; though, in fact, all he could do was recount the events chronologically. Dickie, in bed drinking tea, answered the tentative knock on the door. His response to the surprise return of his son, found on the doorstep with the morning milk, was puzzlement rather than rage. The sight of him provoked two rhetorical questions. 'What are you doing here?' asked Dickie, amazed. 'Oh my God, where did you come from?' asked Ann. Listening to the answer, she said supportively: 'That's all right . . . we were half-expecting you.'

Best was grateful for his father's calm reassurance – 'he told me I'd done nothing wrong', he said – and also his pragmatism. Armstrong had slipped Best a note, which included his phone number. He asked the Bests to ring him. Armstrong wanted to know whether the situation was repairable. Dickie, deeply unimpressed with United's slovenly treatment of a wet-behind-the-ears teenage boy, wanted to know something different: did the club intend to improve its bedside manner? In a call from a telephone box at the end of the street, Armstrong was firmly told that if Best *ever* returned to Old Trafford he would do so entirely of his own free will. He would not be pushed or pressurised.

Dickie stuck to a sagely sensible strategy which, as Best acknowledged, 'gave me time to think how stupid I might have been'. After speaking to Armstrong, and gaining the apology and the reassurances he required, the father sat in his armchair pretending to read a newspaper. He waited to be asked about the conversation, which had buzzed across the line between Belfast and Manchester. Here was a sharp tutorial delivered via catechism.

SON: What did Mr Armstrong want?
FATHER: Well, they don't want you back.

The last sentence, a lie delivered for psychological purpose, was meant to jolt; and it did. Dickie watched Best's features contract and collapse into a spasm of hurt, sadness and deflated pride. 'I felt my insides go cold,' said Best. In that expression Dickie saw how much regret and helpless anguish was already stored up inside him. He saw, too, how much going back to United would mean to his son. Dickie folded the newspaper and told him the truth. Best knew he'd made a mistake in abandoning United. He knew he'd make another by rebuffing them again. 'There were only a few ways to get out of Belfast,' he said. 'You could box, play snooker or be a footballer. My father talked some sense into me. I will never be able to thank him enough.' Listening to his father's advice Best composed a letter to United. His father wrote it. The son signed and posted it. Within two weeks he'd moved back into Aycliffe Avenue.

But, without the woman who ran it, he would still never have stayed there.

In a benign piece of misremembering Matt Busby would say he'd seen George Best practise on his first afternoon at Manchester United. He claimed to have never forgotten the 'clever things' he did with the ball. 'I went along to see how the club's young players were going on,' added Busby. 'They were playing two-against-two . . . One black-haired little squib made a particular imprint on my mind.' If so, Busby was wearing the cloak of invisibility. He went further, insisting that 'Master Best and Master McMordie', as he called them, had actually been inside his office to tell him of their decision to return to Belfast. But neither of them saw nor spoke to Busby. 'I don't remember even catching a glimpse of him. We certainly weren't taken to meet him and we wouldn't have had the courage to speak to him on our own,' says McMordie, who, unlike Best, decided not to accept the return ticket United offered him.

Busby was appalled to discover the trialists had felt it necessary to go home. He took it personally, too, and promptly changed club procedures. He saw the incident as damaging to his reputation and United's. No other arrival, he decreed, should feel the way Best and McMordie had done. He prided himself on creating a family at Old Trafford. The reason why was rooted in his own experiences. He'd known the misery of alienation and isolation.

Busby had once felt a stranger in a strange land – and that land was Manchester, too. As a young player, aged 18 in February 1928, he'd arrived in what he called that 'grim, grimy and great' city from Orbiston, near Bellshill, in Lanarkshire. Orbiston was a hamlet comprising 32 two-room cottages for pitmen and their families. Busby called it 'very clannish'. Its unflattering moniker, Cannibal Island, was fashioned from football, always a combustible affair there. Teams who went to Orbiston and made the mistake of winning would have to flee at the end of the match to save themselves from a beating of a different kind. Opposition players would often sprint for safety in their boots and kit, returning for their clothes the following day when the spitting locals had half-forgotten the score and were less likely to duff them up in retaliation for it. 'They might leave with two points,' said Busby 'but never with their shirts and trousers.' A sniper's bullet killed Busby's father at Arras during the Great War, leaving his mother to raise four children, three of them girls. Busby, the firstborn, had no option but to work briefly in the mines – or, as he put it, 'the earth's intestines' – before football dragged him out of the coal dust and the deepest shafts. Despite Orbiston's slag heaps and filth, as well as the primitiveness of those houses, Busby still longed to see it again because the vast, cobbled sweep of Manchester seemed aloofly inhospitable to him.

He'd signed for City and toiled unsuccessfully at either inside-forward or on the wing. In most matches Busby faded into anonymity. One fleeting League appearance led nowhere except back into the reserves.

At the season's end Busby gratefully boarded the train for Scotland. Only ten weeks later, he said, the return journey to Manchester was made with 'heavy heart and tortured tread'. Busby already thought what he wanted from the game was beyond his capabilities. After another two months he wrote frankly to his fiancée, Jean – the woman with whom he would share 57 years of marriage – and confessed to her: 'I am out of my sphere in football.' He was pitifully homesick and decided to take his broken heart home. 'I have never wanted to be a quitter,' he remembered of that awful, formative period, 'but in those muddled days anything appeared preferable to prolonging the agony.' Trains to Glasgow were so frequent that Busby didn't bother to consult the time-table. He planned to turn up at the station, buy a ticket and wait on the platform. He got as far as writing out a perfunctory letter of resignation to City, resting the paper on the dressing table in his room, and packing a suitcase containing his paltry belongings. He was in his cups. Only the intervention of a guardian angel called Phil McCloy dissuaded him from disappearing. McCloy was another Scot, a full-back capped twice against England and depicted on cigarette cards with wavy, lacquered black hair, prominent eyebrows, as if drawn on with a thick-nibbed pen, and a bevelled chin. He advised Busby to 'give it a little longer . . . you can still make the grade', continuing his persuasive pitch into the small hours of the following morning until Busby relented. Had it not been for McCloy, there'd have been no switch to right-half for Busby, no FA Cup winners' medal for him in 1934, no managerial career.

Busby's circumstances still didn't improve immediately. Pneumonia soon added to his woes. By his own admission Busby was a 'mixed-up kid' who found salvation through the kindness of others. Jimmy McMullan, City's left-half and captain of Scotland's Wembley Wizards, who bamboozled and crushed England 5-1 in 1928, offered him a room in his home. Within those walls Busby found the warmth and stability that had been previously absent. What McMullan gave him, so Busby tried to give to anyone who came to United.

Wanting to replicate the environment McMullan and his wife had created for him, Busby – rather than an anonymous, suited club official – made a point of vetting prospective landladies such as Mary Fullaway. He called it 'the human approach'.

Busby arrived at Aycliffe Avenue in his grey overcoat and a dark, snap-brim trilby and, like an estate agent compiling details for the printed particulars of a sale, dutifully inspected every room for cleanliness and space and also scanned the neighbourhood to make sure it was neither troublesome nor run down. Most importantly of all Busby, who regarded himself as a solid judge of character, satisfied himself that his prospective new employee was a right and proper sort of person. He thought lodgings should be a 'home away from home'. It meant a quiet, cosy atmosphere. It meant at least two square meals a day on the kitchen table. It meant providing comfort and privacy. Busby looked for landladies who were good housekeepers and possessed motherly instincts. He wanted them to be attentive without being over-fussy and to insist on basic discipline and decent manners without being overbearing.

Busby had no doubt that Mrs Fullaway, who he'd go on to call a 'most wonderful woman', fulfilled his and the club's criteria.

She had two sons: Graham, born in 1939, and Steve, born in 1944. The motif of her life was self-sufficiency and she took a stoically indomitable approach to it. Here was a survivor who tackled, without fluster or bluster, the vicissitudes of Fate, however turbulent or unpleasant. She did so without complaint, expecting nothing more than she had and wishing for little more.

Mrs Fullaway was from a generation of working-class Edwardians – born in 1909 in a back-to-back in Wigan – for whom life was generally something that happened elsewhere. It was read about in the newspapers and magazines or glimpsed for a few hours in the smoky darkness of the local picture house, dressed in Hollywood's escapist tinsel or relayed in newsreels that tended to take cheerily positive angles. Her maiden name was Jackson and the task for her parents was the fundamental one facing all those who made do and mended. It was the provision of enough food to feed the family – paid for from whatever manual work was available. Her father, John, was a labourer. Her mother, also called Mary, was a dressmaker, who gave birth to six children – five of them girls. Education and book-learning were considered less important than bringing in a wage. The young girl who would one day become Mrs Fullaway was employed as a machinist in a shirt manufacturer. Marriage to Harold Fullaway came in 1932.

The Fullaways led plain, ordinary lives. After the Second World War, Harold was Works Manager of an electrical firm. His wife – like wives everywhere – juggled the ration book in a different, but no less severe, age of austerity from the one she'd grown up in. Harold played bowls and was a long-standing season ticket holder at Manchester City, admiring a half-back at Maine Road; he was called Matt Busby. Mary liked ballroom dancing and won medals for it. But any life can be utterly reordered in a split-second of upheaval and sorrow. Hers changed irrevocably during a midweek evening at the cinema. It was common then for names to be flashed across the screen if someone needed to make contact urgently. When hers appeared, she picked up her bag and went to the cinema manager's office. She was told that her husband had died of a brain haemorrhage. He was 46; her sons were only 11 and six years old.

Whatever came next was never as cruel or as grim as the shock of sudden widowhood – telling her two young boys about the death of their father, the arrangements for the funeral, the gathering together of the broken remnants of one life and their painful reassembly into a new one. Mrs Fullaway got through her grief for the sake of her boys.

The single parent became a shop assistant at Lewis's department store. She did machine piecework from home. She took in lodgers, which included police cadets and Irish building workers. She made financial sacrifices, going without a few niceties herself to ensure her sons were more than just fed and clothed. 'We wanted for nothing,' remembers Steve. 'If we asked for a new bike, we may not have got one immediately – there was some saving to be done – but we always did eventually. We just don't know how she did it.'

Whoever spent time in her company told stories of Mrs Fullaway that contained common threads. That she had created a home where you never felt uncomfortable about sitting down and staying awhile; that she made everyone welcome by offering them a cup of tea; that she was always friendly and easy going and didn't lose her temper; and that she was also unfailingly modest – though, unlike some, it was not because she had a lot to be modest about. Far from it. She had provided for her family, holding it together at the ultimate point of crisis with the sort of slavish work ethic she expected to see in others – irrespective of whether they made a living from a toolbox or a football. She never advertised what she'd done or had to overcome.

Like Busby, she was a cradle Catholic, who took her God and her faith seriously. Also like him, she didn't want a Protestant boarded in Aycliffe Avenue to take offence at her religious artefacts and symbols. 'What should I do?' she asked Busby, who suggested she remove them. The fact she'd thought of others instead of herself confirmed her suitability to him. She was in the mould of the McMullans.

Best was blessed; serendipity had given him a surrogate mother in an ideal home – a modern lounge papered in red stripes, tropical fish in a square aquarium, a radiogram he could play whenever he liked and occupancy of the front bedroom of the house, which he shared with Steve, who became his friend.

'George is a member of the family,' said Mrs Fullaway. To him, she was 'Mrs F' – a 'nice, homely soul' and 'one of the few people I can trust completely'.

Aycliffe Avenue became his safe haven because she was there. As he made clear: 'Anywhere else and I might have gone home again.'

2

A Glass of Shandy and
a Game of Bingo

When fame arrived for George Best, and the newspapers began to take an interest in Mary Fullaway, she was depicted as a character from *Coronation Street*: typecast as the embodiment of Mancunian hospitality – the doughty, wholesome Northerner of few words, the dutiful and doting carer, almost always photographed doing domestic chores, such as serving a cooked breakfast and pouring tea, or clutching a cloth duster and vacuuming the carpet.

In truth her fetching and carrying wasn't as important as the emotional support she gave Best. Knowing boys will always be boys, and making allowances for that fact, she was discreet and non-judgemental. She didn't nag except when it was absolutely necessary. Best suffered awful bouts of homesickness for another 12 months. The opening weeks were 'hell', he said. 'I was something of an orphan.' Only Mrs Fullaway made him less so whenever he pined for Belfast and his family. 'She always seemed to say the thing that made me feel better about myself,' he explained. He wrote home regularly then. The Biro he used was blue and the paper, thin and lined, came from pads bought in Woolworth. The handwriting was a reflection of Best himself – precise and neat with the flamboyance of curls on the ascending and descending strokes. Each letter ended with a shower of kisses and Best underlined his signature, as if to stress its importance. His salary was £4.1s.9d. and he'd send £1 to his mother, the note folded and tucked inside the envelope. 'I've enclosed a pound,' he wrote to her. 'Hope it helps a bit.' Extra spending money came his way from sweeping the Old Trafford terraces and tidying beneath the seats. Operating on the established principle of finders-keepers, he collected and saved the stray coins that had fallen out of supporters' pockets during a match. 'I mostly got half-pennies and pennies,' he said. 'If I was lucky, I got some silver, like a sixpence.'

He barely filled out his kit, which made him conspicuous on the field alongside robust-looking team-mates. Mrs Fullaway did her utmost to put some meat and muscle on to his bones. She served him bacon and eggs in the morning and steak and potatoes at night. He ate burnt toast because he thought its carbon would give him added energy. 'It doesn't make me laugh when comedians go on about landladies, saying they are steely, flint-faced characters who count the exact number of baked beans to put on the toast for the lodger,' said Best, thinking of Mrs Fullaway. 'I'd probably be a mere shadow of myself if it hadn't been for the nourishing, body-building food she provided, day in and day out.'

He was working under a handicap – a tiresome and now laughable piece of legislation designed to placate the Football Associations of Scotland, Northern Ireland and the Republic. English clubs couldn't then sign youngsters from Scotland or Ireland as apprentices because of concerns about over-poaching. Manchester United could only offer Best 'amateur' terms, which obliged him to combine football with menial employment. It stunted his progress and put him at a pronounced disadvantage. The modern apprentice would see the stricture as abhorrent. The modern Professional Footballers' Association would dismiss it as restraint of trade. Like so much else during the early 1960s it was an irritation endured for appearance's sake – even though it didn't deter clubs such as United from crossing the Celtic borders and taking back whoever impressed them.

Best, caught in this bureaucratic clamp, had no option but to tolerate it, however much he cursed and grumbled. As a 'clerk' for the Manchester Ship Canal Company – a semi-respectable term for office gopher – he worked from 9 a.m. to 5.30 p.m. and trained in the evenings. He took lunch orders, like a café waiter, writing them down with a pencil in a black-bound notebook before accepting payment for the food and returning the loose change. He couriered cigarettes, cups of coffee and tea to workers' desks and sprinted into the centre of Manchester to pick up and deliver letters. 'I was so shattered,' said Best, 'I wasn't strong enough to train.'

Best gathered up his courage and spoke to Joe Armstrong. 'I told him I didn't want to work,' he said. Armstrong swapped Best's white-collar duties for something more inappropriate – lifting and general labour in a timber yard, where his gloved hands would have ached as much as the rest of his body if he hadn't quit at 11 o'clock on his first day. Walking from one shed to another, cradling wooden posts in his arms, Best deliberately dropped them on the ground and walked out. 'I've not come to Manchester to do this,' he said. Though he never appreciated it then, a sign of how dearly United thought of him came from Armstrong's benevolent response. He didn't write off Best as a bolshie trouble-maker. He didn't fly into a fit of indignation, accuse Best of ungratefulness or threaten to cancel his contract. He found a solution. An electrical goods firm allowed Best to train in the morning and work in the afternoons.

He tried to impress in other ways. He cleaned the boots of the professionals with a long-handled brush on the soles and then used a tin of Dubbin on the leather before rubbing in a swab of Vaseline to intensify the shine. 'I wanted the boots I cleaned to be better than anyone else's,' he said.

Long after his career was over, he'd insist with some bravado: 'I had a sense of destiny.' He'd also maintain: 'I knew I was different. I felt different . . . I knew I was never going to be the Average Joe.' In actual fact, before that career properly began, an Average Joe is exactly how he saw himself. Best constantly expected to be pulled aside after a training session to hear what he called those 'end of the world words' – a few polite but clipped sentences that began with the phrase 'Sorry, son', before he was given his boots in a bag. United had the pick of some of the country's prime talent, and Best had seen a lot of it come and go while he remained, which was mysterious to him. These were 'The Disappeared' – teenagers of Best's generation and with his aspirations who had travelled hopefully to Old Trafford, trained awhile and then found themselves dismissed as unsatisfactory. There'd be an apologetic half-smile and a sympathetic arm on the shoulder to soften the blow of such bad news, which always seemed to be delivered when it was least expected. 'You'd turn up one morning, someone wouldn't be there, and you'd hear one of the other lads saying, "They sent him home" . . . A lot of the time you never had the chance to say goodbye,' he said. Best waited for the same fate to befall him. 'Many times I'd walk away from training wondering if it was for the last time.' Blind to the admiring glances he was receiving, unaware of the future already envisaged for him, he remembered: 'No one seemed to notice me.'

Of course, everyone noticed Best. There was a lambent quality about him. He spent hours on the training pitch, volunteering to stay behind to improve every skill. He saw it as both a potential cure for his home-sickness and as a continuation of his education in Belfast. As a boy, he would stand on one side of the road in Burren Way and hit the edge of the opposite kerb with the ball at such an angle that his shot came back to him. He would rattle nearby outhouse doors, using them as target practice, and learned through persistence to strike the door knob so the shot returned to his feet. At Cregagh 'Bud' McFarlane had once urged him to strengthen his weaker left foot. Best went to extremes. He wore a plimsoll on his right foot to remind himself not to kick with it. Throughout an entire match the ball touched only his left boot. This level of dedication was mirrored at United. He repeatedly took in-swinging corners, which he tried to curl on to the centre of the bar. He sharpened the accuracy of his shooting from 20, 25 and 30 yards – again aiming to thud it hard against the woodwork. 'If I could strike the bar from anywhere, I always knew I could find the top or bottom corner, too,' he argued. He would work on his dribbling by reducing the space between the practice poles, making the gap so narrow that only he and the ball could squeeze through it. He did so at speed, weaving like a waiter around restaurant tables. Had he carried a silver drinks tray instead of a ball, he wouldn't have spilt a drop.

Best would strike cross-field passes on the run – and with either foot – and attempt looping centres that would either hit the far angles of the six-yard box or drop directly on to the penalty spot. His feet were so sensitive that Best's party-trick was to place a penny coin on the toe of his shoe and flick it into the breast pocket of his jacket. He toiled away on his heading, too, raising the height of a ball suspended from the ceiling in the gym to improve the spring in his feet and toes and tighten the muscles in his calves. If he found a spare moment, he would use it to juggle with the ball. Even after all this extra training, Best would go on to the open field near Mrs Fullaway's – it reminded him of the patch of land at the end of Burren Way – where he and Steve passed around the sort of plastic ball you could buy cheaply in any newsagent's. The neighbourhood joined in. 'We'd soon have an eleven-a-side game going,' said Steve. 'George loved it. These matches went on until he was really famous.'

Best was adamant: 'No one ever taught me *how* to play.' But, arguing that imitation counts as the ultimate flattery, he assiduously strived to copy others. He watched matches as a student of the game, absorbing whatever lessons he could from them, as if each was a 90-minute tutorial. Best paid particular attention to the pre-match warm-up because no one had any inhibitions about showing off. 'You'd see what players normally only did during training,' he said.

In mid-December 1961, less than four months after Best had signed for United, Real Madrid played a friendly at Old Trafford. Francisco Gento was short, dark and devastatingly quick. He could run 100 metres in 11 seconds. What attracted the 15-year-old Best, however, was a specific skill. Gento sliced his right foot down and across the ball in a chopping motion. It shot ten yards forward and then spun back towards him like a child's top on a string. 'I knew I had to do that,' said Best. 'Next day, I could.'

Someone who would become a boyhood hero also had one of his own: the blond arrow Alfredo Di Stefano – though, when Best finally saw him in the flesh, Di Stefano was more the bald arrow. He looked like a Franciscan monk. He was nonetheless the player Best aspired to be – 'my greatest inspiration', he said. Di Stefano attacked one moment and defended the next, the ball faultlessly stuck to either foot until it was passed with imaginative precision. Di Stefano seemed to have unlimited vision, conceiving the eye as an extruded part of the brain. The goals he scored came in floods. 'He could do the lot and he was just about everywhere,' said Best. Di Stefano was then 35 and, as the master strategist, had steered Real to five successive European Cups, the most recent an unsurpassable 7–3 embarrassment of Eintracht Frankfurt at Hampden Park only a year and a half earlier. Best would tirelessly rerun it, following every tiny step Di Stefano made. An eight-millimetre reel of film of the final was stored in his bedroom at Mrs Fullaway's. 'It's a wonder that my eyes are not permanently bulging considering the hours I've spent watching that match,' he said. Without a screen, Best projected it on to the wall at the top of Mrs Fullaway's stairs, which was the darkest part of the house. Di Stefano and his side swept across the diamond pattern of the paper.

The midwinter weather in Manchester was dismal – blinding rain that turned the pitch to mud. Di Stefano flittered around the length and breadth of it and Best saw himself in the same role. When Di Stefano scored during his first-half appearance, the shot rising between the angle of post and bar, Best spent the following afternoon striving to duplicate it from exactly the same position – despite the protests of the groundsman, who didn't want him on the pitch and tried to chase him off.

A year later Best stood on the terraces at Hillsborough, where he went with a singular purpose: to see Pelé. Santos came to South Yorkshire and made Sheffield Wednesday's energetic, panting game seem crudely Stone Age. Not even the score – 4–2 – reflected the difference in standards between them. Santos began to coast, playing exhibition stuff in slow-time to deny possession to the galumphing opposition. When the Brazilians won a penalty, Pelé played the most complicated game of cat-and-mouse with the goalkeeper. He was like a vaudeville act. He would shape to take the kick before pulling away from it at the decisive moment. A twist of the hips, an angled run or a drop of a shoulder persuaded the keeper to commit himself in a desperate act of second-guessing. He was already moving across his line to anticipate the placement before Pelé's deliberate hesitation left the ball immobile on its spot. 'He must have sent the keeper the wrong way four times,' remembered Best, able to recall each instance. 'By the time he did take it the poor keeper didn't know whether he was coming or going.' One report said that Pelé's approach to the ball before scoring included 'the foxtrot, the two-step and a tango'. The mental notes Best took logged the diagonal runs Pelé made, which meant he was always available to take a pass, and the fact he could ride tackles the way a boxer rode an uppercut or a swinging hook. When Best wasn't watching games, he read about them. Through newspapers and books, and because of an encyclopaedic retention of names and dates, he taught himself about its tactics and history. 'I used to hate Sundays because there was no football. I was bored rigid,' he said, demonstrating a commitment to his trade.

He resolved to graft harder on his game than anyone else. If, as he still feared, heartbreak lay ahead, he wanted the consolation of saying to his parents that he'd done all he could to avoid it. He liked training anyway – the cross-country runs during which he saw others blatantly cheat or slope off for a crafty cigarette, the five and seven-a-sides and particularly any routine that allowed him to improve his ball craft. He couldn't fathom why anyone, given such a chance, would abuse it. Of those who did, he said: 'When I saw them doing it, I knew I was in with a real chance.'

George Best chose to do his work as quietly as possible. Since he preferred to listen, rather than speak, he learned very quickly about the etiquette at Old Trafford. The silence surrounding one topic – the Munich air crash – taught him not to mention it; or even to allude to it.

Thoughts of it were still ever-present, but seldom voiced aloud, and Best felt the inconsolable sense of loss which still permeated Old Trafford. He nevertheless found it 'eerie'; he said that no one spoke about it.

Like anyone else old enough to have been affected by Munich, Best could remember the news when it broke on 6 February 1958, and the way in which the death of a team affected those for whom Manchester United thereafter became 'The Special Club'. The headlines the 11-year-old Best read appeared in the *Belfast Telegraph*.

DISASTER STRIKES FOOTBALL'S MOST FAMOUS TEAM

PLANE CARRYING MANCHESTER UNITED
COMES DOWN IN FLAMES
CRASH SURVIVORS CRITICAL
FIGHT FOR LIVES

The stories below them relayed facts that had to be read at least twice to be believed: the snowy and slushy runway; the ice on the wings of the chartered Elizabethan-class aircraft, bringing the team home from Belgrade after a win against Red Star put them into the European Cup semi-final; the skidding, aborted take-offs after refuelling before the fatal third attempt in which the plane, failing to lift its nose, overran the tarmac and slewed across the grass stopway and into a house, a wooden hut and towards a copse; a wing striking a petrol compound, and the explosion that collision caused.

In the initial confusion the dead were still being counted. Matt Busby's condition was critical. The phenomenal Duncan Edwards clung to life when the severity of his internal injuries ought to have made survival at the scene impossible. Bobby Charlton was thrown out of the wreckage on impact while strapped to his seat; he listened afterwards as a stranger in a nearby bed in the Rechts der Isar Hospital read aloud the names of the victims, each pronounced in a gentle German accent.

Moving images, played and replayed on the television news and then again on a Pathé reel at the cinema, showed the snow falling over the ripped, gaping carcass of the plane and slender pillars of pale smoke, bent on the wind, drifting into a starless night. Scenes of supporters and non-supporters alike drawn to Old Trafford so they could grieve with one another, rather than grieve alone. They stared at a flag flying at half mast, hanging limply against its pole. Even weeks later, when the dead had been buried, it was impossible to conceive that eight of Busby's Babes had perished: Edwards, Roger Byrne, David Pegg, Tommy

Taylor, Eddie Colman, Billy Whelan, Mark Jones and Geoff Bent. Their average age was 23.

The bravest men do not see themselves as brave. Busby, who twice received the last rites, merely thought of himself as another survivor; and, like every survivor of Munich, he asked himself the same two questions: Why did this happen to us? Why hadn't I died? His chest was crushed. His lung was punctured, which meant a fractured foot had to be reset without anaesthetic. To cough brought excruciating pain. Cocooned in a transparent oxygen tent, wanting to die, he said: 'I prayed for the end to come quickly.' The courage he summoned to remain alive was humbly baffling to him. The courage he sustained to restore his own health and rebuild his club was supreme. He spent ten weeks in hospital, leaving on crutches and then learning to walk with a stick. To travel the corridor to his office Busby had to stretch out his arms and move himself along by resting his hands on either wall for support. The scarring along his ribs and breast bone was red and gruesome. His lower back and spine constantly throbbed. The physical imprint of Munich was insignificant to Busby compared to the marks it left on the mind. 'Deep down,' he'd say, 'the sorrow is there all the time. You never really rid yourself of it. It becomes part of you. You might be alone, and it all comes back, like a kind of roundabout, and you weep . . .'

What Munich gave Busby was a more profound appreciation of the purpose of life. Instead of doubting God, or blaming Him for the tragedy, he drew closer still to Catholicism. Mass and confession became a greater solace than before. 'I want to be – and I try to be – a better man,' he said. For him it became a matter of not letting down the dead. He'd told his wife nothing was capable of bringing him back into football. Jean Busby replied: 'I don't think you're being fair to the people who have lost loved ones . . . I am sure those who have gone would have wanted you to continue.' The heartfelt argument was also the logical one. Busby surrendered to it, knowing what the game had meant to the players who had died; knowing also that his abandonment of it would be selfish and pointless and be an abandonment of them, too. It would neither bring them back nor serve their memory. Sculptors could mould statues of the dead in bronze. What else could he create as a memorial to them other than another team; a team, moreover, that would win the European Cup. 'Surely it is the purpose of life to build, to create, to conquer setbacks, to hope,' said Busby. 'I understood at last that to pray for death as I had done was wrong and cowardly. I knew that somehow I must succeed again for the sake of those who had died. Otherwise my life would have no meaning.' The meaning he sought was another Championship – and then the European Cup.

When Best arrived at Old Trafford, the 'new United' Busby envisaged as a tribute to ghosts remained a shaky work in progress.

Busby wanted to grow talent – such as Best – rather than buy it. In the aftermath of the tragedy, he had no option but to reach for the chequebook because otherwise reconstruction would have stalled. To those who had lived through the horror of the crash and felt exactly as he did – Charlton, Harry Gregg and the defender Bill Foulkes – Busby gradually added the components of another side. The inside-forward Albert Quixall was bought for £45,000 from Sheffield Wednesday in 1958. The combative Maurice Setters cost £30,000 from West Bromwich Albion in 1960. In that same year Busby bought full-back Noel Cantwell for £29,000 from West Ham, appointing him captain, and also David Herd, from Arsenal, to provide edge to his attack. From the 1950s and 60s' equivalent of the academy came Johnny Giles and Nobby Stiles, ruthless, soon toothless and also myopic, like a footballing Mr Magoo, who nevertheless always saw enough to impose himself on whoever he was marking. 'There was no such word as "lose" to him,' said Best of Stiles. It didn't matter, he added, whether someone against him was 'six foot four tall or four foot six tall' because he 'got stuck in . . . treated everyone the same . . . played twice as hard as anyone else'.

Busby didn't get everyone on his shopping list. There were unsuccessful attempts to bring John Charles from Juventus and Jimmy Armfield from Blackpool. United continued to misfire; the blend wasn't smooth enough. What Busby needed was a spark of energy and a stroke of flair, which he found in Denis Law – though the fee of £115,000 needed to import him from Torino in 1962 broke the British transfer record. The sum was £15,000 more than the Italians had paid Manchester City for him a year earlier.

As he mopped the dressing rooms, tidied kit and did odd jobs, Best spied on Law and noted his tousled blond hair, his worldly air and immaculate suits. Law looked 'like a modern-day Viking', he said. On the pitch he was different. He held the long sleeves of his shirt against his palms, using the cloth to wipe a snotty nose. Irritation with colleagues who didn't pass to him, or with referees who failed to give decisions in his favour, was apparent on his expressions and in his body language. He contorted his face and made wild arm gestures. Law was like a silent movie star, overacting in an attempt to convey anguished heartbreak or injustice to the audience in the stalls. Around the six-yard box – the point at which he made contact with the ball most often – there were no histrionics. Law, like Jimmy Greaves, was a poacher's poacher. He claimed tap-ins that seemed so simple that Best thought his grandmother could have scored them in her kitchen apron and slippers. Anticipation was his sixth sense. As if it had been foretold to him, Law seemed to know in advance when a ball would bobble or ricochet favourably and so moved into the right position to receive it. The effortless execution of the chance disguised the calculation. Best was bowled over by the short, darting runs he made. Law moved faster than a lizard's tongue in getting where he wanted to go and side-footing or poking the ball in. He also scored acrobatically, with overhead or scissor kicks, and got remarkable goals with his head. If the youth team was playing at home, Best could reach Old Trafford to watch the closing quarter of an hour of a League game. When he did so, it was the zest of Law – not the explosive shots or hurdling dashes of Charlton – that he wanted to see.

In the 1963 FA Cup final against Leicester City – a 3–1 win giving Busby his first trophy post-Munich – Law claimed one of the goals. Best took his eyes off him only long enough to understand who had the tightest grip on the match, controlling it, like a puppeteer in charge of a hundred strings, from midfield. Paddy Crerand possessed what Best described as the 'uncanny knack' of placing a pass so a player could run on to it without altering his stride pattern. Crerand was similar in style to Busby. Both lacked pace. Both, however, compensated for it through speed of thought. 'We used to laugh because he was so slow,' said Best. 'It didn't make any difference. He was far ahead of us thinking-wise. He used to see moves three or four passes before anyone else. He'd pick you out from forty or fifty yards, no trouble.' Crerand cost £43,000 from Celtic, signing only three and a half months before the Cup final and arriving on the very day United marked the fifth anniversary of Munich, which didn't seem auspicious to him. Crerand passed the ball beautifully, either along the grass or loftily, and he knew how to trade tackles ruggedly and take care of himself and protect others. Best said that in 50-50 games, which 'looked a bit dodgy' for United, Crerand made the difference. In response to Alf Ramsey's belief that Martin Peters was 'ten years ahead of his time', Best would say of Crerand's contribution: 'He was the same. He kept the team ticking over.'

Best was besotted with Wembley that afternoon. Going there was a personal celebration for him. The hardest of winters delayed the final for three weeks until 25 May. From December to March, the country resembled the Antarctic – ice here, ice there. The upper reaches of the Thames froze. So did the sea around Herne Bay. Some early round ties were rearranged on ten occasions. The extension to the season meant Best was given professional terms only three days before Wembley, a private signing ceremony on his 17th birthday. Though geography and constant commitments elsewhere prevented Bob Bishop from speaking to Best often, he knew what was happening to him from week to week. 'Bud' McFarlane was the conduit of information gleaned from the family. In conversations with Joe Armstrong, Bishop would also enquire about Best in a roundabout way so as not to make his fascination too apparent. 'The wee fellah's doing well?' he'd ask. With the contract signed, Bishop wrote to Best and told him not to look back. The final line of his letter said: 'You're on your way.'

What Best had seen before only in black and white on a flickering TV screen in Belfast he now saw live and in glorious, abundant colour at Wembley. He'd always recall the vivid greenness of the cut turf, the curve of the stadium decorated with swathes of United's red and Leicester's blue, the scarlet tunic of the military band and the gleam of silver buttons and brass instruments. The pomp and circumstance and hubbub of all of it enthralled Best; and, after it was over, he thought about Law and Crerand and how well he could play alongside them, never daring to hope that this wished-for outcome would happen.

What Busby loved was the game's drama and romance. On what he called its 'great occasions', such as the Cup final, he said it evoked 'wonder and mystery' in him and also 'a sense of poetry'. Once the elation of beating Leicester had ebbed away, Busby saw this Cup final as a step towards higher things rather than the culmination of something. He believed another 'six or seven years' would pass before he could properly recreate afresh what Munich had taken from him. United had narrowly avoided relegation, finishing 19th and relegating Manchester City instead. But, despite the ample consolation of the Cup, his team was deficient. He knew that to win another Championship again – and then compete in another European Cup – required him to draft in one more outstanding player.

Already, he knew which player.

There was more than a watchful sharpness about Matt Busby. He could be calculating, steely and ruthless. This was accompanied by a certain degree of aloofness, which was deliberate – so the sting would be greater if he had to rebuke someone. But he always wanted to do the right thing in the end and he had a sensitivity about relationships. Busby knew George Best was a tender flower.

Even as a pro, Best was reluctant to talk to anyone much older than himself or to someone he didn't know; especially so if they wore a Manchester United shirt. He shrank away from engaging either Bobby Charlton or Denis Law in conversation, and to him Busby seemed a remote and intimidating presence in a suit, tie and trilby. A distant nod in acknowledgement from him was sufficient to send Best scurrying for the shadows. Best saw him mostly from afar, a stately and states-manlike figure who seemed unapproachable because of his status. He was trapped between wanting to impress Busby and wanting to avoid his gaze. Though worried Busby would never know anything about him, he ducked into doorways or dived behind walls whenever he saw him. He admitted that Busby 'terrified me then'. He was in such awe of Busby that he called him 'The Great Man' who was 'a bit of a mystery to me'. Busby consciously tried to make himself less so.

The two of them lived barely a mile and a half apart. Occasionally Busby would take a canny detour and drive past the bus stop at Chorlton-cum-Hardy where Best waited for the double-decker that would take him to Old Trafford. Busby would pull his Jaguar to the kerb and beckon him into the car. The gesture was undercut with a comical element. For Best treated the ride as if his kindly chauffeur was about to kidnap and interrogate him. He sat rigidly in the passenger seat and mumbled incoherently as Busby asked him softball questions and strove to put him at ease. Busby was like a headmaster trying to encourage the quiet boy he knows will one day become the school's star pupil. Best was frightened and worried about saying the wrong thing. He'd snatch at the door handle, yank it open and speed off with a garbled 'thank you' after Busby swept into the car park. Best began to hope the queue at the stop would be long enough for him to hover at the back of it, thus hiding himself from Busby among the office workers and the gossipy housewives carrying their shopping bags. 'I didn't know how to handle that situation,' he said. Busby understood his embarrassment and there were mornings when he tactfully pretended not to see him.

Best's skills more than compensated for his social inadequacies and Busby liked to watch him showboat – the shots swerving in from long range, the back heels and the laid-back, volleyed passes that he distributed after cushioning the ball on his chest or knee. Especially in practice matches, it was the sort of behaviour likely to stoke tempers and cause resentment. These would lead to attempts at instant score-settling among senior pros who had points of their own to make and didn't like being taken for a mug by a bullish whippersnapper. Provided it didn't go too far, Busby wasn't bothered. Best didn't care either. He dodged whatever retribution was aimed at him. Even if the odd challenge caught Best, Busby saw him shake it off as if those thin legs were made of iron. He had a disregard for physical danger. Busby liked all the reports fed back to him: about Best's fantastic appetite for fitness and the slog of training; about his eagerness to talk about the game in the lull after training was over; about his willingness to watch other matches; and about the marked contrast in his demeanour – that introversion off the field and extroversion on it. Contained within this contradiction he saw someone who needed football badly because it alone allowed him self-expression.

Busby did not see – but was rapidly informed about – Best

outwitting Harry Gregg. Had Best seen Gregg coming towards him on a Manchester street, he'd have diffidently avoided him. But, on the pitch, Best said he regarded Gregg as 'just another footballer to be beaten'. And so he beat him. Gregg was familiar with the pimply, whey-faced kids who came from Ireland; Best looked among the tiniest of them, as if he'd wandered in from an Under-14s game. So, as he broke through on the run during a practice match, Gregg reacted in the way that a crocodile does at the sight of a tiddler fish – he supposed he'd gobble him up in one bite. In any one-against-one Gregg schemed to feint right or left and then go the other way; it was usually sufficient to deter kids such as Best. Gregg went through the routine of call-his-bluff and Best left him splayed on the ground as the ball was side-footed into the net. Gregg put it down to beginner's luck – until, of course, Best did it a second time, and then a third. Busby learned it was like watching an old slapstick film in which the small man makes a fool out of his big opponent, leaving him slithering in the mud. 'You do that again,' said Gregg after Best's hat-trick, 'and I'll break your bloody neck, son.' Gregg was only half-joking. He was magnanimous in defeat. 'Next day I was asking all the pros: "Have you seen him?"' he said.

From the outset Busby decided that Best possessed 'more individual ability than I have seen in any other player'. On a pre-season tour in 1962 Busby, sitting in a hotel in central Manhattan on a sweltering June day, told the *Belfast Telegraph*'s correspondent Malcolm Brodie: 'You know, I've got a boy from Belfast who will be the greatest. Remember what I'm telling you.' What Brodie remembered was the conviction in Busby's voice. 'He didn't say things like that without meaning them. He was making sure I paid attention. He just didn't want me to make too much of it. He wanted to keep it as quiet as he could.'

What astonished Busby was the variety of ways Best had of beating an opponent – even, Busby said, 'when it seemed impossible'. He could avoid a tackle on either side. He could chip the ball above the head of a defender and then run around him to reclaim it. The flexibility in his ankles and knees was something Busby hadn't seen before. Because of it he could shield the ball and turn so fast that whoever he left standing looked utterly dumbfounded. In one five-a-side game, which Busby would recount decades afterwards, Best's alacrity of mind allowed him to toe-end the ball against his opponent's shin and then instantly strike the rebound 'cleanly and clinically' past the goalkeeper – the most audacious of one-twos. Busby said that it didn't matter whether or not training sessions were restricted to three, two, or one-touch football to contain him – 'George still dominated them anyway.' He was able to do it, added Busby, because: 'Every aspect of ball control was perfectly natural to him . . . he made the ball do what he wanted it to do . . . he is able to take [it] right close up to someone and still beat him.' He'd seen nothing like him before. 'The things he could do with a ball first made you blink and then made you wonder,' said Busby, who thought Best had three pairs of feet.

In Aycliffe Avenue, Mrs Fullaway noticed the change in him; he was becoming more voluble. There was something resolute about him, too. He wasn't homesick any longer, and she had to nudge him to write home. If he forgot, or became distracted, she'd take the weekly call from Ann Best, understandably concerned that she hadn't heard from him. Every adolescent feels the pull between home and the necessity to break away from it; eventually one – usually the need to stride off on your own path – dominates the other. So it proved with Best. The lad who had once rushed back to Belfast whenever he could, didn't want to go back there now. He was beginning to go out and about, albeit modestly at first, to the bowling alley, the snooker hall or to the coffee bars. And every Sunday night Mrs Fullaway took Best and Steve to the bingo. On the way home the three of them stopped off at a pub, where Mrs Fullaway indulged in one of her own weekly treats

– a bottle of Mackeson – and bought Best a shandy. It was a quiet, contented life.

· No one sensed then – apart from Busby – that Mrs Fullaway was shortly going to be described as 'Britain's most pestered landlady', who had given a roof to 'Britain's most pestered lodger'.

3

The Big Day for the Small Boy

The hardest thing is to do nothing. Other managers would have shaved the maverick edges off George Best, who confessed he was 'a greedy git'. Matt Busby allowed Best to be himself, which meant letting him hog the ball, as if it was his personal property. 'I thought I could keep possession for twenty minutes at a time,' said Best.

In self-defence he claimed such selfish ownership stemmed from his past. 'It was a hangover from my days on the Cregagh Estate where, if you got the ball, the idea was to hang on to it until someone managed to take it off you. In my case they rarely did,' he explained. 'At heart I always remained a kid. I would not pass.' Rather than take the simplest option, he went on baroque runs along the touchline. He preferred not to take throw-ins because he wanted to receive the ball instead of releasing it. And, rapped on the legs inside the penalty area, he often refused to go down – much to Busby's agitation – because doing so meant he'd lose control of the attack. 'I was so proud that I didn't want to fall over,' said Best. 'I didn't want someone to be able to bring me down. I used to think it was an insult to me personally.'

Busby spoke of Best's 'congenital dislike of allowing anyone else to have a kick'. He'd watch him glide around two or three men before being robbed of the ball purely because of his refusal to relinquish it early. 'You would be having apoplectic fits and say to yourself, Why the hell, George, don't you pass the ball?' remembered Busby. As Best admitted: 'If someone said it was impossible to beat four men, I would try to beat five. It was a dare.'

Watching Best in a youth game, Busby tried to instruct him with bellowed advice. Another voice cut in, abruptly interrupting him so the sentence was left unfinished. 'Let him be,' said Busby's assistant, Jimmy Murphy. 'He'll come around eventually.' Busby nodded his head and said nothing more, deferring to Murphy, whom he trusted to know Best better than he did then. Murphy was convinced Best would improve through a kind of footballing osmosis, absorbing what others did around him and learning from it.

A pot-bellied ex-miner from the Rhondda, Murphy was an extraordinary talent-spotter and star-maker. After only a minute's touchline observation he discerned accurately which qualities a player possessed, what he lacked and also whether intensive coaching would buff up the rest. Sent to spy on one starlet Murphy stayed just long enough to see him warm up. During it he registered weaknesses – in control and balance and a lack of crispness in his shot – that disqualified him as a signing. He wasn't cut from the fine cloth Manchester United demanded, so Murphy left before the match kicked off. Best said Murphy was 'one of the boys, a pal – a great character, a lovely man' and that 'everybody loved him'.

Among Busby's strengths was gathering men of character around him. He instinctively took to Murphy after listening to him talk about football to troops in 1945. The war in Europe was over then. Murphy, a sergeant, was NCO at a Services sports centre in Bari in southern Italy and billeted in a white stucco house that, he said, 'looked like a palace' and became known as the 'Baronial Hall'. Busby heard both common sense and fervour in Murphy's words. Speaking to soldiers who had licked Rommel's Afrika Korps in the Western Desert, the fanatical Murphy made football sound as though the game itself had been worth a tank battle or two to preserve it. 'It was his attitude, his command, his enthusiasm and his whole driving, determined action and word-power that caused me to say to myself: He's the man for me,' said Busby, impulsively offering him a role at United. Murphy, also impulsively, accepted it.

Old Trafford had been blitzed in 1941. Two firebombs, aimed at the dynamo and cable works and the engine sheds nearby, blew apart and burned the main stand and split the popular terrace, scorched the pitch bare of grass and destroyed the administrative buildings. Scrub-grass and tree brush grew through cracks in the concrete. The dressing rooms were derelict. There were no training facilities. The ground, which would become 'Busby's Cathedral' and the 'Theatre of Dreams', was a ruin when he and Murphy walked into it.

Murphy, a pre-war wing-half at West Bromwich Albion, was hired to find and develop players that United – with a £15,000 overdraft – were too impecunious to buy. He was aggressive and remorseless in honing and fine-tuning what scouts sent him. He was also charm personified in the living rooms of prospective signings, where he could sweet-talk parents. Busby said one of the favourite jokes at Old Trafford was that Murphy would do '*anything*' – bar adultery or bigamy – to 'serenade the mother of a fifteen-year-old youngster with football talent'. In a tracksuit his language was more bar room than front parlour. It was liberally peppered with expletives, and he'd slam his right fist into his left palm for emphasis as he uttered them. He had no interests other than football, which was something of an obsessive love. His pleasures away from it were the same as the working man's – a quiet pint and a Sweet Afton cigarette. To some strangers Murphy gave the impression of being furnace-fierce and uncompromisingly intolerant. To those who came to know him on the training pitch the crude language helped Murphy express his and Busby's straightforward philosophy, which embraced attacking and defending together – a brand of Total Football espoused long before the Dutch of the 1970s were credited with it. What prefixed and suffixed all the swearing was like a university education in the game, winning Murphy loyalty and immense admiration from those he schooled collectively and in exhaustive one-to-one sessions, during which he worked a player until his feet almost bled. 'Whatever I achieved in football,' said Bobby Charlton of Murphy, 'I owe to one man and only one man.' In the 1950s and 60s he nursed 68 of United's most significant players through the youth and reserve sides and into the First Division. Under him United claimed five successive FA Youth Cups between 1953 and 1957. The Babes had been as much Murphy's as Busby's; though the lack of alliteration, plus Murphy's own dislike of publicity and his reluctance to push himself centre-stage, meant newspapers seldom alluded to it.

Murphy wasn't on the aeroplane at Munich because of a conflict of fixtures: the tie in Belgrade clashed with his part-time position as manager of Wales. The coach, Bert Whalley, died in the seat Murphy would have occupied beside Busby. As Busby recovered and convalesced Murphy became the heart and lungs of United. Alone, biting back his own grief and refusing to make much of it public, he assembled a scratch side and improbably steered them to the FA Cup final, only 83 days after the disaster, and also took Wales to that summer's World Cup finals in Sweden, where Brazil – and a solitary goal from Pelé – denied them a place in the semi-finals.

What Brian Clough once said of his partner Peter Taylor – 'I'm the shop window and he's the goods at the back' – Busby could have coined to describe Murphy, too. Instead, and to his eternal credit, Busby's division of labour created the climate in which Murphy worked unfettered. Busby saw in Murphy something he didn't possess himself; and Murphy saw in Busby a charisma and intelligence for the overall management of the club that he could never attain. Busby relied on Murphy to tell him when a reserve was ready to move into the First Division. He did so with Best.

Murphy knew immediately that Best was unique. He also knew that a unique and quite separate approach was needed to reap the benefits from him. He demanded the lightest of touches where Best was concerned, and Busby concurred. On his instruction United's coaching staff were told to leave Best to his own mercurial devices. He wasn't to be regimentally drilled or methodically coached. Murphy wanted Best to remain as he'd originally seen him – daring and full of tricks. If he made mistakes, these were pardonable. If he continued to hold the ball too long or refused to let go of it, the tendency would be rectified when he matured and became less blinkered. Murphy's defence of Best was: 'How can you tell a genius how to play' and he justified his preferential treatment by recalling: 'There are two players I never tried to coach – George Best and Duncan Edwards.' It wasn't entirely true. At the beginning of Best's career he spent half an hour walking him around a wet practice field. He'd just seen him score nine goals against a team of hopefuls and trialists. In his suit and his street shoes Murphy took Best to different parts of the now deserted pitch, including the penalty area. Oblivious to the splatters of mud on the bottom of his trousers, and the squelching sound every step made, he catalogued the positions Best could have taken and the runs he might have made. Just as Murphy and Busby intended, Best picked up none of the signals that United rated him so highly. Nor did he know his progress was being discreetly tracked and discussed regularly in the manager's office.

When Charlton saw Best as a trainee he said: 'Blimey, he's going to have to grow a lot in every direction to make it.' Charlton soon revised that opinion: 'I saw him play and I could have bitten my tongue off. Sometimes, when he has the ball, you're concerned that no one else is going to get it again – not even if you played until night time.' Denis Law compared Best to 'a skinned rabbit'. What he saw nonetheless was almost a mirror image of himself as a youngster: a pathetically skinny, whippet-like lad. In his teens Law had been the most unlikely player – pasty and diminutive with a narrow face and jug-like ears. He stared at everything through a pair of silver-rimmed, National Health spectacles that didn't disguise a pronounced squint. What was first said of Law would later be said of Best also. How can he play? Won't his legs buckle and break? At Huddersfield, where Law began his career, the manager, Andy Beattie, said in his Scottish brogue that he'd never seen a 'less likely fitba prospect'. After being proved wrong Beattie proclaimed Law was 'a freak'. At Old Trafford one 'freak' instantly recognised another.

What Busby continued to see in Best pushed one question further to the front of his mind: How soon should I play him in the First Division? Conversations with Murphy would weave towards the matter of how Best could be fitted into a team that Busby then thought wasn't capable of taking a League Championship. Leadership is a lonely business, irrespective of who shares the load, and Busby was hooked on a dilemma which he alone could solve. 'He was no yes man,' he said of Murphy, always blowing a bugle for Best, 'but, once having made a point, he would accept that mine was the decision.'

Busby vacillated over Best, originally deciding to pick him against Blackpool in the sixth match of the 1963–64 season – United won it handsomely 3–0 – before recanting. Though meticulous and rational in thought, Busby sometimes let his gut govern his decisions. He had blooded Duncan Edwards at only 16 years and 185 days old. In speaking about Edwards' basic talent Busby could have been speaking about Best: 'He seemed too good to be true. We could find nothing wrong with the lad. What could we work on?' The crucial difference between them – and Busby couldn't ignore it – remained physical stature. Even at 15 years old, said Busby of the muscular Edwards, almost 6ft tall and 13 stone in weight, 'he looked like a man, he played like a man . . . he was a colossus.'

Busby also thought of him as 'indefatigable . . . he would play every day in the week if he could'. Best, though now a shade over 5ft 8in, still looked as delicate as a butterfly. His speck of a body had persuaded heavyweight opponents that he was certain to be a fall-down featherweight, who could be shoved around and battered with impunity. Busby had seen Best confound them. He'd traded tackles on a like-for-like basis, and had never backtracked from a scrap for the ball. 'He was always on the move,' said Busby. 'Anyone trying to kick him kicked at thin air.' For the purpose of self-preservation Best had even got his retaliation in first on occasions, looking so angelic afterwards that no one would have believed it came with malice aforethought.

Busby argued that only 'desperate managers' slotted an untried young-ster into a team they weren't certain could support him sufficiently. Such a move would be cruel, unfair and detrimental to the player. United, however, were winning and the bookmakers' odds installed them among the title favourites. If not now, then when? There were doubts that nagged like a migraine for Busby. What if he was wrong? What if he did play him too soon? What if Best wasn't another Edwards – and, also, wasn't as ready as Edwards had been? He was aware of the adage of acting in haste and repenting at leisure. 'You can do it all wrong and wreck prom-ising careers for the sake of a few months,' he said.

Busby had been cautious and patient in his investment in Best. He'd been anxious not to over-tax him and made sure the nurturing process was unaccompanied by fanfare. Busby was a man of plain words, and he was sparing in his use of them in discussing Best's progress or his prospects to the press. He didn't want Best compared to Edwards or widely heralded in headlines as a Babe of the next generation, which would have brought unnecessary attention and attendant pressures. In fact Busby had personally plotted a course for Best – and only Busby could now decide in which direction to take him.

Still wrestling with these thoughts, he was almost relieved to find his hand half-forced. Ian Moir had already made 32 League appearances for United – and he'd make another 13 more before his career carried him elsewhere – but it's his misfortune to be remembered primarily for the one game he didn't play in rather than those he did. United were only two days away from facing West Bromwich Albion at Old Trafford – a game pitting first against second in the table – when Moir twisted a knee in training.

Murphy had no hesitation in recommending Best as his replacement; Busby stopped dithering. Replacing the unfit Moir with Best, he'd recall its significance with this wonderfully understated description of the decision: 'The big day came for the small boy.'

On the way back from training sessions, Matt Busby's 'small boy' would watch the first team practising and think to himself: 'It'll be twenty years before I get a chance here – and then it'll be too late. I'll be too old.' He'd see Bobby Charlton fizz in shots from the edge of the box or Denis Law impeccably slide the ball into the net from close range and dismiss as 'impossible' his chances of appearing beside them. He'd collect their autographs for friends, sticking a piece of paper and a pen in front of them without a word. 'I just dried up,' he said. Law would give him a friendly tap around the ear to let him know he was accepted.

But, even in the pecking order of the youth team, Best saw himself as not much higher than half way. His contemporary, David Sadler, set the pace. Sadler was three months older, a stone and a half heavier and almost four inches taller than Best. He'd been selected at the start of the season and had retained his place. Best began to mope, asking himself, What kind of chance had I of making the first team with so many young and established inside-forwards towering above me? The more he dwelt on it, the 'more ominous my position appeared', he said. 'I felt I was one of the worst players.'

With no inkling of what was to come, Best's lucky day turned out to be Friday the 13th – the morning Busby wrote out his team sheet. His handwriting was spidery and cramped, the letters squashed into one another, as if he felt the need to save paper. He tended not to finish off his Ts, the small cross stroke usually left hanging well away from the ascender. This is how Best finally saw his name on a 6 x 4 piece of Manchester United stationery, the club's name curiously printed in dark blue rather than a rich red.

Best presumed he'd be in the Central League team; he'd even told his parents as much. His omission left him sadly scanning the A and B teams in the Lancashire League. Finding he wasn't included in either of those, his heart almost dropped out of his body. 'For some reason, which I can't explain, I decided to look at the first team,' he said. He found Busby's uneven, ballpoint scrawl had listed him at the bottom beside one word written in capitals: RESERVE. Since substitutes weren't permitted then, Best was distraught rather than ecstatic. 'I managed to behave in the way that makes so many people despair of me having any sense at all,' he said. He assumed United were dropping him as a punishment. He could think of three possible reasons. He'd been playing poorly. He hadn't trained hard enough. He had said or done something that had displeased the coaches. 'I had this idea that I was going to be left without a game,' he added. The downcast Best assumed he would be used as an odd-job man – someone to 'help with the boots and other dressing-room chores', he said. He slunk back to his digs, fretful about his future and also the prospect of making eye contact, let alone embarking on a serious conversation, with either Busby or his senior players such as Charlton. 'I wasn't used to speaking to anyone in the first team and too many others in the reserves either.' He spent the night turning in his bed, half-wishing 'someone would fall downstairs and break a bloody leg or something so I could get in the team'.

Memory can be a fickle beast. Best subsequently gave slightly different accounts of the hours before his debut. In the first he reports for the pre-match meal and finds Old Trafford's groundsman and Joe Armstrong offering him congratulations and the traditional 'good luck'. The perplexed Best can't understand why 'a lot of fuss' is being made 'over someone who is a reserve'. Not until Paddy Crerand tells him: 'Don't you be hitting your crosses too hard today,' does Best begin to appreciate what lies beneath the advice. He queries the meaning of what Crerand has said.

BEST: What's going on? What are you talking about?
CRERAND: You're playing today. Don't you know? Hasn't the boss told you? Everyone else knows.

In another version Best remembers Busby strolling casually along the aisle of the team coach. He lowers his head and leans across Best, giving him the news above the sound of the engine. 'You're playing today, son,' he says. Best initially thinks Busby is talking about United's A or B team. He believes he is being dispatched back to the Cliff for what will be 'another game in front of three men and a dog'. The sentence doesn't impact properly on him until he hears Busby add the crucial words 'against West Brom'. In a third recollection Best excludes the early exchanges, which are baffling to him, and fuses together Crerand's explanation and Busby's crouching beside him. In a fourth Busby calls him into his office to tell him the news. 'I nearly died,' he said.

The consistent theme is Best thanking Busby for protecting him against the possibility of stage fright. He called it his first direct experience of Busby as a 'master handler of men' and a 'super-manager'.

Best was the last person to know of Busby's intentions. The evening before, Mary Fullaway had been glumly informed about what her lodger believed would be his skivvying duties at Old Trafford the following afternoon. At Saturday lunchtime, however, she caught the radio bulletin about Best's selection before he heard it himself. At home in Belfast Ann Best sensed what was going to happen in an extraordinary and unexplainable instance of precognition cum mother's intuition. On the Friday evening she turned to her husband and said: 'You know, I think our George will be playing in the first team tomorrow.' Dickie Best gently told her what he knew to be the truth. 'He's travelling with the reserves.' His wife was convinced otherwise, her conviction unshakeable. 'No,' she insisted. 'He's in the first team. It's almost as if I can see it.' At 12.30 p.m. the next day she was monitoring the radio like Mrs Fullaway. Afterwards she was able to repeat exactly what she heard: that Busby was taking a 'big step' in calling up 'a Belfast boy, a lad called George Best'. She almost fainted.

What came next stayed with Best for ever, fixed and unchanging, in a montage that was structured and sequential. He remembered a shirt-sleeve September morning – summer fading into autumn – that was 'sunny and warm . . . when people would be better off on the beach or playing cricket'. He remembered the coach arriving at Old Trafford, where he looked along the congested pavements and across the car park at the fans in scarves and toting rattles. He remembered the faces who stared inquisitively at him with the sort of puzzled gaze that said: 'Who's that?' As Best said: 'Nobody knew me. Few had ever heard of me . . . Most probably thought I was there to help with the kit.' He remembered some supporters slapping the coach windows, smudging the glass with the palms of their hands, or giving him the thumbs-up. He remembered the number 7 shirt, pristine on a hanger, waiting for his slim back. He remembered the scent of liniment and cigarette smoke. He remembered, as the clock ticked towards three o'clock, another conversation with Busby in which he was told in a 'quiet, persuasive way' to play the game that came naturally to him. He remembered nodding out of respect and because it was expected of him; though he knew there was no other way he *could* play.

Busby wouldn't forget Best's debut either. He'd always strictly rationed his games, as if hiding him away like a secret weapon. In two seasons Best had played just four Central League reserve matches – and the first of those was just three weeks before his grand baptism. His other games comprised two FA Youth Cup ties, 15 A team appearances and 40 for B side, the lowest rung of the ladder.

Busby was used to novices looking as though the guillotine's edge or a public stoning, rather than an admiring full house, awaited them. The muffled sound of a chanting, eager crowd infiltrated through the walls of the dressing room and intimidated them. Busby had seen players pace the dressing room as if determined to wear a hole in the tiles. He'd seen others curl into a foetal silence, knees drawn towards their chest. Their skin was the colour of plaster and a mongoose-stare filled their eyes. He'd seen a lot puke and retch or clutch their bellies in mad dashes to the toilet bowl. Even United had its share of those for whom waiting for the start of a match brought different kinds of torture, which meant varying eccentricities or displacement strategies were needed to counter them. Charlton was constantly talkative, his tongue releasing the tension inside him. Shay Brennan would light a fag, the smoke rising from behind the door of a lavatory cubicle. Nobby Stiles would slide in his contact lenses and then repeatedly order his things on his peg, as though the hand of an invisible intruder had stolen something in the ten seconds between each rechecking. To settle himself, even Jimmy Murphy was partial to a small shot of Scotch, the bottle concealed in the team's wicker skip. Busby knew when a player needed bolstering, and he would mutter comforting platitudes to him. In such circumstances he understood that the reassuring timbre of his voice was more important than what he actually said. But, where Best was concerned, Busby found himself all but redundant. Best was unperturbed and also imperturbable. He acted as though he was about to take part in nothing more arduous than a morning's training.

Only on the very stroke of an engagement does a commander truly find out whether one of his combatants can handle the big battle. Best was nerveless. Watching him discreetly, the incredulous Busby saw Best sit cross-legged in a corner of the dressing room, as though preparing to drift off into yoga meditation. He watched him turn the pages of the flimsy match programme from front to back and then from back to front again. There wasn't much to read. Busby's column was anodyne, extending a 'hearty welcome' to the opposition. The pen pictures of Albion's 'playing personalities' were strictly factual. The centre spread gave the sides in formation, the presses rolling before Best's call-up, which meant Moir's name instead of his own was in print. Advertisements framed the rectangular layout – one for a car dealer's, another for a raincoat company and a third for Manchester's Saturday-night *Football Pink*. Best hardly spoke; for once not because he was too shy, but because there was nothing constructive to say. He got changed slowly, folding his shirt and jacket as though about to pack them away in a holiday suitcase. Busby recognised it was neither callowness nor ignorance. He merely possessed what his boss would say admiringly could not be 'measured, anticipated or practised . . . he was completely oblivious to pre-match tensions'. Best put it another way: 'I never once felt the slightest twinge of butterflies . . . I just couldn't get worked up about it.' After half an hour, Busby thought Best was 'playing his three hundredth game rather than his first'.

One thing threatened to throw him off his stride. Ask any pro at the highest level what struck them most about their debut and the answer is usually the same: the noise. So it proved for Best. Decades on he could still hear it. The slight incline of the tunnel meant that someone at the back of the team line was able to see only a slender bar of terracing before becoming fully visible to the crowd. As Best emerged into the afternoon light, the thunderous and throatily raucous acclaim for United overwhelmed him, almost pushing him backwards as though he'd been shoved in the chest. He had envisaged nothing like it and so was unprepared. To stand in a crowd such as this – as Best had done often – was no substitute for standing in front of it. The hairs on the back of his neck bristled, and the decibel level rose as one section of Old Trafford's oratorio competed to outdo another. As the sound swept down and across the pitch, it grew louder and then even louder still, as if it had no peak. This was the way Best imagined Bedlam to be – a pounding and thumping racket comprising whoops and cheering cries, shouts and blasts of shrill yelling. But he couldn't have told anyone what was being yelled exactly; for nothing emerged from this wall of noise that was sharp and distinct. Best had to shake his head to clear it and press his forefingers hard against the lobes of his ears to hear properly again. (He retrospectively likened it to the sensation you feel during take-off on an aircraft.) One word, chopped into syllables, became comprehensible to him above the roar: U-ni-ted. 'I felt like a gladiator coming into the arena,' he said. The effect it had on him was everlasting. 'Even later in my career, playing at Liverpool or Benfica . . . or in front of 130,000 at Real Madrid, nothing quite compared with that first time,' said Best. 'It will be there until I die.'

Best hadn't been over-bothered when his team-mates began calling the left-back who'd be marking him a 'killer' and a 'cruncher'. His response was the dismissive: 'He'll have to catch me first.' Aware Graham Williams was supposed to carry 'a wooden club in either foot', and also thinking about his bellicose reputation, he half-expected to see someone forbiddingly tall with tree-trunk legs and an expression of pure menace. Williams was 25. Like Best, he'd made his debut aged 17. Unlike Best, he was solidly and stoutly built. Best still reckoned he was 'small' for a full-back and cockily thought to himself: 'Georgie boy, you've got nothing to worry about.' His attitude hovered between the blasé and the contemptuous. 'I set out to do the same things as I would have done if I'd been with my mates on the park in Belfast,' he said.

Best pushed and ran the ball rapturously around Williams. He nutmegged him with typical audaciousness, nipping past him in a wide semi-circle. Williams tried to muscle Best out of the match and because of it he was booed and cat-called, like a pantomime villain with a waxed moustache. It was nothing Williams hadn't heard before; he was a hard man's hard man and had the equipment to play that role. As the jeers for his treatment of Best intensified, Williams turned and began blowing kisses to his critics nearest to the perimeter wall. One tackle caught Best flush on the left ankle and sent him sliding towards the touchline. Maurice Setters ran across to confront Williams. 'Fancy kicking little boys,' he said tartly. 'He doesn't play like a little boy,' replied Williams, who'd later say: 'He was like dog shit. He got everywhere.' Best gathered himself up and tried not to limp away, already knowing the bruised ankle was swelling beneath his sock. Had it happened two seasons later, after the Football League finally relented and allowed substitutions, Busby would have taken him off at half-time. He reluctantly switched Best to the left wing instead to ensure United retained numerical parity.

There was another debutant on the pitch. Campbell Crawford had been told the previous day that he'd be marking Charlton. His instructions were rudimentary to say the least. 'If Charlton dips his shoulder to go one way,' he was told, 'he will go the other.' Crawford was 19, an attacking, speedy full back, who weighed almost 11 stone and matched Best for height. He'd faced him before in the Central League and knew what to expect. The exchanges between them were tit-for-tat, a three-quarters-fit Best doing to Crawford what he'd done to Williams or losing out to a stretching leg that stole possession from him. 'You lucky sod,' was the phrase most often swapped between them. Crawford would never face Best again.

That game was a dishevelled affair, and Best looked like a foal on ice during much of it. The attendance was 50,453, though three times as many would retrospectively claim to have been there to see something that ought to have been a five-star ballet turn into a clodhoppers' dance. No one refers to the result or to the frugal entertainment in a game settled by a solitary goal from David Sadler after 65 minutes. No one cares about the context of the match other than what it represented historically for Best. Were it not for Best, the fixture would be ignored – another statistic in a dusty, put-away record book. But, as Busby stressed, Best 'had pulses racing' from the start. None more so than Busby's own. He wondered whether what he saw was 'really true' and asked himself: 'Was I just dreaming?' Busby crucially learned two things about Best that he had suspected but could not confirm before sending him out against Albion. The grand occasion galvanised rather than diminished him; and his airy attitude was not a fake front designed to disguise self-doubt. 'I have known many examples of players who are absolutely wonderful at practice,' said Busby. 'Come match day, they have left all their wonders on the training ground last Tuesday. The hottest property . . . can freeze on the big day in front of the big crowd.'

Best passed his test. He had taken on Williams, who looked perfectly capable of dicing him into quarters. He'd run at him and taken the ball beyond him. He'd made him lunge and curse. And he'd survived the sort of challenges that would have forced the faint or tender-hearted into instant surrender. Busby had seen Best get whacked on the knee and rapped on the calves and studded along the shins. He'd barely winced. Further confirmation of his astonishing agility and deftness on the ball wasn't needed. But there was also evidence of these for Busby – those small moments that can escape all but the connoisseur's eye in the helter-skelter rush of a match. 'There's something in the really gifted player that hits you,' said Busby, outlining his belief that what he always searched out was 'instinct'. Unquestionably Best possessed it. His first touch was always exquisite, killing the ball stone-dead before taking control of it. The pushes and nudges Best performed at full pelt were exquisite, too. He could run as fast with the ball as without it, and a swerve sent him slaloming away as defenders tried to recover both their dignity and their bearings. Some would slip in his wake and then chase after him, legs pumping furiously, as if pedalling an invisible bike. Others were dizzied by him, the defender staggering away like someone who had never walked before. Busby saw flashes of all this against West Brom. He also saw that the perfectionist gene in Best meant he was still dissatisfied. He hadn't scored. He hadn't dominated. Even the fact he'd played the first pass in the build-up to the goal wasn't enough for someone who, despite his age, had visualised himself waltzing from half-way line to penalty area before slipping the ball into the net and then taking an extravagant bow in front of the Stretford End.

Mrs Fullaway made Best a celebratory meal of egg and chips, a dish he regarded as his caviar. The following morning he cut out the match report from *The Pink* and posted it along with a quickly scribbled letter to his parents. In 12 lines he recounted the 'fabulous experience' of coming out of the half-darkness of the tunnel. He also claimed – tongue-in-cheek and adding an exclamation mark for effect – that Williams was a 'madman', who 'almost broke my flippin' ankle!' So as not to appear arrogant or complacent, he didn't confess what he really felt. 'I knew I'd arrived,' said Best later. 'I knew then what I'd always believed – that I'd find it easy to play in the First Division.'

The First Division, however, would not find it easy to play against him. In both pre and post-match interviews Busby usually gave nothing away. 'It's very dangerous to shout,' he'd say, 'because in my profession every twenty-four hours can make you a fool.' Busby didn't like to make outlandish forecasts in case these proved to be wrong and were subsequently used to ridicule him. If asked, he spoke about Best in a factual, deadpan manner, as if there was nothing much to say about him or his performance. The act was intended to dampen anticipation about him. Best, said Busby, was 'a promising individual at the birth of his career'. He made it sound as if no one – especially him or his coaches – knew whether or not Best would thrive or flare briefly before fizzling out. But in an interview he gave earlier in the week to the *Observer* – well before Moir's injury made Best's inclusion certain – Busby revealed what he really thought. The piece was published on the morning after the win over West Brom. His remarks about Best were almost throwaway, and slotted into the penultimate paragraph.

'And we've got an Irish boy here called Best and if he doesn't make a bloody genius I haven't seen one. . . it's all there – the heart, the ability, everything.'

Within one year and 16 days of his debut – encompassing only 28 League appearances – George Best was already fêted. At the end of his first season *Soccer Star* magazine realised no team photograph of Manchester United would be complete without Best in it. The problem was that no such picture then existed. Its editor resolved the problem by having Best's head clumsily superimposed on someone else's shoulders. Ironically that someone else was Ian Moir. Best had already been called a 'thin-faced Beatle', a sobriquet bestowed by the *Daily Express*, who also said he was 'a boy among men in his team'. He was likened to Stanley Matthews and Tom Finney and also spoken of as a prospective Garrincha, the 'Little Bird' Brazilian who had dominated the World Cup in Chile two years earlier. Best preferred the reference to Garrincha to comparisons with either Matthews or Finney. He signed one letter to his parents 'Garrincha George'. In another he proudly told them: 'The crowd think I'm another Johnny Berry,' who was also a winger and a three-time League champion at United in the 1950s. Seeking an analogy for his remarkable rise Busby settled on the description of Best as a 'new comet'. Best referred to the same period as 'The Explosion'. The detonation occurred against Chelsea at the end of September 1964. Best pinpointed the date as the most momentous of his nascent career. 'For the first time I realised what could happen and what was going to happen,' he said of the clamouring attention of fans and girls and the media. 'My name was plastered on every newspaper.'

What Best did on a Wednesday night in West London was 'mesmerising' according to Busby. According to everyone else it was miraculous. No one could contain him because no one could catch him. Whether on the left wing, where he began, or on the right, where he drifted, Best beguiled. Everything he'd ever done on that uneven patch of grass near his home on the Cregagh Estate he now did in the upturned bowl of Stamford Bridge. Even among those with allegiance to Chelsea, there was eventually a longing on the terraces for Best to get the ball; for in getting it he would do something memorable with it.

Busby anticipated it. This defining performance had been coming ever since his unexpected recall three months after his debut. After his ankle healed, Busby decided it was sensible to let Best build up his stamina in the Central League and thicken up his torso and legs on the training pitch before summoning him again. The decision to bring him back was another made through expediency. A double-header against Burnley, squeezed into the week between Christmas and New Year, began ignominiously – a 6–1 thumping at Turf Moor. Best, then at home in Belfast, was called back as a reinforcement. The telegram Busby sent him didn't make promises, which led Best to erroneously believe that he was needed only as cover. He brokered a deal that now – as it must have done then – seems impudent. He wanted to return to Belfast immediately afterwards to finish off his festive holiday.

The game was role-reversal; United won 5–1. It brought Best his first goal – a right-foot drive from the fringe of the box – and a piece of advice from Busby that served him well then and afterwards. Confronting Best were two of the most accomplished full-backs in the Football League: John Angus and Alex Elder. Both had been around the block; both had won a Championship medal; both had reputations as meanly uncompromising competitors. Best said Busby had a 'laid-back' approach, a 'soothing voice' and he didn't rely on long convoluted speeches to pass on insights, which always sounded like suggestions instead of orders. He'd speak to a player as if the two of them were having a casual, very private conversation. At half-time Busby, ever so gently, told Best how to master Elder.

'*You're running flat out as soon as you receive the ball and he's catching you over that first four or five yards. Don't try to go at breakneck speed as soon as you get the ball. Go at three-quarter speed. That way the full-back adjusts his pace accordingly to make the tackle. Just as he commits himself, accelerate away with a burst of pace. He won't catch you then.*'

Best tore into Elder and acutely embarrassed the doleful Angus, who was like a man trapped in a revolving door.

Busby didn't like to discuss a game in its immediate aftermath. The dissection of it – if necessary – would take place on Monday. He didn't want to say anything in the heat of the moment that he might regret over the rest of the weekend. Some of his praise was shared in the same manner. 'If you'd played well he always let you know,' said Best, whom Busby sought out 48 hours after seeing him treat Angus and Elder as if the pair of them were raw starters. 'Well done, son,' said Busby, tapping Best on the elbow before moving on. 'I felt,' said Best, 'as if Jesus Christ had spoken to me.'

From then onwards – as the second half of the season unfolded gloriously in front of him – Best was celebrated as the wonder of the First Division rather than a novice, which is how he judged himself. He was a fast developer. There was a parade of exceptional performances – against Arsenal (3–1), Tottenham (3–2), Bolton (5–0) and another defeat of West Brom (4–1). Rarely did a win not bear something of Best's stamp. Headline writers relished his name, which was short – handily fitting into a single-column drop – and could also be used as a pun, however predictably, in such phrases as:

**THE BEST OF GEORGIE
THE BEST MAN FOR UNITED
BEST OF THE REST**

There was scarcely any televised football; both the BBC's *Match of the Day* and the Sunday afternoon hour of League highlights shown in the regions had yet to feature on the schedules. So those who read about Best were often surprised when he appeared in front of them. 'I was mistaken for a mascot and an autograph hunter,' he said. Dickie Best cited his son's size as the sole reason for his apprehension about whether or not his impetus would continue. 'I thought he'd be killed,' he said. 'I'm more than surprised at the wee fellah making the grade.'

Best did so because of his remarkable resilience. Without it he'd never have been able to dwell on the ball long enough to use it decoratively. He walked off with vivid, blue-yellow bruising on his calf and his thigh. He ignored the odd flaying arm in his face, an elbow in the ribs or chest, a push in the back and even the sly dig in his kidneys. The verbal threats and insults didn't disturb him either. 'Someone was always saying he'd break my leg if I made him look stupid,' said Best. Other defenders would warn him that 'the hard man of the team' was preparing to smash him against the railings. It only made them sound feeble, like a weakling threatening to fetch his big brother. Best saw these as playground games. What propelled him on was the need to be better. 'So many kids before me had been hailed as the golden boy a shade too soon . . . That wasn't going to happen to me,' he insisted. The lack of TV coverage meant that coaches couldn't constantly watch and rewind film to chart Best's movements or try to detect faults. Busby cautioned that the following season would be more arduous still than the last because defenders knew what to expect from him. Familiarity didn't breed contempt, explained Busby; it did, however, mean that Best's opponents now had a lot of knowledge gained through experience. No one would have described Best as a one-trick pony – he had an entire book of those – but there was a feeling that he'd have to go up another gear to make an impact again. Best, unflappable as ever, looked at it another way. However much full-backs had learned about him, he'd learned equally as much about them. And the conclusion he reached was this: he was too quick and too agile for them. The game at Chelsea proved it indisputably.

In *The Football Man*, his beautiful study of the beautiful game, Arthur Hopcraft wrote: 'Sport can be cruel to men. Football can make a man more ridiculous even than drink can.' That floodlit night at Stamford Bridge was cruel to Ken Shellito because Best made him look ridiculous. Hopcraft attributed the return of the verb 'to dribble' to the football writer's vocabulary entirely to Best; Shellito knows why. Best often said: 'I play as I feel.' Against Shellito he felt exhilarated and unstoppable. The humbling of Angus and Elder was tame compared to the torture inflicted on him. Best gave an artist's exhibition revelatory in its execution and coruscating in its range.

It is said that man responds to those landscapes in which he instinctively feels he belongs. Best had never played at Stamford Bridge before; but he knew he belonged there. The architecture was unimpressive. There was rickety-looking double-decker seating on stilts beside the modest main stand, its footballer's weather-vane twisting atop a white-fronted pediment. There were wide, open spaces behind each uncovered goal and 20-floor high-rises could be seen in the middle and far distance. But something indefinable in regard to the ambience of the ground and the atmosphere inside it never failed to inspire Best. He was roused whenever he went to Chelsea, which became one of his spiritual homes. 'Something about it used to lift him,' said Busby.

Best went into the game thinking for the first time that United might lose it. The sides were locked beside one another at the head of the table. Chelsea were called Tommy Docherty's 'Diamonds'; Best thought of them as 'young lions' – Bonetti and Venables, Tambling and Hollins, Harris and Houseman. But what was billed as a titanic struggle between teams turned instead into a one-man show. Best's supremacy of the ball and of the match was such that, writing in *The Times*, Geoffrey Green said that Shellito 'must have felt that he was trying to push back a genie into his bottle'. The *Daily Express* argued that he 'baffled . . . rocked . . . and finally crushed' Chelsea. The *Daily Mirror* report dwelt on the reaction of the 60,000 crowd: 'At the end they stood and acclaimed him. They gave him their hearts . . . who will forget it?' Reciting those lines out loud would always leave Dickie Best dabbing tears from the corners of his eyes.

United won 2–0. Best scored the opening goal, after intercepting a back pass, and created the second with a high chip that Denis Law headed in. Around these two goals he caused havoc. If you were to take a pencil and try to trace on paper the paths Best cut across the pitch, you'd be left looking at a mass of curves and cross-hatchings, diagonal lines and tight, uninterpretable squiggles. Best talked about his 'usual lack of tactical discipline', stressing that he 'switched and roved about the forward line'. He savaged Shellito more than anyone, beating him at will. He went outside him like a sports car passing a lumbering truck. He nipped on his inside after throwing him off balance. The nutmeg – already one of his trademarks – was done whenever Shellito attempted to spread himself in Best's path. And, as the game progressed, he grew ever more unorthodox. As Shellito loomed over him, Best crossed his legs at the knee, stepping over the ball with his right foot and kicking it with his left. He then turned his back on Shellito and pirouetted around him as if the ball was tied firmly to his foot. Near the end he took a pass on the run and stopped it so suddenly that Shellito dashed three yards past him before realising that Best was heading in the opposite direction.

Shellito was recovering from a severe knee injury, which had damaged his ligaments and cartilage and restricted his movements. But he never tried to bring Best down or pull his shirt and he didn't resort to whacking him on the ankle as Graham Williams had done. 'If someone beat me legitimately and because he was better than me, I had to accept it,' said Shellito virtuously, as if wanting to uphold Corinthian ideals. 'I didn't like to kick wingers to stop them. That wasn't how the game should be played.' The left-back, Eddie McCreadie, had no such scruples. He did kick, and the blows his boots struck soon persuaded Best to switch back Shellito's way. 'I told him to bugger off,' said Shellito. 'He hadn't been gone long enough to give me a proper break.' The only thing that released Shellito was the final whistle. When it mercifully came, the vanquished willingly went up to the victor. Shellito sportingly dropped his colours in solemn salute, clasping Best by the hand and wrapping an arm around his shoulder. 'My difficulty about facing him that day – and any other – was trying to decide which way he'd try to go past me. I knew that he didn't know what he'd do until the last moment. So how was I supposed to tell?' asks Shellito. His agony was wittily summed up by Paddy Crerand, who insisted Shellito left the field suffering from 'twisted blood' as the result of Best's mazy sprinting. 'If you want to know the truth,' says Shellito now, 'everything was twisted.'

Best didn't know what to say in return to the congratulations Shellito offered him. He mumbled a 'thank you' and said 'hard luck', half-waving towards the teeming terraces. He then dropped his chin to his chest as he walked off, as if feeling disorientated.

What he'd done had yet to register fully with him. It did so only in the silence of his hotel bedroom the following morning. He awoke, made himself tea, spread the national newspapers across the bed and began to read them, turning first to the match report, to relive 'those moments when everything I tried seemed to come off'. He told himself that United's team 'was going to be special – and I would become special with it'. Best claimed he could 'feel' this without being able to say why or even explain the depth of his conviction.

The next seven months would affirm it because, as Best said matter-of-factly, 'I was born with a talent other people would have died for.'

4

Everything I Do is Off the Cuff

A clip of film less than ten seconds long defines the early impact George Best made. It's a miniature portrait of him – 'The Young Footballer as an Artist'. Contained within it is all his precocity and audacity. It showcases a goal, another scored against Chelsea, the team Best treated the way a dog treats a lamp-post.

That goal begins from the most innocuous circumstances. The goal-keeper, Peter Bonetti, bowls possession to his right-back, Eddie McCreadie, who accepts it close to the angle of the area. There's no danger to McCreadie and nothing to alert him either about what's to come. He stills the ball with his right foot and glances around and then ahead of him, as if he has the rest of Saturday afternoon and also Sunday morning to play it lazily where he wants. Best isn't even in the camera shot.

McCreadie is choosing the channel along which he will strike a long pass. He's unperturbed and has eyes only for the far-off scene. He sees his forwards on the half-way line, arms raised and pleading for the ball to be pumped at them. When Best does appear in the picture and begins to cross McCreadie's line of sight, the defender pays no serious atten-tion to him. He doesn't take into account how fleet of foot Best is; how rapidly he can cover ground and shut him down. Best is within six feet of him before McCreadie feels the urgency to clear up-field. In hoofing the ball he fails to get sufficient elevation on it. In the same moment Best begins to turn, his back and the number 11 on his shirt half-facing McCreadie. He charges the kick down, the ball striking both his outstretched right leg and then his left heel. McCreadie is forced to swivel and chase towards his own goal-line to retrieve possession, regarding it as a routine chore – a mistake that can be rectified with simple tidying up. It is a crass misjudgement. Best is quicker and smarter than McCreadie and he gets to the ball before him, toe-poking it in a high loop and immediately heading off in pursuit of the drop. McCreadie is initially flat-footed, stranded. There's no other team-mate, apart from Bonetti, in this area of the Old Trafford pitch. Bonetti is a hapless bystander anyway, able only to shout advice, which is drowned out by the noise of the Stretford End, banked behind him.

On his own, panicky and confused and without a rational thought in his head about what to do, McCreadie manages to scamper backwards and momentarily shields the ball from Best; he can feel his breath on his neck. He decides – again riskily and misguidedly – to play a pass back to Bonetti with the outside of his right boot. Best cuts across him, the challenge forcing McCreadie to change the plan and slide into a tackle, which he loses. He begins to topple over and the ball dribbles weakly off his left foot. He looks a damned fool. He is sprawled, ignominiously, on his front, scrambling to get up and pressing both hands into the turf. He slips again, as if the grass has been greased, and so has a worm's view of what comes next. Best lets the ball run a foot inside the area. He's at a 15-degree angle from Bonetti's goal; and Bonetti, who has not known whether to leave his six-yard box or stay inside it, is standing in front of his near post. Anyone else, confronted with such improbable geometry, would have sent a firm centre towards the penalty spot, where David Herd is waiting to claim it – and where Denis Law is waiting beyond him. Not Best. He pays no attention to either of them. What he does instead is instinctive, stemming from the certain knowledge that his skill won't let him down. As he strikes the ball Best looks like a model posing in the Football Association's coaching manual. He leans back slightly. His left foot is planted solidly beside the ball. His right is drawn. Outstretched arms give him perfect balance. He uses his instep, giving the lob curve and loop and spin. In his heart Bonetti knows he is beaten as soon as he sees the ball rise off Best's boot. He pushes himself upwards, throwing his right hand at it, and hoping beyond hope that even a feathery touch with his long second finger might deflect the effort sufficiently to save it and him and McCreadie. But the mathematical and trigonometrical calculations Best makes are infallible, as if he's surveyed the land and everything in it and worked out the height and weight, and also the velocity and dip, he needs to achieve to clear Bonetti and find the net. The ball evades the keeper's jump by an inch and drops a foot inside the far post. Herd, who had been expecting the pass that never came, leaps into the net to retrieve it, scarcely crediting what he's witnessed. Bonetti is baffled. He rests his hands on his hips, briefly swivelling towards the vanquished McCreadie, who is upright again, trudging across the muddy area with dirty knees and looking at no one. He doesn't need to be told – through word or glance or gesture – that the goal is his fault. The ridicule of the crowd is punishment enough.

Geoffrey Green evoked Gertrude Stein when writing a memorable line in *The Times* to remind anyone who had forgotten that all goals, whether scored with a searing shot or scuffed messily over the line, count equally: 'If a rose is a rose is a rose, then a goal is a goal is a goal.' Best's, precipitating a 4–0 rout of Chelsea on a mid-March afternoon in 1965, was a full bloom. What *Match of the Day*'s two gantry cameras preserved was a piece of individualism as good as anything else he'd ever produce. No one who sees it tires of doing so again. Shown at normal speed you recognise the pace and the tenacity and the nobility of the finish. Shown in slow-motion you also see the full range of abilities needed to score it. Most of them are impossible to teach.

The goal was precious to United, then hanging on in a three-cornered contest for the Championship. The table still didn't look promising for them afterwards. United were three points away from Chelsea (when only two were awarded for a win) and one adrift of Don Revie's Leeds, freshly promoted. Best was already impatient. He wanted to own immediately what most players don't win at all or attain only at the mid-point or the end of a career. 'I set my heart on a Championship medal right from the start,' he said, thinking only Leeds were capable of denying him.

In any argument between the crimson petal and the white Best was grateful to be on the west of the Pennines. He didn't merely dislike Leeds. He loathed them to the extent of expressing borderline hate. 'They would say anything to provoke you. They *were* dirty,' he explained, insisting that trait ran through them like fat in streaky bacon. He added that Leeds were the only side that obliged him to wear shin-pads for protection. His antipathy towards them is distilled into a two-line joke he frequently told.

'Why is the Elland Road pitch so green?' asked Best. 'Because of the amount of shit they put on the field.'

George Best's early boyhood crush wasn't on a footballer. It was on the fictional Hollywood character Zorro, the dashing Spanish nobleman who wore a black sackcloth mask and a black silk cape and righted social wrongs with a rapier in one hand and a bullwhip in the other. After watching him at the cinema near his home Best tied his school gabardine around his neck, pretending it was Zorro's cape, and took part in imaginary swordfights on the pavement. He came to play the way he saw Zorro fight. Zorro mocked his opponents. He outwitted them through cunning instead of force. He taunted them to the extent that most became embarrassed and then angry. That was Best's aim, too. 'If I could rile whoever was there to stop me I knew there was more chance of them making a mistake,' he said. 'They were too preoccupied trying to get their own back to think sensibly.' Early on, and irrespective of reputation, he always tried to stick the ball through opponents' legs to prove who was the boss on the pitch. Nor was he averse to letting someone know verbally that he regarded them as his inferior. 'You're too slow' and 'too old', he would tell them, or 'not good enough'.

He did things no one else could do. Against Burnley, during an FA Cup tie, he made two goals while wearing only one boot; the left came off in a tackle. United were losing 1–0 and there were less than ten minutes to save them. Not wanting to waste a second, Best tried to throw the boot over the touchline, where someone unhelpfully hurled it back at him. So he carried the boot in his right hand, laying on each goal with a foot that had only a stocking to protect it. Newspapers christened him 'The Bootless Wonder'.

There were defenders who would take small shuffled steps, like stammered speech, towards him, each hesitation highlighting a reluctance to commit themselves. Others would foolishly tear towards Best in a futile effort to crowd and hurry him into a mistake. Whatever technique was employed against him, Best found an answer to it. He was rarely corralled or confined to the touchline. 'Sometimes,' he said, 'I'm marked by even two or three defenders. Often, I can see the defender thinking that the only thing I can do is pass. This is often the time I choose to dribble . . . Zorro fought when his opponents expected him to run.'

He was easily piqued. When David Sadler griped that he was holding on to the ball too long, Best took offence. In retaliation he decided that his first ten touches during the next game would all be passes to his friend. 'He must have been a bit bemused,' said Best, 'because he was playing centre-half that day.' Other objectives were more virtuous. While still an embryonic player Best had accepted a challenge from another friend, John Fitzpatrick, to get a goal direct from the kick-off in a youth game. The grass was invisible beneath two inches of snow. Best took the ball across it, beating umpteen attempts to stop him, before popping the ball into the net. 'Is that what you wanted?' he asked Fitzpatrick, skittishly. When he knew a match was being televised, Best dearly wanted to score from the half-way line, and would frequently attempt it without success, always believing his next long-range shot would bring him a goal so memorable that *Match of the Day* would have to screen it during the opening credits. 'I would look up and see if I could lob the goal-keeper. If I thought it was on, I wouldn't hesitate to try it.'

The game in the 1960s was a particularly brutal business. It could turn into a free-for-all form of caged combat. If contemporary strictures – about high tackling, challenges from behind, elbows and the use of studs – had been in force then, most games would have ended seven-a-side. In getting under the skin of defenders Best substantially increased his chances of leaving the field on a stretcher. But, during his first full season in Division One, he didn't think that *anyone* was fast enough to catch or pin him to the turf. 'And if I did feel any pain, I didn't show it,' he said. 'I got up fast and tried to pretend I'd barely been touched.' Zorro did that, too.

The most uncompromising of the defenders were as mean as bare-knuckle fighters who believed the Queensberry Rules were for cissies. Ron 'Chopper' Harris of Chelsea called himself a 'butcher' and knew how to carve the joint. With that scarred-looking, scowling face and narrow eyes, Tommy Smith at Liverpool looked as if he might eat someone whole and be found chewing on their bones afterwards. Aged 69, Dixie Dean had part of his right leg amputated after a blood clot. Entering a room full of fellow amputees he looked around him and announced quietly: 'I see Tommy Smith's already been here.'

But Leeds – or 'Dirty Leeds' as the terrace fans were soon chanting

– had the blackest reputation for Best. Some thought of them as the antithesis of fair play. Don Revie preferred to think of their approach as an example of 'professionalism', a term used derogatorily in current parlance to describe something underhand. In Revie's vocabulary 'professionalism' meant employing modern methods. Unquestionably, his was a skilful side; but the glint of hard steel within it was sometimes flashed too often to reveal the finery beneath. If either were playing today, Billy Bremner and Bobby Collins would be booked simply for getting off the team bus.

As Best saw it, fish rots from the head down. The sort of team Leeds became followed inexorably from the kind of person Revie was – the polar opposite of Matt Busby. Best argued that football was basically a 'simple game', which ought never to be over-complicated. 'I don't like tactics. They bore me,' he said. 'Everything I do is off the cuff. That's where the buzz is for me. I just like those spontaneous moments.' What Best found particularly pointless were chalkboards used to elaborately illustrate where the opposition might attack or the movements a specific player could make. In Busby, he was paired with a manager who thought identically.

Revie was a tactical fundamentalist, a man whose search for fine detail bordered on obsessive-compulsive disorder. He liked to plan and scheme intricately and regarded as scripture the dossiers that were exhaustively prepared beforehand on each team. For him the training pitch was a testing laboratory where his strategies were refined. Revie thought scientifically, as if he was searching for some missing particle in a player's make-up that would, once found, provide the foolproof answer to every football problem. The philosophical gulf between him and Busby was cavernous. Busby concentrated on beauty and believed that 'coaching is for ordinary players', who he strove not to sign in the first place. He wanted United to play uninhibitedly. 'Have fun,' he'd say. 'There's no other point in playing.' The tactical talks he gave – only occasionally using magnetised discs – were brief and never deeply technical or overbearingly complex. Dismissing as a 'waste of time' any effort to give players a list of dos and don'ts, he seldom went beyond the opposition's fundamental strengths and vulnerabilities. Busby was no tactical dolt, however. He read other teams as well as the life-lines on his own palm. He knew how everyone else played; though, more significantly, he knew how he wanted United to play. He said his over-riding concern was to set 'a pattern' and forge 'a complete under-standing' between his players. He saw it in his Babes as well as in the Real Madrid of Di Stefano and Puskas and the Double-winning Spurs of Danny Blanchflower and Dave Mackay. 'To create it the first job is to make a player aware of what his own position demands,' he said. Anyone under Busby was expected to know the idiosyncrasies of his colleagues. The ideal, he added, was to establish 11 'thought-readers' who knew what the others were going to do. 'I have always believed that a great team is based on blending the skills of great players. I have never been convinced that great tactical systems, or that playing by numbers, is a guarantee of success.' When Alf Ramsey was operating with the wingless wonders of his 4-3-3 formation, Busby picked wingers nonetheless. He sent out his sides with the instruction to entertain and told them: 'Play to the best of your ability. The results will follow.' Nowadays, this sounds rather eccentric, as if Busby were living in an Arcadian past. But, while Revie was more concerned with nullifying the threat against him, it was imperative to Busby to win by attacking. 'We didn't play all this 4-3-3 and 4-2-4 rubbish,' said Best. 'We played the old formation – two full-backs, three half-backs and five forwards. That's the way we always played it. We could give teams a two or three-goal start and still win. If some of us had an off day, the others played well.'

As Busby and Revie duelled in 1964–65, the cultural clash was a subtext of the tussle for the Championship. When Busby spoke about his outlook, he'd say: 'There is nothing wrong in trying to win, so long as you don't set the prize above the game,' which is what he believed Revie was doing. But, ever tactful in such matters, he didn't want to disturb the harmony that existed in public between them. He concealed reservations about Revie and declined to condemn what he saw as spite and nastiness in Leeds which he – as well as Best – thought resulted in legitimate physical contact becoming deliberate thuggery for the purpose of eking out the points. Busby damned Revie with the faintest of praise; Revie was 'shrewd' and 'firm' and an 'intense character', he said. 'I saw that he would sweat it out as he would insist that his players would sweat it out.' Still reluctant to be more explicit about Leeds, Busby merely added: 'I would be less than honest if I said I had agreed with some of their tactics on the pitch.'

Some of their tactics off it were repellent, too. In mid-April Best and United went to Elland Road for what the news-boards, tied to railings and lamp-posts, trumpeted as 'The Championship Decider'. Chelsea, while slenderly in front, had played a game more than either of them. Walking down the tunnel Best felt what he said was a 'terrific pain' in his right calf from a kick. He turned to find Collins, Leeds's captain, snarling behind him. 'That's just for starters,' he told Best. The words were pathetic and prophetic. The match needed a United Nations ambassador to control it rather than a referee. One high, wild and crudely dangerous tackle cum hack followed another. Best, constantly bruised by Collins, fought back. He barged and dug him in the ribs and took his legs away from him. He saw Collins slide across the cinder track. The reply was a scything challenge taking Best near the midriff. He was still rolling and twisting when Collins stood broodingly over him, his face contorted and his teeth bared. He looked like a mad imp who had escaped from its cathedral niche and put on a pair of shorts. Collins growled to no one in particular: 'You'll have to get him again – he's still moving.'

With Nobby Stiles and Paddy Crerand, United were no pacifists. A Stiles tackle cleanly lifted Collins off his feet in retribution. The game was played in a howling gale, and Best remembered seeing Collins flung through the air and almost float on it, as if his whole body was as light as a paper bag. He dropped against the concrete base of the perimeter wall and lay crumpled against it. What Collins did to Best, so Stiles did to Collins afterwards, leaning across him for menacing effect, baring the gap where his front teeth should have been and yelling: 'Every time you come down our right-hand side and kick George, you filthy bastard, I'm going to hit you like that – only harder.' Best heard Collins appeal for the referee's protection. 'Did you hear that, ref?' he asked, holding his lower back. 'He said he's going to do me every time I come down the right side.' The referee, dismissing him with a wave of his hand, said: 'Well, if I were you, I'd stop going down their right hand side as from now.'

When a football match broke out, one kick of the respectable kind settled it – a left-footed shot dispatched from the edge of the box in the 14th minute by John Connelly, whom Busby had signed for £60,000 from Burnley. The goal was one of 89 United scored – six more than Leeds. But, despite the flair up front, undeniably prodigious, United took the title and fulfilled Best's first ambition because the defence leaked fewer goals – 39 in 42 games – than any other team in the Football League. Leeds conceded 52. Those statistics matter because what separated the champions from the runners-up was goal average. When the number of goals scored was divided by the number of goals conceded, United edged the mathematics by .686.

The penultimate fixture – a 3–1 win over Arsenal at Old Trafford – settled it. Usually Best was so relaxed before a match as to be almost comatose. Often he'd still be getting changed or tying the laces of his boots when the order came to go on to the pitch. In the hour before kick-off he'd drink Bovril and talk to his friends at a refreshment bar not far from the dressing room. When Busby asked 'Where's George?' someone would be dispatched to drag him inside only a quarter of an hour before kick-off. Against Arsenal, knowing how much the result meant to United and especially to Busby himself, Best confessed: 'Even I felt the strain.' The knot in Best's stomach and the nervous crackle of expectation among the crowd led to misplaced passes and missed chances. Denis Law had such a horrible gash on his right knee that seven stitches were required to close it. He poured cold water from a hosepipe on to the joint to numb it, and then wore strapping so tight that he moved like the Tin Man in Oz. On one leg he scored two goals. Leeds were at Birmingham City, the bottom club, and soon 3–0 behind. Celebrations began on the Stretford End. But Best, looking at the scoreboard, was horrified: Leeds pulled one goal back, and then two and, finally, a third. Walking off the pitch, he heard a voice from the crowd shout: 'Leeds won 4–3.' Only when photographers and crates of Moet appeared in the dressing room did Best understand that he'd won his Championship medal after all. 'There was enough champagne for us all to have a bath in,' he said.

Busby was choked. While the race was ongoing he didn't dare admit how dearly he wanted to win it. 'I would like the League title – but then I'd like the lot,' is as far as he went. To Busby, the Championship was a necessary means to an end: what he considered as another stride towards the Great Dream. 'I think this team can reach the upper heights. I think we can win the European Cup,' he said.

Best was thinking that, too; but still didn't fully appreciate the integral role Busby saw for him.

As if it had been celestially scripted, George Best's first full season for Manchester United poignantly coincided with Stanley Matthews's final appearance in the Football League. One Wizard of the Dribble, then 50 and knighted in the New Year's Honours List, gave way to another.

Matthews was still scrupulously fit and lean-looking and would later regret that he'd retired at least two years prematurely. According to him the longevity of his career, which began in 1930, owed much to a set regime: early to bed, teetotalism, a practically vegetarian diet and a punishing training programme that was self-devised. The first newspaper profiles of Best drew a picture of someone similarly abstemious, dedicated to perpetual improvement and living an exemplarily quiet, chaste existence. He was portrayed as the goody-two-shoes son every mother wanted. An interviewer found Best playing cards at the kitchen table and listening to records in Aycliffe Avenue. He blushes as Mary Fullaway says in front of him: 'He's a grand lad. No trouble at all. He doesn't smoke or drink and eats everything up I serve him.' Best claims he has no time to spare for women, puts his money regularly into a savings account – he's already got nearly £1,000 – and doesn't go to dances. 'I can't twist or shake,' he says.

The past is always another country, and things are done differently there. In the mid-1960s newspapers were printed in smudgy monochrome. There were only three television channels, and the BBC considered it acceptable to screen *The Black and White Minstrel Show* on one of them. The average house price was £2,500. Since a pint of beer was less than 2s., you could get drunk on £1. You had to drink quickly, however, because the pubs were closed for most of the day. It cost just 4s. to stand on the terraces; 8s. to buy a decent seat. More than 70 per cent of men and over 40 per cent of women smoked. There were more coal fires than gas or electric ones. The shops shut on the Sabbath. The roads and motorways weren't clogged with traffic. There were those who saw the future as a continuation of the present, the moral and social values of the 50s being upheld in an unchanging static world – except for a new gadget in the kitchen every now and then. Viewed today – especially by those born during the last 20 years of the old century – the decade of Best and the Beatles doesn't appear overly glamorous or even glittery. But the 60s undeniably swung and were seminal, shaking the entire social framework. The way we live now is rooted in the way that generation lived then. For Best, it was giddy bliss to be young. The 60s were a Wordsworthian-like heaven, a Golden Age. Everything was changing – fashion, music, attitudes and ambitions. There was mop hair of the 'Love Me Do', 'Ticket to Ride' Fab Four. There was the aggressive dissatisfaction of the Rolling Stones and the Who, determined then to die before old age claimed them. There were Mary Quant mini-skirts, then the sight of Twiggy in knee-high boots and the boutiques of Carnaby Street. *Time* magazine declared London to be the '*fin de siècle* city of the world'. The carnival parade passed most provincial cities by. Not Best's own, however. Manchester was locked into the heart of the revolution. Former pubs spruced themselves up and became cabaret venues. Nightclubs were places in which to be seen. From its studios on Cross Street, Granada Television created Granadaland, a landscape of soaps, kitchen sink dramas and industrially earthy comedies in which Northern folk and Northern accents, previously considered impenetrable and coarsely vulgar in the quaint Home Counties, became familiar and accepted. The joint jumped. The Beatles performed weekly on a programme called *Scene at 6.30* even before Beatlemania began. The BBC transmitted *Top of the Pops* from Manchester, too. Every group, every actor, every comic and everyone else who was someone went to the North West.

Those were the days indeed and Best revelled in them.

He represented the future. Matthews represented pre-war anxieties, post-war austerity and the stuffy and stiffly repressive 1950s. Best was the footballer of the new age; and he represented the new confidence of the young. Matthews was redolent of the participants in *The Saturday Men*, a 1962 fly-on-the-wall, warty television documentary that shows football as common industry and footballers as working men.

The camera is allowed into the dressing rooms and the boardroom at West Bromwich Albion. However rehearsed some of the scenes look now, irrespective of how cautiously clipped the dialogue sounds, the 26-minute programme accurately reflects the game as it was then and the insecurities of players aware of the brevity of their profession. Lack of fitness, the whim of the manager or the displeasure of a director means losing your wage and your club house. Training takes place on a pitch almost entirely shorn of grass. Dotted around it is a low wooden fence, a patch of bare trees, a row of telephone poles and distant houses with squat roofs, smoke corkscrewing from chimneys into air already black. The changing room is tiled and without home comforts. Refreshment is weak orange squash poured into chipped mugs. The showers are like pit-head baths. You dry off afterwards standing on a folded copy of a newspaper so as not to wet the floor. The manager shuffles uncomfortably in the oak-panelled boardroom. He is surrounded by plump, balding men who are elderly or middle-aged and treat him as a lowly subordinate, asking questions such as: 'I'd like to know how the boy went at outside-left?' The manager fiddles with his pen, glances at the sheaf of papers in front of him and says: 'I recommend that we play the same team again next week.' The directors agree, as if sanctimoniously giving him benediction. The players gather around the team sheet, pinned on to a baize-covered noticeboard in a well lit corridor. What follows isn't so much a tactical talk as a testy telling off. Far more assertive without the directors' patronisation, the manager accuses the under-performers in his side of 'going into your shell' and launches into what is supposed to be a tub-thumping speech. The language is neither original nor rousing: 'You've got to keep fighting lads . . . the game's never lost until the last whistle . . . there's no excuse for packing it in . . . points are absolutely vital . . . we ask for one hundred per cent for ninety minutes . . . we're all in the same boat.' Those he's left out resemble mourners peering into a grave; a few look as though salty tears are coming. Like everyone else in the country who punches a card to clock in and out again, the players are seen collecting their wages in brown packets. On match day the team arrives on foot and wearing sports coats and slacks. One of them pulls out his top set of dentures and slips them into his jacket pocket, smacking his lips together afterwards, before going on to the pitch. When the cheering stops at 20 to five, the player goes home. Scarcely anyone bothers him until the following weekend begins.

What *The Saturday Men* confirms is the footballer as an ordinary being with a few, unfancy perks. He uses brilliantine in his hair. He lives on the same street as the fans, his house – usually a terrace or a semi-detached – indistinguishable from the others. He travels on a corporation bus to the game. The interior decoration of his living room – the wallpaper, the furniture, the gilt-framed replica prints and the china ornaments on the fireplace mantel – is almost identical to his neighbours'.

The cosily arranged and predictable 'at home' features, appearing occasionally in *Picture Post* or another of the photographic-led weekly magazines during the 1940s and 50s, posed him like a store window mannequin: Nat Lofthouse in a high, white collar and tie, a patterned tea-towel in his enormous, thick fingers, as he dried plates and left them in the kitchen rack; Billy Wright reading beside a small, tiled hearth – his legs tucked into his chest – as a matronly landlady in a pinafore darns his black socks on the sofa behind him; Cliff Bastin mowing the over-long grass of his back lawn and still wearing a black, buttoned-up waistcoat and a formal pair of laced shoes; Bobby Robson gazing up at his mother as she pours him tea at the table from a bulbous brown pot. Sometimes there'd be recreational pictures snapped on the golf course or a tennis court: Len Shackleton addressing the teed-up ball in a pair of billowing plus-twos or John Charles on the baseline, the wooden racket looking no bigger than a soup spoon in his enormous hand. There was the odd reminder that a footballer couldn't live on football alone: Tom Finney, a plumber's wrench poking from the top pocket of his greasy overalls, emerging from beneath a housewife's blocked sink. The striking thing about all these black and white images is the fact that even the youngest face seems middle-aged. Lofthouse could be pushing 40 rather than 30; Wright, then only 26, seems a decade older. Even Robson wouldn't automatically pass for the 19-year-old that the camera captures. He already appears to be in his early 20s.

Best wasn't like this. He didn't look as any other footballer had looked before. He looked instead like a singer from *Top of the Pops* or a guitarist on *Ready Steady Go!* Compared to his predecessors, he inhabited a different, fresher world. The clothes he wore, the length of his hair, his nonchalance in front of the photographer's lens – all these illustrated the division between the mid-60s and what had come before. It was the optimum time to be young. Old conventions were disappearing as new conventions were established.

Each generation falls into the common trap of supposing it is infinitely superior – wiser, sassier, more knowledgeable and surer of what life can offer it – than the previous one. It certainly seemed so to Best. He used the phrase the 'good old days' either ironically or derogatorily. Best said he was 'grateful' to have been born in 1946 rather than 1926 because 'we don't have to stick rigidly to the short-back-and-sides and wear-your-club-blazer-at-all-times routine of the past'. Anyone criticising either his appearance or his opinions was told: 'There's room for freedom of expression in football now and I'm afraid it's up to the older generation to accept it.' To someone in their late teens even a 25-year-old appears ancient, as if eons separate them. 'At nineteen,' said Best, 'thirty-five is so far away it's not even worth thinking about. It's only when you get there you realise there's still a long way to go in life.' And some of the 'older generation' to which Best referred weren't even 30. He took out two insurance policies, insisting each was 'for my old age', which he then defined as being 'thirty-two to forty'. He was 18, going on 19. The nucleus of United's title-winning squad had an average age approaching 28. Most of them, including Bobby Charlton and Denis Law, lived lives of peaceful domesticity. Saturday night for the married men meant a quiet restaurant meal with their wife or a few hours of television after tucking the children into bed. 'I thought none of them liked me because no one suggested going out,' said Best, not understanding the responsibility of wedlock or parenting.

He established a social circle of his own away from Old Trafford. Too often he'd be cornered by someone wanting to talk about football or someone else telling him that so-and-so was a better player than him. His group became known as 'Our Crowd' or 'The Chaps' and Best was its epicentre. Like the sun, everything revolved around him. He chose who could belong and who couldn't. He avoided most parties, which he found 'boring'. He neither sought nor wanted a multitude of good companions. He liked the group to be close-knit, protective of one another. Best picked only those he liked – and never because of social status or for show. There was Danny Bursk – slim, curly brown hair – who worked in the fur business; Eddie 'Freight Train' Hindle, a brawny rep for a clothes company; Malcolm Mooney, also in the rag trade; Frank Evans, who'd go on to be a British bullfighter in Spain. Best found a soulmate in the blue half of Manchester when Mike Summerbee arrived at Maine Road in the summer of 1965. Though only 22 – 18 months older than Best – he'd made more than 200 League appearances for Swindon. The adjustment from small town to big city was muddling for him at first. 'Everything in Swindon closed at ten o'clock at night,' said Summerbee. 'Everything in Manchester was open until five o'clock in the morning.' Chance brought Summerbee and Best together. Summerbee went into a coffee bar called Kardomah in St Ann's Square – 'imagine a downmarket version of Starbucks', he says – and spotted Best sitting at a table. Their rapport was instant, as if boyhood friends had been reunited. Both came from tight communities and, as Summerbee remembers, 'we were still trying to sort out what life was about'. Summerbee describes the friendship as 'brotherly', and thinks the easy chemistry between them began because neither found the need to 'talk shop' to start or sustain a conversation. 'We hardly spoke about football. He'd ask about my match and I'd ask about his – and that was the end of it as far as the game was concerned.' One would meet the other's team coach when it arrived back on Saturday night from an away match. 'There was a solace about it, too,' says Summerbee. 'We didn't feel alone in Manchester.'

Best's closest friend and confidant was Malcolm Wagner, less than a year older than him. Bursk introduced them. 'What do you do?' asked Best after the polite, preliminary small-talk was over. 'I'm a hairdresser,' replied Wagner, also a very good musician. He'd played in a Manchester band called the Whirlwinds, the early incarnation of the group that would become 10cc and go on to record three UK number ones. The friendship, which began with that straightforward exchange, never broke. Best forever turned to Wagner for advice and counsel and relied on him for practical assistance. He was both the friend you hope to be and also the friend you hope to find for yourself. The pair became socially inseparable.

What Best later became started in the months after Manchester United's Championship success. There was the carousing and the social-ising and – to a very modest extent – the drinking. For at the beginning he would sip the odd beer and nothing else. He turned down free pints from club and pub patrons, politely telling them: 'I don't really drink.' Wagner emphasises: 'We'd go to the cinema and then to a nightclub for an hour of two. Going out was never about the drinking then and George didn't drink much at all.' Best still failed – as Matthews never did – to understand that the human body, especially one still developing, was meant to rest as well as play. Late nights became the norm. 'It was a bit daft,' he said. 'I was living twenty-four hours a day and letting myself get really run down.'

Club rules stipulated that curfew at Aycliffe Avenue was 10.30 p.m. There were 14 houses in the cul-de-sac, each kept respectably by, among others, an ex-publican, a teacher, a printer, a retired Bolton Wanderers scout and several husband and wife pensioners. One of Mary Fullaway's next-door neighbours was a window cleaner, who stored his ladders at the back of his house. This was useful to Best. He'd borrow them to climb into – and sometimes out of – his bedroom to avoid being seen. So would women. Steve Fullaway would be fast asleep when one of them, believing he was Best, tapped him on the shoulder. The window cleaner regularly awoke to discover those ladders were not where he'd left them the night before. Best arrived back so often in the early morning that Mrs Fullaway gave him his own key, a unilateral decision made without Matt Busby's knowledge or approval (which wouldn't have been given) and designed not to break her sleep. She seldom knew what time Best got in. She would nevertheless wake him from a deep sleep for breakfast at 7.30 a.m. by rubbing his nose, which he 'hated'.

Busby had a better intelligence network than the British security services. The whereabouts and predilections of his players were unfailingly fed back to him through telephone calls, letters, a discreet word passed on at the golf club. A chain of contacts voluntarily gave him information about who had been seen where, when and with whom. 'If you had a glass of lager, he would get to know about it,' said Best. There was no shortage of misinformation, too, usually relayed with bad intent. Busby's daily post brought anonymous accusations and all kinds of malicious tittle-tattle. He had learned what to ignore and what to take half-seriously. Busby cautioned his team: 'You can be sure, if you do anything wrong, somebody will tell me.' Also, he gathered evidence with his own ears and eyes. If someone looked haggard or was dishevelled in appearance, Busby wanted to know why. If a stray remark, perhaps overheard on the practice pitch or in the dressing room, set an alarm faintly ringing, he'd investigate surreptitiously.

Busby began to hear reports of Best's extracurricular activities. There was a consistency to the stories, which gave them credence. Alcohol wasn't an issue. What worried Busby were the hours Best was spending in nightclubs when he should have been tucked up in Aycliffe Avenue. At the beginning of the 1965–66 season, Busby thought Best seemed curiously lethargic. His form alternated between the barely acceptable and the abysmal. Best admitted: 'I was going on to the field tired [and] coming off it shattered.' In defence of the Championship, he scored only once in the first eight League matches; United won just twice. Busby assumed Best's slump was temporary, a drop in performance stemming predominantly from the lavish and laudatory publicity he was getting. Busby thought the need to live up to the hype was making Best overanxious. He was still a pup, after all. But, as the displays worsened, he settled on an alternative reason. The inevitable followed: Best was summoned to see him.

Busby never dressed players down in front of one another and he believed managers who did demeaned themselves and eroded their own authority. 'Private flagellation is as painful and as lastingly effective as the public variety. But it preserves the offender's public dignity,' he argued. 'Public punishment is sometimes a sop to the pride of the man who decides to inflict it.' Old Trafford's referees' room was located in the tunnel to the pitch. If Busby wanted to drop or rebuke someone he would station himself there and beckon inside the unfortunate recipient of the bad news. He'd solicitously enquire how the player thought he'd been performing. Gentle interrogation would often persuade the player to admit his shortcomings, which was akin to dropping himself. As if Busby was determined to make an impression, Best was called to his plainly decorated, sparsely furnished office. Busby had a broad, dark oak desk on which two telephones sat. His high-backed chair was raised a few inches above the three chairs placed in front of it. Anyone occupying one of the guest seats felt as though Busby was peering down on them.

Again Busby preferred to coax rather than demand. Even if he was screaming inside, he didn't betray it. He didn't slap the wooden top of the table or shake a balled fist at Best. The anxiety he displayed crossed his brow in a flutter and he explained with uncompromising lucidity what Best must put right. He looked weary. He wasn't playing well because of it. He flinched at the things he'd being hearing about Best's frenzied socialising. Busby was direct in his advice:

'You've done the hard bit, son, you've got to the top. Staying there is easy if you only think about it.

'Avoid the hangers-on. Concentrate on your work. Look after your money.

'This is a European Cup season. I want to win it. You know how important the trophy is to the club, don't you?'

Best couldn't say in mitigation that his nights out relieved strain. Busby wouldn't hear of it. His views on such an excuse were uncompromisingly hard-line. 'One wrong way of reducing tension is to go boozing in a nightclub,' he said. 'Another is simply to stay out longer than orders permit. These methods may well take off tension, but they take the edge off performance, too. Such novelties must be stamped upon no matter whose toes are bruised.'

A chastened Best listened as Busby told him he was 'a bloody idiot'. Even his silences were loaded with meaning and his stares of disapproval left Best feeling as if he'd grown smaller in his chair. Busby dropped him and Best felt the pain of it. He promised 'never again' to put 'pleasure before playing'. He accepted that 'you need a lot of sleep to play football'.

Best viewed Busby as an incarnation of his grandfather George Withers. 'They were very similar,' he said. 'Both were hard when they needed to be. But they were lovable, too. I found it difficult to get around or con either of them.' Not wanting to humiliate Best across the back pages, Busby told newspapers that Best needed time off because he was still a teenager fatigued by the unstinting demands of the League season. 'He'll be back quickly enough,' he said. Best simply lied. 'I think I've been too greedy,' he said. 'I've been wanting too much of the ball and not doing enough with it. I have spoilt myself.' When his father rang to discover why his son wasn't in the team, Best lied again because he was too ashamed to tell him the truth.

Unquestionably, he was his mother's son; and he was used to getting away with a bit of mischief. As Ann Best's firstborn he was indulged like an only child. Since he'd always been forgiven indiscretions before, so he always expected to be forgiven them again. He disarmed with charm. 'If I ever felt a little cross with him,' said Mrs Fullaway 'he'd put on a wide grin from ear to ear and I wouldn't have the heart to be too severe.' Best did likewise with Busby, who failed to figure Best's character into the equation when determining the degree of his punishment for this first offence. He believed that the cold shower of his words would tug him into the disciplined ranks. A similar approach had worked for Busby in the past. Shortly after Bobby Charlton went to Old Trafford, Busby heard he'd been drinking beer though under-age. 'He was very young,' said Busby. 'So I sent for him and I told him: "If I ever hear you have been drinking beer again before you are old enough, you will be for it." It was a long time before he had his next glass of beer, and certainly not before he was old enough.'

Like so many of his vintage, Busby found the upheavals of the 1960s perplexing. The decade was an unfathomable, rolling mystery to him. It was as if he'd been transported to another planet, strikingly similar but also – and paradoxically – so distinctly different from the one on which he grew up. Much of it seemed peculiar to someone born when the frock-coated, wing-collared Herbert Asquith was prime minister and Edward VII was king. The pop and cultural scene was particularly confusing to Busby, who knew almost nothing of the charts. When the Beatles stayed in the same London hotel as United's squad, he mistook Paul McCartney for Freddie Garrity, the 5ft-tall lead singer of Freddie and the Dreamers. McCartney courteously corrected him. 'We're the Beatles, Mr Busby.'

Busby mistakenly thought that underneath his trendy clothes Best was a youth exactly like Charlton had once been, and that respect for the smack of authority would have the same effect in the 1960s as it had done in the 50s. He didn't appreciate how Best saw things. In the coming years, as he became high maintenance, Busby would be criticised for his saintly forbearance and for being too gentle on Best. He would claim this was an 'illusion'. But there is no doubt that the trauma of Munich made Busby more liberal than he otherwise would have been. The big stick wasn't brought out for Best. 'I suppose I was softer on him than I should have been,' he conceded, eventually. 'I had lost the other lads. That maybe made me more lenient with those who came afterwards.'

Best missed only three matches: two in the First Division, the other in the preliminary round of the European Cup. What Busby missed was the chance to draw a line that Best dare not cross. He was sure emollience and patience would pay off in the end.

Both of them reaped a bad harvest from the misjudgement.

5

A Ticker-tape Parade
of Banknotes

It was a requirement in the 1960s to be able to do something impressive and worthy before becoming famous. There were no asinine television reality shows to transform a duffer, lacking qualities or qualifications, into a so-called personality. The newspapers didn't usually alight on the untalented and, through pretence, build them into somebody speciously starry. Fame was a much more select club then, and only those combining charisma and ability were allowed into its VIP lounge. But it was possible to gain admittance overnight. Lack of choice meant TV was a communal affair – everyone watching the same thing at the same hour – and each letterbox in the country had a morning or evening newspaper stuffed into it. A solitary TV appearance or a full-page interview was capable of making you a household name.

Already, George Best believed this: 'The story of my life couldn't have been better written even by the editor of a boys' adventure comic.' But that adventure had hardly begun. Neither he nor Matt Busby expected what was to come.

The critic Clive James wrote that 'as long as there have been human beings, there has always been fame'. He also recognised that 'fame turned into something different' during the 20th century. 'Suddenly,' he said, 'there was more of it.' And James identified the 60s as the period that fame broke into a run because this was a time conscious of itself, partly because of those who became famous during it. Normally reputations are built incrementally. It can be difficult to pin down the tipping point: that exact moment when fundamental change occurs. Not so in Best's case.

Writing after the instantaneous success of *Childe Harold's Pilgrimage*, the poet Lord Byron announced: 'I awoke one morning and found myself famous.' That morning was 10 March 1812. Nothing links the Georgian romantic poet to the Elizabethan romantic footballer – except this. For Best also awoke and found himself famous. And he did so coincidentally on 10 March – 154 years later in 1966. Like Byron, Best was a stupendous success overnight – lionised and desired. Like Byron, he thought everyone had gone 'stark mad'. And, also like Byron, his life was never his own again afterwards.

After Manchester United won the League Championship, he began to think of himself as 'a star' on the basis that 'everyone wanted to speak to me'. Best, Denis Law and Bobby Charlton – and chiefly in that order, too – were described in newspapers as the club's 'Holy Trinity'. Mail began to dribble in for Best. Autograph books were pushed in front of him. The occasional fan rattled the letterbox at Aycliffe Avenue. It was a gentle prelude compared to the tumult and the intense fan worship that was coming.

It happened like this.

A hot night in Lisbon. Benfica versus Manchester United in the quarter-finals of the European Cup. The Portuguese, one of the behemoths of Europe and twice winners of the trophy, had lost the previous season's final to Inter Milan, and the loose-limbed Eusébio was recognised as the continent's premier player. No one had beaten Benfica in the Estádio da Luz in 19 ties. No one really expected United to break the sequence despite going there 3–2 ahead from the first leg. That result was only half-satisfying to Busby. He regarded it as too narrow to be decisive for them. Two years earlier he'd seen his team – including the Holy Trinity – crushed 5–0 in the same city by Benfica's rivals and inferiors, Sporting. He travelled to Lisbon again more in hope than expectation.

Best always insisted he had a photographic memory of games that qualified as his most significant. He could recall the images of them as if film were unspooling in front of his eyes. This is what he saw. There were the Portuguese fans beating incessantly on the windows of United's coach, the slow turn of the wheels carrying it on a stop-start journey through the traffic. There were the other supporters waving four fingers and a thumb to remind him – as if this was necessary – of what Sporting had inflicted and what Benfica and Eusébio would surely better. There was sniggering at his long hair and sideburns; men tugged at their own hair and made snipping gestures, pretending to hold a pair of scissors. There was the heavy-headed, gold eagle, Benfica's emblem, guarding the entrance with its blade-beak and razory talons. Inside the dressing room there was Paddy Crerand whacking a practice ball against a long mirror and smashing it. There was the superstitious among them – fretting among an already fidgety team – that the break had cursed them as surely as the Lady of Shallot had once been cursed. There was Law telling Crerand: 'You crazy bastard. We don't stand a chance now.' There was Busby's cautious order to be 'tight' during the opening 20 minutes. 'Make them do the early running,' he said.

As a boy Best was entranced by European competition well before there was an organised tournament to win. Dickie and Ann Best couldn't afford a television. A neighbour allowed Best to watch the challenge matches that Wolves' far-sighted manager, Stan Cullis, arranged at Molineux against Spartak Moscow and Honved, a team with six of the Hungarians – Ferenc Puskas among them – who had shattered England's sense of superiority and arrogant entitlement by whipping them 6–3 at Wembley in 1953 and then 7–1 in Budapest in 1954. On an 11 in screen Best saw Wolves in satin shirts, glimmering and shimmering under floodlights that still remained a rarity in the Football League of that era. The picture was misty and shadowed and it broke up when the signal grew weak. To Best, however, the broadcast was spellbinding. 'I always wanted to play in Europe after seeing Wolves,' he said.

He'd made 17 European appearances before this one: two in the Cup Winners' Cup, 11 in the Fairs Cup and four in that season's European Cup. Nothing he'd done before compared to Lisbon. Nothing after it compared to anything any British footballer had then experienced. The game was over as a contest during the first quarter of an hour. When United were supposed to be conservatively focused on restraint, Best was rampant. As Busby drily observed, Best must have pushed wedges of cotton wool into his ears during the team talk.

The film of the game is now as smoky-grey and faded in places as the transmission of those Wolves matches had been. Not even such poor, perished stock, however, diminishes what Best does. A free-kick from the left touchline curls into the box. Best is between two white-shirted defenders who watch the flight of the pearl-coloured ball instead of paying attention to him. The lights are harsh, the shadows cast coal-black and each player's points, like clock hands, at 20 to four. Best starts his sprightly run from the lip of the area and makes a timely, springy jump off his left leg, which allows him to twist his head on to the ball as it arrives slightly beyond the penalty spot. The goalkeeper, wearing an undertaker's colours, comes out of his six-yard box, his right fist clenched in preparation to make a punch. Best is already airborne, two inches above the marker who ought to have picked him up. He presses his shoulder into that defender's collarbone to give himself even more leverage and he directs his header goalwards, the ball arcing over the keeper into an unguarded net. Only six minutes have gone. Another six elapse before his second arrives – one of the most boldly uninhibited he will ever score for United. A long kick up-field, out of Harry Gregg's shovel-sized hands, drops like a military shell three-quarters of the way into Benfica's half, where the unchallenged David Herd, spotting Best as he chases towards him from deep, heads it into the space in front of him. There's no need for Benfica to take immediate action. Four players stand between Best and the long dash he must make from there into the box. But each is too complacent and also moves with a bovine sluggishness. Best snaps to it. His goal is gorgeous, and he unfurls it like a bolt of gold-threaded silk. His first touch – with his right foot – takes him clear of the initial attempt to deny him possession. The second – also with his right – side-steps the defender approaching him head-on and beats another who comes at him from his flank. His third touch, after he has pushed the ball at speed into the area, is flicked past the keeper, haring off his line. Best's three touches – and his acceleration – have carried him 40 yards as fast as electric current. Benfica, still groggy, concede another goal three minutes later. The howling, 75,000 crowd is in catatonic shock. United win 5–1; Eusébio doesn't get a sniff of the ball.

The bowler-hatted columnist of the *Daily Express*, Desmond Hackett, writes of British football reaching 'an Everest peak' in Lisbon. 'Call them Magnificent United,' he adds. Busby, less poetically, calls it his 'finest hour', as if remembering Churchill. Afterwards Best, elated but dazed, is in the dressing room watching those around him, as if standing outside the scene. 'I'd done something that no one else could have done,' he says. 'After it was over, it felt as if someone else had been out there.' Best described it as 'the game that changed everything' for him. He was putting it mildly. A crazed-looking youth chased him with a sharp, curved knife and asked to cut off a lock of his hair. The bikini-wearing women on the beach outside United's hotel in Estoril were transfixed, every look an unspoken invitation. He went to sunbathe in

85 degrees and found himself pestered for his autograph. Newspaper reporters from Portugal queued to speak to him. Best was given a folded copy of *Bola*, its main headline printed in black and red ink. He asked for a translation. 'A Beatle called Best smashes Benfica,' he was told; and that comparison to the pop group, who by then had sold 150 million records worldwide, stuck rigidly to him thereafter. He was now 'The Fifth Beatle'.

Best prepared himself for the saucer flashes of the photographers' cameras, which he knew would be waiting at home. On one of the tacky tourist stalls, selling souvenir beer tankards, mantelpiece trinkets and enormous toy donkeys, he bought a tasselled straw sombrero with the spare escudos in his back pocket. The stallholder told him he'd woo the girls with it. The sombrero was wider than a dustbin lid. He had to hold it on with his left hand as he walked. On the aeroplane Gregg told him to take it off. 'Throw that bloody thing away. Great players don't need gimmicks,' he said, tersely. Gregg didn't appreciate Best's motives. He and Mike Summerbee were about to open a boutique. Best called it the 'Mod Shop for the extrovert male' and said he wanted to do 'something out of the ordinary' to attract attention. This was an advertisement for himself. In a basic search for meretricious look-at-me publicity he had the chutzpah to stroll on to the tarmac wearing the sombrero along with a leather jacket and a pair of sunglasses. He had the deportment of someone all-conquering, who knows also that wherever he stands will represent the centre of the room.

In today's showbizzy world, where stunts are choreographed and the costumes are much more ornate, his use of a cheap prop looks absurdly tame. But this was the 60s – and the sombrero counted as a novelty. One photograph demonstrates the sartorial difference between Best and other passengers. On the tarmac he radiates the ethereal beauty of a pre-Raphaelite; he had it so he flaunted it. In the background are businessmen dressed in dull suits and trilby hats. The *Daily Mirror*

– then selling more than 5 million copies daily – put Best and his sombrero on the front as well as the back page. The goals he'd scored featured on the news and again during Saturday's edition of *Grandstand*. How differently the public now viewed Best became apparent to Summerbee as he walked beside him through Manchester shortly afterwards. Summerbee saw traffic halt suddenly and pedestrians stop and stare at the mere sight of Best. Some women blew kisses. Others shouted his name and waved. A few were dumbstruck, mouths hanging open. 'Drivers wound down their windows. People turned to look at him and point,' said Summerbee. 'Something fundamental had changed. He came back from Lisbon as a superstar. Everyone was talking about him. Everyone wanted to meet him. He couldn't go anywhere without being watched and followed. It was eerie in one way, unreal in another.' The Mod Shop opening was a continuation of it, the 14 x 14ft floor chaotically congested. The 'customers' pretended to buy while ogling Best and left behind fan letters and love letters and photographs for him to sign. There was jostling outside, onlookers pressing so hard against the window that Best was afraid the glass would shatter. At the door more people waited their turn to wriggle inside.

Within a week there were three unopened hessian sacks of letters heaped in a corner of Best's bedroom at Mary Fullaway's. Another two sacks were waiting for collection at Old Trafford. The boot and back seat of his car contained more mail. Even the deep brim of the sombrero, casually thrown on top of his wardrobe, held cards and letters, too, which he eventually tipped on to the bed. The newspapers couldn't print articles fast enough to sate the public's appetite for information about him. Busby, like Best himself, thought all this was a passing fad. The dogs would bark; and then soon enough the caravans would move on, parking themselves outside someone else's door, which is why Busby sensed nothing harmful or too distracting about the attention. But United won only one of their next four League matches. Nor did Best score in the three appearances he made. Busby nonetheless said nothing of substance to him about his boutique or the fact he'd become – instantaneously – a hero, worshipped as an individual in a team game. United were still expected to win the European Cup at a canter. Even Best was convinced no one would stop him or them. Their next opponents, Partizan of Yugoslavia, held no fear for United. They were only mid-table in their own 'First League'.

P. G. Wodehouse once wrote: 'It's just when a fellow is feeling particularly braced with things in general that Fate sneaks up behind him with the bit of lead piping.' Best was feeling braced. He was pleased with himself, too. And, sure enough, the lead piping was about to hit him. He tried to ignore the discomfort in his right knee, which had begun to stiffen and lock. Heat and ice treatments got him through matches. 'I'll make it through to the end of the season,' he said to Jimmy Murphy. Only a month after Lisbon, during the semi-final in Belgrade, his cartilage collapsed. He lay on his back near the goal-line, hands covering his eyes, a stiletto shaft of pain running through his body. United lost the first leg 2–0 and the tie 3–1 on aggregate. Best watched the return on television from a hospital bed and missed the season's last six weeks. Real Madrid beat Partizan 2–1 in the final in Brussels. 'We could have beaten Real,' was the view Best took.

United's failure – and his own absence from it – had no effect on Best's popularity. Every day then was still like a new toy to him, and he saw no interruption to the joyous sequence of his weeks.

There is no self-creation without self-conscious effort; and, once he was fit again after his summer recovery, George Best put a lot of energy into making sure he was seen and heard. 'Sometimes I did it shamelessly,' he said.

He understood what to do, where to go and how to act to please the print-led media. He also realised that any relationship with it was based on mutual dependency. With that airport sombrero, he'd recognised how straightforwardly publicity could be garnered. More of it now came with forethought. With remarkable frequency, he backed into the limelight.

'To some extent I cultivated the stories around me,' he admitted. 'I liked having my photo taken. I liked seeing my name in the papers . . . everything was a bit of a leg-pull, really. I knew what made a good photo. I knew what would get me a headline.' Best even admitted: 'If a photographer asks me to stand on my head, I'm willing to do it.'

In his first two seasons at Old Trafford he'd continued his boyhood hobby of collecting clippings and photographs, which were cut out and sent home to his father. As interest in him turned into a fixation, he gave up. Best's name appeared so frequently that he had neither the time nor inclination to monitor what was written about him; and he'd have needed a packing crate to ship all the paper to Burren Way. For the football periodicals, he was the obvious – and profitable – cover and poster boy. A centre-spread or good cover photograph of Best could add 5,000 copies to the sales figure. His thoughts, as well as gossip and comment about him, spilled into the pop papers, such as the *New Musical Express* and *Melody Maker*, the political and cultural press, including *New Society*, the *New Statesman* and *The Listener*, the children's comics and the fashion magazines – *Vogue* and *Paris Match* among them – and the expanding female market. Established titles such as *Woman* and *Woman's Own* knew Best appealed to a sizeable slice of its readership – irrespective of whether or not the reader found the offside rule as impenetrable as an Einstein equation. Even when Best did nothing he was still interesting. He created news by walking down a street.

At Old Trafford, he'd brought shampoo and a hairdryer into the dressing room when everyone else used red carbolic soap and a towel. Every morning, except match day when the club badge had to be worn, his team-mates waited to see what outfit Best had chosen. Sometimes he was as colourful as a Christmas tree, the boutique owner a billboard for his own stock. Dandyish about his appearance, like no other footballer had been before, he gave off a coolness of style; though he could have worn a burlap sack and still looked as graceful as Beau Brummell. He changed clothes up to three times a day and still found something new to wear. Malcolm Wagner trimmed his hair almost daily, too. Best owned more shirts than the Great Gatsby. Some, as elaborate as a floral arrangement and costing 15 guineas each, were worn once and discarded. Others were never worn at all. 'I buy half a dozen a week,' he explained. 'I throw them out without wearing them.' He preferred vivid and warm colours – pinks and reds, dark blues and rich purples, tangerine and soft yellows. He was seen in hipster trousers cut from garish plaid of the sort that Scottish lairds once went hunting in. Another pair were rose madder on one leg and dark red on another. A third pair, similarly head-turning, were cadmium lemon. A fourth were a sulphurous yellow, as though Best was worried about not being seen in the dark. This painter's palette was Best's response to the conservative garb club etiquette had obliged him to wear during his seasons in United's youth team. He didn't defy convention then in case Matt Busby – a suit or slacks man – disapproved. 'I used to wear very quiet clothes,' he conceded. 'Now, if I see something smart, no matter what anyone else says, I buy it.' He was partial to thick sweaters – cardigans with lapels, polo and turtle necks. He had a penchant for jackets with jagged dog's-tooth patterns or vertical stripes, each luxuriously lined. One of these was black and white, like a butcher's apron. He also wore what he described as his 'cowboy outfit' – another pair of checked trousers, a thick black belt and a suede waistcoat. He bought – or was given – so many clothes that his bedroom at Mrs Fullaway's resembled a gents' outfitters after a tornado had ripped through it. The wardrobe and chest of drawers in his bedroom soon became unfit for purpose. What couldn't be put away was strewn on the carpet until Mrs Fullaway arranged the jumble for him. His shirts were hung or folded, carefully laid on his bed or stacked on the floor. Shoes and boots with Cuban heels and elasticated sides were tissue-wrapped and stacked in boxes, too. Mrs Fullaway asked him to get rid of some of his clothes because she could neither vacuum around them nor dust the furniture properly. Best claimed to have curbed his extravagance only after feeling an unexpected twinge of guilt. 'I thought of my dad and how little money he made,' he said.

His idea of a scaled-down wardrobe still seemed to anyone else of that era like a department store of clothes. The inventory comprised: 20 pairs of slacks, around 40 shirts, a 'pile' of sweaters, one overcoat and only two suits. 'I feel a bit restricted in a suit, shirt and tie,' he explained of his reluctance for formal dress.

In 1963, the new arrival in Manchester United's first team, Best earned £17 a week – still four times more than Stanley Matthews had picked up for winning the FA Cup at Blackpool a decade before. Three months earlier he'd apologised to his parents for not sending them housekeeping because 'I've bought a mac . . . my other is finished.' By 1966 he could have bought mackintoshes by the truck-load. His salary was a basic £125 a week. The average salary in Britain was £1,300 a year. A new home cost less than £3,500. There were crowd bonuses at United, too: an extra £1 if the attendance was over 35,000; £2 if it went above 40,000; and £3 for 45,000 or more. Between the 1966–67 and 1968–69 seasons Old Trafford's average gates were more than 50,000. With other incentives – for winning and for being in the top six – Best progressed through a ticker-tape parade of banknotes. His only dilemma was how to spend them. The epicurean lifestyle was comfortably afforded. Busby thought the sums United paid reflected 'the star salaries' of the 'new footballer'. The 'new footballer' to him was 'the smart man about town'. This was an Identikit of Best.

Again thinking of his father, Dickie – as well as his father's friends in the shipyards – Best was sympathetic towards anyone who thought he had a cushy, overpaid existence. He'd seen men, backs bent like hooks, trudging wearily to the docks, silently wishing their life away in a longing for the monotonous hours to fly by and release them from the drudgery of manual labour. 'Compared with a man who sweats his guts out working in a factory, my earnings are money for old rope,' he said. 'Football isn't a job.' Best had a habit of saying precisely what was on his mind; even though that mind regularly changed its opinions, sometimes hourly, which frequently left his rhetoric outrunning his judgement. Some things should have been left unsaid. What were taken as solemn pronouncements should have been read as the half-baked thoughts of someone in a hurry and still groping with the realities of his life. He certainly had no inhibitions about declaring his long-term intention to be Midas-like in an accumulation of riches. At 20, he said: 'I like to think that by the time I am twenty-five I won't have to rely on football. I'd like to be so well off that it wouldn't bother me.' Asked what he thought counted as 'well off', he replied 'sixty thousand pounds'. Within a few months Best realised he'd underestimated his earning potential. 'I like money. I want as much as possible,' he said with the candour of a child. 'What I'd like to be is a millionaire.' Best couldn't have aroused more comment if he'd announced plans to marry into the royal family. In 1966 there were fewer than 100 millionaires in Britain – all of whom would count as billionaires today. Declaring his ambition so frankly, and at such a ridiculously tender age, didn't endear Best to that section of the public who weren't fans of football and considered him to be flash, smart-alecky and swollen-headed. His precocity, and the brazenness of his intentions, riled them.

Best was never avaricious. On the contrary. He never went searching for money. It came looking for him in numerous sponsorships, endorsements and public appearances. He did them without demur and usually without asking how much he was being paid.

Apart from the clothes, a few items of jewellery and a record collection, Best wasn't materialistic or ostentatious. He didn't acquire possessions for the sake of them; people were more important to him. His only indulgence was an E-type Jaguar, attractive because Hollywood's Steve McQueen was regularly seen behind the wheel of one and also because the car was known as 'The Greatest Crumpet Catcher Known to Man'. One Jag was replaced by another, each costing upwards of £2,500 (enough to buy three terraced houses in parts of Manchester), which he parked on the kerbside outside Mrs Fullaway's. 'I was a sucker for it,' said Best, who didn't know what to spend his earnings on. 'If I walked past a showroom – even if I'd only had my car a month and I saw a better one – I'd get rid of the old one because I had the money.' Best was frank enough to confess he did it because it cultivated a playboy image.

He seldom checked his bank account because cash in itself meant nothing to him. Provided there was enough to cover what he wanted to buy, Best didn't bother about finance. He summed up his attitude to his earnings in two typically easy-going sentences: 'I don't have to think about the cost of anything,' he said. 'Sometimes I feel I ought to worry more about money.'

Someone else did that for him.

Ken Stanley was a workaholic and he belonged to a substantially different era from the players he represented. He connected well with their managers who, like him, had known poverty, and survived the Great Depression, the unrest of the 1930s and the Second World War. The football men who would eventually become knights – Matt Busby and Alf Ramsey – regarded him as scrupulously trustworthy.

Stanley was 5ft 8in with thinly winged eyebrows and hair that receded to the dome of his oval head and made him look older than his years. But, just as George Best did, he prided himself on being immaculately groomed: sober suit, plain shirt and tie, a waxy, mirrored sheen to his black shoes. It was the uniform of the good salesman, and the thing Stanley sold convincingly was himself. He chose his clothes to impress in boardrooms, where deals were struck, and in domestic living rooms, where the mothers and fathers of Britain's richest football talent were won over. He didn't belong to the 1960s. He was, however, attuned to them.

As a presciently astute businessman, sharply aware of the commercial power of the 60s' footballer before any of them properly cottoned on to it themselves, he became one of the first and most powerful sporting agents in the country. He corralled thoroughbreds into his stable.

Born in 1922, one of nine children in a squashed terrace, he grew up in the slums of south-west Manchester. His original flair was for table tennis. It took him to the World Championships, aged just 14, and then guaranteed a regular, if modest, living. Though lacking a 'killer' trade-mark shot, he was considered to be an impressive all-rounder, as well as an inventive tactician, who could have become world champion if the war hadn't taken him elsewhere. As player and part-impresario, he toured in exhibitions of the sport, appeared at Butlin's holiday camp and shared a court with basketball's entertainers, the Harlem Globetrotters, and a troupe of jugglers. During the 1950s, when sportsmen earned a pittance but played in front of packed houses, Stanley was aware that self-promotion was the way forward. He developed a branded range of equipment – bats and balls in particular – and opened table tennis academies in the North West of England. He also turned disused cinemas into five-a-side football arenas.

His life changed because of the sunshine of 1959, a gloriously dreamy summer that seemed endless. Even in February the thermometer was recording unseasonal temperatures – as high as 19 centigrade in London. From the second week of May to the third week of October, it was so warm that curtains were thrown wide every morning on to unblemished skies, and it was so bone-dry that water shortages were threatened. No one wanted to be cooped up indoors, which meant Stanley's tables and pitches went unused. He became a manager at Mitre, a Huddersfield-based firm that began in a tiny tannery during the early part of Queen Victoria's reign and grew to dominate the market through technical innovation. Mitre's speciality was the panelled football. His role proved to be a key that opened many doors. Stanley travelled non-stop, hobnobbing and cordially getting along with everyone. He was well-informed about any schoolboy capped internationally. 'It's all about contacts,' he said.

Long before the Football Association accepted defeat in the High Court, Stanley saw the end of the maximum wage, believing it was unsustainable. It appalled him that venerated footballers weren't better off than men at the pit-face or the lathe. It was unjust, too. The money clubs made was shared disproportionately, most of it going into the wrong pockets because the owners or directors greedily creamed off more than was decent. Not even football could set itself apart from the rest of society or plead for preferential treatment. Industrial and employment relations were changing, and the game couldn't expect its feudal practices to remain unchallenged. The footballer was a man like any other; someone who was legally and morally entitled to be fairly treated in the workplace. He couldn't be discriminated against because he kicked a ball. And he couldn't be dismissed as inconsequential, like a medieval serf whose movements and pay were restricted on the whim of a club's board. Stanley knew the FA would be forced to concede another thing: that the players' union could no longer be brushed aside or vilified as a bunch of militant, rabble-rousing extremists. The charge wouldn't stick because the union had right on its side. The implications in all this, as Stanley also appreciated, would be the most far reaching since professionalism in football was legalised in 1885. Out of it football would be fiscally reordered and the richly talented would emerge with vast earning potential and widen the game's public appeal. 'Football was climbing out of the clog and shawl era at last,' he said.

Stanley was the man who saw tomorrow. He spotted his opportunity, the chance to break away from Mitre and establish himself as an agent. He acquired the signatures of the schoolboy internationals he'd tracked: Gordon Banks, Billy McNeill, John Greig, Billy Bremner and Alan Ball. As a one-man band he operated from the family home. His office was in a spare bedroom and, unable to afford secretarial support, he typed his own letters, the house alive to the repeated rat-a-tat-tat sound of his fingers thumping down hard on the keys. Rapid expansion followed. By the mid-60s his 16-hour days took him to the top floor of a former solicitor's office in central Huddersfield. The town and the address – 19 Railway Street – may have suggested dinginess to anyone who had never visited them. But seven rooms with high, rectangular windows over-looked St George's Square and the handsomeness of its Georgian architecture. Stanley's office was wood-panelled and contained floor-to-ceiling bookshelves. He sat at a mahogany pedestal desk longer than a single bed. His dozen employees affectionately called him Mr Ken.

As a former professional sportsman, Stanley knew the sacrifices required to become an international, the competitive edge necessary to retain that status and the mental and physical toll it took simply to stay in condition. He'd done all these hard miles himself; particularly the days-upon-tedious-days of practice in the hunt for unattainable perfection. He knew about Kipling's twin impostors, triumph and disaster; he'd been in form and out of it. He'd experienced sleepless nights and sweating anxiety before big matches; and he had gone through periods of self-doubt and questioned his abilities. His background enabled him to empathise genuinely with whomever he enticed on to his books. He'd coached extensively, too, and learned the importance of patience and trust in regard to teaching youngsters to prepare for a pro's life. In discussing what he'd been through himself – and what he could pass on because of it – Stanley emerged as a reassuring presence for parents, who knew he had their boy's well-being at heart. He was also a convincing tutor cum surrogate father figure to the son, who felt he'd be safe and cared for.

Anxious to sort out ethical wrongs, Stanley was aghast at the sight of those he diplomatically referred to as 'semi-con-men who jump in and talk players into signing contracts that prove to be far from marvellous deals'. He considered pirating reprehensible and criminally exploitative. He asked: 'If you were a football player and you went to the ground and there were fifty touts selling posters and pennants and postcards with your picture on and you weren't getting a penny, you'd be bloody mad, wouldn't you?' As a my-word-is-my-bond sort of chap, Stanley's high morals won him respect.

Initially Stanley's competition for signatures was thin. There were only a handful of agents – most of them operating out of London – and each lacked the creative vigour he possessed. Stanley had a geographic advantage, too. 'All the best players were in the North then,' he explained.

He was treading a lot of virginal territory. The footballer as a serious face for the high street retailer and the blue chip commodities was still a rarity. The game's popularity had always drawn advertisers. The wares being sold, however, were either targeted towards the working classes, who crammed on to the terraces, or the weekend player. As far back as 1898, when the kit comprised shirts with grandad collars, breeches and knee-length socks, Forfar Athletic endorsed Elliman's Embrocation, a pungent concoction of athletic rub that came in fat jars and stank out dressing rooms. By the 1930s, as everyone puffed away blissfully ignorant of the carcinogenic effects of nicotine, Dixie Dean urged 'all young footballers' to try the toasted tobacco of Wix cigarettes. Similarly Stanley Matthews was photographed in his England shirt as the face of Craven A, which the manufacturers claimed was the epitome of 'smooth, clean smoking' (the word *clean* was even underlined with a broad pen-stroke). Only slightly more sophisticatedly, Johnny Haynes, the first player to earn £100 per week, became the suave Brylcreem Boy, succeeding the swashbuckling Denis Compton. Haynes was pictured in a dinner jacket and black bow tie. The sleek, combed swirls and the sharp parting of his immaculate hair appeared beneath the caption: 'Who is *this* man of the world?'

As the 60s found its step and rhythm, Stanley saw wider horizons for his clientele, which went further than flogging liniment, cheap fags or hair grease. Stanley thought that the modern footballer needn't be confined to pushing football gear, such as the basic boots and balls. He sensed it wouldn't be long before television – as it did through *Match of the Day* – screened a game weekly. He believed it would improve the profile and lift the earnings of the most talented performers in the same way that *Sunday Night at the London Palladium* had successfully turned some previously unknown showbiz entertainers into household names. He recognised the axis shift in the world around him, too; and, more-over, he understood that the changes it wrought were sure to precipitate others equally as seminal. Stanley decided the 60s, like all decades, would have its transient fancies. But he accepted early on and unequivo-cally that attitudes and values – predominantly among the young – were fundamentally different and would remain implacably so.

Even when Harold Macmillan proclaimed the end of the 50s as the period of 'You've never had it so good,' there wasn't a lot of milk and honey to go around – particularly for those on low wages. Stanley nonetheless followed his instincts. Demographics and his own hunches told him that the baby-boomers wouldn't be as passive or as class-obsessed as earlier generations. They would strive and aspire and be niche consumers.

He knew one player who would specifically meet that market.

* * *

'Handling George Best is an endless task,' said Ken Stanley, who conceded that 75 per cent of his business originated through him.

He'd recruited Best when almost no one outside Old Trafford knew of his existence. The tip came from Denis Law, already on Stanley's books, who informed the agent that he was 'outstanding, brilliant and something very special'. Stanley didn't hesitate; Best was signed in the same summer Busby made him a pro.

Post Lisbon, Best's account demanded its own staff. Three secretaries administered his fan club and sifted through the mail. He received 5,000 letters per week, which made slitting them open a full-time task. A lot of correspondence came from overseas, especially the Far East, and the scribbled address on the envelope was regularly rudimentary:

George Best
Footballer
Somewhere in England

Best estimated that one in five letters came from schoolboys, who wanted a signed photograph and asked him the same question: how can I become a professional footballer? Other correspondents, less innocent, pleaded for cash, the begging always supported by appeals to the heart. Their sob stories told of family misfortune or urgent medical need. There were chancers cum speculators and flimflam men striving to part Best from his cash through convoluted get-rich schemes or investment opportunities. More disturbed writers were convinced that Best was a deity to whom God had given powers to heal the sick. They asked him to cure cancers, make the maimed whole again and enable the mute to speak. And then there were the letters from besotted females, varying in age group from the barely pubescent girls to the flirting married mothers, who ought to have known better. There were wedding proposals, invitations to parties and nights out, and pleas for

Best to become a pen-friend. The anxious wrote for emotional support, as if Best was an infallible agony uncle who could guide them through growing up. The souvenir hunters asked him to send them a piece of clothing or a lock of hair. Had he given in regularly to the latter request, Best would have been practically bald within a month. Much later, when Best advised anyone who wanted a strand of his cut-off hair to write to Malcolm Wagner at his salon, The Village Barber, there were so many requests that Manchester United apprentices were commandeered to put it into envelopes. 'Everyone wanted something from George,' said Stanley.

When starting out, Stanley had self-generated marketing and promotional ideas. Agents weren't embroiled in transfer negotiations then; and businesses weren't convinced that footballers were marketable. Stanley's bible was *The Blue Book*, the yearly almanac which gave product and statistical performance data on companies. His pitches had to be carefully prepared from the information he gleaned. Knowing the onus was entirely on him, Stanley thought of a scheme before hand-picking the firms he believed were suited to capitalise on it. He still had to persuade the commercial community that an established link to a footballer could either turn them a profit or improve the word-of-mouth reputation of a company. He also had to show, step-by-step, the often sceptical chairmen and directors of that company how it would be achieved; for most of them didn't know the difference between Bobby Charlton and Charlton Athletic. Stanley wrote to newspapers and suggested stories or features that would both cast his clients in a favourable light and provide interesting copy. He then produced the cuttings as evidence of the sort of exposure a business could potentially expect. 'The companies didn't come to you then,' he said. 'You had to go to them. And you also had to convince them that football could realistically work for them.'

Best alone changed the dynamic. The crisp phrase Stanley relied on to emphasise his commercial attraction was the much quoted: 'George could sell stair-rods to people who live in bungalows.' Stair-rods were almost the only thing to which Best's name, face or signature was not attached. 'Whenever my phone rang,' said Stanley, 'it was usually someone wanting George. People came to us. We didn't have to go to them.' Stanley had to sign and counter-sign on his behalf. Until May 1967, when Best reached his 21st birthday, British law regarded him as a minor. It rankled Best, who pointed out: 'I was old enough to fight for my country and get killed doing it. How can I be a minor?'

The arrangements Stanley made for him were lucrative. Throughout the second half of the 1960s no British sportsman or woman banked as much as Best. Not Ann Jones, the 1969 Wimbledon women's singles champion. Not Tony Jacklin, who won the Open in the same year and the US Open 11 months later. Not Henry Cooper, Britain's heavyweight champion, who had twice fought the then Cassius Clay. And none of his footballing contemporaries – including Law and Charlton – competed in the same league in regard to earnings or had the same allure to businesses. The 1966 World Cup made Bobby Moore widely recognisable. His wife, Tina, advertised Bisto gravy on television. Moore modelled suits for the Queen's designer, Hardy Amies, plugged Vitalis hair tonic and promoted the matey spirit of the British pub in *Look in at the Local*, a paean to homely licensed victuallers. In a TV commercial he threw darts at the treble 20 and mechanically spoke the stilted lines he'd been assigned. Moore did make £3,000 from a Kellogg's commercial before the 1970 World Cup. By then Best could earn £5,000 simply from cutting a ceremonial ribbon to open a supermarket. The *George Best Annual*, a combination of full-page pictures and ghosted articles, sold 120,000 copies yearly.

In 1968 he earned more than £100,000. In 1969 his income rose to £5,000 a week. In both years his basic salary was only £130 to £140 a week. Best was everywhere – on TV, on roadside billboards, on the front, back and inside pages of newspapers and magazines. Added to his football endorsements – staple revenue generators such as plastic balls and bags, shin-pads and trainers, kit and goalposts – were goods that swept across every age and social class: chewing gum, sausages, apple pies, Spanish oranges, cereals, eggs, petrol, slippers, shoes (men's, women's and children's), ties, jigsaws, colouring books and collectors' cards, crisps, lollipops and sweets, bedspreads and bedding, socks, sunglasses and hairspray. Best didn't sell only clothes; he also sold his own brand of hangers on which to put them. And he didn't only sell his own knitwear; he also sold – to those nifty with a pair of needles – the knitting patterns that allowed the same sweaters to be made at home. There were pyjamas, too – though Best questioned the purpose of them with a confession reminiscent of Marilyn Monroe who, when asked 'do you sleep with anything on?, replied with a two-word answer: 'The radio.' Best's query to Stanley was slightly different: 'I don't wear pyjamas. Does anyone these days?'

The relentless pushing of the Best brand chimed with Stanley's philosophy that sportsmen had no option but to capitalise when the going was favourable for them. He didn't see it as a mercenary act. For Time, as Stanley argued, wasn't inclined to offer second chances. 'Most businessmen reach the peak of their earning capacity from thirty onwards,' he said. 'Most sportsmen are at the top at twenty or so and ready to finish at thirty . . . It is surely only common sense that they should make the most they can, consistent with it not encroaching on their playing activities.' It underscored Stanley's belief that 'footballers of today have the glamour and appeal that film stars had in the old days'. What he couldn't fathom was the inability of some businesses to understand it. 'If you want to sell something, footballers have just about the biggest pulling power in the country,' he added, amazed that he had to reiterate it.

Stanley could afford to be picky. In turning down more offers than were accepted, he showed principled restraint as well. He had three fundamental rules. The first two were: 'I never interfere with the football career and I never allow the commercial side to intrude on club time.' The third, which guaranteed smooth relations with Old Trafford, was the sensible: 'I always ring Matt Busby first and get his approval of the proposition.' Stanley knew Busby well and consequently rejected approaches he judged would compromise Best, or those that seemed tacky. Busby wouldn't have allowed them. Stanley turned down a football pools' company because he didn't want Best tinged, however lightly, with gambling or betting. He waved away film makers, who wanted him to act, and pop producers, who wanted him to sing on records.

Commercial commitments were fitted around his socialising. Best wouldn't adhere to a structure, the blocking off of specific days each month dedicated to promotional duties. Stanley couldn't work out Best's reluctance to embrace them entirely. Nor could he curtail his spending. 'As fast as the money rolled in, it rolled out again,' said Best. 'I don't really have any clear idea where it went.' Best had a habit of agreeing to divert money – sometimes several thousand pounds – into schemes and only telling Stanley about them afterwards. 'I'd say "Yeah, great",' said Best, 'and never checked up on what was happening to it. I lost a lot of cash that way.'

Stanley went as far as going to Aycliffe Avenue and enlisting Mary and Steve Fullaway's support to teach Best the principles of micro economics. 'Can you tell him that every sixpence he gives away is actually costing him a pound?' asked Stanley, exasperated because he'd tried – and failed – to explain it himself. At first Best was indifferent to soaring levels of income tax – 19s. 6d in every pound – that Harold Wilson's government forced on high earners. Somehow the message got through to Best, whose subsequent dislike of the Inland Revenue grew out of the amount of tax taken from him during the 60s. He would eventually ask to be paid for some appearances in cash. 'Get the readies,' he'd say, stashing the money in drawers and cupboards rather than putting it in the bank. Tidying up one of his sock drawers Mrs Fullaway once came across £30,000 in cash – another win for Best against the Revenue. Stanley was fortunate in this respect. His son, David, was only a year older than Best, which meant each could relate to the other. Chaperoning him through appointments, David Stanley found Best shy and sweetly vulnerable, which added to his engaging appeal. 'My father thought George could charm the backside off an elephant. He was right. I saw hard-headed businessmen go weak at the knees when he spoke to them. If he was late, he'd apologise. Within thirty seconds no one would care that George hadn't been on time. He'd give them his smile and all would be forgiven.'

For Best, the waitress pouring the tea had parity with the managing director in charge of the company. 'He was full of humility and always courteous, and he looked on everyone as being equal. He had an open, trusting nature and he saw himself as a real person connecting with real people,' added David Stanley, who also marvelled at Best's phlegmatic attitude and his patient kindnesses and tolerance when tetchiness or annoyance would sometimes have been forgivable. 'If someone was rude, he wasn't rude back. If someone was a bother, he tried not to notice.'

If Best planned to make his excuses and leave because a situation or an engagement had become too much for him, he'd merely use a code developed with his friends. 'OTW,' he'd say. It was an acronym for Over The Wall, a signal for what he described as 'The Great Escape'.

Of course, there was no escape for Best. His fame was about to swell into something neither he – nor anyone else – could control.

'That's when the madness began,' he said.

PART TWO

More Tears Are Shed Over Answered Prayers

6

Birds and Bees and Shiny New Toffees

Every morning, noon and night was an unfolding entertainment for George Best, which he compared to 'some bloody great roundabout with music playing'.

He was constantly restless, admitting: 'I never stay in. I can't sit in the house.' Then he went further. 'I can't sit down for five minutes on end. I've got to be on the move all the time. Wednesday to Saturday, it's murder. I know I've got to stay off the town and get to bed by eleven. But it drives me nuts. The only thing that keeps me sane is remembering there'll be a party on Sunday and Monday and Tuesday.'

But, as the idolatry grew, so did the nuisances.

A Premiership player is well screened from intrusion. Appointments are usually arranged after protracted negotiation and detailed haggling about time and protocol. Interviews are nearly always done because there is a product to promote.

Best was ridiculously accessible. He was difficult to find occasionally only because he went wherever the mood – or one of his pals – took him. In these pre-mobile phone days, Ken Stanley had a scroll of possible numbers for him: those of favourite clubs and bars, friends and associates and Mary Fullaway's. To find Best was a process of elimination. It was possible to walk into his boutique and run into him on the shop floor. Or you could ring the store and discover that, on a whim or during a bored moment, he'd decided to answer the call himself. There were only two Fullaways in the Manchester telephone directory – Mary and her eldest son, Graham. It remained that way until its constant ringing at all hours lifted it off the hook and Mrs Fullaway went ex-directory for her own sanity. Even doing that didn't make much difference. 'No matter how hard I try to keep my number quiet, it always leaks out,' complained Best, regularly awoken in the middle of the night by anonymous callers who hung up as soon as he answered. 'I suppose it could be the boss checking up on me,' he said, wryly.

Fans would wait in clusters on the pavement outside the house in Aycliffe Avenue for Best to leave or arrive. Much braver souls opened the gate, strolled along the narrow concrete path and knocked on the door. 'They always want to see George's bedroom,' reported Mrs Fullaway.

As Best drove through Manchester, he would find himself tailgated by drivers and could escape them only by breaking a succession of red lights. Wherever he went he was hassled for his signature. He couldn't eat a restaurant meal without interruption. It reached the stage where Best wouldn't bother to have a starter from the menu. He'd choose a main course and hope he could finish it before being bothered. To eat three courses, Best would have had to order in three different places and run from one to the other.

At first he took the constant pestering as a compliment and his affable nature meant he dealt with hysterical clamouring for his attention with astonishing equanimity. Sometimes there was a deep comedy attached to the public's reaction to him: Best unable to open his car door because of the heaving crowd around it; Best unable to walk three steps along a street before an autograph book or a scrappy piece of paper was pushed in front of him; Best darting into alleyways or stores to avoid newspapermen or fans – and then finding more of them irrespective of where he hid.

He couldn't go to the cinema without turning up late and leaving early. Best said: 'I'd wait until the film started, and everything was dark, before I took a seat. And then I'd get up a minute or so before the end and stand near the exit. I never saw the opening or the closing credits.' He couldn't stop at a traffic light without a supporter rapping their knuckles against a side window or on the windscreen of his Jaguar. He couldn't go into a shop to buy a newspaper or to a bar to unwind with a drink and expect to be left alone. He was pounced on and cornered, captive to the pub bore who wanted to talk football.

On the terraces Best received the sort of heckling that is unbelievably mild compared to the witlessly crude and facile abuse directed at current players. The most common taunt was the basic: 'You don't have to tackle him. Just wait until he trips over his wallet.' The cloth-caps, considering Best effeminate because of his fondness for clothes and his long hair, yelled: 'You're just a big girl' and asked: 'Where's your handbag?' He'd once emerged from the tunnel at Anfield carrying one, which he'd borrowed from a tea lady and draped over his left forearm. Occasionally an empty beer can appeared from beyond the perimeter wall and landed at his feet. During a stoppage in the game he'd pick it up and pretend to take a drink before lobbing the can on to the track. 'You expect stick from the opposition crowds,' he'd say, 'and you soon ignore it or handle it in a way that doesn't provoke.'

There were also cranks to handle, whose malign intent was relayed to him in unsigned hate mail. Stanley braced Best for it, warning about the warped minority who'd be angry, jealous, censorious and strictly puritanical or just extremely hostile towards him for no discernible reason. The anonymous, vicious letters did come and were written in vivid coloured inks (usually green or red) and contained screaming capital letters. The poison pen was his 'worst enemy', he said. 'They are almost certainly the work of twisted minds – but they still hurt.' Best was lambasted as loathsome, radically subversive and a corrupting influence on the young. He was promised hellfire. One writer, signing himself Ashton-Under-Lyme, would post two or three letters a day and complain vilely about everything he did. The older Best would learn to shrug off the comments as either deranged or irrelevant. The younger Best could never grasp why he aroused such hatred or what motivated someone to express it so graphically. He tried to dissuade the critics from buying a pad of Basildon Bond and a stamp, announcing: 'All my letters are screened. I don't get to read the worst ones. It's pointless to send them to me.' The letters continued to arrive anyway. Some were sent directly to Matt Busby. Cross-referencing the venues and times of where Best was supposed to have been sighted, Busby frequently found him in two places – and often three – simultaneously. One letter said Best had been seen fall-down drunk in a street. Another claimed he'd been losing money in a casino the night before a match. Busby dismissed the clearly malicious and checked out only the dispassionate writers, who stuck to cold facts, because he knew Best obeyed one golden rule. He didn't stray far from Aycliffe Avenue on a Friday evening.

It seemed to Busby that Best was appearing in the newspapers every day. Since Busby had never encountered such a situation before, he had no strategy to handle it. Duncan Edwards had never opened a boutique. Bobby Charlton wasn't a fashion model. Denis Law didn't get into the gossip columns. Busby again assumed the frenzy around Best would blow itself out. People would get tired of him and interest would wane. In the meantime he'd address each accusation against him as it arose. Best vigorously defended himself. 'Do you think I would run around the city night spots in the early hours of the morning before a match?

You could have a job to catch me in a public house even *after* a match,' he said.

The desirable Best found he was always on show. Wherever he went, women followed. If his Jaguar was unprotected, he'd return to declarations of love and devotion scrawled across the bonnet, the boot and the driver's door. Best's colleague John Connelly made the error of parking beside the Jag and came back to discover two dozen females waiting for Best. 'I couldn't get into my car,' he said. 'George's was covered in writing and the wipers were jammed with notes. After that, I made a point of finding a space as far away from him as possible.' Those messages in lipstick or eyeliner could be removed with a damp cloth. Those scratched into the paintwork with a nail file or a ballpoint meant a respray. Best repeatedly drove to the garage to book a paintjob or to order new wheel hubs after finding them stolen or damaged. One woman spread herself over the Jag's bonnet and refused to move until Best left the driver's seat and gave her a kiss on the cheek, the traffic banking up behind him and the sound of distant car horns filling the Manchester air. Someone tried to steal one of the wheels. Someone else tried to jemmy the number off Mrs Fullaway's door with a screwdriver. Mrs Fullaway also went into the living room one morning to find a teenage admirer had opened the downstairs window and was sleeping on the sofa. She insisted the girl leave in exactly the same way as she'd arrived, uninvited. Other girls would rap the window to attract Best's attention. 'Girls ring up all day long – even until two o'clock in the morning,' said Mrs Fullaway. 'When I answer all I hear is a lot of girlish giggles. The girls only want to boast they have spoken to George.'

The players' entrance at United – a wooden red door – was besieged after every game by hangers-on, more autograph hunters and troops of women who wanted a kiss and a hug from Best. Letters were slipped into his pocket asking for a date. Some made far more forward propositions. Others wrote their telephone numbers on the back of photographs that showed them seductively pouting or scantily clad. Best liked to slide a maroon or white handkerchief in the top pocket of his jacket. In the scrum outside Old Trafford, it would be taken from him as a souvenir. Best went through a drawer of handkerchiefs before exasperation obliged him to pin one to the inside of his pocket. The pin didn't deter the shrieking pack, who ripped it away and left a tear in his jacket. 'Sometimes I was lucky to get out of there still wearing my shirt,' he said. On match day he arrived and departed Old Trafford in a taxi, which ferried him to and from the secure spot where he'd left his car.

He'd received letters – slid-in Polaroid photographs enclosed with them – that were so sexually explicit as to qualify as top-shelf porn. They regularly read simply: 'Dear George, I want you to fuck me.' A telephone number was always included on the off-chance Best found the offer or the image instantly irresistible.

There were *doppelgängers* in Manchester and London who called themselves George Best. One impersonator drove a white E-type Jaguar like his own. Another conned a woman during a holiday in Italy. At Old Trafford Best received a letter demanding to know why 'he' hadn't contacted her. 'You said we should write to each other,' she wrote. Realising she'd been deceived, Best rang her telephone number, tucked into the top right-hand corner of the letter, to tell her the truth. He'd never been to Italy on holiday then (it was 1967). A maxim says nothing is so obnoxious as other people's luck – especially where sex is concerned. Best's luck with women brought him resentment. 'If you were an envious sort of person,' says Mike Summerbee, 'you couldn't be with George because he was the centre of attention wherever our group went. His friends accepted that. Some strangers didn't.' Husbands or boyfriends accused him of trying to steal their partner away; and there were many women who were willing to be stolen. 'It was insane,' said Best.

He couldn't go to the toilet alone in case he found an aggressor waiting for him. He remembered a story about Bill Shankly. A fellow beside Shankly in the urinal did a quick double-take, spun to speak to him and pissed down the Liverpool manager's trousers, soaking the right leg. 'An amazing number of people walk up to you while you're trying to take a pee and want to shake hands with you,' said Best.

Even at 21 years old Best talked about his dreams of leaving all this – an early, tell-tale admission that foretold the upheaval to come. 'Have you ever felt like wanting to get away from it all?' he asked. 'Have you ever felt like stealing away into a quiet corner, taking your thoughts with you? Have people ever got on your nerves so much that you have wanted to stand up and scream? I have heard celebrities ask questions like this before and there are times when I know exactly what they are getting at.'

The *Sunday Times* once persuaded George Best to appear in its colour magazine wearing only a pair of navy shorts. He rested a dark panelled football on his right hip. He was photographed both face-on and from behind. The article was called 'The Price of Genius'. The idea was to illustrate the damage a career in football did to the body. A line was drawn from each limb and muscle, a brief caption attached to it. 'Cartilage removed from right knee,' said one. 'Feet and ankles get the strongest punishment. Best's now have to be strapped before a game,' said another. What the piece didn't comment upon were the marks on his neck, imprints on the flesh no defender had made. They were love bites.

Near the end of his life the Poet Laureate John Betjeman was asked whether he had any regrets. 'Not enough sex,' he said. This is not a sentence Best ever spoke. Before the end of the 1960s, he'd say: 'A couple of years ago the boys and I worked out how many girls I'd taken out, and it came to seven hundred and fifty. Now it must be well over a thousand.' Those who knew him say the figure is not boastful exaggeration. 'It became impossible to keep count,' he said, much later, of his horizontal life. In his *Histoire de ma vie*, Giacomo Casanova logs only 122 lovers, which practically makes him a virgin compared to Best, who said he saw nothing wrong with leaving one girl at midnight and being with another 'half an hour later'. He claimed to have slept with seven women – 'lucky seven', he said – in one 24-hour period.

It wasn't always like this. In his early years at Aycliffe Avenue, as soon as Mary Fullaway noticed his interest in women – and their interest in him – she began to feel 'a bit anxious', she said. She didn't know whether Best had ever received the standard lecture about the birds and the bees. Afraid he might be embarrassed or compromised, she thought it sensible to educate him about the facts of life in case he got himself – or a girl – 'into trouble'. 'I thought I'd better have a little talk about the kind of girls to beware of,' she said. The talk didn't last long. 'I soon realised he was howling with laughter,' she explained. Mrs Fullaway would add, correctly, that half the women in Britain wanted to mother Best and the other half wanted to marry him. 'His problem is that he tends to fall in love so quickly,' she added.

Best would always remember his early crushes and his attempts to date a girl he described as 'the school model'. Her boyfriend and his friends threatened to 'beat' his 'head in'. He remembered other girls poking fun at him then because he was so skinny. And he remembered falling for Steve Fullaway's girlfriend, writing her a note because his accent was still so broad that he couldn't be certain she'd understand him. 'A few days later Steve had the note. I was so embarrassed.' Best began to see her nonetheless. 'Her mother used to work during the day. I used to sneak over to the house. Her mother came home early and we were upstairs.' Best believed he'd escaped without being seen after dressing, tiptoeing downstairs, opening the front door quietly and sneaking away. He didn't know that her mother, washing dishes at the sink, had watched him scuttle off. 'I thought I was being clever,' he said. Best still found it difficult to overcome his shyness. At 17 he couldn't summon the courage to approach a girl in a Manchester bowling alley. Best stared at her so intently for four hours that she finally asked why he hadn't gone over to speak to her. 'We started a mad, passionate affair. I thought this was the love of my life,' he recalled. The relationship ended when Best returned to Aycliffe Avenue after a holiday in Belfast to find she'd eloped with a sailor. 'It shattered me,' he said. 'I was going to take my life and never love another.' He changed his mind very rapidly.

The writer Fay Weldon, recalling the liberating consequences of the Pill, made available on the National Health Service in 1960, said: 'As soon as you could have sex without babies, everyone just had sex all the time.' It was certainly true for Best. He spent a great deal of time having sex or chasing it in an era when women were called 'birds' or 'dollies' or an amalgam of the two, when jack-the-lad male chauvinism was rife and the decade was labelled permissive. It's a rule that everyone's love life is funny apart from your own. Best's was portrayed this way. He was the Soccer Playboy. It wasn't so much *Match of the Day* as Mattress of the Day for him. The women were always Georgie's Girls, a lame pun on the 1966 film *Georgy Girl*. 'Sex,' he said, 'is like scoring a goal.' He expanded on that theme later on, claiming the run towards goal was like an erection and the scoring of a goal itself compared favourably to an orgasm.

He didn't have to seduce. Women came to him, which was just as well because he didn't possess the practised patter of the confident lothario. In the beginning he spoke slowly and softly, almost in a whisper, and his lips barely moved. Often his head was slightly bowed, as if he was afraid of making eye contact as he spoke. He avoided initiating conversations with strangers. Indeed, whenever possible, he avoided gatherings in which they might occur. In crowded rooms he liked to stand in a corner. Chat-up lines got stuck on his tongue. Summerbee always had to speak on Best's behalf. 'I used to say to him, "Come on. Hurry up. Make your choice. There are ten in a queue for you. Which one are you interested in?" Then I'd go and talk to her as he stood beside me, not saying anything.'

Every Manchester United player was given a 4 x 3in, 16-page red-leather booklet containing the club's 'Training Rules and Playing Instructions'. Within this tiny bible were 16 commandments, which Matt Busby dictated and signed. These ranged from basic hours of employment to distribution of kit, adhering to the Old Trafford doctor's advice on diet to possible penalties about unauthorised absences from training and a stern, pre-emptive warning to dissuade players from bringing friends into the dressing room 'under any pretext whatsoever'. Specific guidelines were given, too, about nicotine and alcohol. Rule 11 stipulated: 'Smoking is strictly prohibited during training hours and players are earnestly requested to reduce smoking to the absolute minimum on the day of a match.' Rule 13 said: 'Any player rendering himself unfit to perform his duties through drinking or any other causes will be severely dealt with.' That Busby felt it necessary to put all this into cold print said how much he wanted to remind his team about decent behaviour and good practice. But Best was also aware of another, more important regulation, that curiously, didn't appear in that booklet. It did, however, appear in his contract. Clause Five read:

The player shall not . . . live in any place which the Directors of the club may deem unsuitable.

Unmarried players were supposed to 'reside' only in the digs approved for them by the club – for reasons United condescendingly claimed were based on the principles of 'proper attention and good food', as if a footballer lacked the intelligence to find himself a decent meal every day or to dress himself in the morning. The restriction appears crudely anachronistic and the attitude attached to it bizarrely strait-laced to us now. Busby, always devoted to family life, nevertheless didn't want the bachelors in the team to live alone and get into mischief. In the mid-60s, however, Best and Summerbee were single and free. Best said: 'I realised I was in the perfect position for pulling birds. I had the limelight, the publicity, the money.'

He and Summerbee began renting a one-bedroom flat together at a peppercorn rate. The flat was in a red-brick Victorian house in Crumpsall, a suburb of North Manchester, and the two of them got involved in its interior decoration. They put down a green, flowery carpet and found comfortable furniture and curtains to complement it. Hanging behind the bathroom door were two towelling dressing robes – one red and white for United, the other blue and white for City. The flat became a weekend bolthole and gave Mrs Fullaway in particular some respite from her lodger's late-night cum early-morning comings and goings. The fact that it had only one bedroom frequently meant there was a race between Best and Summerbee to occupy it. 'If you didn't get there first,' said Summerbee, 'you were on the sofa.' Taxi drivers were asked to take convoluted routes – involving deliberate wrong turns and U-turns – to try to conceal the flat's exact location from the women taken back there. Best dreaded the prospect of arriving in the early hours to find half a dozen girlfriends waiting for him on the front step. He was anxious to preserve the secrecy of the flat's existence from Busby, too. But, like almost everything else Best did in and around Manchester, Busby found out about its existence. Believing wild oats had to be sown somewhere, and assuming Best would settle down shortly, he made no strenuous attempt to get him to relinquish it. Newspapers then were less inclined to go digging for dirt on sportsmen anyway, which meant Busby wasn't likely to wake up and discover Best salaciously splashed across a Sunday red top in tabloidese that yelled about the love nest below a headline font thick enough to announce a war.

Best took as a defeat women he couldn't get into bed, among them the actress Jane Asher – once her romance with Paul McCartney had ended – and Dusty Springfield (he didn't realise she was a lesbian). He was seen with models and actresses, beauty queens and pop singers. Most were prominent in the 60s and are forgotten or half-forgotten names now. Best was quickly smitten by women he saw for the first time. His friends asked why he didn't settle on one girl. He'd rub his thumbs and index fingers together, as if taking the shiny paper off a sweet, and say: 'I like unwrapping new toffees,' which didn't make him sound too much like Galahad. Every summer, during June and part of July, Best went to Spain, where he'd find women 'throwing themselves at me', he said. According to Best: 'Sex was no big deal. You fancied going to bed with someone and they fancied it. That was it. There was no embarrassment or guilt or anything. Thank you very much and move on. It's terribly easy.' In retrospect Best became angry with himself for speaking glibly about his relationships and tried to refine his comments. 'It was more than one night stands. It was never sordid,' he insisted.

The liberal attitudes of the age suited his libido all the same and he couldn't resist adding: 'I love the company of girls and I see nothing wrong with sleeping with as many as I can.' He enjoyed the pleasure of the chase as much as the capture. 'The one who pretends she doesn't care is the one I'm interested in,' he said.

His first steady girlfriend was Jackie Glass, a film scriptwriter, who said of him: 'There are more sides to George than there are panels to a football.' Glass was likened to the model Jean Shrimpton. The comparison didn't do her justice; she was more gorgeous than that. It was attraction at first sight. He was smitten in a fraction of a second after seeing her in a nightclub. So much so that someone who loathed dancing and who, strangely, couldn't do so rhythmically because shyness inhibited him ('I shuffled a bit,' said Best) asked Glass' boyfriend for permission to dance with her. It was his only hope of getting her alone. Her boyfriend made the mistake of agreeing. 'Everyone was looking at us,' she said. 'I didn't realise no one had ever seen George dance before.' Glass describes Best as 'romantic – but not in a hearts and flowers kind of way'. He took a train from Manchester to London, where she lived, simply to persuade her to catch the next train back with him. If the phone rang at two o'clock in the morning, she'd answer 'Hi George' because he was the only person she knew who rang up in the early hours. Sitting in a cinema, and seeing her name suddenly appear on the screen, Glass went to the manager's office thinking that it must be an emergency. 'I'd imagined every possible calamity.' The manager handed her a white envelope. Inside was a note from Best: '*I Love You. G.*' When she took him home for the first time – the family lived close to Best's boutique – Glass' mother didn't recognise him. 'What do you do?' she asked. Glass' father, however, had raised a football devotee after taking her to watch Busby's Babes in the 1950s. She had prayed for Duncan Edwards after Munich. 'I was a United fan,' she says.

Apart from her physical attractiveness, Best was drawn to her intelligence, independence and extrovert personality. She spoke French like the French, and also wrote in French. She mixed with the film director Roman Polanski and his wife-to-be, the actress Sharon Tate. 'She had talent,' said Best, which was important to him. 'You always wondered whether a girl went out with you because of who you were,' he said. 'Ninety-five per cent want to know you because you're rich or well known. That's why I like dating women with minds and careers of their own. They didn't have to be seen with you to be someone.' Glass encouraged Best to be more outgoing. She recommended books to him, which began his penchant for reading. She took him to exhibitions. She spoke to him about films. Best called it 'an education'. She was part of the mixed-up world Best found himself in. 'He couldn't go anywhere, really,' said Glass. 'It was difficult for him to do anything spontaneous that was ordinary or normal, such as visiting an art gallery or going into a bookshop. Or even just popping somewhere for a coffee.'

She experienced the sinister side to the craziness, too, when a malicious caller rang a radio station to claim she and Best had been killed in a car crash. The story was believable because Best's record on the road suggested he drove like Mr Toad. He'd mishandled the gears on one of his first cars and gone into a low wall, demolishing most of it. He'd been fined for speeding in 1966. He was fined again – and had his licence endorsed – in 1967 for driving without due care and attention after knocking down a woman, who fractured her pelvis. At the end of that year his E-type, which Best claimed skidded on black ice, collided with a parked van. He bruised his head and gashed his knee. So the radio station broadcast the unverified piece of hearsay, which swept across Manchester. Glass' father, panic-stricken, went to the boutique and found Best and his daughter unharmed, ignorant of what was being said about them. 'He just came across, hugged me and said "Thank God",' said Glass. The old saying is true: a lie can travel half way around the world before truth pulls its boots on, which is why the *Manchester Evening News* found it necessary to publish a front-page story to confirm that reports of Best's death were exaggerated. His family were contacted in Belfast before the false rumour reached them. Even after the *Evening News* report, and the bills outside newsagents' shops, the rumour refused to go away. He'd be stopped in the street and hear people say: 'I thought you were dead.'

Glass also witnessed the esteem in which Best was held. In a London restaurant he was approached, very courteously, by a man with long, dark hair, chiselled cheekbones and a blade of a nose. He bowed deeply to Best from the neck and apologised sincerely for troubling him during his meal. 'You are a true artist,' he explained as the prelude to the inevitable request for an autograph. As ever Best signed willingly. When the man left, Glass asked:

'Do you know who that was?'

'No,' said Best, blankly.

'Rudolf Nureyev,' she said.

George Best never arranged to take out a woman on a Saturday night in case Manchester United lost. 'I don't know what sort of mood I'm going to be in,' he said. 'So I don't chance it.' Best was adamant, too, that women never interfered with his football, which he claimed meant more than socialising to him. Everything was subordinate to the game then. He trained dedicatedly, always willing to practise long-range shots and in-swinging corner kicks, which grazed the far post, before taking a solitary ball into the centre of the open field for half an hour or more. Occasionally Matt Busby and Jimmy Murphy stood in the middle distance to watch him juggle and demonstrate his affinity with it. Best's shirt was always loose. His socks were always rolled to the ankle and he'd play his keepy-uppy, as if not bothering to concentrate. With neat, short taps, or the odd flick on to his knee, Best passed the ball from one foot to the other. He'd then knock it over his head and back heel it into the air again, retaining possession before it fell. He'd extend his right leg to make it more difficult for himself, and then do the same with his left. The thud-thud noise of boot on ball echoed around him. Busby knew Best could have achieved this all day and anywhere – on a street corner to the accompaniment of accordion music if necessary. 'I did it because I loved it,' said Best. 'I liked having a ball to myself.' Repetition never dulled the routine for him.

He thought historians should mark the 1960s with a huge asterisk to establish it as the era in which 'football was most fun'. He didn't mind the scarred pitches or the fug of blue fag smoke drifting from terraces and he also accepted the Kung Fu kick-like tackling as an occupational hazard. 'The ambition was to score goals and plenty of them,' he said. 'I went out to put on a show.' Talent, distributed throughout the First Division, made the nil-nil draw (almost) as extinct as the unicorn, he added. Spurs had Best's favourite forward, the opportunistic Jimmy Greaves, who was capable of both scoring outrageous solo goals and appearing from nowhere, as if sprung from a concealed trapdoor in the area, to plunder from close range. Everton had Alan Ball, who exhausted the opposition with performances that were perpetual motion. West Ham had Bobby Moore, always immaculately patrician, and the technically proficient Martin Peters. Liverpool had Ian Callaghan and Peter Thompson and the underrated Roger Hunt. Rivalry sharpened in Manchester once City reorganised under Joe Mercer and Malcolm Allison and drafted in the collaborative arts of Mike Summerbee and Colin Bell. And there was Leeds, where facing Norman Hunter was like meeting a cannon-ball in full flight and Best found Paul Reaney got close enough to him to see the pink, cob-webbed veins in his eyes. 'If I'd decided to go for a piss during the game,' said Best, 'he'd have stood next to me in the urinal and got his boots splashed.' There was camaraderie within the football world then, said Best. He'd find Bill Nicholson slapping him on the back at White Hart Lane. He'd hear Bill Shankly greeting him at Anfield with the raspy growl of this promise: 'Eh son, don't bother – you're going to get beat today.' Best admired the verve of the Scots: Jim Baxter, who strolled through matches with an imperial languor and was capable of landing a pass on a silver dollar from 75 yards, and Jimmy Johnstone, who went where his instincts took him at Celtic, which usually meant beating all-comers at least twice.

Honours were well distributed during that decade. There were seven different League champions – and also seven different FA Cup winners. No one was wholly dominant for more than a season. 'Anyone,' as Best stressed, 'could beat anyone else.' To compete in the European Cup then meant becoming champions again. There wasn't the luxury of finishing fourth – as teams do today – to qualify for the early phase of the competition. Best was conscious of the fierce urgency of *now*, which he sensed at United. Sand was slipping through the hour glass; Busby didn't have many years left as a manager. Losing to Partizan in 1966 was distressing enough for Busby to say pessimistically to aides such as Jimmy Murphy: 'We'll never win the European Cup now. We are not meant to win it.' In using 'we' in that sentence, what Busby also meant was 'I will never win it'. The April of his discontent accentuated his misery towards the domestic game, too. Fixture congestion floored United. Nine games were packed into 25 days, and Busby won only two of them. The team just ran out of puff. There were even defeats against Aston Villa and West Ham, both embedded in the bottom half of the table. The corollary of striving to win everything was to win nothing. United, tipped for a treble before the month began, lost the FA Cup semi-final to Everton and the League to Liverpool, ten points superior. 'I was downcast,' said Busby, who considered retirement after finishing an inadequate fourth. Again, as she'd done in the months after Munich, his wife Jean was decisive in talking him out of it. He'd come so close. Why give up – especially when his side still respected him and future success seemed so probable? The World Cup finals were coming. How could he watch the competition and *not* be eager afterwards for the campaign that was to follow? And surely a life with United was far preferable to a life without them? To try to argue against the truth of it was pointless for Busby. One other thing swayed him – a chance encounter, which he found humbling. Busby was driving to Old Trafford when he stopped at a zebra crossing to allow a group of blind schoolchildren to pass. 'There I was down in the mouth about some adverse results in the game of football,' he recalled. 'There were those kids unable to see and facing a lifetime like that. As I sat and watched them my despair lifted and I told myself: Get your priorities right, Matt. At least you can do something about the European Cup.'

So, in preparation for the 1966–67 season he went through the previous one as if conducting a forensic examination. Every game was studied. Every player was picked apart. The title was the door through which he had to pass before the culmination of his managerial career. 'We must have a real go to win it,' he said, not feeling the need to say more. For what more could he say?

Busby decided he couldn't go on expecting United to consistently outscore the opposition. Sometimes you were bound to fail – if only because of the law of averages. Two statistics dominated his thoughts. United had hit 84 goals to Liverpool's 79 in the previous League season. But the glaring difference between them had come at the other end of the field. Liverpool had conceded a mere 34; United had conceded a whopping 59 by comparison. Strength in defence, which meant eradicating mistakes there, was Busby's priority. He didn't want to diminish the carefree elan United showed going forward. He did, however, see the need for them to be more conscious of what he called, like a plumber discussing a malfunctioning pipe, 'leakage and seepage'. In mid-September Busby made what Best regarded as his most decisive move. He signed the goalkeeper Alex Stepney from Chelsea for £55,000. 'He wasn't flash,' said Best. 'He just got on with his job.' From then on Best was sure no one would stop them. 'I just knew. I could *feel* it.'

The country was aglow because of football. The pub talk after that end of July day of sun and showers at Wembley was about two numbers – 4–2 – and also about Hurst and Moore, Charlton and Banks, and Stiles and the tracksuited Alf Ramsey. The game attracted a new audience. Even people previously uninterested in it now wanted to watch and learn and debate its merits. Best saw England beat West Germany. He sat on the wooden benches beneath the royal box, rolled programme in his hands, and longed for something impossible: to be beside his clubmates Charlton and Stiles. With him, there'd have been no need for extra-time; and so no need either for those 'was-it-or-wasn't-it' arguments about whether the whole ball had crossed the line. Best thought he'd have run the German full-backs, Höttges and Schnellinger, into the turf. Deprived of that stage, he sought to build another wherever he went during the season to come. He felt exactly as Busby did; United had a League to win.

Fully fit again, Best scored ten First Division goals to claim his second Championship medal in the month of his 21st birthday. United won the title by four points. The kernel of it was a 20-match unbeaten run, beginning in late December and continuing until the season's end, which held off Nottingham Forest and Tottenham, separated only by goal average.

Effectively needing only one point from their penultimate game, United were resplendent against West Ham at Upton Park. Busby missed the opening minutes, arriving in his seat to see West Ham kicking off. He didn't realise Bobby Charlton had already scored; he hadn't heard the crowd's reaction to the goal. Those sitting beside Busby supposed he knew what had happened, and so didn't remark on it. Even at half-time he went into the dressing room believing the score was 3–0 instead of 4–0 and urged his team not to become complacent.

Analysis of that Championship is nearly always perfunctory. It is ignored as a necessary preliminary, a chore to be gone through before the main event. In an autobiography, *Soccer at the Top*, Busby devotes only five words to it – a plain statement of fact: 'We won the Championship again.' He doesn't gloat about it. He doesn't even say, as though inviting others to look up the figures, that United conceded the second-lowest number of goals in the division – 45; or that 14 of those went into the net before Stepney arrived.

Best chose the win at West Ham as one of his six most memorable matches at United. The result – 6–1 – typified the fact Busby remained adventurous and reflected his 'attack and attack again' attitude and also what had gone before: the 5–3 licking of West Bromwich Albion, the

4–1 and 4–0 defeats of Burnley and Blackpool, a 5–0 trouncing of Sunderland and another five goals to bury Leicester City. United had been given the odd whacking: 4–1 at Forest, 3–1 at Leeds. Whatever Busby said about being tighter at the back, Best observed nonetheless that the players 'still thought we'd score more goals than anyone else'. This was true – 84 compared to West Ham's 80, the second-highest total in the table. 'It was gaudy, heady football,' he added, remembering the 'air of triumph' about United at Upton Park. There's a smudgy black and white picture of them celebrating there. It's a shooting-gallery line of players either bare-chested or wearing V-necked white shirts. Steam from the showers mists the room, giving the edge of the picture a ghostly haze. United are toasting themselves, glasses half-filled with champagne. Busby had brought the first bottle with him. No sooner was it drunk than he was asked about the European Cup. 'There it was,' he said of it, 'high in the sky shining at us like a star, beckoning us.'

And so the effort to reach it began again for him. He looked upon the 1967–68 competition with anticipation and also a now-or-never trepidation, always thinking of Munich and what it had denied him and the dead. 'I am sure the 1958 European Cup would have been ours, and after it, ours and ours again,' he said. Best was devout in his belief that United would win it for Busby this time, saving him from more grief. He knew – as Busby and Charlton and Bill Foulkes also knew – that the season represented a watershed. He saw other European landmarks ahead for him – but not for this United and not for that trio, combined age 126. The desire to win the Cup for himself was equalled by his drive to ensure he honoured them; and also those men he knew only from photographs in boys' annuals and the newsreels. With each round, Best became increasingly convinced of the certainty of what he felt in his bones. 'We were going to win it.'

So much of what occurred on the route to the final takes second billing or is skimmed over. Busby seldom lingered over it, ticking off each match as if always impatient to get to the absolute heart and guts of his story; what he called his 'Magnificent Obsession', and the hunt for 'The Holy Grail'.

The draw was kind. Hibernians of Malta, genuine minnows, were beaten 4–0 on aggregate. A bumpy pitch of compressed sand and gravel enabled the part-timers to claim a face-saving 0–0 draw at home. Next came Sarajevo, overcome 2–1 in the two legs. It was the first occasion since Munich that United had chartered its own aircraft – a BAC-111. The Bosnians tackled at waist and chest height to compensate for flagrant deficiencies in fundamental skill. Three of their players were booked, another sent off. Best was clogged repeatedly, his flesh black with bruising. Busby condemned it as some of the most heinous tackling he'd ever witnessed. Somehow Best survived. Another side with the attitude of hit men awaited United in the last eight: Poland's Gornik Zabrze, based in the Silesian coalfields. Gornik were beaten 2–0 at Old Trafford. For the return Best trooped behind the Iron Curtain equipped like a Boy Scout on a camping expedition into the wild. Soup and two pounds of tea, plus a heater on which to boil them, were packed along with his kit. 'I didn't expect it to be like the Ritz out there,' he said. The game ought never to have started. The pitch was covered in a two-inch layer of packed-down snow. Beneath was a sheet of ice. The wind chill slashed the temperature to below zero and sleet began to fall like grain. The players slid treacher-ously and skated maladroitly on a surface that made control difficult and finesse impossible. The extreme foulness of the weather made chasing the game – as Gornik were compelled to do – more arduous. There was a solitary goal for them, eked out 20 minutes from the end. United doggedly clung on. 'I don't think I've ever been colder,' said Best.

What separated Busby from his dream – so close he could almost touch it now – was Real Madrid. United went from the freezer to the furnace, taking a solitary Best goal for protection. At Old Trafford, Real policed Best so closely he could hardly breathe. One chance was none-theless enough for him. Real were unaccountably lackadaisical, allowing Best to roam unmarked around the penalty spot. The closest defender to him was marooned on the edge of the six-yard box. Best's block-busting shot, struck with his left foot, billowed the roof of the net like a fisherman's big catch. There was still a gloominess about United. Busby was publicly upbeat, declaring his conviction that 'this is our year' while privately speaking aloud his doubts about whether the unanswered goal Best had given him would be sufficient in the Bernabéu. He described it to Murphy as 'our last chance'.

In Poland, Best would gladly have worn a sheepskin coat and scarf. In Madrid, he found the conditions stifling; so chokingly hot, he said, that 'you had to pass the ball – it wasn't a night to go it alone'. Busby gave the advice he always did.

'Keep it tight early on.

'Find a team-mate.

'Play without fear.'

A game of high stakes is always fraught and nervy. So it proves until the final 13 minutes of the first half when, inexplicably, United implode. Real score three goals and United drag one back fortuitously, the ball going in off a Real defender. United slink off the pitch, swallowed by misery. The dressing room is as silent as a funeral parlour. A manager can be overrated and what he says is often forgotten or ignored as soon as a match starts or restarts either through circumstance, forgetfulness or wilful disregard. But Busby, surveying the depressive mood and the slump of bodies in front of him, recognises that the flood of goals amounts to more than the loss of the lead; it means a loss psychologi-cally, too. It isn't just that United are dispirited; and that seeing Real buoyant makes this acuter still. Busby had pessimistically admitted to Murphy on the way to the dressing room: 'Well, I suppose that's it.' What lifts him out of his dejection is the need to seem strong and also the simplest of mental mathematical calculations. Busby has never been so wily. Never have so few of his words amounted to so much. He waits until almost the last moment. United are about to haul themselves back on to the pitch before he speaks two sentences:

'Don't forget that we came here with a goal. You're still only a goal behind.'

The way he says this and the timing of it – spoken firmly, like an order, but also in a reassuringly calm and authoritative manner – makes the difference. 'We'd been moping and feeling sorry,' said Best. 'We went out a foot taller than we came in.' Real contribute to their own downfall through conceit, the assumption their job is done. United find themselves with space to play in because the Spaniards hang back and give it to them.

The rest belongs to the Busby legend. How Nobby Stiles, provoked by Real's star Amancio, 'The Witch', lashes out and floors him; and how, incredibly, neither the referee nor his linesmen notice the punch. How David Sadler claims a far-post equaliser, unaware he's scored it. 'I didn't know where the ball had gone,' he said. 'There were a hundred and thirty thousand people in there and suddenly they were silent. I thought: Has something happened?' How, most implausibly of all, the goal that sends United to Wembley for the final – 4–3 on aggregate – is swept in by the outfield player least expected to score it. Foulkes, the veteran at 36 years old, is not a defender who ventures into the nose-bleed territory of the opposition box unless a set-piece demands it. What prompts him to say to Stiles after 75 minutes, 'Stay here, I'm going up' is something that he can't explain. Gut instinct, perhaps. Precognition, maybe. Urged on by some voice from the recent past, hopefully. Best goes on one of his trademark bursts in which he hugs the right touchline before nutmegging the left-back. And, when he looks up, the only colleague in support of him is Foulkes, who drops three paces back to receive the cross. Best, who thinks he is seeing a mirage in the Madrid heat, rolls the pass to him. Foulkes's finish is as clinical as Denis Law's would have been. 'It all seemed so unreal,' said Foulkes, 'like I was frozen in time.' Foulkes scored only seven goals during a United career spanning 566 matches and 19 years. What distinguishes the most important of them is the lack of celebration following it. Foulkes doesn't give an astronaut-on-the-moon-like leap of ecstasy. He doesn't attempt a cartwheel or beat his chest and snarl defiantly. He doesn't even bolt so his team-mates have to catch him before the congratulations can begin. He only turns towards his own half, slightly spreading his arms and softly clenching together the fingers of both hands. His face is almost stony. At first Best couldn't fathom this impassiveness, as if Foulkes was in a trance. Only later did he understand the thoughts – and images – that must have been whirling through his mind then.

Of men who would never age, would never go grey and would always wear United Red.

7

In My Beginning is My End

The night before every game George Best imagined himself playing in it. 'I would plot what I was going to do,' he said, 'and then I would go out and do it.'

He framed everything in his mind's eye: the architecture of the ground, the swaying crowd jammed inside it, the ball as it came to him. He heard the noise from the terraces and the shouted instructions from the bench, and even the swearing and vulgar curses of his intimidators. 'You try to destroy him mentally,' he said of opponents. For Best, that psychological process began during his private dress rehearsal. Relatively rare when he began practising it, this motivating mental drill – quiet meditation lasting up to an hour – is standard now among athletes taught to prepare brain as well as body for their sport. Modern-day coaches believe positive thought generates confidence and enhances performance. Best understood the benefits as far back as the early 1960s. A correlation between attitude and results was obvious to him. As if taking a grandstand seat, he saw himself as others would do from beyond the touchline and created a near flawless image of each step and every intricate movement he planned to make, such as the upper-body twists and the fast turn of his feet in possession. He visualised the wide spread of the field and the routes – some of them quixotic – he'd take to cut his way through it. There'd always be a dribble and a nutmeg, a shot crisply struck to bulge the net and a long-range chip spinning beyond the goalkeeper's reach. There'd be something more elaborate and irrepressively clever, too – an impudent back heel, a pass trapped with his backside, a high flick over his marker and a chase around him. Best would see himself galloping clear and then turning around to wave goodbye. He always saw himself doing all these things in isolation – the lone man against 11 others – because it made him feel invincible. In these testosterone-fuelled battles Best was never caught, shackled or outclassed. His mind wouldn't allow it. The defender was always outwitted, left on his backside or seen falling face-down like a red-nosed clown.

Best imagined the European Cup final in the same way

At Wembley, old foes awaited him – Benfica and Eusébio. Best saw the sweep of the stadium, the march out of the darkness of the tunnel into the mid-evening light of late May. He saw the pitch, bowling green-smooth. He saw a solo show eclipsing everyone else around him. Best always went at everything he did with everything he had, constantly asking more of himself. 'I always expected to be number one,' is a sentence he spoke a lot. It was never sufficient for him to reaccomplish something. There was an urgent need instead to be much better than before. He set himself tests for each match: to score from a certain distance; to push the ball through an opponent's legs a specific number of times; to hold it for two minutes and then three. 'I did it to put myself in a position where I had to do something special,' he said. If Best didn't achieve what he'd plotted to his absolute satisfaction, he'd consider himself to be a failure. 'I'd feel as though I'd let people down,' he explained.

By his gold standard, the 1967–68 season as a whole counted as a failure so far. Only winning the European Cup could atone for it.

He'd come close to giving Manchester United another Championship, scoring one barnstorming League goal after another – 28 in total – as the title race focused exclusively on Manchester, after first Leeds and then Liverpool were squeezed out of it. In the derby games United had won 2–1 at Maine Road in September and City had won 3–1 at Old Trafford in March. Before both of them Best and Mike Summerbee would seek out one another. 'I'd tell him not to make me look stupid,' said Summerbee. 'Otherwise, I wouldn't buy him a drink that night.' The turning point, shifting power from United to City, came with three games to go: United lost 6–3 at West Bromwich Albion; City won 2–0 at home to Everton and moved in front of them in the table. And then, on the season's final afternoon, with City ahead on goal average anyway, United lost again, beaten 2–1 by Sunderland at Old Trafford. City disposed of Newcastle 4–3 at St James' Park.

Best and Summerbee made a pact in advance of that final Saturday. Whoever lost the Championship would buy the bubbly for the other at Manchester's Cabaret Club. Summerbee was late and didn't expect to find Best there because his melancholia after a League defeat was severe enough. The meal Mary Fullaway cooked him would be only half eaten or not eaten at all and he'd spend at least 48 hours going over a game, trying to pick it apart. After losing a title, Summerbee supposed Best would be inconsolable, his mood beyond black. But, when he arrived at 1 a.m., Best was on his own at a table, the champagne sitting uncorked in a silver ice bucket and two clean glasses beside it. 'He said "well done" and we had a drink. That's the sort of bloke he was. Though he was feeling terrible, he didn't want to let me down or spoil my night.'

There was a consolation prize for Best. He'd taken the football writers' Footballer of the Year award – the youngest ever recipient – in a land-slide vote that exceeded 60 per cent. The silver statuette wasn't enough for him. He wanted what Stanley Matthews and Alfredo Di Stefano, and Denis Law and Bobby Charlton, had already won: the Ballon d'Or – Europe's Oscar, the premier prize for an individual player. If he won the European Cup he knew he'd win the Ballon d'Or too.

Benfica had clinched the Portuguese league for a fifth successive season. Six of the side – Coluna, Graça, Augusto, Torres and Simões as well as Eusébio – had been to Wembley before, losing the World Cup semi-final to England. The club was offering them £1,000 apiece to beat United. Their passage to Wembley had been twitchy on occasions, however. In the first round Best's boyhood heroes of Glentoran scared them at the Oval, where Eusébio scraped an equaliser with four minutes left. The goal, which seemed then to simply cover their embarrassment, giving them a 1–1 draw, became priceless after the Irish League part-timers held them 0–0 in the Estádio da Luz – a result that the rest of Europe took to be a misprint next morning. Benfica snuck through on the newfangled away-goals rule, the first occasion it had been implemented. There was a steady 2–1 aggregate win over St Etienne next and a more comfortable one – 3–0 – against the Hungarians Vasas. Juventus couldn't bar Benfica from the final, the Italians beaten 3–0. Best looked at those ties and was unimpressed. 'I thought we'd stroll it,' he said.

He saw his performance royally crowning the match. He'd get the ball and never give it back. He'd stretch the Benfica defence until it twanged. He'd outshine and outmaster Eusébio. In the closing quarter of an hour – the result a foregone conclusion – he'd perform his most beguiling tricks. It would be a cabaret performance, savoured and remembered. 'Nothing gives me more pleasure than making a fool of somebody,' he said. He was going to turn Benfica into fools. A world-wide audience of 200 million would watch live on television. In Manchester the roads would be almost empty of traffic, the streets devoid of people, the pubs and bars without TVs silent, pints unpulled. The soaring challenge Best set himself was this: 'To score a hat-trick and take Wembley by storm.'

No man is exempt from thinking silly things. The misfortune is to think about them seriously. Best demanded too much of himself, doing so because he thought absolute perfection was attainable and consistently repeatable. We have to take into account the fact he was only 22, almost entirely ignorant then of the discrepancies between practice and theory. The old adage claims nothing excellent is wrought suddenly. Best's four-and-a-half-year rise from obscurity to eminence had seemed to disprove it. He was accustomed to triumphs and used to getting whatever he willed. He assumed Wembley would be like a robed coronation for him.

Everyone knows what happens next. Knowing, however, diminishes neither the impact nor the meaning of the match for a city, a club, a manager. Never has a European Cup final contained within it a sub-plot so intensely emotional. There were two Manchester United teams at Wembley – the present one and another that had died on an airfield. In the build-up each was as conspicuous as the other. Because of it there was solidarity for one club from every other. Rivalries and grievances and the pettiness of historical disputes were put aside. Even those who weren't fond of football found themselves wrapped in the human strand of the drama and strenuously willed United on, as if a red and white scarf had always hung in the hallway. It wasn't necessary to understand or to like football – or even to have any allegiance to the game – to feel compassion towards the participants of this one. The heart led you on. In the fortnight between the semi-final and the final George Best found the comfort of strangers wherever he went. United were suddenly Britain's team. 'Everyone wished me luck,' said Best, aware also of the subliminal message in each salutation.

The living were made aware of their accountability and sense of duty to the dead. They couldn't fail those ghosts and dare not lose either for the sake of the survivors, who, as Best knew, would find defeat unbearable. It seemed to him that a grand alignment of events – the tenth anniversary of Munich, the form he was in and home advantage – was a portent. To him the result, however it was achieved and irrespective of the margin, looked predetermined, as if Fate was offering Matt Busby small consolation for the cruelty of its earlier act. To beat Benfica was never going to bring closure for those who had been on the aeroplane and came home again as far different men. But it would mean that their decision to carry on playing – when playing had seemed almost blasphemous – had fulfilled a purpose and was also a fitting service for all the dead and their loved ones.

Much of the game is dreary. The prospect of defeat inhibits and stifles. Much of the film of it is speckled and grainy. The BBC's copy is prefaced with an apology for minor glitches in the coverage, a few blank seconds unrecoverable because of cracking or splitting.

What you notice first is the brightness of the sinking sun, slanting over the tunnel end of the ground, and the hard, elongated shadows it casts, which are as thin as a church spire and splice the immaculate mown squares of the pitch. Manchester United's support is banked there, and everyone seems to be carrying a banner or waving a home-made flag, the red and white cotton rippling in the heavy air. Those without flags tautly hold a striped scarf between outstretched hands. Some have made cardboard replicas of the European Cup, as flat as stage scenery and covered in stuck-on baking foil, which catches the light. Others brandish a Union Jack bought from one of the street hawkers lining Wembley Way. This is Wembley as it used to be – the huge, semi-circular spaces behind each goal, the rows of photographers clustered tightly beside the posts, the low wire fence surrounding the pitch, free from the garish clutter of perimeter advertising. The squat twin towers rise from the rim of its curved roof, the flags atop of each barely fluttering on their poles. Nor is the occasion lace-trimmed or draped in grand ceremonial pomp. There are no national anthems, no red carpet, no dignitary to meet. The teams line up alongside one another near the centre of the pitch, waving half-heartedly at the crowd, who seem far away from them.

The same loop of images, as familiar as old friends, is seen whenever the action is shown.

There is Bobby Charlton running towards – and then rising to meet – David Sadler's cross in the 53rd minute. Benfica have seven players in the area. Not one of them is within five yards of Charlton. The ball flashes off his bald, glistening pate and drops inside the far post, the goalkeeper Henrique watching statuesquely from his line. A blur of pale leather flies across him.

United 1, Benfica 0

There is Graça's equaliser 11 minutes from the end, his shot razored past Alex Stepney on an angle. United's distraught, fatigued defenders glance away from the ball nestling in the net. It is left there for almost a minute because no one wants to retrieve it.

United 1, Benfica 1

There is Eusébio breaking away in the closing moments. He fastens on to a flighted pass, a muscular surge taking him between and beyond two defenders. Even watching Eusébio now is to believe he will score. You momentarily flinch in anticipation of the goal to come and the suffering to Busby as a consequence. You see the ball whipped past Stepney, and then resting in the same bottom corner as Graça's shot. With Eusébio on the stampede towards him, Stepney knows what he does in response will determine whether United survive or perish here. Three different thoughts spark across his mind in less than two seconds. First, he prepares to dive at Eusébio's feet to smother the chance. Second, after the ball sticks on the turf, he supposes Eusébio will chip him. This is what Jimmy Greaves would do in the same position, and so he readies himself for it. Third, he realises Eusébio has decided on an entirely different option. He's going to blast the ball. He'll try to score with sheer brute force. The expression on his face, the set of his body, make this certain. Stepney retreats, ever so slightly, in anticipation. On the bench Busby is groaning, 'Oh, no . . . not again,' so audibly that those close to him hear each word. Near the half-way line Best, a helpless observer, is conscious of time slowing down – it's as if Eusébio is moving imperceptibly, every stride consuming a full minute – and also of the silence around him, the crowd hushed and shaken by the awful thought that United and Busby are going to lose after all. Then, finally, Eusébio shoots – and Stepney, like the circus strongman catching a cannon-ball, stops and holds the effort cleanly against his chest. The thunderous impact of ball against breast bone jars him to his left. 'I thought we were done for,' said Best, who felt relief flood through him and overwhelm two other emotions, which were frustration and guilt. Best had been a lame disappointment so far. No hint of a hat-trick. No dominance. No sustained eye-catching skill. The Ballon d'Or would not be his like this.

On a scouting mission near the end of the season Benfica's coach, Fernando Cabrita, watched Best strip Newcastle bare, claiming a hat-trick – including two penalties – in a 6–0 rout at Old Trafford, which could have brought another half a dozen goals if United and Best had wanted them. Cabrita also sat through a recording of the 1966 tie in Lisbon, entranced by Best, and told his coaching staff afterwards that the teenager on the screen was much more potent now. In tactical discussions he was obsessed with Best. If he couldn't be blocked or blotted out, Cabrita knew there was no chance of beating United. If Best got loose, and began to roam unchecked, no system or formation Cabrita could devise was foolproof against him. He decided Benfica would be cagey, concerned with containment rather than creativity, and that the defence needed to get over-physical with Best. Intimidation was the strategy, the slender reed on which Cabrita's hopes hung.

The game was barely three minutes old when the white-shirted Jacinto callously tripped Best from behind. Best turned and marched towards his assailant, anger rising inside him. Jacinto pretended to be unconcerned, purposely leaning into Best as he ran past him, clipping his right shoulder with a thrust designed to threaten and unsettle. This is how it was for Best in the following hour and a half. He was hauled down and pushed over and all sorts of niggly antagonism, such as shirt tugging and ankle tapping and sly digs in the ribs, the chest and the back, were committed to subdue him. Cruz even stood on his face. One tackle sent him across the field in a half-cartwheel. A second – after a defender's boot was rammed against his left shin – left him spread-eagled, his Prussian blue shirt and shorts grass-stained in the fall. A third saw him slither on his belly again. Best climbed to his feet and gesticulated towards the referee, demanding protection and censure for the wicked challenge. The referee stared neutrally at him as if to say with a shrug: 'What else do you expect?' A disgusted Best shook his head, knowing a further appeal was futile. Benfica's fear of him was greater than their fear of a referee's reprimand. The tolerant official allowed him to be fouled repeatedly. Best was kicked out of his stride. 'I was given no chance at all,' he said.

Before the start, within the hospital-white walls of the dressing room, he hadn't been his usual nonchalant self either. He fiddled with his kit, fussed around his bag and paced the floor – things he'd never done before. Someone who maintained nerves never affected him was finally nervous. What became apparent after kick-off was Best's anxiety – transmitted by facial grimaces, the sight of his chin dropping on to his chest, the open palmed gestures of failure to team-mates, which were used as a means of apology, and hands-resting-on-hips exasperation with himself and almost everyone else. Nothing went right for him. The ball bobbled out of his reach. Or it was nicked away by a toe poke or a shoulder charge, a blatant obstruction or a shove. Or he found himself double-marked and had to rid himself of possession for the betterment of the team. Only twice in normal time did he sparkle. In the first instance he made a half-chance for himself, robbing the dilatory Cruz before Henrique slid out of the box and cleared the ball with his feet. In the second he tenaciously robbed Simões outside the area and then sprinted into it. The sort of opening he'd exploit in any other circumstance was finished feebly, his shot sliced into the side netting. Best was mortified. He tugged abstractedly at his right sock, jammed around his ankle, to avoid meeting the gaze of those who were waiting in the box for a cross – or a goal – and then jogged sluggishly up-field again.

He was grateful for extra-time. 'The chance to start again,' he said.

The day before the final Matt Busby kicked a ball around on the Wembley pitch. He wore a smart grey jacket, fastening the centre button, a white shirt and narrow tie. A pair of Ray-Bans shielded his eyes. The sunglasses made him look like an elderly member of the Rat Pack or a Mafia godfather. Those who saw Busby appreciated the type of player he had been before the war. With a pale brown ball under his control, there was a military uprightness about him. His bearing was regal. In this pose it was possible to glimpse a 24-year-old Busby, who had originally come to Wembley for the FA Cup final of 1933 and who then returned to play in it again in 1934. In the crucible of those two finals – the first lost, the second won – Busby forged some of his managerial philosophy. In '33 Manchester City committed what Busby always regarded as a tactical blunder of the first magnitude. The players arrived one hour and 45 minutes before kick-off and didn't know what to do with themselves after inspecting the stadium. In the dimly lit dressing rooms, some smoked and others wandered like lost souls, hearing the terraces gradually fill above and around them. 'The entire team was ready to start the match at two fifteen p.m.,' he said 'With each moment of passing time, the nervous tension increased. We were as unprepared for a game of football as any team could be.' Everton beat them 3–0. In '34 City fell behind. 'Not until about twenty minutes from full-time did things turn in our favour,' remembered Busby; Portsmouth were beaten 2–1.

From those experiences Busby learned lessons. Relax your players. Choose your sentences carefully so as not to subdue or overawe them; for the balance between the two is gossamer-thin. Make sure your emphasis is on what's to come – not what has just happened. Busby had done this in the semi-final against Real Madrid and invigorated United. He did so again.

During the game he had smoked busily away, a few discarded butts at his feet, and the forward crouch of his upper body and the frown on his face betrayed his apprehension. 'I could see the tension take us over as we got closer to the prize,' he said. 'After Benfica scored I wanted full-time to come.'

Aside from the goals, plus Alex Stepney's save from Eusébio, there had been few chances. David Sadler fluffed one of them appallingly – shooting in haste and repenting immediately, slapping his hands against the spot on the ground where he'd slid his effort wide, as if a divot in the turf was to blame. Eusébio had bent a shot from almost 20 yards on to the bar. Stepney could not reach it because he did not see it leave the boot or burn through the air until the ball was already past him. He only heard the solid crack it made against the woodwork.

It was immaterial to Busby now. He knew what he said – and how he appeared to his players – would decide where the Cup went. He needed to convince them that another half-hour in humid conditions was an endurance test, easily passed, rather than a calamity, impossible to overcome. He stubbed out his cigarette. He thrust back his shoulders and strode on to the field. He told his team to stand up in case their leg muscles stiffened. Since Busby was used to crisis management no one looked calmer, less perturbed about the gruelling slog ahead than he did. He relied on oratory that was simple and sharp. He delivered it without edgy hesitations.

'Just don't give the ball away.

When you make a pass be certain it reaches your man.

Play your football.

Keep attacking them.

They're more tired than you are.'

George Best had set his heart on giving Busby what he wanted. 'I didn't want to think about what I could say to him if we lost,' he said. 'I wasn't sure I'd be able to look him in the eye and say sorry.'

Best, thinking about how ineffective he'd been and beating himself up about it, heard what Busby said and knew he was right. Benfica were tired; whereas Best had energy to spare. He'd been allowed to go on no long run. His calves were sore only because of the stud marks on his skin, which made it tender. Best reached a decision. He was going directly for goal as soon as *any* opening presented itself. If a pair of Benfica boots trampled all over him again, he'd get up without protest and recover possession. Whatever the physical cost, he was going to win the Cup for Busby.

He did it only two minutes later.

To think about the final is to see Best during and after the fabulous goal he scored. Watching and rewatching this goal, the impudence, as well as the effortless craft and cold courage, continues to amaze. The essence of successful magic is always misdirection. When coins or playing cards are materialised out of thin air and other things appear and disappear, what fools us is a visual illusion – the magician's ability to divert attention and bamboozle. Best deceived in this way, too.

The move began prosaically – a short back pass from Shay Brennan to Stepney and then his heaved, hopeful kick down the middle, falling midway into the Benfica half. Brian Kidd – on his 19th birthday – out-jumps his marker and nudges the ball on. It's as if Benfica, sapped of strength, have dozed off and awake to the threat Best poses only when preventing it is already beyond them. Best is left with only one defender and the goalkeeper to beat. He's almost 30 yards out and three other defenders are charging back, panic in every stride. Best gets to the ball fractionally before Cruz, who is directly facing him, and smartly sends it between his legs. Cruz is sent spinning, unaware of where to turn next. There is no possibility of catching Best now. Through necessity rather than choice Henrique is dragged off his line in an attempt to narrow Best's options and his angle. The goalkeeper advances past the penalty spot as Best – unrushed and steady-eyed – transfers the ball from his right to left boot. There's a fractional repositioning of foot and his body to send a fake signal about where he intends to go. Henrique misreads each of them. He ends up hedging his bets, wobbling from one side to the other in his reluctance to commit himself. It seems as if Best has him on a lead and is able to pull him in whichever direction he chooses. Henrique drops to his left at precisely the same time that Best goes to his right with a stride as niftily elegant as a dance step. The keeper is still rising off the floor as Best takes the ball clear of him. The net is at his mercy. He thinks about milking his moment – *the* moment, which he knows, as it is actually happening, will be replayed for ever. Busby is always telling Best not to take on too many defenders. He wants his moves to be reducible to a few bold lines. But Best can hardly ever resist the temptation to do more than is necessary; and he always sees himself – another of those images he visualises the night before every game – taking the ball around a keeper, stopping it on the line and then getting down on his stomach to head it in. He thinks about doing so now. 'I only chickened out,' he said 'because the bugger got up too quickly. Mind you, if I'd tried to do it I might have given the boss a cardiac arrest.'

Best simply rolls the ball into the net with his left foot. Henrique makes a final attempt to stop it, throwing himself forward as the pushed shot crosses the line. He slides along on his chest as he does so and becomes entangled in the net. Best doesn't see this. He has already turned away, right hand raised during a joyous dash.

United 2, Benfica 1

The goal tears the heart out of Benfica. Kidd almost immediately poaches another with his head.

United 3, Benfica 1

What Busby has spent more than a decade longing to win is sealed for him at last in eight devastating minutes during the first half of extra-time. Charlton, finishing off the Portuguese, sweeps in his second.

United 4, Benfica 1

'For an infinitesimal blank in time I didn't know what had happened,' said Busby, trying to comprehend the enormity of what United had achieved. 'Then the blast of what seemed millions of decibels hit me. We had won. But it seemed to have come so suddenly after the years of waiting.'

Best is the last United player to touch the ball before the whistle goes. When it does he is too tired to do anything at first except lift both arms in weak triumph. There is a crush of people near the touchline and Busby emerges from the bench, smoothing his tie. What Best always remembered was his expression. 'He looked as if he should have had a halo over him. He had one of those faces that lights up, like the pictures you see of saints,' he said. The bags beneath Busby's eyes were moist and glistening.

In the dressing room Charlton, dehydrated and emotionally spent, tried rubbing his own sobs away and sat down because he could barely stand. Crerand was on the verge of collapse, too, and began to vomit through exhaustion. Kidd tried to mask his tears behind his hands. Stepney, fumbling for a cigarette as he sat beneath his peg, began to cry, too, without knowing why – 'huge, baby tears that rushed down my face', he said. The spray from uncorked champagne streaked the bulbous trophy, and what remained was swigged directly from the bottle.

But Best – though he disguised it – didn't feel as the others felt.

He always experienced the sense of anti-climax once any game was over. He never really wanted a match to end. As a boy, he had to be dragged off the park or the street during kickabouts. If Best was playing well, he was determined to go on playing. If he wasn't, he felt the compulsion to run and pass and shoot until his form clicked. 'I'd have carried on playing until I dropped,' he said. 'And I had the same feeling wherever I went.' Wembley was like this for him. Even as United began to coast, knowing Benfica could summon nothing potent to stop them, Best wanted the final to go on until he'd accomplished something else that bore his exclusive stamp. He hadn't taken Benfica's rigorous clamp-down on him as a compliment. He saw instead his failure to break it as a mark in his debit column. It meant, he said, there was no 'high' for him after the Cup was won – only the nagging thought that he ought to have done a lot more. He experienced what he described as a 'few pangs of remorse'. Best said it was both 'the greatest night of my footballing life' and 'one of the most unsatisfying'.

What Best did against Benfica would have brought a lifetime's satis-faction to anyone except him. What satisfied others, however, didn't satisfy Best. At the year's end he won the Ballon d'Or – his 61 votes beat Charlton's 53 – and the memory of that goal in the final swayed the electorate. But the pinnacle of club achievement was diluted for him because he felt personally unfulfilled. There was no reason for Best to feel so negatively. But the fantasy he'd played out in his mind about his part in the final was absurdly grandiose. It meant the reality of the match was almost always sure to deflate him. He declared his perfor-mance to be deficient. Nothing anyone could say could fully convince him otherwise. Best thought he'd let himself down and was over-apologetic about it. Whenever he spoke about it, he tended to add a prefix or a suffix to his reminiscences that downgraded his own contribution. The phrases he used varied in structure and tone – ranging from sorrow and regret to obvious irritation – but never in content. 'I didn't play as well as I should have done . . . I wasn't as good as I'd been throughout the whole of that season . . . That night I never really got going or did myself justice.'

John Aston had the rip-roaring game Best envisaged for himself. He was quick and assertive and confidently outstripped – and then outstripped again – his full-back Adolfo, who suffered public torture. Aston beat him at will. At one point he gave a perfect demonstration of push and run in which he chased his own pass and outpaced Adolfo at leopard-like speed. Benfica were so obsessively preoccupied about Best that Aston – an afterthought to them – was given more space and latitude. He played the game of his life. Aston had been so nervy beforehand that he'd suffered stomach cramps on the coach and had wandered around the dressing rooms, where he found a toilet. 'I stared at it, and suddenly thought there must have been some famous backsides sitting on that with diarrhoea in the past thirty years.' That thought made him laugh his anxieties away. Rated alongside Aston's performance, Best reproached himself for being only a minor collaborator rather than a virtuoso force. He felt a sense of dislocation, and claimed not to regard himself as 'part of the laughter and the tears' afterwards. 'I was there but I didn't belong,' he said.

After the adrenalin of the final had drained away, only emptiness remained – an awful hollowness he thought no one else properly understood.

Seen in the context of what came later, George Best's response to these mixed emotions carry a dark foreboding. 'I went out and got drunk,' he said.

In the early hours of the following morning no excuse was needed to open another bottle of champagne. No one noticed – or cared – how much was consumed. A hangover was the consequence of success. His boozy overindulgence was just one of many, and perfectly legitimate in the circumstances. But Best said he drank so much that he could only ever recover fragments of the final from his memory. Eusébio's shot, and Stepney clutching it to his chest. His goal, the ball travelling so slowly into the net that sometimes in his dreams he saw Henrique catch it. Swapping shirts with Benfica's Simões, his own dripping in sweat. Hugging Matt Busby on the pitch, the way a son would hug his father after a long absence. The upward climb of 39 steps – sandwiched between Bill Foulkes and Paddy Crerand – to the velvet-covered royal box. Bobby Charlton receiving and then lifting a trophy, which looked too big to carry unless he clutched it close to his weary body. The glary arc light that followed the team on a lap of honour, the soundtrack of Cliff Richard's 'Congratulations' – a cheesy tune that grated on Best – blaring from the public address system. He recalled nothing of leaving Wembley or the banquet that followed at London's Russell Hotel. No matter how hard he thought about them – what he'd done, where he'd gone, who he'd met – Best couldn't shake any subsequent events loose from his mind. Not Busby crooning along when the Joe Loss Orchestra played Louis Armstrong's 'What a Wonderful World' and singing it to himself repeatedly. Not Duncan Edwards' parents picking a way to Jimmy Murphy's table and telling him: 'Duncan always said that United would win the European Cup and we are so proud he was proved right.' Not the handshakes and the back slaps and the sight of Busby again, his reflection in the polished curves of that Cup. Amnesia struck Best. 'Almost everything was a blank. I don't know what I did,' he confessed, ashamed that the postscript was erased because of drink.

What he did, however, was this. He put his medal and the souvenir shirt into his bag, changed his clothes and stole away from the reception once the preliminaries were over. A night porter found Best a taxi, which took him to Jackie Glass's flat in Chelsea. She had watched the game on her small black and white TV, dancing around the living room after her boyfriend's goal. He had promised to spend the night with her – irrespective of the result. He arrived after midnight and brought a present, a silver chainmail purse bearing a Benfica crest, which Eusébio had given him as a gift. 'He seemed drained of emotion,' she remembers. United's prayers had been answered. But, as St Teresa once wrote, 'more tears are shed over answered prayers than unanswered ones'. In its way that epigram became the epitaph for United and the '68 European Cup winners. Like everyone else, Best thought then that history would record the win as the first of many in the European Cup. The possibilities seemed endless for Manchester United and for him. 'It *should* have been the start of something wonderful and beautiful,' said Best, seeing Wembley in retrospect instead as 'the beginning of the end'.

His features, as much as his feet, were his fortune. The camera loved his face. But, with a twist of irony, one of the most poignant photographs ever taken of him doesn't show it. He's on the half-turn, the white number 7 visible on his back. His shirt hangs loosely over his shorts. His socks are crumpled. His right arm is raised in acclaim and also to acknowledge his accomplishment. To look at it enables you to see what Best saw in front of him a half-second after his Wembley goal that night. There's the curvature of the tunnel end, the crowd amorphously massed there, the faint white blocks of the scoreboard, which is about to change, the stubby shadows which the floodlights cast, the cut strips of pitch, each narrowing to its vanishing point. What this picture freezes is the summit of Best's career – though no one could have anticipated it then. Now, because we know what happens to him, it carries the underlying sadness of something lost and long over. He will never again experience ecstasy like it. There will be no second and third acts for him. Nothing he does will rank beside this. Busby will never win another trophy. Best will never win another medal.

8

Golden Boots and Diamond Studs

George Best would still go into the fish and chip shop closest to Aycliffe Avenue and take back cod or haddock wrapped in a newspaper for a late-night supper with Mary Fullaway and his friends. But that newspaper almost always included a story about him. He was more famous than ever after Wembley, a personality as much as a footballer. Whatever he did brought him a headline. Whatever he said was reported. Wherever he went fresh demands were made on him. 'I'd be a liar if I didn't say I enjoyed it,' he said. 'I was caught up in the whole thing.'

Best had signed so many autographs he supposed everyone who wanted his signature had already got it. Now he signed twice as many again. He stood for 'hours and hours', he said, after personal appearances. 'The people who've organised them have said I'm not going to sign any more – then I insist I will.' He hated being stopped in the street, tolerating it only because 'I don't like to upset anyone if I can help it. I've never refused – unless someone's been rude to me.'

Mrs Fullaway continued to serve as an unofficial secretary. If she wasn't answering the phone, she was at the door accepting books and pictures to be signed or taking in post or dealing with cold callers on the step or hangers-on who loitered at her blue-painted gate. Contemplating the inconveniences she underwent on his behalf, Best pondered: 'I don't know how she coped. People banging on the doors at all hours. The phone going non-stop. The amount of mail that piled up. Journalists on the street outside and sometimes trampling across the garden. The stories about me and the way I came and went.'

Bill Shankly said that fame was 'the price you pay for doing your job well'. Fame for Best eventually became a punishment, which increased by degrees.

Best had to travel almost everywhere by car. To go on foot meant being bothered or needled. Car horns would be honked. He said he saw vehicles 'run up each other's backside' because drivers stared at him and forgot to look at the road in front of them. 'Walking past a bus stop – to me that became a big event,' he said. 'I'd see a bus stop, say twenty to thirty people waiting, and you'd guarantee half of them hate you and the other half love you. There'll be two or three who want to smack you in the mouth and half a dozen want an autograph. Another two will have read something about you and want to question you about it. Rather than run that gauntlet, you cross over and take the long way round. Your whole way of life becomes like that . . . You can't imagine what it was like at the real height . . . If it wasn't serious, it would be funny.'

It was impossible to count the number of letters he now received or the number of promotional offers made to him. Like a vampire, he found darkness preferable to daylight because it partly concealed him. 'I could hide a little bit at night,' he said. Best was in perpetual demand and he could name his price for his presence. A boot deal with Stylo brought him £20,000 outright, plus 5 per cent of the purchase price for every pair sold. The company's advertising guaranteed 'Best fitting. Best comfort. Best Ball Control', as if Best's gift was soaked into the leather. Stylo budgeted on sales of 2,000 to 3,000 in the first 12 months after launch. Best sold them 28,000 pairs. The range quickly passed the

£250,000 sales mark, which prompted the gleeful manufacturers to present him with what it called 'Golden Boots for a Golden Boy'. However corny, Best *was* golden to them – they ought to have made his studs out of diamonds to reflect his worth – and also to the others who approached his agent Ken Stanley. Among them were Great Universal Stores, which paid Best £15,000 in return for two afternoons of modelling catalogue clothing in a cluttered, sweaty studio every six months. GUS was the equivalent of a superstore that came directly into the home. The catalogue contained nearly 500 pages, weighed over 4lb and sold goods on hire purchase – everything from kettles to fondue sets, portable typewriters to chunky ashtrays, teak nests of tables to gold-plated carriage clocks. In today's expensively cut, designer Premiership, where players are seen out-of-kit in Armani, Dolce & Gabbana and Gucci or Paul Smith, Best's collaboration with a catalogue store seems a low-key and almost menially ignominious role for someone of his stature. Stanley saw the wider benefits and his far-sightedness reaped them for Best. Since the early 1960s Britain had been developing a credit-driven mentality, which GUS catered for. Though Manchester based – occupying an enormous Victorian warehouse less than four miles from Old Trafford – the operation had more than 2,500 mail order and retail outlets nationwide, distributed in excess of 3 million catalogues and its boardroom was described by *The Times* as one of the country's ten most powerful. GUS catalogues were passed between friends and neighbours, which pushed Best into more living rooms than ever before. He dominated its section on men's fashion, dressed in high collars, various plain and striped double-breasted jackets and an assortment of fine knitwear. The catalogue presented Best to a markedly different audience. He maintained he didn't 'love or like very much' the role of the model, which was thrust upon him. Once the photographer clicked away, what came out of the dark of the developing room glowed nevertheless and suggested he had been born to do it.

Tesco, expanding its chain, offered to pay him £500 every time he snipped the ribbon on one of their new supermarkets. The company had 100 openings planned country-wide, and the only possible inconveniences were motorway travel and the fact some flagship stores needed him on Saturday mornings. He turned the company down.

He didn't earn 50 per cent of what he might have done because he was so blasé about supplementing his footballing income. Best lived for the moment, the here and now, and didn't care much about the weeks ahead, let alone the years. 'I thought this was what I was going to do for the rest of my life,' he said, which made him reluctant and stubborn about doing what his contract stipulated. Best was paid £35,000 to promote the hair and cosmetic brand Fore, a pun deliberately, if unsubtly, chosen to suggest his sex appeal (presumably because the slang from which it originated – *phwor* – was considered too blatant or common) and to appeal to golfers. Best didn't understand the golf connection. He didn't play golf. He didn't like the sweaters middle-aged golfers wore.

The company hired a helicopter to take him and Malcolm Wagner to London and installed them in hotel suites. Filming a television advertisement in London's Hyde Park – Best, surrounded by a posse of models and, incongruously, Afghan hounds – was scheduled for 8.30 the next morning. 'Bit early,' said Best, the real meaning of which was: 'Too early for me.' Not unexpectedly he met a woman that evening and slept at her flat rather than in his hotel bed. When Fore's top brass arrived to accompany him to filming, Wagner gallantly tried to cover for his friend, an attempt which fell at the first fence.

'Where is he?' asked Fore's agitated managing director, already aware Best was AWOL.

'In his room,' replied Wagner, trying to think how he could be tracked down.

'Find him or I'll sue him,' he was told.

Wagner got a number for the place where Best was staying. The phone rang for a long time before he answered. Wagner got the response he'd been dreading. He listened as Best insisted. 'I can't be bothered. Get my stuff out of my room. I'm off back to Manchester.' Fore's representatives were close enough to hear whatever Wagner said. To placate both them and Best he was sensibly noncommittal. 'I'll be round in a bit,' is the only comment he made. Wagner had to explain to Fore that Best needed to be coaxed rather than bullied; and that only he could do the coaxing. Wagner set off for Chelsea in a taxi, the head of a convoy, moving at Keystone Kops-like speed, which comprised the Rolls-Royces, the Bentleys and the Jaguars of Fore's boardroom. He found Best, feet up, watching TV, like someone who'd got lucky on a lads' weekend in London. 'Are we getting off home then?' Best casually asked. Wagner convinced him to stay. Why abandon the models? Why not 'give it a go', he said. Best thought Fore would resent his original non-appearance and he didn't want to be grumpily harangued by men in suits he didn't know. 'Once we show it'll be as right as rain,' Wagner assured him. Best got to Hyde Park five hours late. The light was fading, and the original script needed to be tweaked to accommodate the constraints of the clock. Fore's executives were twitchy, fearing the worst. An entire day's shooting – not to mention the cost of hiring models, publicity photographers, cameramen and lighting and sound engineers – seemed certain to be wasted. In these situations, however, Best was a natural performer. He possessed what the critic Kenneth Tynan once identified as the 'ease' of the actorly stars. Everything was nailed immaculately in one take that lasted 90 seconds – the walk, the glance, the smile. The director yelled 'cut' and Best sauntered off to Manchester again. The chaps from Fore slapped themselves on the back.

It showed nonetheless that sometimes Best was awkward simply because he could be. He also got bored easily, a trait which became apparent early on. 'He was always restless and training took up only a few hours a day,' says Steve Fullaway, remembering Best in his teens. 'He would find out where I was working and I'd suddenly see his shadow over my shoulder. He'd watch what I was doing because he didn't have anything to do himself.' When Manchester United were in the ascendancy, and the football was good, it assuaged that boredom and stimulated him. When, post-Benfica, it began to sour and go bad, Best began to exhibit the self-destructive symptoms which, much later, blighted him.

For what Best envisaged as the beginning of a golden age for United – he saw them matching Real Madrid's haul of European Cups – became instead one tortured, bare season after another.

Within a fortnight of Wembley, Matt Busby was knighted in the Queen's Birthday Honours alongside 29 others who rarely appeared in the public's thoughts. The list comprised industrialists and entrepreneurs, a professor of history, QCs and the alderman of a provincial council. Despite a penchant for playing the populist card, the prime minister, the dumpy Harold Wilson, rarely sprinkled handfuls of glitter on these gongs; though MBEs to the Beatles in 1965 was a stand-out exception. Only the crustiest of the upper classes begrudged Busby his recognition. Alf Ramsey had been knighted for winning a World Cup. Busby, it was widely acknowledged, deserved nothing less than to match him. Wilson reflected the country's mood.

Busby was to United what Lord Reith had once been to the BBC. He seemed irreplaceable. Not wanting him to go anyway, the board simply willed him to continue and fancifully hoped the status quo would remain into infinity. What hindsight infallibly tells us is that a combination of his knighthood and the trophy ought to have persuaded him into retirement.

As soon as the Cup had been won Bobby Charlton noticed the weariness in Busby as he came on to the pitch, the ravages in his face and

The school prefect reports to the offices of the *Belfast Telegraph*, where he and Eric McMordie are the centre of attention before their trial at Old Trafford.

Early days. He emerges from the tunnel, in front of Tony Dunne and Dave Gaskell, and then signs autographs for already adoring fans.

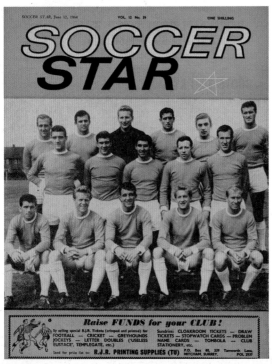

The editors of *Soccer Star* superimpose his head on to another's body to add to the magazine's sales appeal.

Even in a dingy dressing room he still looks like a model-in-waiting.

Bob Bishop: the man who had a talent for finding talent. Next to him is Sammy McIlroy - another of his star finds.

Mary Fullaway became Britain's most pestered landlady to Britain's most pestered lodger. The lodger relaxes inside with his daily newspaper.

…ooking particularly natty – handkerchief in top pocket – outside his Aycliffe Avenue digs in 1965.

'Looking after George Best is a full time job,' said his agent Ken Stanley, who made sure his client got more endorsements than any other sportsman in Britain in the 1960s. One of them – an obvious publicity stunt – promoted cycling. Beside him is David Stanley, Ken's son.

The bamboo frame of George Best in the mid-1960s and his pursuit of a ball against Chelsea at Stamford Bridge in early 1966.

A self-advertisement. George Best knows exactly what he's doing – generating publicity for his new boutique – by arriving back in Britain wearing this dustbin lid of a hat. He's now El Beatle – and the scorer of two goals against Benfica in the 1966 European Cup quarter final in Lisbon.

Seldom a hair out of place. Malcolm Wagner makes sure his friend is perfectly groomed for his close-up in a TV commercial.

The mod shop entrepreneur was the perfect billboard for his own clothes. But, as Mike Summerbee (right) once said: 'Do we look like businessmen?'

body that Munich had caused in someone only 59 years old. 'He really was, I felt, an old man,' said Charlton. David Sadler had the same opinion. He used almost the same words, too. 'The boss looked very old, which he had never seemed.' Sadler went further, looking at Busby at the Russell Hotel banquet and then ruminating to himself: 'I wondered if there was anywhere to go from here, even in defending the Cup.' Charlton and Sadler recognised then what few others did. Busby was worn out – mentally, emotionally, physically. But Busby didn't feel as if he could quit even when the urge to do so overwhelmed him. He was aware that others – fans, directors, players – wanted him to press on and try to retain the Cup, completing the equivalent of a politician's last hurrah, before resigning. As the representative of the soul and the spirit of the club, he saw it as his solemn obligation to continue – even while sensing he no longer possessed the constitution or the rigour for a job that had ripped so much out of him.

The team had aged alongside Busby. Charlton and Shay Brennan were 31; Paddy Crerand was 29; Bill Foulkes was five months away from his 37th birthday. As Crerand confessed: 'A few of us were past our sell-by dates. Changes were needed.' Still preferring to groom talent rather than buy it, Busby couldn't lean on his scouting network. Finding and signing the next George Best was more strenuously competitive now. Busby accepted a 'different United' would have to be built. He also knew someone else would have to do it; and that he had no ready-made successor in mind to recommend categorically to his directors. The prime candidate, Jock Stein, was embedded at Celtic. Another, Ron Greenwood, was devoted to West Ham. Don Revie then had only one trophy to his name – the League Cup – and his approach, as well as his tactics, were incompatible with Busby's. The up-and-coming managers, Brian Clough at Derby and Dave Sexton at Chelsea, had still to prove themselves. Also, just 73 days separated the end of the old season and the beginning of the new. Even if Busby had stepped aside then, United would have found it impossible to complete an orderly handover of power. The unanimous choice, negotiation and appointment of a replacement wouldn't fit into such a tight time-scale. So Busby pressed on.

In doing so he couldn't be disloyal to those who, by winning the Cup, had been loyal to him. 'Loyalty is responding to loyalty in kind,' he said. His dictionary definition of the word was the noble 'being human'. Best arched his eyebrows quizzically and said: 'He was sentimental in hanging on to players when he shouldn't have done.' Busby made minimal changes, convincing himself – but no one else – that the squad he possessed had another profitable nine months' running in its legs. With a hefty slice of the money the Cup brought him, he signed the winger Willie Morgan from Burnley for £117,000. The fee amounted to £4,000 more than the entire European Cup side had cost him. With a lot of stylistic aping and posturing, rivals tried to copy Best – though all of them ended up resembling one another rather than him because no one could duplicate exactly what he was capable of producing at will. Morgan resembled Best in physical appearance only; he wore his black hair long. 'He wasn't in the same class as what we [already] had,' said Best.

Returning for pre-season training, Best immediately sensed that United had become cloy. The pinnacle had been reached. Busby's aspirations had been sated. 'I felt what was going to happen,' remembered Best. 'It seemed to me that afterwards everyone just breathed a sigh of relief, and said: "The European Cup, that's been our dream, that's what we've fought for all these years, especially after Munich."' He heard players talk about Wembley as representing 'the end' whereas he was still covetous, greedy for prizes. 'For me it wasn't even the start of it,' he added. 'I was only warming up . . . I was hungry . . . I was someone who wasn't going to reach my peak for another seven years.' He added bleakly: 'You could almost hear the energy and ambition sighing out of the club. Everybody was talking as if the good days were over.'

The good days *were* over.

The 1968–69 season distressed Best throughout. 'Something was missing,' he said. 'There just didn't seem to be that sparkle. I struggled on.' For weeks at a stretch United looked as though impostors were wearing their shirts. Between the beginning of October and mid-January, Busby won only three First Division games out of 16. 'Whereas previously I never believed anybody could beat us, it quickly got to the stage where I was worrying about going on to the park because I knew sooner or later some good team like Leeds was going to give us a thrashing,' said Best. Somewhat harshly he considered United to be 'one of the worst teams' to have won the European Cup so far. His optimism about the coming seasons was based purely on the assumption that Busby would spend – and then spend again – to guarantee United became more successful than Real Madrid had been. 'We're going downhill unless we buy some new players,' said Best. He was proved right in less than 12 months.

Emblematic of his miserable state and the stresses Best faced were the two legs of the World Club Championship against the Argentinians of Estudiantes. The games were warfare with a ball. Busby ought to have known better than to agree to the challenge in the first place. Celtic, champions of Europe before them in 1967, had gone to South America to face Racing Club, another Argentinian team. A play-off, staged in neutral Montevideo, was mayhem. Six players were sent off – four of them Celtic's. This was a grubby competition. Brian Glanville, writing in the *Sunday Times*, called it that 'dreadful abomination'. What appealed to Busby was being labelled, indisputably, as the world's greatest.

The brief highlights contain more than grisly X-certificate tackling and dirty tricks. What's obvious is the sight of Best, his strength being sapped, under pressure in an already declining United. All Best's troubles appear in microcosm here. The sense of futility he feels. The storm flashes of temper because of it. The need to exact retribution and the disciplinary punishments meted out to him as a consequence. Estudiantes were deliberately savage. As Best said: 'You'd go into a tackle and your opponent would apparently ruffle your hair in what seemed, from the terraces, a friendly little gesture. Then he'd yank at your hair and you'd feel your scalp was coming up. Or there'd be an arm thrown around the body, in another apparently matey gesture, except that the fingers gripped into the flesh and you felt you were being attacked by killer crabs.' Kidney punches, spitting, elbows or head butts in the face, eye-gouging and a knee in the back of the leg were common skulduggery. 'If you held the ball you were in danger of your life,' said Best. The Estudiantes players responded to the merest brush of a tackle by rolling on to their backs and writhing, as if acting in a hysterically bad, over-theatrical death scene. The hosts won 1–0 in Buenos Aires in a stadium innocuously called La Bombonera – the Chocolate Box. Glanville more accurately said it was 'a bear-pit' and the *Daily Mirror* described it as 'The Furnace of Football'. The locals, remembering the infamous 1966 World Cup quarter-final after which Alf Ramsey condemned the Argentinians as 'animals', took out their ire on Nobby Stiles, christened '*El Bandido*' – the Bandit. The match programme called Stiles 'an assassin' and said he was 'brutal, badly intentioned and (a) bad sportsman'. 'Fucking charming,' said Stiles, who was sent off, an outcome as prede-termined as the culmination of a Greek tragedy. Stiles protested after being incorrectly waved offside – a decision peculiarly reached by the referee rather than his linesman, who didn't flag. 'The referee's blind,' Stiles told Charlton, who had played him clear. The referee, overhearing the remark, asked him to repeat it. Stiles, again turning to Charlton, said: 'He's fucking deaf as well.' Best put his safety first and foremost. 'Fifty-fifty balls I just didn't bother with. I just stood out of the way,' he said before criticising the club and Busby. 'We should never have come here. It was ridiculous.'

On a rainy, mid-October night at Old Trafford – for part two of this horror flick – Best was pulled down inside the opening minute when the ball was ten yards away from him. Shortly afterwards he was sent spinning sideways into the air after a vicious boot in the shins. In another incident he side-stepped a horrendous, swinging kick that could have split open his stomach and chest. The beatings continued, the officials abysmally ineffectual. Best was barged into the advertising hoardings, cropped at the ankle, studded in the thigh and calf. With United drawing 1–1, he could tolerate no more of it. The chief culprit, Hugo Medina, elbowed Best full in the face to add to the other wounds he'd inflicted on him at five-minute intervals before yammering threats in his ear. Violent aggression meant violent defence. Best snapped, lashing out and toppling Medina with a swift right hook, delivered without even looking at him. The two of them were sent off. Best didn't bother to wait for the referee to point him towards the dressing room. He went there of his own accord. He was a walking portrait of desolation, a consuming sadness and anger in his expression, which betrayed how bewildered the abrupt change both in United's fortunes and his own had made him.

Only the defence of the European Cup offered the chance of redemption. United reached the semi-finals mainly because a benign draw paired them against Waterford in the first round, Anderlecht in the second and Rapid Vienna in the last eight. None of them possessed a sling-shot and a stone capable of killing a giant. AC Milan, much more formidable, were United's semi-finalists. Outcomes in sport can hinge on micro-measurement. Less than an inch – a debate about whether a goal had or hadn't been legitimately scored – brought defeat. United chased a 2–0 deficit from the opening leg in Italy. In the return Best – who else? – made a goal for Charlton after 70 minutes, venomously struck. With renewed vigour United went at Milan again, convinced an equaliser had come after Denis Law poked at a shot. Best was sure the defender responsible for clearing it had done so with his hand. He was equally sure that the ball had crossed the line. The referee didn't see the hand and didn't believe the whole of the ball had gone over the line. He waved aside the appeal. The momentum and the tie were lost.

Best was used to collecting trophies. These had come so easily he had taken them for granted. Only one previous season – 1965–66 – had failed to bring him a winners' medal before this one. Now he recognised the variance between United's aspirations and his own expectations. With prescience, he said: 'The way things were going I was not likely to achieve anything more.'

United were lame in the League, finishing a pitiful 11th – the chasm of 25 points split them from the new champions, Leeds. Best brooded over a succession of defeats against rank inferiors, such as Burnley, Southampton and Ipswich. Attendances declined because of it. On the season's opening day more than 61,000 had gone to Old Trafford. By early March fewer than 37,000 watched them crush Queens Park Rangers 8–1, a rare demonstration of United's old selves. The evidence of Busby's error in staying on was contained in the admission he made to his players before the announcement of his retirement, which came four months before his official departure in May 1969. 'I'm getting too old for this. It's time for someone else to have a go.'

Danny Blanchflower, the most erudite and shrewd footballer-turned-writer of his generation, believed he had seen almost everything in the game until George Best illuminated it as a teenager. Witnessing the effect Best had on a crowd, he asked two pertinent questions. Could he consistently satisfy what was expected of him from the terraces? Did he have the armour to withstand the accumulated pressures? Blanchflower then added a portentous observation. 'It is hard to believe that one boy can be blessed with so much talent, and that Fate will not take some sort of quick revenge on him.' Blanchflower meant a career-threatening injury. Given Best's will-o'-the-wisp approach, and the way he infuriated defenders, he practically asked to be kicked. And if, as the title of that famous German novel claims, the goalkeeper does have a fear of the penalty, then a player like Best had a secret fear of a tackle that could, on purpose or accidentally, break his leg or split his ligaments. In a signed column, ghosted for him, it is noticeable how frequently Best mentions the prospect. 'I could break my leg in the next match and then it would all be over,' he'd say. 'You can't let it worry you or you'll be afraid to cross the road.' Best was worried nonetheless. 'There are times when you get a deep-down black sort of feeling about the physical risks,' he conceded. 'You feel the odd shiver run down the spine. Playing my style means a constant battle of wits and I guess I must be very quick-witted.'

Sometimes victors are by victories undone; but neither Best nor Blanchflower thought it would be true at Old Trafford. Both, post the European Cup, saw Manchester United steamrolling on unstoppably. And Blanchflower saw Best alone initiating a sustained period of dominance. Of course, so did Best. He understood why Matt Busby had stayed on for another season; and also why he'd then chosen to make public his decision to go during the middle of it. He didn't begrudge Busby that indulgence. Best did berate himself for timidity nevertheless. Callowness dissuaded him from giving a voice to his dismay about United's lackadaisical attitudes after Wembley and the club's lack of preparation for the future, which he described as 'tragic for me'. On several occasions he thought of approaching Busby and asking for a meeting. He almost went to see him in mid-August after United had won only two of their opening six matches. He considered doing so again in late autumn after a run of draws and defeats. He made it a New Year's resolution to call on him in the first week of January. Each time Best talked himself out of it. He said: 'I was only a lad . . . Who was I to tell the greatest club in the world that I thought something was intrinsically wrong with the set-up? Who was I to walk into the boardroom?'

As United's League results worsened, and Busby didn't buy to halt the descent, it became apparent to Best that the burden of carrying the club into another era was going to fall disproportionately on to him. The weight of it was troubling, chiefly because he'd imagined Busby – or Busby's successor – tailoring a team around him and making it fit, so his solo artistry could flourish. Now it seemed to him United were banking on that solo artistry being enough in itself. If United were going to be successful again, Best would have to be self-sufficient. 'I wasn't old enough to take it,' he said. 'If I'd been three or four years older, it might have been different. At twenty-two, I didn't want the responsibility of carrying anyone. I just wanted to enjoy it.' But Best wasn't enjoying it. The 19 League goals he scored in Busby's final season couldn't stop a slide into pessimism and the evisceration of hope. The statistic was a pyrrhic triumph for him anyway because it hadn't led to a Championship or a Cup. Avoiding a lowly finish was no reason to be cheerful. His goals needed to serve a better purpose than that. 'I didn't feel the satisfaction I'd been getting in the previous five or six years,' he said. 'I kept quiet about it . . . Inside it was gnawing at me all the time . . . I used to run things over in my mind until I couldn't think about them any more.'

Blanchflower was another of the players Best, the boy, had aspired to be, and he got close to him because of it. Best would always take Blanchflower's telephone calls and talk to him after matches. According to Blanchflower, the private Best was more fragile than the public persona. 'You could see it in his eyes,' he said. 'He'd say one thing – about being well and fine – but his eyes told you another, far different story.' What the spectator saw was someone coolly in control, almost insouciantly so. 'What I saw,' said Blanchflower, 'was someone who experienced a lot of mental anguish in those seasons immediately after the European Cup.' Blanchflower recognised Best's needs, which were becoming a neurosis. The need to be superior on the field. The need to always win. The need, above all, not to let himself down by failing to be or do either of those things.

'A genius is different from the rest of us,' said Blanchflower in an adaptation of the Ernest Hemingway line about the rich. Manchester City's coach Malcolm Allison contemporaneously explained the quandaries of working with one. For Allison, the 'star' player, such as Best, required exceptionally delicate handling. 'The most difficult thing is for a star player to maintain his star qualities consistently,' he said. 'Average players are easy to coach because a coach knows exactly what they are capable of. On their way to stardom they present few headaches. Because everything is new and interesting and a challenge, they are prepared to battle against all situations. But once they become star players your problems start. Marking gets tighter, opposing teams start to prepare for them and suddenly the game becomes hard. You have to stimulate their enthusiasm and keep working at their game.' Allison's assessment can be read in three ways. As a warning to United. As a summary of Best's career to date. As a prediction about the next phase of it. Each proved accurate. Allison said of football: 'The game is like being in love. You've got to suffer to enjoy it.' The doubts Allison had about Best were based on whether he'd continue to believe that suffering was worth it. Just as Blanchflower correctly diagnosed Best's character, so Allison correctly judged his response when the tide turned against his team.

Best's happiness and equilibrium were based on achievement, and he'd presumed success at United would be seamless. He also wanted the public to leave a ground talking only about something he – and he alone – had been able to accomplish: an incident good enough to be discussed on the way home, over a pint in the pub that night, during the rest of the weekend and then again on Monday morning at work. 'I think of myself as an entertainer,' he said. 'I'd think I'd let people down if I didn't put on a show and I would be disappointed with myself.'

Fame and tranquillity can seldom be bedfellows. But he was able to handle his renown as adequately as anyone could have done – until the edifice Busby had built began to chip and crumble because no one kept it in constant repair. What happened to Best in the coming years as a consequence grew out of the sort of person he was and the temperament he had. With United ambling and losing, he began to wander. In her London flat Jackie Glass received occasional calls from Busby politely enquiring whether she knew where Best could be found.

'There just wasn't any one person strong enough to hold the team together after the European Cup,' said Best. 'The whole thing just seemed to collapse.' Change, he added, didn't come 'rapidly enough', which led to 'disaster – all the way down'.

Busby's botched succession began it. He'd failed to groom a candidate and establish him unequivocally in advance as his number two. The 105 days separating the announcement of his retirement in January 1969 from the announcement of his replacement in mid-April raised expectations that were never going to be met. Busby's choice of Wilf McGuinness was calamitous. If you are going to step into someone's shoes, you'd better take the same size; especially when the shoes belong to a colossus.

McGuinness was only 31, a Mancunian devoted to both United and Busby. As a wing-half he'd played alongside Duncan Edwards and those who lived and died at Munich. With the Babes of 1956–57 he'd won a League Championship and also owned two England caps. But his career, once so full of promise, ended with the simultaneous break of the tibia and fibula of his right leg during a routine tackle. The crack and sharp snap of the bones sounded horrendous to those who heard it. Busby recruited McGuinness for his coaching staff because he considered him to be an erudite thinker. He recommended him to Alf Ramsey, who was then rearranging England's backroom staff. Rapidly establishing himself within it, McGuinness schooled England's youth team, which at various stages included Harry Redknapp, Tommy Smith, Ron Harris and Peter Osgood. In 1966 Ramsey, greatly impressed, commandeered him to work alongside the England squad during the build-up to the World Cup finals and promised: 'If we get to the final – and we *are* going to get to the final – you'll be there.' His word was a binding contract. McGuinness was given a seat on the bus taking England to Wembley and another inside the stadium. At the end of that afternoon of sun and showers, joy and controversy, Ramsey made sure McGuinness was in the dressing room as the trophy passed from player to player. At that evening's victors' banquet, he sat at the manager's right hand after a place was cleared and set for him on Ramsey's instructions. The next step was to give him control of England's Under-23s. At Old Trafford McGuinness moved from being Busby's youth coach to take charge of the reserves. Returning to Wembley for the European Cup, he volunteered to lay out the kit. Best saw nothing in this – or his overall record – to suggest it made him a fitting substitute for Busby.

No manager in the Football League came close to matching Busby's European Cup, his six Championships and his two FA Cups. But, as frothy speculation filled the hiatus Busby had created, Best took it for granted that someone of stature would be hired. McGuinness' promotion disappointed him. He didn't see him as another Busby in the making. Nor were Best's previous dealings with him reassuring. He was ambivalent about McGuinness in public. 'There was a time,' said Best, 'when I regarded him with some suspicion. When I was younger I got the impression he was telling on me whenever I did something wrong.' Best moaned that McGuinness gave him 'some very hard times in training' and also 'used to have right old goes about my so-called late nights and the reputation I was getting in some quarters'. In between the criticism Best offered a placatory qualification. 'I now realise,' said Best, as if he'd undergone a road to Damascus conversion, 'that this was a strong United man – a man who felt the club was the one thing bigger than any personality in it – and he really was doing the right thing by me.' Best added that McGuinness was 'totally dedicated' and said he had a 'deep respect for him'. As endorsements go, it was standard and noncommittal. Also included in it were two prophetic sentences. 'I've had my brushes with him in the past,' he said. 'Could even be that there will be some in the future.' He'd be subsequently more forgiving, claiming: 'To be quite brutal, whoever took over was going to have the toughest job in the country and the most impossible and the least rewarding. If someone had offered me the job, I'd have said no.'

Busby had decided at least six months earlier to anoint McGuinness. But McGuinness – the bookmakers' 6-1 shot – was ignorant of it until less than 24 hours before the press conference. Busby sought him out. 'Wilf, tomorrow, I would like you to come in looking smart, wearing a collar and tie.' McGuinness was too circumspect to ask why. 'Oh, right,' he replied, knowing then what the request really meant.

In a kind of arranged marriage, McGuinness was made chief coach, a defensive move designed to protect him against some of the stresses of taking over. He'd be responsible for fitness and tactics and he'd select the team. Busby would look after transfers, wages and discipline and he'd speak on behalf of the club. 'I'm here to help,' Busby told him, which confused rather than clarified because it opened up what McGuinness saw as 'grey areas'. 'I didn't know how much he wanted to do,' he explained. The earliest charge against McGuinness is that he said yes to a job he was unqualified to take. But how could he have said no? For the chance might never have come again for him. It's impossible not to feel sorrow for McGuinness. Busby spoke about preserving 'pattern and continuity'. If he wanted a protégé to do so

– and also to mould the type of bootroom community that allowed the handover of power at Liverpool to be successful during the 1970s and 80s – he ought to have been more inclusive. McGuinness should have always been at Busby's shoulder in 1968–69 to signpost the promotion to follow, as if it was simply natural evolution. When it came, however, McGuinness' elevation was a semi-shock. Sitting beside Busby, and smartly business-like in a white shirt and his tightly knotted European Cup tie, McGuinness was soon answering three fundamental questions put to him in front of the television cameras and assembled newspapermen. These were the same questions Best asked himself.

Was he too young and too inexperienced to cope with European Cup winners?

How could he effectively boss those players who had been his equals – or superiors – for so long?

Did he have sufficient charisma, authority and gravitas for the job?

Even seen at its very brightest, Busby doesn't come out of this episode well. He was asking someone who had never managed a League club before, let alone one of the most prestigious names in the world, to achieve what he no longer believed *he* was capable of achieving himself. Seen at its very worst, it looks as if Busby – fulfilling the role no manager beneath him could ever fully ignore – had decided to dabble by proxy. This would have been more awkward with an outsider; and Busby was always suspicious of those who lacked United's family lineage. Among the confidants on his staff only McGuinness fitted the exceptionally narrow criteria that Busby set down. He wanted 'someone in his early thirties or older, but no more than forty-five'. Jimmy Murphy was then 59 (and didn't want to take over anyway) and Jack Crompton and John Aston senior were both 48. 'He must be experienced because we are not in a position to experiment,' added Busby. 'He must have already proved himself as a leader who commands respect.' McGuinness, given £80 per week, immediately discovered Best, Denis Law and Bobby

Charlton were earning higher salaries than him, an irregularity that Busby ought to have resolved in advance. Busby also retained the grander manager's office. He was like a king, half-willing to abdicate the kingdom but not the throne room.

Like all men given the thankless task of following a legend, McGuinness was burdened from the beginning. He was passionate, committed and unquestionably talented. What he lacked was wisdom. At that time – and in those circumstances – he had no chance. The job would have been too big for most people. It was certainly too big for him. He was caught in Busby's penumbra. Nor could he clear the hurdle of being 'one of the lads' in the morning and the boss in the afternoon. The swiftness of the promotion didn't allow for a careful transitional period during which both McGuinness and the players might have become accustomed to the change in his status. McGuinness needed to put a respectable working distance between himself and his team. But he was the instigator of some typically masculine banter and joking in the dressing room, which could now be misconstrued as criticism or complaint or as some Delphic pronouncements loaded with multiple interpretations. As Best also said: 'In some quarters there was resentment that he now held the reins.' He thought some players 'found it difficult to look up to him . . . or to take orders'. He also sensed 'that one or two just wouldn't [or] didn't feel like giving one hundred per cent for him'.

The unprepared have to learn as they go along. Inevitably McGuinness made more errors of his own to compound those Busby had already committed. Inexplicably he chose not to sufficiently pick the encyclopaedic brain of Murphy, who had mentored and then befriended him. Murphy, acutely hurt at the rejection, was effectively sidelined. McGuinness was also obliged to move into Murphy's office. United under McGuinness began the 1969–70 season abysmally – no win from the first six League matches. The second and fourth of these games were defeats against Everton, who would become champions that season. United lost 2–0 at home and 3–0 away to them. The combined scoreline – Manchester United 0, Everton 5 – was only partly obscured by the fallout from the decision McGuinness made before going to Goodison Park: he dropped both Charlton and Law. 'When I announced my team,' said McGuinness, 'it was more like I'd dropped the atom bomb.' Charlton was omitted for tactical reasons; Law because McGuinness thought he was labouring with groin trouble. McGuinness later conceded that leaving out Charlton was 'rash' and deliberately misquoted Oscar Wilde to chastise himself for going too far. 'Losing one world-class footballer might be construed as careless,' he said, 'but losing two . . . well, it doesn't bear thinking about.' McGuinness remembered he was 'practically crucified' in the press, who wrongly – but perfectly reasonably – read the runes and deduced the following message from them: he was brandishing a clunking iron fist and exhibiting an 'I'll show you who's in charge' attitude. In actual fact, desperate for points, McGuinness was only trying to win a match.

The change of manager unsettled Best because it brought other changes with it.

Only a year and a half after winning the European Cup, he was already looking at it, plus the period beforehand, as if it were prelapsarian. 'The club really did have a certain special thing about it,' he said of the mid-1960s. He missed those days when Busby put on a scarlet tracksuit, pulled on a pair of old boots and trained. 'Because of his age he wasn't going to run around much. He joined in the seven-a-sides that we had. If the ball came to him he passed it to somebody. In that one little thing he became one of the boys, really,' said Best. He also liked the fact that after training, he and others – usually Charlton and Law, Nobby Stiles, Paddy Crerand and Shay Brennan – would congregate in a kitchen above the offices. 'We used to go there every day for a cup of tea, sit around and chat.' Those cosy get-togethers mostly belonged to the past, too. Best watched United's squad splinter into cliques. 'One by one, they were falling out,' he said. This was the scene as he described it:

'Players going off in twos and threes, talking behind each other's back, which I had never known. I'd seen it with the team just before us when they started to break. I didn't realise it at the time because I was so young. It does happen if teams of players have a certain degree of success and all of a sudden it's not there.'

There were arguments in training, he added, and 'moaning about this and that'. Lots were drawn to allocate who shared with whom in a room on away trips. 'To me it was unbelievable, really, that it had got to that stage,' said Best. 'There were three or four players who were saying, "I hope I don't get with him".' Best always roomed with David Sadler. He was still rooming with Sadler afterwards. 'We fiddled it,' he said.

The team had the odour of rising damp about it. He tried to convince himself things would improve, never believing it. As a reaction to the pasting Everton gave them – plus the fact United had conceded 11 goals in four matches – McGuinness paid £80,000 to Arsenal for the Scottish centre-half Ian Ure. Or, more precisely, Busby persuaded him to make the investment against McGuinness' instincts. Best was aghast. He sometimes got changed with the youth or reserve side. In the dressing room he was asked what he thought of Ure's arrival. 'Not good,' he said. In training he then made a point of taking the ball up to Ure and nutmegging him. As Ure turned, so did Best – nutmegging him again in the other direction to make a statement. The squad lacked depth and there were only mini-revivals and false starts as the season unwound. An odd pair of wins was punctuated by sequences of draws or defeats. The corner was never emphatically turned.

Busby was adamant that he never interfered with the team. He certainly wasn't overbearing or dictatorial towards McGuinness, who would sum up the relationship between them like this: 'He didn't want to ride roughshod over me, and I didn't want to be seen running to him every time there was a decision to be made.' But McGuinness did concede he ought to have been more forceful in wrenching transfer cash out of Busby. Knowing how poorly furnished United had become, McGuinness unsuccessfully tried to wrestle Malcolm Macdonald – the barrel-chested, bow-legged goalscorer – from Luton, the full-back Mick Mills from Ipswich and Colin Todd, who read the play in front of him almost as well and cleverly as Bobby Moore, from Sunderland. Busby blocked approaches for Mills and Todd, branding them as 'too expensive'. He was myopic about what was happening to the market, where fees were rising. Six-figure deals were becoming the norm. A month before McGuinness' first season began, Leeds paid a record £166,000 for the striker Allan Clarke from Leicester City. A month or so before it ended, Spurs handed over £200,000 to buy Martin Peters from West Ham. Even newly promoted Derby, under Brian Clough, willingly spent £100,000 on the Welsh international Terry Hennessey from Nottingham Forest. Clough would eventually get Todd for £175,000 as well. Busby, it seemed, thought 1970s players should still be available at 1950s prices.

As if inheriting Busby's mantle didn't come with enough cumbersome baggage, McGuinness also had to maintain United's cultured style of play to satisfy the connoisseurs. The Cavalier approach, rather than Roundhead regimentalism, was obligatory. To win wasn't enough. There had to be an artful quality attached to it. There wasn't enough derring-do about McGuinness for Best's liking. To him his approach seemed stolid in comparison to the purity of Busby's 'go out and enjoy yourselves' instruction. A side which had predominantly concerned itself with one another for seven years was now told to dwell on the opposition, too. McGuinness relied on a board with magnetic discs to lay out formations and discuss tactics. While this was the modern approach, it appeared to Best in particular as the equivalent of lecturing the Beatles on how to carry a tune. He took it as an insult. Best thought McGuinness had been led astray by the influence of Ramsey, whose world champions he considered to be 'a bit too conservative for my tastes'. The arrows and squiggly diagrams McGuinness drew were a yawning bore to him. 'Everyone had a specific role on the field, unlike Sir Matt's day,' said Best. Sometimes, he said, a mischievous hand would surreptitiously slide an extra disc or two on or off the board. In full flow McGuinness could find he was talking about two teams that comprised either 12 players each or only ten. Where Best was concerned, whatever was said in these pre-match briefings went into one ear and directly out of the other, never stopping. He played as he saw fit. He was irked about, but could comfortably deal with, being told what role to play by simply ignoring the order. What could McGuinness possibly say about such insubordination if it led to a goal or the making of one? To anyone else Best's behaviour looks arrogant, mutinous and deeply undermining. To Best, who saw nothing amiss with his attitude, the ends justified the means.

Best camouflaged a struggle he was having with himself. He looked around him and saw incremental deterioration in the team. This wasn't United as he knew it. This wasn't Old Trafford as it had been. 'The family', as he called the club, was breaking up. He wanted to speak out. Instead, wishfully thinking that one morning he'd find everything miraculously hunky-dory again, he declared his primary aim was to play on for another decade at Old Trafford. 'People are asking what there is left,' he said. 'You've done everything, they say, suggesting that from now on it's all going to be an anti-climax. They must be joking.'

The statement was reassuring when Best made it. But at the same time he was saying all the right things he was also starting to do all the wrong ones.

9

And the Award Will
Be Posthumous

The misconception about George Best is that alcohol alone wrecked him and his career. It ignores the reason why he drank. The football was to blame.

There was something intensely driven about Best, a raging competitiveness in his character that led him to extremes. He conceived nothing else but being number one in a team that was also number one. He despised losing at *anything*. At Manchester United he had run faster, kept the ball off the ground longer, trained harder and beat more defenders than anyone else. Away from it, trivial competitions, such as cards or dominoes or flipping the most beer mats off the edge of the table and catching them cleanly, had to be won, too. Best would insist competitions like these went on – sometimes interminably – until he was successful. Friends would be kept awake until the early hours simply so he could beat them. To do so was a matter of personal pride for him. To lose was a weakness. Someone thinking and acting this way was always going to find regular defeat impossible to accept.

Neither Best nor those closest to him could definitively identify the point at which he sought out drink as a remedy for those losses on the field. He guessed it was 'around 1970 and 1971'. The dates coincide with the beginning of United's bleak midwinter – those years when supremacy was surrendered and mediocrity became the norm for them. Best couldn't cope with it. He couldn't cope either with the pressure of being seen as the only player capable of reviving them.

Addictions blight and poison incrementally; their work is often done in secret. So Best's problem wouldn't become blatantly apparent – either in his complexion or his behaviour – for some time to come. He also possessed an extraordinarily strong constitution and continued to work vigorously. Bill Shankly thought 'you could see the fitness shine out of his eyes', and Jimmy Murphy regarded Best as 'the hardest trainer I've ever seen'. He sweated out the alcohol without giving it a second thought. He still scored goals. He was still gorgeous George, healthily pink, because binges rarely blemished his skin and didn't puff out his face or give him a pot-belly. If the odd blotch appeared, he hid it behind a beard. In the beginning, the various stages of his drinking – the long, slow descent from one level to the next – slipped by, almost unnoticed. But the youngster who'd once sipped weak shandy with Mary Fullaway after Sunday night bingo had long ago developed a taste for something more potent.

He'd got drunk for the first time in the late spring of 1964. United's youth team had gone to Switzerland to compete in a tournament organised by amateurs Zurich Blue Stars. Despite playing 31 games in the preceding five months – one more appearance than he'd made during the whole of the previous season – Best was included in the squad because United liked pot-hunting. Matt Busby and Murphy considered the FA Youth Cup as paramount; not only because it allowed them to prepare players competitively – 'the young team makes men of them', said Murphy – but also for the kudos. The Babes had been blooded this way. Busby had no qualms about using first teamers, such as Best, in that competition – even if it infringed its spirit and added considerably to an individual's workload. With Best, United had won the Cup a month earlier. More than 50,000 watched them beat Manchester City in the semi-final over two legs. Swindon Town were then brushed aside, 5-2 on aggregate, in the final. Busby now wanted his Youth Cup winners to bring back another piece of silverware. Best wanted to unwind.

One hot afternoon he and John Fitzpatrick went to a bar with two team-mates, David Farrar and Eddie Harrop. The virgin drinker gulped down three pints of lager for appearance's sake. It was gassy and strong and tasted harshly on the tongue. He began to feel woozy, as if his brain were a roundabout that someone was gently pushing. Fresh air accentuated that sensation. Best's face was whiter than milk. A taxi driver, fearing he would be sick over the upholstery, originally refused to allow him into the car. Best wound down one of the back windows, sticking his head out of it in case of an emergency. Barely able to put one foot in front of the other without wobbling like a buckled wheel, he was propped up by the arms and conspicuously dragged through the glass doors of the hotel. Busby and Murphy were occupying window seats in the café opposite the entrance – counting the players out and then counting them back in again. Even from a distance Busby recognised that Best wasn't self-propelled. But a drink or two was a rite of passage for someone of his age; so Busby let it pass. In his room Best's belly began to churn. He retched and puked into the toilet bowl. 'I felt like I was dying,' he said. Fitzpatrick, forgetting to collect his own room key, lay in Best's empty bath. 'I just hoped,' said Best, 'that there wouldn't be a knock on the door and I'd open it to find the boss staring at me.' Farrar and Harrop were unaffected. 'We were physically bigger and we were used to the odd drink,' said Farrar. 'What I remember is George being sick *everywhere*.' The following morning Best, tightly wrapped in the blankets of his single bed, had to be shaken awake. 'We've got to go training,' John Aston told him. Best opened one eye and mumbled back: 'Some of us need to train,' supremely confident of his own abilities by now.

Afterwards Best made the usual promises about 'never drinking again'. He wasn't over-fond of beer – usually lager with a splash of lime – because it bloated his stomach. Within a year he was drinking vodka and lemonade. Vodka didn't catch on his breath. If anyone was nosy enough to ask, Best could plausibly lie to avoid being reported to Busby. 'It's flat lemonade,' he'd say. Drinking then had a practical purpose. With a drink inside him Best didn't feel so shy. Every sip was the acquisition of Dutch courage. During the initial years of his celebrity Best didn't mind being looked at in the street – 'it was a marvellous feeling', he said – but he disliked finding himself in unfamiliar places where he knew almost no one. Alcohol was his release. 'After a drink,' he explained, 'I might loosen up sufficiently to chat to one or two people.'

In the mid-60s he and Mike Summerbee settled into a Saturday-night pattern. There was usually a meal at an Italian restaurant, Arturo's, where both Busby and Joe Mercer dined quietly with their wives. At another table Best and Summerbee would act out a cordial charade, sipping soft drinks to give the impression of being responsibly upright professionals, before peeling off for a typical young man's night of entertainment. 'We'd always go and say goodbye and be perfect gentlemen,' said Summerbee 'The wives were always telling us to take care of ourselves and we always promised we would. The managers knew where we'd be going and why, and there was never any bother about it provided you didn't turn up the worse for wear on a Monday morning.' The bar, pub and club crawl that followed began in swanky surroundings and ended in a shebeen, where alcohol was sold after normal licensing hours. The shebeen that became one of Best and Summerbee's favourite drinking holes was in Moss Side, a hotel called the Clifton Grange, belonging to Philomena Lynott, the mother of Phil

Lynott, who'd later become lead singer of the band Thin Lizzy. The Victorian house was popularly called 'The Biz' because of its showbusiness clientele, mostly comprising cabaret acts, singers and dancers. Philomena, who opened it in 1966, soon became 'Auntie Phyllis' to Best because of her homeliness and her willingness to listen as he talked about whatever was on his mind.

The Biz was accessed via a metal fire escape. You knocked on the door and waited for a peep-hole to swing open so 'Auntie Phyllis' could see who was calling. You were then 'signed in' by an existing resident to circumnavigate the licensing laws. Inside, the chairs and sofas were wide and comfy and rubber plants and small ferns in pots stood between them. Deep purple drapes were hung at the window, shutting out the light completely. Since there was no clock on the wall, the hours passed without anyone knowing whether it was still dark or the sun had risen in a blaze. No one cared. 'When those curtains opened,' said Summerbee, 'it could be half past ten or eleven o'clock in the morning.' The drinkers would blink to protect their eyes from the sudden glare. Philomena made Irish stew in huge brown pots, serving it up as either a late-night meal or a hearty breakfast at noon. Best would often arrive from a gambling club, handing Philomena his winnings – 'a thick wedge of rumpled notes', she said – in an envelope, which she'd put away for safe-keeping until he left. She bought an enormous Ludo board and Best would play that game endlessly. 'He liked the atmosphere and the friendliness he found with us. My regulars were like a family,' she said. 'And we all loved George.' She banked at the same branch as Busby, who would tip his hat whenever he saw her. 'I used to wonder if he knew that I was partly responsible for keeping his star player out at night.'

In 1967 Best also found a pub that suited his odd preference for obscure, scruffy, spit and sawdust surroundings. 'Typical *Coronation Street*,' he said. The Brown Bull was another piece of Victorian architecture comprising browny-red, Flemish bond, Accrington brick. It curved around the corner of Chapel Street in Salford beside the railway arches, not far from his boutique. The building would tremble when a train chugged by. The exterior – or at least its middle tier – was attractive: sash windows and miniature Corinthian columns. The thin letters of its two-foot high signage stretched below a shallow pitched roof. The interior, however, was typical of the rough boozers depicted in kitchen sink dramas: a pair of slatted swing doors, the floor sticky from spilt beer, the long bar and tables cut from brown oak, the once mustard and white walls and ceiling stained by the nicotine of strong cigarettes. Best liked it this way. The publican was a former American GI, Billy Barr, who spoke with a Texan drawl. Purely because of Best's patronage the Brown Bull was transformed in less than a month from unknown, backwater ale-house and stopover for travelling salesmen to well-known drinking den, a leap in status accomplished without altering the decor. Word about the pub, which Best envisaged as his hideaway, soon grew to the point where Barr was obliged to vet his customers. The Brown Bull was close to the Granada Studios and soon drew anyone of distinction filming there as well as the starlets. The pub, which never closed for Best, infuriated Busby. Firstly because he could never accurately recall its agricultural name, describing it as the Black Cow or the Pink Calf, and secondly because Best used it like a home-away-from-home, where he drank beside a clientele that were friends or others who were desperate to call him a friend. He said the Brown Bull was a 'mad house'. There'd be various games and challenges, which included picking up a chair by one leg, passing a bar stool to someone while lying on your back, doing push-ups in the middle of the floor, jumping through knives, playing football between tables, holding gunfights with soda siphons and arm wrestling. One game, called Jacks, required a pack of cards. The first person dealt a jack had to order a drink, which usually meant asking Barr to mix the spirits. Some of these concoctions – brandy, whisky, Bacardi or vodka – would have stunned a racehorse.

The person who got the next jack had to taste it. The recipient of the third had to gulp it down in one. The fourth jack paid the bill for the drink. Barr, grateful for the customers Best brought to his modest pub, passed him his own key as a thank you. Best served himself whatever he liked and whenever he wanted it. Sometimes he'd sleep in one of the spare rooms on the upper floors, awaking to find passengers on the double-decker buses peering at him because he'd forgotten to draw the curtains. 'The parties would go on all night,' said Best. 'It really did become an institution . . . they packed to the doors every night, almost.' Twenty years on he conceded: 'The time I spent there probably did more to me as an athlete than any other single factor.'

There was a long-established drinking culture in football. Few thought it was harmful for players to sup pints on a Thursday night because there was still a day and a half for it to pass through the system before kick-off on Saturday. As far back as 1904 the Spurs captain, J. L. Jones, wrote of beer as being a 'recognised article of diet', which made it impossible to ban. In the 1930s Hughie Gallagher was accused of being drunk on the pitch. In the 1940s Tommy Lawton would laugh about the post-war England team sneaking out of a hotel through a toilet window and escaping to a bar the night before an international. At half-time during the 1950 FA Cup final, Denis Compton took a swig of whisky before Arsenal claimed the trophy. And in the early and mid-1960s Glasgow Rangers allowed Jim Baxter to run up a weekly drinks bill in a hotel, which the club paid without quibbling, and Bobby Moore arranged after-match nights out on the field, telling opposition players where he'd be going and inviting them along. So the fact Best drank wasn't considered abnormal – despite the fact the amounts he was drinking often led to him blacking out afterwards.

There were nevertheless portents of the overindulgence to come.

Only 13 days before the European Cup final, Best collected his Footballer of the Year award. He downed one glass of vodka after another and later danced on a nightclub stage with a line of chorus girls, still clutching his statuette. 'I wouldn't let go of it,' he said. During the one-night stand that followed Best was so drunk that he attempted to undress himself without putting down the trophy. Realising it was impossible to remove his trousers while standing up, he decided to sit on the bed. By his own admission he missed it 'by four feet' and hit the floor with a clatter. He didn't let go of the statuette. The girl, who had taken him back to her flat, had already undressed. She was now brushing her hair in a mirror and turned around to look at him dismissively. 'Some player of the year,' she said. Best promptly fell asleep. The following morning, the rain lashing over London, he huddled inside a doorway to wait for a taxi and dozed off again cradling the award, wrapped in brown paper, in his arms. A policeman jarred him out of his slumber. The brief exchange that followed has both sweet comedy and bitter tragedy entwined within it because you know similar, but more sinister, exchanges will follow in the 1970s.

POLICEMAN: What are you doing here?

BEST: I'm the Player of the Year

POLICEMAN: Bloody looks like it. What's that?

BEST: My trophy.

POLICEMAN: Show us then.

(*Best unwraps the parcel for him, revealing the distinctive silver footballer on a plinth.*)

POLICEMAN: Very nice too. But I'd go back to your hotel if I were you or you'll get pneumonia and the award will be posthumous.

As the 1969–70 season began there were clues that Best's life was beginning to go awry.

There was a predictability about his visits to Sir Matt Busby's office and the rigmarole of what each said to the other. Misdeed, confession and consequence were played out as *déjà vu* moments. Time and again the same themes – the hours and the company Best was keeping, the extent of his commercial interests – were revisited and left unresolved. On every occasion Best would apologise and look contrite. He would often use the 'bloody idiot' defence and claim to have learned a lesson. Promises were piled on promises – each as worthless as the ones before. 'I used to sit in front of him and nod yes,' admitted Best. Busby would think that everything had been amicably settled and then find his protégé had reoffended.

What the other players feared was Busby's disapproval. Paddy Crerand observed that the rebukes Busby delivered generally weren't about bellowing. Such a patrician man preferred not to go into a rage because to do so was an affront to his dignity and composure. Busby didn't have to shout to make his point. He could wound with a shake of his head or a glance; for both were capable of withering the recipient before a word was spoken. 'You always felt embarrassed that a man like that should give you a dressing down,' said Crerand. 'He'd never demean you. He'd make you feel a bit ashamed that you'd done something that wasn't proper.' With Best, his mentor tried everything from persuasion to punishment, which included docking his wages. He showed him uncritical tenderness. He gave him the sort of fiery telling-off that could have immolated an entire forest. He mixed arm-twisting with dire warnings. Busby also preached the glories of matrimony with a revival-ist's zeal. He wanted his players to find a bride early on, build a home and settle down in it – a pram in the hallway. What Busby thought Best needed was a good woman; of course, what Best thought he needed was several of them. A wife, said Busby, would quickly convert Best from night-owl to home-bird. Mike Summerbee had got married the previous summer, choosing his best pal as his best man. Best couldn't resist a joke shortly before the service began. 'The church was in the Peak District,' said Summerbee. 'Before the ceremony he took me out of a door at the back, pointed to a wall in the distance and said: "See that? You can run down there, jump over it and you'll free. You'll never get caught.'" Busby hoped Best would follow Summerbee's example. 'Any special young lady?' he'd ask him regularly. 'Have you never thought of marriage?' he'd ask again. Best, who'd broken up with Jackie Glass, would tell Busby he daren't marry – 'in case I fall in love with one of the bridesmaids in the middle of the wedding'. He'd then declare, as one of the country's most eligible single men: 'I'm a confirmed bachelor.' But Best had previously spoken of marriage to Glass. 'Soon after we started dating, George introduced the topic,' she said. 'As we had only known each other a matter of weeks, I thought he was joking. Whenever he brought the subject up, talking about what good-looking babies we'd have, I'd get embarrassed, laugh it off and not give him a direct answer. Barely out of my teens, and with George just twenty-one then, I felt we were still babies ourselves.'

Best used to wear a plain gold chain around his neck. For their first Christmas together, Glass bought him a gold disc which she had engraved with the word 'Yes' – her answer to his proposal. Eventually, says Glass, the two of them 'drifted apart'; though Best attempted – and failed – to woo her again. 'I managed to resist George when he tried to get [us] back together. Not because I didn't want to, but because I knew it wouldn't work and I couldn't envisage a future for us. He was not the type of man to turn away the girls . . . and I was not the type to turn a blind eye.' A coda reflects no credit on Best. He bought two more gold disc medallions of his own – one for Malcolm Wagner, the other for Danny Bursk – and had each inscribed identically. They were used as a clear, if unorthodox, way of sending a message to women for sex.

Ken Stanley believed Best had reached the stage where 'he could go anywhere, do anything'. Without exaggeration Stanley added that Best was so influential that he could ring the Lord Mayor of Manchester on a whim and say: 'Close the city down for ten minutes while I have a think.' The Lord Mayor, said Stanley, would 'have bloody well done it' without hesitating. What Best did instead was less ambitious. He asked a Danish newspaper to track down a mystery woman on his behalf. She'd asked him to sign an autograph before a friendly in Copenhagen a week before the season started. He gave an Identikit description of her – long-legged, blonde and blue-eyed, a profile which fitted 95 per cent of his courtships and probably 96 per cent of the female population of Denmark under 25. The newspaper published an appeal and sent Best four photographs received in response to it. He immediately recognised the woman in one of them. She was 21-year-old Eva Haraldsted. What Best did with her address, which was also included, made Busby apoplectic. Within eight days of meeting her, Best was talking publicly of hearts-and-flowers love and marriage and the tabloid press announced their engagement. She was photographed at Aycliffe Avenue helping Mrs Fullaway with the washing-up. Within another 91 days the relationship was over. Within a further fortnight Best was being sued for breach of promise, an anachronistic piece of common law tort, a form of which began in the medieval age. Again, Best was at fault. He told a newspaper that the romance was 'over' before he informed Haraldsted. That night Best was 'silent and preoccupied' until confessing he wanted to break up with her. He eventually paid £500 to settle the case out of court – his own solicitors suggested the amount – after initially saying he would 'get rid' of his assets to prevent her receiving 'anything', which was a ludicrous overreaction to a situation he'd created. 'I fell in love with a pair of knockers, basically. It could have happened to anyone,' he said. What Best envisaged as 'a fling' got out of control because he lacked maturity, which is the line Busby took when Best was summoned to see him. Like everyone else, Busby learned about the story only when it appeared on the front page of the newspapers, which he read over breakfast. And, also like everyone else, he was flabbergasted. 'I got to the ground as fast as I could,' he remembered. The obvious observation Busby made – what are you thinking of; you don't know this woman – was met with logic even more obvious: 'You're the one who's always telling me to get married,' said Best.

Busby was aware Best had previously been in an on-off relationship with a married woman. He disapproved and told Best so. What he didn't know was this: the woman had become pregnant and her and Best's child – a girl – was born that same year. For the sake of her marriage, and her daughter's future, the mother asked Best not to contact his daughter. He agreed reluctantly, always fulfilling that promise. Best liked children; he just didn't envisage being a father at 23. That he'd become one, without being able to see his baby, made him more conflicted and mixed up than even Busby imagined.

More complications followed. Best seduced the second wife of the barrister George Carman, who was part of the northern judicial circuit and later became one of the most celebrated QCs in the country after successfully defending the Liberal leader Jeremy Thorpe on a charge of conspiracy to murder. In separate cases he'd win libel damages for both Tom Cruise and Elton John, too. A sequence of unlikely events led Best into Mrs Carman's bed. Carman was hired to defend Paddy Crerand, charged with assault following an incident outside a nightclub with the man Haraldsted had begun to date after Best and two other men, one of whom got his jaw broken. Inside the club Best had asked the disc jockey to play and replay the Beatles 'Get Back', a jibe aimed at Haraldsted so she might, as Best said, 'actually go back to Denmark where she belonged'. Her new boyfriend, his brother and a friend sought revenge. As he did on the pitch Crerand protected Best, who was called as his chief defence witness. To make sure Best appeared, Carman thought it would be sensible to allow Best to sleep in the spare room of his house the night before the trial. That evening Carman, Best and Malcolm Wagner went drinking. Each got drunk. At home Carman fell asleep on the sofa; Best went upstairs and slept with Mrs Carman. At three o'clock in the morning he rang Wagner to admit what he had done. If Carman found out, asked a concerned Best, did Wagner think he would still defend Crerand? Betraying no sign of knowing what had happened, Carman cleared Crerand of the charge. Things didn't end there. Carman appeared on Best's behalf in another case two years later. Best concurrently began an affair with his wife, which lasted several months and ended the Carmans' marriage. He was even brash enough to park his E-type Jaguar outside the house. Carman approached a gangland figure in Manchester and asked him to break Best's legs in retribution. He was rebuffed. The gangster he chose turned out to be a fan of Best's. He told Carman he didn't get involved in domestic disputes and warned him that, if Best was harmed, he'd know who'd done it. 'I'll come after you,' he said to Carman.

This was the self-destructive phase of Best's early life, dominated more than ever by screw-ups and screwing. He would look back on it and admit he was 'amazed' that someone hadn't 'done me in' because of some of his affairs.

'I was drinking too much over long periods and getting depressed easily,' said Best. These depressions, he explained, were 'brought on by football' and were caused because he said 'the old thrill' of the game had gone.

Like so many celebrities before and after him George Best complained about the media's tendency to be meddlesome and to denigrate whomever it had previously flattered. 'As soon as you're on that pedestal someone always wants to drag you off it,' he said. He'd always been given a goodly share of flak for his hair or his clothes. Now there was a harder edge to the criticism. 'Towards the end of the sixties the papers were interested in digging for dirt on me. They started pestering my friends and my family for some new scandal. They would dig and dig until they found something. I'd have to have been Superman to do all the stuff I was reported doing. There were times when I was said to be in six places at once with six different women.'

Best needed to grow up. Off the field the bad publicity about the breach of promise suit painted him blackly. On it he was getting agitated because Manchester United weren't winning. He had an awful, pit of the stomach belief that United were heading for a long and irreversible slump and he believed no one else cared about it. If Best was brought down, he began to over-protest, giving the impression that he deserved immunity from the inconvenience of being tackled. If a team-mate made a mistake, he was quicker to moan about it – and he expressed his displeasure loudly. If a game was going against United, his proclivity to retain posses-sion to the detriment of others became more pronounced than ever. He wouldn't pass, even if he saw someone in a decent position, because he assumed the attack would dissipate without him at its helm.

Best had rarely got into quarrels with referees before; now these were becoming regular occurrences. In early December United lost 2–1 against Manchester City at Maine Road in a League Cup semi-final because of a late penalty. Best was adamant Francis Lee had dived to con the referee, Jack Taylor. With Best continuing to grump and snipe about it as the teams left the field, Taylor refused to engage with him. To get his attention Best petulantly slapped the ball out of his hand. Taylor sent him off near the tunnel. For both demeaning the game and bringing it into disrepute the Football Association suspended Best for 28 days and fined him £100, which was like lifting a halfpenny from a rich man's pocket. The length of the ban was the true hardship, and it took into account who Best was – and what he'd become. The newspapers reproached him for failing to set a consistently shining example to the young and impressionable who idolised him. He was accused of becoming whiney and brattish and spoilt, far too headstrong for his own and United's well-being.

Without him United began to win, stoking a debate that hinged on three questions: Did the team need Best? Did the superstar make harmony on the pitch impossible? Would Wilf McGuinness be better off without him? McGuinness dismissed the arguments as ridiculous and the general criticism of Best as sensationalist. As soon as the suspension ended, McGuinness picked him for a fifth-round FA Cup tie at Northampton.

There is a photograph of a 17-year-old Best taken in United's boardroom in 1963. He is polishing the FA Cup, which United had won the previous May. He is already the dedicated follower of fashion; he wears a deep red cardigan with off-white stripes, brighter even than the ugly patterned wallpaper decorating the room. The trophy glistens, the light of the photographer's flash bulb reflecting off the point where its designer, Fattorini and Sons of Bradford, carved the words, THE FOOTBALL ASSOCIATION CHALLENGE CUP, across its silver belly three years before the Great War began. Best was handpicked for the picture. United wanted to prove it possessed players of the future capable of winning the Cup repeatedly. Best believed it was so.

The FA Cup mattered then. Heavy with romance, the final was every season's showpiece – a shared, longed-for day during which the commemoration and formal ceremonies of tradition were performed, as if each had quasi-religious significance. Best avidly followed the finals of the late 1950s and early 60s on television. First Aston Villa and then Bolton had beaten United; Wolves had given a comprehensive thumping to Blackburn, and Tottenham, captained by Danny Blanchflower, swept over Leicester City to claim the Double. On that Saturday night he and his friends congregated at the end of Burren Way and replayed the game among themselves. 'I always had to score the winning goal,' said Best. 'I wouldn't go home until I'd done it.'

Best was besotted with Wembley's pomp and rituals and the grandness of the Cup: the smartly uniformed marching band, the community singing from small white song sheets, the early notes of 'Abide With Me', the ribbon of red carpet, the new smart suits and the fresh kit each team wore. The Cup attracted those who watched football only once or twice a year. For a week beforehand, and during the celebrations afterwards, the teams were the centre of attention for those who had a ticket and the millions of others who would watch from an armchair. Best wanted a winners' medal. He wanted to wake up on Cup final morning and find the newspaper back pages' headlines had been written around him.

Regularly he saw himself at Wembley in a Cup final. In his daydream United led by two goals. There were fewer than 20 minutes left on the clock. What he used to describe next was a football fantasy, a fairytale in a plumed hat. He even referred to himself in the third person as he began to tell it.

'George Best will produce the greatest show of individual talent ever seen on a football field. As the Manchester United thousands are singing their songs of praise victory seems inevitable. The Cup is going back to Manchester. . . It is time to show off.'

Showing off to Best means trapping a high-flying, 75-yard goalkeeper's kick against the turf with his bum cheeks. 'Imagine the roar that rends the air at this spectacular show of virtuosity. The rank impudence of a player so much in control,' he says. Best sees himself laying off a pass. He hears Denis Law admonishing him. 'Stop taking the mickey,' Law warns, wagging a finger, too. Best ignores him. 'This is Wembley . . . the Queen is here . . . and the television cameras . . . and millions of people are watching the match in their own front parlours. I sweep past the left flank of the opposing defence bouncing the ball on my thighs and never let it touch the ground.' In the closing minutes United are given a penalty, which he takes. Best puts himself in the mind of every spectator, each of whom he says will think: What will 'the showman' do this time – back heel it in? The answer comes in a shouted boast to the goalkeeper: 'It's going in off the crossbar.' And, of course, it does. Even this outrageous act isn't enough for Best. He still hasn't finished. A centre arrows across the face of the goal. Only Best can reach it. 'It's mine and it's at headable height,' he insists. But he does not head it. 'Denying all known laws of balance and past practice I fly into a headstand and volley the ball into the foot of the net with my feet.' Best insisted these tricks were possible. 'I have done them all in training,' he said.

The Cup galvanised him. He longed to send his parents tickets to watch the final. Their seats would be close to the royal box. Every season he wasn't able to do it was like a broken promise.

Best lost in the semi-final in 1964. West Ham beat an overtired United 3–1 on a Hillsborough pitch so sticky and churned after pouring rain that Best could almost feel himself being sucked beneath it. He was only 17 then, and defeat didn't scar the heart as much as others would do later on. Best thought there'd be other, better chances awaiting him. He was a loser again in 1965. After one spitefully competitive but goalless game against Leeds – on another impossibly boggy surface at Hillsborough – United succumbed 1–0 in the replay at Nottingham Forest's City Ground. Again Best consoled himself with thoughts of another, more prosperous day ahead. Already Matt Busby had won two FA Cups and also reached another two finals. Surely, said Best, Busby would claim his hat-trick eventually? But a third chance came and went in 1966. Best missed the semi-final against Everton at Burnden Park because of his damaged cartilage, which required surgery. Without him United went down 1–0, and Best saw Everton win the Cup on a minuscule portable television that nursing staff wheeled into his private room on a trolley following his operation. 'It increased my ambition to win it,' he said. By now Best should have known that, however much he cherished the Cup, the competition would do him few favours.

He continued to travel hopefully, convinced that 1970 would be different. Nowhere in the First Division's Championship race, and without Europe to stimulate them, United concentrated on Wembley. It was important to Best to sustain his interest in this flagging season. And it was more important to McGuinness, for whom the Cup represented protection against critics – both within the club and outside it – who were still mockingly sceptical about his credentials.

Northampton were stuck in the Fourth Division after falling from the First, and then through the rest of the League, in successive seasons. The town succumbed to that condition known as Cup fever. Houses were draped in maroon bunting. Flags were hung from windows. Shop fronts were decorated with colour photographs of the home team and cardboard cut-outs of the Cup. A local butcher gave the players T-bone steaks. Admission prices were doubled – from £1 to £2 – in the knowledge no one would refuse to pay or think the charges hellishly exorbitant. Northampton shared the County Ground with Northamptonshire Cricket Club. It was one of only two three-sided grounds in the Football League. An extra stand had to be built for the tie, which Northampton harboured aspirations of winning because the conditions seemed ideal for an upset. The pitch looked as if a farmer had driven his ploughing tractor from box to box to churn it up in preparation for crop-sowing. The rutted soil was sprinkled with bucketfuls of sand in a token effort to fill in the ruts and smooth them. What grass remained was scrubby and pale after late January and early February frosts. This was a surface for shire horses. There was also a forceful wind, bending the flags at each corner and on the half-way line, which assisted the long ball Northampton relied on, as if firing mortar at an enemy.

Best would look back on the match as 'one positive, definite, absolute highlight of my career'. For, as he calmly added, 'the goals just kept on coming'. He said the six he scored – in an 8–2 win – were his way of 'taking out my anger' against the doubters and the FA.

Best had worked so tirelessly to prepare that he collapsed with exhaustion during training and also insisted he always knew 'something special' was going to happen for him that afternoon. The boast was made well afterwards and didn't reflect the truth. As he waited to go out he agonised about what awaited him, fearful that if something went terribly wrong – if United allowed an inferior side to beat them – he'd be held responsible for it. He imagined all sorts of condemnatory headlines. In the cramped dressing room Best sat with his back propped against white-washed walls and listened to the stomp of feet on the wooden floor of the main stand above him. In the corridors outside were mail-sacks, heaped up and firmly tied with coarse string to stop them from bursting. They bulged with letters for him. These had been sent 'Care of the County Ground', each writer unaware whether Best would even play when the letter was posted. Northampton didn't know either. His name wasn't printed in the programme's team line-ups.

The YouTube clips of what he did are still constantly replayed. His first goal was scored in the 27th minute and his last in the 87th. The opening one is a straightforward back-post header. He rises, like a bird startled by the sound of gunshot, to meet it. His second came after a drilled, 30-yard pass, which he takes with the lightest of touches and plants in the far corner. The hat-trick comes in the second half, a shot buried into the roof of the netting on the rebound after the original shot ricochets off a defender's knees. Best betrays no emotion. To look at the emptiness of his expression it's as if he's derived no pleasure from scoring; for what he set out to do has already been accomplished. It's the same with his fourth goal – a glancing header – and also the fifth, slid in after outpacing his markers. He smiles enigmatically. There is no need to make an elaborate song and dance about it. He remembered the quietness of the County Ground as his goals went in. 'I get a tremendous kick out of the sound of silence – the stunned silence that hits the home supporters,' he said. The keeper is Kim Book, brother of Manchester City's captain Tony. The gem in the bag of Best's half-dozen is the sixth. Anyone who views it can only feel an awful pity for Book. Best only needs to dart around one tackle before he and Book are one-on-one. Best avoids the challenge effortlessly, like slipping through a door that is ajar. He knows how to exploit the chance. He's aware of the space and the time he possesses. He's aware of the position of every other defender in close proximity. He's aware of what needs to be done. Book is compelled to come and meet him. This is an uneven duel and he loses it badly, embarrassingly. You can hear the whirring of Book's mind. Where will he go? How will he beat me? Best wriggles and shapes to play the ball with his right foot before dipping on to his left. Fractionally before Best does so, Book commits himself. He goes to his own left – making the wrong choice – and his knees shake and then slowly collapse beneath him, as though the joints have been removed. Best is walking the ball into the net now and Book – like Benfica's Henrique in the European Cup final – is on the ground looking up at him, as if begging for help in getting up again. Best, after ramming in his shot, leans against the left post, almost hugging it because he is out of breath. His lack of match fitness has caught up with him. The right sleeve of his shirt and his white shorts are smothered in mud.

The next morning's banner headlines are the easiest to write because cliché can be legitimately fastened to hard fact to create them:

SIX OF THE BEST

There were no more grandstanding performances that season; George Best contributed only cameos. His form was fitful, his spirit flagged.

Manchester United won only three games after beating Northampton, including the FA Cup quarter-final against Middlesbrough. With each defeat or draw Best, crestfallen, thought about the recent past, which now seemed so distant to him, and a Manchester United team at its zenith for whom winning had seemingly come with minimum effort.

Everything was becoming a strain and a slog. The current side wasn't good enough. The current manager wasn't capable of moulding a new one.

Best began to think Wilf McGuinness had him under surveillance. He watched him like Orwell's Big Brother watched Winston Smith. 'My biggest worry was his determination to keep an eye on me,' he said. 'Probably because I was single and my reputation with the girlies wasn't designed to give a football manager an easy night's sleep. Whenever we went away from home he seemed to spend every moment of the day trying to anticipate my next move. I don't know why he bothered.' Best felt fenced in, which gave him the urge to break out and be more rebellious than he otherwise would have been, irrespective of the damage caused. He embarrassed McGuinness – and himself – before the Cup semi-final against Leeds. In doing so he didn't give a hoot for the authority of his boss.

United and Leeds had already taken chunks out of one another in a goalless tie at Hillsborough. On the day of the replay at Villa Park, Best mooched around the hotel near Birmingham. He tried playing cards and grew tired of it. He attempted to watch television and became irritated by it. 'I was bored,' he said, as if to excuse what happened next. His roving eye alighted on a married woman – 'chic, self-possessed' and with 'exquisite legs', he said. She was reading John Le Carré's espionage novel *A Small Town in Germany*, pretending not to notice or acknowledge Best. When the two of them passed on the stairs, however, Best said hello and she asked him to autograph a photograph, which was conveniently in her room. Best agreed to visit her after his pre-match meal. He tried not to rush his food, fearing that McGuinness would suspect an ulterior motive. 'It took me all my time to stay at the table,' said Best. 'I had one thing on my mind.' McGuinness was much smarter than Best imagined. 'I didn't have to be Hercule Poirot for my little grey cells to start buzzing,' he said of the charade.

McGuinness was soon standing outside the woman's door. With him was the hotel porter, clutching the master key. 'I've never seen him so angry,' said Best. The manager immediately ordered Best to his own room. 'I was fuming, absolutely blazing . . . he had taken me for a fool and not opened the door,' said McGuinness. Expecting a public lecture, Best saw McGuinness vanish down the stairs and into the bar instead. He leaned over the banister and heard him order a whisky. 'He was sweating,' said Best, due to board the team bus in an hour. 'I did an about turn and went back into the woman's room and stayed there. I clambered into bed and made love to her. When I had finished I said: "Excuse me, I have to go now and play in the semi-final."'

Best was always astonished that Muhammad Ali, for example, refused to have sex for six weeks before going into the ring. 'I don't believe the nonsense that making love before an event affects your performance on the pitch,' he said. There is no telling evidence – either physiological or psychological – to suggest sex before competition is bad. Some sports medicine studies say it can be beneficial to sportsmen because it stimulates the production of testosterone, which enhances aggression. Had Best's display against Leeds been exemplary, his dalliance in advance of it wouldn't have mattered and medical science could have used him as a positive textbook example. But he was abysmal. 'I played like a wanker,' was his honest assessment. He fluffed his one, glorious chance to take United to Wembley and send his parents those Cup final seats. When, late on, Best got clear he tried to walk the ball into the net on a quagmire pitch. The ball got stuck in the mud and Best fell over it, face-first. 'I lay there wishing the ground would open up and bury me,' he said. The tie again finished goalless, and Leeds won the second replay 1–0.

Nor was this an isolated incident. In London Best met a woman outside a restaurant. He booked her into the team hotel and left his own room to go to hers. Almost sprinting along the corridor he found

McGuinness looking out of a window near the lifts. 'I almost walked into him,' said Best, who made a U-turn and padded softly back to his own bed, expecting the coast to be clear shortly. Ten minutes passed. As Best tentatively peered down the same corridor, trying to avoid being spotted, he saw McGuinness hadn't moved. He was still there an hour later. 'He virtually patrolled up and down outside my door for the rest of the night,' said Best, continually ringing his date to promise a rendez-vous that couldn't take place. He finally got into the woman's room at breakfast. By then, she'd lost all interest in sleeping with him.

On each of these occasions Best made the trek to Sir Matt Busby's office to explain himself. 'I was spending more time in there than him,' he said. Busby had once allowed Best to bring a woman, who he'd only just met, to travel with the team. United had just won the 1967 Championship; Busby was so happy that Best could probably have brought a burlesque chorus with him. Now the two of them spoke about sex without using the word. Euphemisms were traded instead.

Where Best was concerned Busby subscribed to one of football's great truisms: 'Players are as fallible and as vulnerable as the rest of us . . . footballers are ordinary mortals with ordinary mortals' weak-nesses,' he said, driving himself mad trying to correct Best's. 'He talked quietly to me,' said Best. 'He screamed at me. He suspended me. He fined me. He put an arm around me. He did everything humanly possible.' Busby still couldn't exert any lasting control over Best. 'I can't live with him twenty-four hours a day,' he'd say, shrug-ging his shoulders in half-surrender because his chivvying and chas-tisement had failed.

Managers have to be cold-hearted when it is necessary. In the past Busby had been. Other individuals, whom he perceived as militant or in breach of discipline, were smited. Foremost among them was Johnny Morris. As far back as 1949 he sold Morris, a crowd favourite at inside-right, for a then world record fee of £25,000 to Derby. Morris, at 24, was the youngest of United's '48 FA Cup winners. He challenged Busby over wages and bonuses and also tactics. At the Cliff, Busby proposed practising with five men in the defensive wall from a free-kick; United had leaked a goal after using only four the previous Saturday. Morris deliberately antagonised him by insisting the addition of another player wouldn't make any difference. Sensitive to attacks on his authority Busby made the error of inviting Morris to support his theory with practical proof. Morris took inordinate pleasure in smashing the ball into the top corner of the net. Busby and Morris were soon at loggerheads again. When Morris failed to regain his place after injury, he began to train half-heartedly. Busby confronted him publicly on the training pitch, and Morris walked off, unresponsive to a warning that he'd never kick another ball at Old Trafford if he crossed the touchline. 'He had to go,' said Busby; and go he did.

There were two crucial differences between Morris and Best. Firstly, Morris was expendable. Busby knew United would still prosper without him. Best was irreplaceable. The thought of selling him to a rival was inconceivable to Busby. Secondly, Busby had never found any common ground with Morris: 'I've tried every angle. I've bullied. I've used flattery . . . I just can't get through [to him],' he said. Best was different. He inspired genuine, paternal love from Busby, who referred to 'the boy underneath the man' to emphasise how impressionable Best remained. 'Fathers everywhere know that lads let down dads,' he said of Best's waywardness. 'A man does not give up on sons who love him as he loves them.' Fathers still don't always understand sons. Best admitted that Busby 'could not relate' to his fame or his clothes or his lifestyle and 'could not come up with the right advice'. But his special relationship with Busby, as much as his unchallengeable status in the team, meant he was allowed more leeway and leniency than anyone else. He was forgiven, excused and appeased. All along Busby hoped Best would experience an epiphany and mend his ways. Which is why he did something as a man that he would never have done as a manager. In dealing with Best, he stuck to tactics that were unsuccessful.

10

The Glass Menagerie

Everyone wants a home of their own eventually. So did George Best. He couldn't go on indefinitely being the superstar in the spare bedroom of Mary Fullaway's terraced house, a Jaguar parked outside the front gate. And Sir Matt Busby tacitly acknowledged he couldn't, like an over-protective parent, continue to dictate where someone lived.

Others who had dominated the cultural whirl and swirl of the 1960s and become its idols had bought themselves mansions. John Lennon was swapping Kenwood – his 22-room home in Surrey – for the 72-acre Georgian manor house Tittenhurst Park near Ascot. Mick Jagger owned Stargroves, a Georgian manor house with towers and turrets and a drive that seemed to stretch further than a motorway. Even Bobby Moore was living in a Georgian-style house with a bar and a staircase, which his wife, Tina, said was 'like something out of *Gone With The Wind*.'

The pop stars had butlers to fetch and carry and chefs to make them exotic dishes. Best still had Mrs Fullaway, who served potato pies, spaghetti Bolognese and cooked him his favourite meal, Steak Diane. In Aycliffe Avenue Best's bedroom was smaller than Lennon's or Jagger's walk-in wardrobes. He slept in a single bed under cotton rather than silk sheets and covered them in a fluffy canary-yellow eiderdown. He watched television in the lounge – he'd bought Mrs Fullaway a colour set – and listened to records on the radiogram. Sitting on the sofa, he'd create abstract hobby-craft pictures in rectangular wooden frames. Mrs Fullaway continued to spoil him. 'What's that Mrs F?' he'd say. 'You're asking whether I'd like a cup of tea?' And off she'd go in her pinafore to boil the kettle. Best never took Mrs Fullaway or her hospitality for granted and he treated her and Aycliffe Avenue with a gentlemanly respect. He never swore in front of Mrs Fullaway. Nor did he invite a guest to the house without asking her permission.

Although Aycliffe Avenue was nominally his base – he kept his clothes, his money and the rest of his belongings there – Best roamed. His living arrangements became chaotic because he preferred the peripatetic exist-ence of a gypsy. As his close friend, the journalist Michael Parkinson, said: 'He slept in more beds than a travelling salesman.' He would book into a city centre hotel after a night out or he would bunk down where he could.

Life in Chorlton-cum-Hardy was also becoming difficult because everyone – especially the press – knew where to find him. And, since Aycliffe Avenue was a cul-de-sac, Mrs Fullaway's could be put under siege by fans and photographers and a fevered media. The front-room curtains had to be drawn. The phone had to be taken off the hook. Knocks at the door had to be ignored – unless a pre-booked appoint-ment was made. The simplest of strategies smuggled Best out of the house. Steve Fullaway was the same build and height. He would order two taxis to turn up five or ten minutes apart from one another. When the first arrived, he would pull the hood of a dark duffel coat over his bowed head and dart into the passenger seat pretending to be Best. 'I hoped at least some of the waiting journalists would follow me so George could get out,' he said.

Finally, for everyone else's sake as much as his own, Best decided to move. Leaving Aycliffe Avenue was a wrench. It was like saying goodbye to Burren Way all over again. Mrs Fullaway waved him off just as his mother had once done. Best once said of Busby that 'he would be honest with you' and then assume that 'you would offer him the courtesy of being honest' in return. But to side-step the pesky Clause Five in his contract, Best fibbed to him. He said his parents would be living with him 'eventually'. The time-scale was unspecific. Best pretended he was telling the truth. Busby pretended to believe him. The hollow compromise avoided a conversation that neither would have relished. Best adored both his father and mother. But he was like any other son in his early 20s, who had long-ago flown the family nest and knew he would never go back there again permanently. He wanted to retain his independence. He didn't want to be under anyone's watchful eye. Telling your parents early on Saturday night that you might not be back until Sunday afternoon would have been too inhibiting for him. And what could he possibly have said to his mother about the women who would arrive, stay awhile and then depart never to be seen again? Sex was another addiction for Best. The more he had, the more he wanted. Looks were important but not essential in a bed-mate for him. 'Some of the greatest girls don't look like models, you know,' he said. But, with his parents in the bedroom across the hall, how could he have maintained his reputation as a Romeo at all? Busby consoled himself with the thought that home ownership could be the making of him. He had no inkling of the sort of house Best had in mind.

The architect Frazer Crane designed The Village, a development in central Manchester comprising 12,000 square feet and made up mostly of semi-derelict warehouses which were beautified and billed as the North's version of London's Carnaby Street. A main attraction of The Village was Edwardia, which Best launched as his second men's boutique – his name alongside the shop's title, which was emblazoned in shaded capitals.

Originally Best had seen himself settling snugly into a renovated country house or a stone cottage where roses bloomed around the door. There were three imperatives for him: privacy, a snooker table and a sunken bath. Crane persuaded him that a modern man needed a modern house – something innovative, custom-built, state-of-the-art and statement-making. Best was seduced by the thought of Crane's expansive vision, forgetting instantly the olde worlde charm and rusticism of thatch and beams and pastoral living. He decided the architect was right. A futuristic house would better fit his image as the playboy parvenu and confirm him as someone who set trends rather than followed them. Best bought half an acre of land in Bramhall, Cheshire. An 18th-century cottage called Wren's Nest had once stood on the site and its former grounds provided him with an established apple orchard and a panoramic view of the distant, brown-green roll of the Pennines. During the year it took to build the house Best admitted: 'I've spent a lot of time trying to understand the plans.' What Crane created – a split-level, flat-roofed, Scandinavian-influenced construction in brick, tile and glass – became the most gossiped about house in Britain during the second half of 1970, after Best moved in. At the beginning of 1971. *House and Garden* magazine featured it beneath the headline 'MR BEST BUILDS HIS DREAM HOUSE' and called it 'probably as compact and spectacular a bachelor's home as any in Europe'. Even *The Times* dispatched a reporter there and covered half a broadsheet page with its article. This was particularly noteworthy because *The Times* then was very much the toffs' newspaper of record – its front page had carried nothing but advertisements until as late as May 1966 – and it generally eschewed 'celebrity' coverage, as though doing so counted as a vulgar lowering of standards. The tone adopted in the report about Best's house sounds snooty, as though no one knew whether an upper-crust readership would be fascinated and mildly amused at the sight of the place or dismiss it as appallingly common. 'What happens,' the piece asked, 'when a 23-year-old footballer decides to commission a firm of architects to design his first house?'

What did happen was this. For approximately £36,000 – more than seven times the national average price of property – Best got two bedrooms, a 1,050 square foot L-shaped lounge with 40 foot-long windows made from tinted, one-way Belgian glass set into German frames, an enormous games room, a functional galley kitchen, a bar with beer on tap and a wine cellar, a staircase made of stainless steel and Sicilian marble and under-floor heating throughout. Electronic wizardry galore was installed. Everything was push-buttoned and remote-controlled. An ultrasonic beam dropped the colour television dramatically from a false chimney breast of white ceramic tiles. The swish of every curtain and the operation of both radio and hi-fi were governed by a flick of a switch, too. So was the opening and closing of his front door and the two-car garage. All this was a wondrous tomorrow's world to ordinary working families, many of whom didn't have their own telephone, regarded the dishwasher as space age and longed for a colour TV.

In a line of riddling speech that today would guarantee him a paragraph in *Private Eye*'s Pseuds Corner, Crane said he sought to 'interpret [Best's] performance in the design of the house'. Whatever that piece of pretention actually meant, the new homeowner made sure no one walking into the house would have known he was a footballer. Nothing in it indicated his profession. Best wanted no trace of it to be seen. There were no action photos, no framed shirts, no trophies. At Aycliffe Avenue Mrs Fullaway, worried about burglars, had put his medals into a black plastic bin bag and hidden it under the bed. Best decided to send everything back to his parents and he bought his mother a square display cabinet to store them in. Bright, fat red roses with emerald stems were painted on to the glass. 'I had this house built to make sure I had somewhere to get away from football,' said Best. 'I was determined to have absolutely nothing even remotely to do with the game inside it.' The interior was sparse. The rooms looked as though Hopper or

Hammershoi had painted them to reflect quietude and introspection. Best was sold on the ideal of simplicity, lack of clutter and a subdued tonal range of colour. Minimalism was the key. He chose square-shaped, black-hide sofas and chairs and tobacco-coloured Axminster carpets. 'I wanted lots of white walls and rich plain colours such as burgundy, deep green, midnight blue,' he explained. 'I can't stand vivid colours like lime greens, pinks, violets. When I get home I want somewhere restful and soothing. My life is frantic and noisy and I want a home which is a complete contrast.'

Best didn't usually flaunt his wealth or gloat about it. But he had come a long way from a council house on the Cregagh Estate to this. He'd grown up in an area where to own your own home was an unaffordable fantasy. Very few of the men who went to the shipyard every day could have scraped together enough for a deposit on a house without two lifetimes-worth of assiduous saving. As he looked around his living room, and gazed through a wide window into the far and middle distance, he thought about that fact and felt a swell of pride and satisfaction. It was a tangible sign of high achievement. The house told everyone he was a success. Best really believed he was starting afresh and putting the upsets of the recent past behind him. The house would help him handle the pressures of playing football because he could isolate himself from them and relax. He was going to learn to ride a horse. He was going to buy himself a dog. He was going to write an autobiography that he said would 'put the fear of God into people'. He was going to spend 'a lot of time alone'. Best said he thought of the house as his hermitic 'refuge', his 'castle' and his 'palace' and added: 'It is going to mean a whole new way of life for me. I won't have to keep going out because I'm going to have somewhere to stay in.'

There was soon trouble in his shut-away paradise. The first problem was the sunken bath. It was big enough – eight feet by six feet – to accommodate United's first team and one or two of the opposition.

But the water pressure was so low that it took more than two hours to fill. Occasionally the taps would start to run without Best touching them, stopping only when an inch and a half of water covered the Italian mosaic tiles. He began to receive small electronic shocks from the door handles because some of the carpets were nylon based. The snooker table was too long for the games room. The standard cue couldn't be used from the baulk end. There was a discrepancy between the ambition of the house's high-powered gadgetry and the reliability of the technology. The electronics sometimes went haywire. What could go wrong did go wrong. In a frantic few hours, which felt as if he was at the centre of an enormous practical joke, Best found the garage door opening and closing repeatedly, like a giant mouth, the lamps and lights constantly flickering on and off and the TV vanishing up and down the chimney. 'It was mad,' he said. Whenever an aeroplane passed low overhead, the signal from its radar threatened to scramble the electronics in the whole house.

Best was so houseproud that he'd willingly show off the property to whichever newspaper or TV station asked to see it. He gave them the grand tour. He posed outdoors standing on the concrete raised platform overlooking his ornamental fishpond. He posed indoors slumped comfortably across his sofa and sliding a slice of bread into the toaster in the kitchen. He allowed the *News of the World* to stage a tacky competition for readers to name the house. The winning entry was Che Sera, which encapsulated Best's entire approach to life.

Best assumed he would be left alone now. But all the publicity, which he had sought, stoked an insane amount of interest. The public didn't only want to read about Che Sera, they also wanted to see it for themselves. There were no gates, walls or fences to protect him from those who were rude enough to trespass. Within a few weeks of moving in, he wanted to move out again. Aycliffe Avenue had given him more privacy than Che Sera.

Even before it was built, Best likened himself to 'some sort of specimen in a glass case'. Once inside it, that is exactly what he became. He was like a zoo animal and people arrived, singularly or in groups, to see him. They tramped across his garden and climbed the veranda stairs, as if Che Sera was a National Trust property, and stood over the fish-pond. Some stole the fish, taking the larger ones away in pet shop tanks and the tiddlers in jam jars. 'I started off with a couple of hundred and ended up with three or four,' he said. The more brazen souls cut up pieces of his lawn or walked directly up to his windows and tried to peer straight in, leaving fingerprints and breath marks on the glass. In one photograph a woman in a headscarf, wearing a long beige mack-intosh and sensible, stubby-heeled shoes, does exactly this. She couldn't see Best – but Best could see her and others who were lingering impa-tiently in the background, waiting for their turn to gawp. The eyes of these voyeurs would widen, he'd remember, and their noses would be pressed flat against the window. Best could stand a few feet away, flicking two fingers at them or gurning his own face into a hideous expression. The one-way glass gave him complete anonymity. Weekends were the worst. Every Sunday a coach full of tourists would chug into view, blowing black exhaust fumes, and park close to the house. A few picnicked on Best's lawn, leaving greased paper and bottles strewn across the grass. 'I thought about setting up a stall selling cups of tea, sandwiches and hot dogs,' said Best, who learned to stay away from his home until nightfall. There were days when he needed a police escort to get into or out of his own road.

The architectural community christened Crane's design a 'masterpiece of modernism'. The public were far less flattering. The response was grunts of disgust. Crane's grand design was too far ahead of its time for them to appreciate it. Shiny white tiles were chosen for the exterior of the house, signifying the difference between contemporary materials and the red brick that built the Victorian homes of the North West when sooty factory chimneys made it an industrial and textile powerhouse. The verdict of the average housewife and her husband was damning. They thought the tiles made Che Sera look like a public toilet. As if to prove it, one local 'critic' allowed his dog to piss against them. The house was mocked as a 'Superloo' or 'George's Convenience'. 'Not only did I have to put up with all this,' said Best, 'I then had to read that the people who came insulted the place. Charming, wasn't it?'

Kings are notoriously touchy to criticism. But Best was attracting a disproportionate amount of it and provoking an exceptional level of vituperation. He was being observed, scrutinised and judged by everyone. But this was more than pedantic or pernickety criticism.

Best got unsigned letters in masculine handwriting that promised to 'bash your windows in'. Other warnings were more ominous. 'There were direct threats to blow the place up,' he said. 'I wonder what sort of mentality it takes to write a vicious letter and not have the courage to put a name to it. I've never really discovered what these cowards expect to get out of it. I mean, do they sit back and imagine me quivering with fear, or bursting into tears or something? I'd love to meet one of these blokes face to face so I could find out what makes him tick. That's if he could say anything at all after receiving a right-hander in the mouth.'

On the street Best had begun to encounter hostility and provocation that were so scabrous that only the presence of the green-eyed monster of jealousy could explain it. He received daggered, full-on stares of loathing from strangers, who tried to rile him. There were thrown-down gauntlets, challenging him to a punch-up. Wherever he went there was a risk of becoming embroiled in a brawl. 'It's almost impossible to relax,' said Best 'Everywhere you go it is glares or stares. The stares aren't so bad. But the glares, the hatred? Hell, what have I ever done to them?'

Best put it like this: 'I can go nowhere, do nothing without people staring, trying to pick fights. Men will come up and try to pick a fight because a friend of a friend has told them that I was looking at their wife in some club. They will jostle me in the bar and then accuse me of trying to cause trouble.' Others would openly challenge him about the standard of his performance for Manchester United. 'They wait for me to make a mistake on the pitch and then they start. My God, do they start. They tell me to do so many bloody things – shave off my beard, cut my hair – as if all that would make me into what they want me to be. Jesus Christ had a beard and long hair and they didn't want to change him. It's not that I have a persecution complex. Just that they all seem to pick on me . . . I'm so nervy now I even look over my shoulder to see if anyone is following me or watching me.' Some of the most yobbish and disgusting behaviour he encountered was from those who spat at his feet or tried to spit in his face. 'Even going out for a coffee became an ordeal,' he said.

He began to understand Sartre's definition of hell as being 'other people'. If the doorbell rang at Che Sera, he would peek through the curtains before deciding whether or not to answer it. If he needed shopping, he would send someone else to fetch it. If he was invited anywhere, he had to work out how to get there and back without being noticed or followed by journalists. He'd call a friendly policeman, who was prepared to escort him on to the road at a crawl and then allow Best to break the speed limit. The drivers behind him couldn't follow because the policeman in the patrol car, still travelling within the law, would have given them a ticket.

Best only went to places he regarded as secure, a spot where the landlord, the manager or the owner could find him a discreet niche in which to hide because encountering someone with a drink inside them meant things might get nasty.

Best began to feel claustrophobic and talked plaintively about the need to get away from what he summed up as: 'The pressure cooker in which I live, play, sleep and breathe.'

At least once a week he went back to Mrs Fullaway's for a meal, grateful to find Aycliffe Avenue exactly as he'd left it, as though he'd just slipped out for an hour. She and it were two of the stable elements in his life. 'He can come here whenever he wants,' Mrs Fullaway said when Best packed his bags. 'He knows he's welcome and there will be a cup of tea waiting for him.' Best had continued to rent his old room – at £30 per week – to repay his landlady for her loyalty and kindness and love. He wanted Mrs Fullaway to retire instead of taking on another boarder. 'You've done enough,' he said to her. 'It's time to put your feet up.' At her kitchen table, the irony of his situation struck Best. He was retreating to a safe harbour because the one he'd chosen for himself already felt threatening. Malcolm Wagner had tried to dissuade Best from building Che Sera. After buying a newly built town house in Salford for himself, he suggested Best should purchase the one beside it. 'We could have a connecting door,' he told him. 'You can have company when you want it and privacy when you don't.' Best suggested Wagner live with him instead.

He possessed all the luxuries and privileges a man could ever want: everything others most desired and envied. There was the adoration on the pitch and off it. There were the women, most of whom looked as if Best had handpicked them from the pages of *Vogue* or *Playboy*. There were the exclusive nightclubs and the bars. There were the sports cars. There were the clothes. There was money to pay in cash for whatever he wanted. Best was good at concealing his feelings. 'I can hide my emotions well,' he admitted. He could look and sound calmly nonchalant. So to the outsider, who knew Best only through television or newspapers, there was a relaxed looseness about him. He was the content sybarite.

The reality was different.

The boutiques, despite his branding, were in financial peril (he'd started up a third, called Rogue, after snipping the opening ribbon on

Edwardia). A decision about whether to sell up or invest more into the businesses to save them needed to be made; an enormous amount of capital was required to do so. Ken Stanley stepped in to unpick the mess and muddle of the accountancy, sorting out the debts accrued through disinterest and mismanagement. The shops were soon merged into another entrepreneurial group, which retained Best's name on the signage and his presence as a figurehead.

In a show of ostentation he swapped his Jaguar for a white Rolls-Royce. He'd wanted one ever since the Bee Gees had given him a chauffeured ride around Manchester in theirs. A Jag wasn't uncommon on the roads of the city. A white Roller was almost as rare as the sight of a camel on Deansgate. Best could go nowhere inconspicuously in the car. He sold it within three months, making a profit only because his name was in the logbook.

With indignation, he complained about his lack of privacy. 'Until I came along, the press weren't interested in what footballers did off the field,' he said. 'I was the first player to dominate the front pages as well as the back.' There was no disputing the accuracy of the statement. But Best didn't properly acknowledge his complicity in the arrangement. He had been a willing volunteer in glossing his image. He'd played to the gallery he was now trying to avoid. In one seemingly innocent example Best once claimed to a reporter that he'd briefly broken a holiday in Majorca – and would be flying back there that afternoon – specifically so Wagner could cut his hair in Manchester. 'I don't want anyone else to touch it,' he said. 'The sun makes it terribly hot when you have long hair.' Asked how much the haircut had cost him, Best replied: 'Including the airfare it's fifty-six pounds, twelve shillings and sixpence.' This was the summer of 1966. The economy was in such dire straits that the recently reelected Labour government was about to announce a six-month wage and price freeze. It is immaterial whether the reporter either knew Best was spinning an elaborate joke, but used the piece anyway, or didn't know and took what was said to him at face value. But in allowing it to go so far Best let the press assume that nothing was off-limits and he'd be impervious to – and uncaring about – whatever was written about him. Newspaper editors also quickly realised that sending a female reporter to his boutique gave them an excellent chance of getting something quotable out of him. Even if Best wasn't there, he could be tempted into the shop with a phone call from a friend that passed on these two connecting pieces of information:

A) Some reporter wanted to see him.

B) She was (as he put it himself) a 'bit of all right'.

On a slow newsday Best, like the patron saint of newspapers, was someone to whom journalists could always go for a decent or half-decent story. He couldn't keep them at bay now.

It was as if he was living on the run, staying out because the prospect of returning to the lonely captivity of Che Sera was too ghastly to contemplate. 'My life was going insane,' he said.

'A man can crack up in many ways,' wrote F. Scott Fitzgerald, whose own cracking up came after mortgaging himself physically and spiritually to the hilt. George Best did the same.

The symptoms he displayed, slowly at first and then much later in a rush, would be diagnosed today as clinical depression. There was a constant restlessness about him. He awoke early in the morning or in the middle of the night. He took no pleasure from things that had once had been his stimulus, including football. Anger and resentment began to surface. And there was use and abuse of alcohol, gradually developing into a dependency. Every case of depression is different; almost always there is no single cause to precipitate it, but rather an accumulation of events and issues, which are often rooted in change or loss. Best was mourning the 'death' of his once dominant team and immersed in failure and futility at Manchester United. 'Instead of revolving around me, the team now depended on me and I lacked the maturity to handle it,' he said. He had devoted himself to United; he couldn't pretend that the club's poor results didn't matter. 'We were getting worse,' said Best. 'It got so bad that I didn't want to wake up in the mornings . . . We were losing and I felt this terrible emptiness.' He'd been convinced the new house would change everything. He soon realised it was a folly, no place to build a life, and a symbol of the wider malaise affecting him. 'It was a disaster,' he said. 'I dreaded going home. I was a prisoner.'

Another worry – and a major one, too – were his parents. The strain he was experiencing seeped into their lives as well; especially his mother Ann's. 'That's the sad part,' he said of his difficulties. 'You get so many others involved.'

Dickie Best was his first football teacher. The father saw the son kick a ball and instantly understood there was something remarkable about how he did it. The photograph he took with a Kodak box camera in 1947 – Best, aged between 15 and 18 months, on the street outside his maternal grandparents' home – is not a routine family snap. You wouldn't turn the page in the album without stopping. One look would automatically lead to a second and then a third. The Best he would become is recognisable in the infant. He'd always say, 'What makes a great player is balance. You can't do anything without it.' The photograph shows he possessed it at birth. His head is studiously over the ball. His body is perfectly positioned, the ball under control near the kerbside. You can imagine him running along the concrete with it after the camera ran out of film. Dickie would urge him to practise and then practise again. He encouraged without being pushy or overbearing and didn't interfere. 'I could have scored five or six goals or I could have had a stinker,' said Best. 'He never said, "I thought you were brilliant" or "You had a stinker". He knew that I knew.'

Best was nonetheless his mother's child. And she idolised him. At

Old Trafford Ann proudly wore a red trouser suit with white piping, a United pin badge attached to the left lapel. When the Bests got their first phone, she insisted it was red, too.

'I was closer to her,' he admitted, adding he was 'more like her' in most respects as well. The relationship between them has been picked over and analysed microscopically more than any other in Best's life because, during the 1970s, her alcoholism ran concurrently with his own. Ann was teetotal until she was 44. Her first drink in 1967 – a Pimm's and lemonade – coincided with the period when Best's fame had begun to take wing.

Fame can be a terrible burden for those who experience it through association. Ann, a private woman, found herself thrust in front of the public against her will and wishes. It was just about manageable when the publicity was good. It was torture for her when it turned against Best. 'This was hitting her harder than I ever imagined it could,' he said. Her two elder daughters believe she was also going through the menopause; though seldom did her generation speak of women's health issues.

While Best knew his mother had started to drink, he was ignorant of its scale. 'I thought she was only having a glass of wine or two,' he said. Before the destructiveness of that drinking became apparent to him, Best even announced he wanted to buy a 'suitable public house' in the countryside, which his parents could run. A fish and chip shop, which he'd bought earlier for them, had been sold. To him the pub seemed a logical replacement for it. His opinion began to change during a party at Burren Way to celebrate his parents' silver wedding anniversary in June 1970. Best watched his mother leave the room at regular intervals to drink on her own, which she then denied doing despite becoming progressively tipsier. Drinkers are experts in fiction, fooling themselves as much as trying to fool everyone else about how much is being drunk and how often, and attempting to

disguise the effects. Best still didn't entirely recognise the early, calamitous signs of his mother's condition any more than he recognised
them in himself. And only in the coming year – as he moved into
Che Sera and began to take stock – did he make the connection
between what was happening to him and what was happening to her.
'My mother had become ill from the drink, which I felt I was the
cause of, really,' he said.

Inquisitiveness about him became borderline harassment and then
blatant intrusion for Ann. She encountered critics of her son in shops,
at bus stops and in bars, who had a particularly caustic, viperish side
to them. She received a catalogue of his alleged deficiencies in a cloak-
room where a woman told her, 'I think he's a disgrace to Ireland' before
continuing her tirade. After half a minute of listening to it, Ann unchar-
acteristically slapped the complainant across the mouth. In a pub one
man spoke continually to her of his dislike of 'big-headed Best' and
left without ever knowing she was his mother. 'I'd learned to bite my
tongue,' she said, referring to the earlier incident. If a stranger enquired
whether she was 'George Best's mum', Best said she always wanted to
deny it. The Bests made no attempt to capitalise on or exploit his name,
declined to ask for money from him – 'they always felt they were
begging, which was ridiculous', said Best – and tended not to mention
any disturbance in their own lives. Only by reading about it in a newspaper did Best find out of his father's part in a seven-week unofficial
strike, which reduced the family's income. 'Why didn't you tell me?'
he asked. 'We didn't want to bother you,' said his father. Purely through
obligation Ann took part in a television advertisement in which Best
promoted sausages. It was mocked up in a kitchen almost as big as the
entire square-footage of Burren Way's ground floor. He had the only
speaking part, an unimaginative six-word slogan that played on his
surname to extol the virtues of the product. Ann found it excruciating
to appear in front of the cameras. Every forced smile for every tedious

take – and there were more than a dozen of them – made her long for the wretched thing to end.

She never sought – nor liked answering – questions from lone news reporters, who arrived unannounced, or entire packs of pressmen, who left imprints of their shoes on the front lawn. Just half a dozen average strides carried you from the gate to the doorstep of the house. Frequently she had to negotiate her way along the path through a tangle of uninvited visitors. When stories about Best were unfavourable, bringing another unsavoury headline, she drew the venetian blinds during the day, and ignored a thump on the window, the rattle of the letterbox and appeals for a comment. When he went home, the family sometimes found out about it first from journalists who, tipped off about his boarding of a Belfast flight, rang to enquire whether he had arrived. When he did, the house was besieged. 'Our door was swarming,' she'd say. Dickie rode the requests for quotes from journalists. She had hated dealing with them and once, able to take no more of the pestering, she rebuked a reporter on her doorstep; sadly, she'd been drinking before she did it. He'd knocked repeatedly, refusing to give up until she came out. When she did, her 'no comment' was a blast of invective. 'You're nothing but a drunk and everyone knows it,' said the reporter. 'What's more, without people like me, George wouldn't be where he is today.' The laughable idea that journalism was responsible for her son's career pushed her into a counter-statement. 'Without people like George, you wouldn't be in a job,' she replied.

For every good story written about him Best calculated that there were twice as many to break his mother's heart. He tried to persuade her not to read them; or, if she did, not to believe what was being said. 'I know it was hurting her, killing her,' he explained. Best flinched whenever he remembered how she'd questioned her mothering skills, as if these had been deficient, before defending him. 'I sometimes think I could have advised George a bit more at times,' she said. 'I don't know if it would have made any difference. We are what we are. I wonder if the average fellow would have behaved any differently given George's money and opportunities.' Ann thought what he needed was a wife. 'I'm sure that's the basis for most of his troubles,' she added. 'He has the fancy girlfriends. I'm not talking about them. I'm talking about an ordinary girl with her feet on the ground, who would cook for him and care for him.'

She wanted a wife to be a friend to him, too – someone to whom he could 'open his heart' she said. The mother was then able to identify the one problem that made all the others so hard to solve. 'He finds it terribly hard to confide in people.'

George Best would look back on his Che Sera period and describe himself as a 'lonely, mixed-up Irishman who couldn't come to terms with what he wanted from life'. He added: 'I was fed up with everything – and everyone – around me.'

Both personally and professionally he had reached a turning point. The problem was he didn't know how to turn. 'I used to think that playing football was like having a birthday every Saturday,' said Best. The teenager who had lain awake every Friday night planning how he would play the following afternoon was nearing his 25th birthday. 'And I wasn't thinking of the matches at all,' he explained. Ken Stanley suggested he should try to live quietly and ration his socialising. 'I don't want to. I don't want to be like everyone else,' Best said to him. So a pattern was firmly established. The drink. The late nights that turned into early mornings. Mishaps and slip-ups and rotten publicity. Best convinced himself he could handle whatever he drank without jeopardising his health or his career. 'Instead of having six or seven drinks, I'd have ten drinks and then a dozen drinks,' he admitted. Almost every difficulty he encountered radiated, like spokes in a wheel hub, from the central problem of that drinking. No amount of sane persuasion could get him to stop. Best, nearing his tipping point, began to walk the extra mile in imbecility.

Punctuality had become a bone of contention. He started to regard an appointed time as a matter of negotiation and didn't discriminate. Everyone was kept waiting. He was late for meetings and commercial work and he became crotchety about them. 'I get myself into a heck of state,' said Best. 'I'm not sure where I'm supposed to be at any given time.' David Stanley had to make strenuous efforts to locate Best, who dodged telephone calls and wouldn't answer the door. Sometimes Stanley had to scurry across Manchester to find him.

The beard became thicker and the excuse Best gave for growing it was 'laziness'. He said he didn't want to shave twice a day. The facial hair was actually a mask, hiding mild marks and stains on the skin that the alcohol was now causing. One Manchester United director asked Busby: 'When are you going to get him to shave off his beard?' Giving him a dismissive, sideways look, Busby, guessing the real reason why Best had grown it, said: 'If you can guarantee to me that if he takes off his beard he will be a better player then he will have it taken off tomorrow.'

If only Best had been able to talk about his drinking and the reasons for it. If only he hadn't recoiled from discussing his emotions. He said he didn't 'really need other people all that much' and didn't have to 'lean on them emotionally'. Each of those claims was an attempt to explain away and partly validate this one: 'I tend to keep my thoughts and worries locked up.' More revealing was another admission: 'I don't find it easy to get really close to people. Or maybe I should say I don't find it easy to let them get close to me. In fact, when I'm getting involved it makes me uneasy.'

Mike Summerbee thought his friend was a lonely type of person, and Best offered confirmation of it, admitting he was a 'bit lonely' even as a child. 'I've never called on anyone and asked for advice, which I suppose is a sad thing to say. I always figured I could sort myself out without bothering anyone else,' he said. 'I would far rather sit on my own and be depressed than talk to somebody.' He liked his own company for the silence it brought. 'To me there's nothing worse than somebody who thinks they've got to talk two to three hours at a time . . .' Sometimes he would just disappear for a few hours or an entire evening. 'I'd go to places where I was known quite well,' he said. Within 15 minutes, added Best, someone would still ask him: 'What are you doing on your own?' It left him with a dilemma. 'I can't turn around and say I want to be on my own,' he explained, 'because right away you're ignorant, you're rude and anti-social [and] you don't want to talk to people. I end up with them giving me their problems. As soon as that one goes another comes in.'

The prospect of being exploited made him wary of forging relationships. Scepticism became a necessary default setting. He would search a face and try to interpret the motives lurking behind the eyes. He'd be asked to invest in or to endorse something. Or he'd be invited to a function, the purpose and success of which would be solely dependent on his presence. On being introduced to someone new Best used to ask himself two questions: Has this person got anything to gain from being in my company? Is it you they want as a person or you as a personality? He wasn't always good at sifting out the specious or superficial. In the end he conceded, gloomily, that it was a chore to decide who wanted to get to know him for self-gain. 'I will never be able to tell those who want me because of myself or those who want me as a footballer.' With complexity nevertheless comes contradiction. Best still found it difficult to shake his head and say no to anyone. He wanted to please. So displacement was rife. He was always putting things off. Asked to make a personal appearance, he would reply with an instant 'yes' because acceptance caused him less hassle than a refusal at the time he made it. It meant he wouldn't have to listen to five minutes or more of compassionate pleading or hear a drawn-out explanation of *why* a particular event needed him. In giving his answer Best sounded so sincere that whoever requested his presence would go away convinced an unbreakable deal had just been done. Posters would be printed, tickets sold, advertising space booked. As Best's friend Malcolm Mooney once said of him: 'He told lies beautifully.' He owned up to regularly saying one thing when he meant the other. 'Sometimes I would agree to go to three things held at the same time in different parts of the country,' said Best, who usually ended up attending none of them – and telling no one in advance – before offering excuses that everyone knew were lies. Many of his conversations began with an apology because of it. In this way problems – such as those at United – were allowed to fester because he had a propensity to retreat from them. His defence mechanism was always denial and a crass expectation that ignoring a situation would make it go away. He did it knowing full well what the outcome would be.

'I would sit down, have a couple of drinks and they'd disappear for a bit. The next day it was ten times worse,' he said.

PART THREE

No One Knows How it Feels to Be Me

11

Searching for the
Orange Balloon

With hindsight comes wisdom. As soon as he knew Sir Matt Busby was retiring, George Best should have plotted a different course for himself. Instead of building Che Sera and staying at Manchester United, he ought to have gone abroad. He accepted as much, finally concluding: 'It might have been a good thing just to go out of the country for a few years and play somewhere else.' Best subsequently went further. He said he should have asked for a transfer and 'gone like a shot'.

There were offers from Spain and Italy. Real Madrid, looking for another Alfredo Di Stefano and a second Ferenc Puskas, were interested. Best was reluctant to commit himself to Franco's capital then. Juventus, without a Scudetto since 1967, would have packed his cases for him. John Charles, who won three Championships there, told Best so. The move, he said, would reinvigorate him. Charles intimated that the money Best could expect overseas would make his salary at United look like a handful of small coins. Juventus, bankrolled by Fiat, had given Charles a rent-free apartment, a new sports car, bespoke suits and silk shirts. He'd also bought himself a 17th-century villa overlooking the

Po valley. On the streets Charles was treated like a member of the royal family. 'I hardly ever carried money because no one would allow me to buy anything. Everything was on the house,' he said. Charles also added that he'd be so closely marked in Italy that, when he played anywhere else, it would feel as if the pitch was twice normal size. He thought Best could only benefit from the experience – both in regard to his football and in widening his horizons. He reassured Best that, like Denis Law, he could return to Manchester a year or two afterwards and resume his career there.

The architect Le Corbusier paid tribute to Turin as 'the city with the most beautiful natural location in the world'. It still wasn't beautiful enough for Best. And, as he told Charles, Serie A contained defenders who tried to remove your ligaments without anaesthetic. Best spoke no foreign languages and wasn't inclined to learn one. The Italians were also too puritanical in their attitudes towards drinking for Best's liking. Moderation was the rule for players. A glass of wine was acceptable; a full bottle was not. Johan Cruyff thought Best should have gone to Holland. At club and national level the Dutch were having a renaissance. Feyenoord had won the 1970 European Cup. Cruyff's Ajax would win the next three. 'For a player like George, the style of Ajax was a present from heaven. He should have played for us,' said Cruyff. 'He would have fitted in perfectly.'

But United was Best's club; and Manchester was his city. The foundations for Che Sera had been dug and laid and the house was quickly more than a skeleton. 'I never dreamed of playing for anyone else,' he said, a willing captive at Old Trafford after signing a seven-year contract. Best agreed to United's terms – £170 per week – without haggling, not knowing that the other members of the Holy Trinity, Denis Law and Bobby Charlton, were earning more than him. He signed despite a sense of foreboding, too. 'I was doing everything I wanted to do,' he added. 'It was perfect. Then all of a sudden it looked to me as if it was going to be nothing. I felt it inside and it was hurting me. I could see failure and doom and all sorts . . . If someone had given me the choice of having the most beautiful women in the world or of winning the European Cup every couple of years, I would never have looked at another woman. All I wanted was for us to be the top club in the country as long as I was there. I couldn't see it happening.'

At the beginning of the 1970–71 season, the weekly newspaper *Inside Football* voiced what others were thinking, describing the 'tragedy of a genius' and insisting Best was 'at the crossroads'. He was 'failing to deliver the goods', it said, likening his diminished contribution at United to Shakespeare 'getting an additional dialogue credit' or Caruso stuck 'in the Sadler's Wells chorus'. 'What the hell is the matter with the man?' it raged. 'Perhaps he feels there is no challenge left.' It warned of the 'yawning abyss' that lay ahead for Best unless he bucked up. The article was a summary on his present state and also a piece of flawless clairvoyance. Its predictions came true soon enough.

Wilf McGuinness was promoted from chief coach to manager. Best still saw the sack as the only conclusion to that story. While others spoke of the Championship, he thought United would have to pedal hard to stay out of the bottom half of the table and gleaned no satisfaction from being proved right.

A sequence of spluttering performances brought a paltry three wins from the opening 13 First Division games. The title was out of reach before the leaves turned russet in autumn. In December Aston Villa, then an unprepossessing Third Division club, beat United over two legs in the League Cup semi-final. That defeat, catastrophic for McGuinness, came two days before Christmas. Three days after it he was summoned to see Sir Matt Busby. As Best always said about such encounters: 'He never did it to hand out the sweeties.' McGuinness never forgot the words Busby used. He looked at him gravely, like a doctor passing on the gloomiest prognosis, and said: 'The directors have asked me to take over the team again.' United were 17th in the table. McGuinness could not take in what he'd been told. United was his life. The job was his dream. Busby was the man he worshipped. McGuinness' wife was pregnant with their third child. 'I was demoralised, heartbroken, horribly hurt on both a professional and a personal level,' he said. McGuinness dissolved into irrationality. In search of a bottle of whisky in the directors' room, he found only sherry and drank several glasses. Then he began to head-butt the wall. 'It bloody hurt,' he said. Busby reflected afterwards that McGuinness' failure was rooted 'in the handling of players he had been brought up with', also observing that 'young soldiers promoted to lance corporal in their own platoons sometimes found it embarrassing'. He then added: 'Probably it was our fault for choosing Wilf.' The disingenuous word in that sentence is 'our'. Busby sheltered behind collective responsibility when there was no elaborate hierarchy at Old Trafford. He was the power in the boardroom. Busby admitted what Best had known all along. 'It is my opinion, too, that he was then too inexperienced to handle [the team] and get a full response.'

Drinking was taking priority over the football for Best. He missed the train taking United to a game at Tottenham. He failed to turn up for practice on Christmas Day. Busby often fell into the trap of thinking of Best as forever 17 years old, the doe-eyed, spindly boy he'd originally seen. 'I have to sit back and remember he is a grown man,' he said. He tried to be placatory. 'I think George is a fraction away from being the best player in the world. I am only holding back from putting him on top to keep him on his mettle.' The follow-up sentence outlined Busby's basic plan. 'The thing with George is that you have to keep him going,' alluding to the need for clever cajolement. At least Busby acted quickly. What he didn't appreciate was the depth of Best's desolation. Busby thought sorting out Best's problems on the pitch would cure his misadventures off it, too. This was a terrible misdiagnosis.

Best made a spectacle of himself over an eight-day stretch in January 1971. It was like something from the Theatre of the Absurd – both funny and not funny at all.

His disciplinary record was worsening. He'd been sent off in an international against Scotland the previous April for throwing a clod of mud at the referee. Domestically he'd collected three bookings inside 12 months for various displays of petulance, a tally that seems trifling by today's standards but counted almost as a public flogging offence then. Best was waiting to be called in front of the FA's disciplinary commission when he received a fourth caution for a sliding, fractionally late tackle on Manchester City's full-back Glyn Pardoe. The tackle broke Pardoe's leg in two places. The referee – barely ten yards away from the challenge and almost square on to it – didn't stop the game and didn't dive for his book and pencil either until City's players implored him to speak to the linesman, whose view of the incident was obscured by Pardoe's back anyway. When the derby was shown on TV the following afternoon, Malcolm Allison, City's coach, and Jimmy Hill, then working as the analyst on *The Big Match*, each exonerated Best from intentionally going over the top. Pardoe's injury was so devastating nonetheless that it impaired circulation to his foot and, at one stage, surgeons thought amputation might be necessary. Allison said Best was 'clearly distressed' afterwards. So was Allison. 'I was spitting with him in the heat of the moment,' he said. 'I didn't want to look at him afterwards, let alone speak to him.' Some newspapers called it a tackle 'to cripple'. That same weekend the plate glass window of Best's boutique was smashed with a brick, vandalism he assumed had been carried out by a City supporter to exact revenge.

Given Pardoe's plight, United's general disarray and Best's own falling apart, the FA hearing was already a headline event. Best, knowing what awaited him, got drunk the night before it and was too hungover to travel to Lancaster Gate on time. The train pulled out of Manchester without him. Busby persuaded the FA to delay the lunchtime tribunal until 4.30 p.m.; Best made it there with half an hour to spare. He vomited in a corner of the lift – at least he didn't splash Busby's shoes – before escaping with a £250 fine and a six-week suspended sentence. Another, much more ridiculous pantomime evolved from it. Busby left Best out of United's Saturday game at Chelsea after he absented himself from training without excuse or explanation. But Busby couldn't get hold of Best to drop him. He had to ring Malcolm Wagner to pass along the message instead. Still expected to travel with the team to show some unity of spirit, Best missed the London train again. Impulsively, he went to Manchester airport, flying to London and then preferring to go to the Islington flat of a girlfriend, the actress Sinead Cusack, instead of Stamford Bridge. 'I didn't really know what I was doing or why,' he'd say contritely after being found out. 'I was just so bloody mixed up that I just wanted to get away for a few days . . . I just had to get some peace and quiet . . . I suppose I took the coward's way out.'

On Saturday afternoon Best watched *Grandstand*, waiting for its teleprinter, clacking like a loom, to bring him the results. United's 2–1 defeat of Chelsea ended a sequence of ten matches without a win for them. 'All the experts said the team was better without me,' said Best. The headline news, however, was about Best's snub to Busby. By Sunday afternoon the media had found Best and turned him into a hostage in Cusack's flat. It arrived like an invading army, and so did an over-ebullient mob of teenagers, who crowded on to the narrow pavement outside. The front pages, as well as the back, were filled with the unfolding farce.

Inside the flat, behind lace curtains, Best was in a woe-is-me mood. He was 'very worried' and 'very miserable' said Cusack, who also confessed she 'quite honestly didn't understand' his problems. Television cameras arrived, the arc lights creating a white glow in the winter darkness. Surreally Best and Cusack found themselves watching the live scene being played out below them on the BBC's *Nine O'Clock News*. The screaming fans, clutching autograph books and scraps of paper to be signed, managed to get into the building after the lock of the main door broke. The stairway was jammed. The younger fans cried in pain in the crush. Fists beat and thumped on the door of the flat before police arrived in a squad car and a van to remove these unlikely intruders. One reporter made it through the begging mob. 'I want a few words,' he shouted above the din. Best appeared in a blue, roll-neck sweater and a smart pair of black trousers. His reply was brief: 'What you want,' he said, 'is a broken nose – get out.'

The hullabaloo demonstrated a disproportionately intense and voyeuristic interest in whatever he did. 'Prince Charles wouldn't have got as much [coverage] as I did,' said Best. An obscure Scottish Conservative backbencher posted an Early Day Motion in the House of Commons, which read: 'That the Best is the enemy of the good', a reference to Voltaire's poem *La Bégueule*. To protect himself against opposition claims of paper-waste and facetiousness, he claimed it was both Celtic wit and a way of asking a serious question about slavish devotion to football and footballers in modern society. Another anonymous backbencher asked why the police used money and manpower for Best's benefit. Even *The Times* weighed in. It unprecedentedly decided to devote its third leader column to the castigation of Best. The other topics chosen that day were an analysis of the chancellor's ailing economic strategy and the state of communist parties across the globe. In comparison, a footballer who'd merely gone missing to spend a weekend hiding in a girlfriend's flat was fluff. Beneath the headline 'The Price of Indiscipline', *The Times* censoriously lamented that: 'These are sad days for lovers of the game.' Its anonymous writer then proceeded to pump a lot of bombast into 600 words. Among the 'distasteful features' of football, the paper pontificated, was the 'growing indiscipline of many stars off the field'. The piece didn't name Best until the end; but there was no doubt who it regarded as the primary culprit in the slow degradation of the British game.

> The successful player can now become a wealthy man quite quickly. Much of his money is likely to come from the businesses he may run, or be associated with, or products he may sponsor. He may get caught up in the show business whirl, with all the temptations and opportunities that involves. This is liable to make it harder for the player to retain his sense of proportion and enthusiasm for the game, and for the club to exert its control over the player. The club have launched him, but once he is in orbit as a star he is no longer dependent upon it for his wealth or his fame.

The moving finger writ, and having writ moved on. Other headlines were bleak for Best, too. 'How Good Was George Best?' asked one, the deliberate use of the past tense suggesting his career was over. 'Hero or Villain?' queried another. 'Is He Getting Too Big for His Golden Boots?' read a third. There was a question mark attached to every aspect of his life. In Belfast, his mother – door-stepped by journalists – reiterated that her son could only express his anxieties by running away and hoping the distress signal would be picked up and understood. In Manchester, Busby said he'd considered reporting Best as a missing person and added he felt 'terribly let down'. 'I thought I could confide in George as much as he would confide in me.'

The reckoning in Busby's office isn't particularly important for what was said afterwards or for the punishment – a 14-day suspension – Best received. The published photographs, which showed Best sitting demurely beside Busby, were eloquent in conveying an inner turmoil. Occasionally Best smiled. But those smiles rapidly sank beneath the surface of his features. He is subdued, as if on medication and also in need of several nights of unbroken sleep. The eyes are empty, his gaze glazed or distracted. He seems dismally alone and is caught staring down at the floor or towards the ceiling. He looks as though he can't wait for all this to be over. Neither he nor Busby spoke specifically about what was said during an hour-long meeting. It was 'private and personal' according to Busby. It was 'something I can only talk to the boss about', according to Best. He protested eventually that 'football reasons' alone – the role he was asked to play in the team – were pivotal. He even claimed there'd been a strategic method behind the madness of dashing off to Cusack's flat because it forced that showdown with Busby. He made it seem as if his manager was suddenly icily unapproachable and impossibly unsympathetic. The preposterous premise of the statement went unchallenged. Anyone astute, however, saw through it like glass. Michael Parkinson met Best in Manchester and noticed he was 'pale and tired'. Parkinson went on: 'I told him frankly that I couldn't swallow the story and believed there was something else, something more deep-seated and disturbing.' Best still tried to pretend otherwise. 'Nothing,' he said, shaking his head at Parkinson. 'I mean, what matters to me more than football?' he asked, rhetorically. Parkinson observed then that the pattern of Best's weeks, outwardly so glamorous and enviable, was actually 'a ritual he goes through with all the enthusiasm of a performing dog'. What no one knew was that Best had broken down in Busby's office in the process of unburdening himself about his house, the team, his businesses, his boredom, his mother, his insecurities. 'Those tears were real,' said Busby. 'George wasn't kidding. He was upset because he'd upset me.'

What Best required was semi-prohibition, practical guidance, a professional support network, regular counselling and some discipline to his days. Such support rarely existed then; and certainly not for a footballer such as Best. No club provided it because most of society hadn't emerged from the Dark Ages in regard to the recognition and treatment of psychological trauma and depression and also nascent alcoholism. Busby came from a generation of stoics. You made do and mended. You didn't complain. You worked things through yourself. And you seldom discussed your feelings. Busby wasn't equipped to be the amateur psychiatrist. So he sent Best to a professional one. 'I think you need to go and talk to someone,' he told him, not wanting to use the words 'shrink' or 'psychiatry' in case it sounded intimidating. Knowing what Busby meant anyway, Best, tongue pressed firmly into cheek, told him: 'You must be crazy if you think I need a psychiatrist.' He went to the appointment, pretending not to know why questions about his past and his upbringing were relevant to his current behaviour. Best remembered being stared at over a pair of dark-framed glasses. The psychiatrist wrote notes on a pad and Best, pretending to be listening, counted spots on the wallpaper. 'At some point I thought this is madness,' he said. 'I'm sitting here being interviewed at great cost by some prick who is going to tell the club what they already know – that I'm as daft as a brush. And I started laughing. He looked at me in a funny way and then jotted something down.' When Best reflected on it, the realisation of what he'd sat through brought resentment rather than enlightenment. 'I got mad. They sent me to a headshrinker because they thought I was mentally sick,' he said, still refusing to accept he needed clinical help. The club didn't press Best to continue the sessions.

The conundrum for United was finding a solution to something no employer like them had encountered before. It was a journey without maps. Busby did what he could. With whispered instructions, during or after training, he set Best targets – to beat a particular player or to go on a specific run – that would rouse him out of numb lethargy.

United had won only a paltry five First Division matches under McGuinness. Busby led them to a further 11, which hauled them into a respectable eighth in the table. In the opening half of the season Best had scored only six League goals. With Busby in charge, the change in

Best's energy and attitude was transparent. He claimed another 12, praying each one might persuade Busby to retain his grasp on the team for another year or two until a dauphin was established.

'You know I want you to stay on,' said Best to Busby during the season's final month.

'The job needs someone younger now,' was his deflating, but not unexpected, reply.

His flood of goals gave Best the confidence to ask Busby for tangible recognition of them. He precociously asked to be made captain instead of Bobby Charlton. 'I wasn't being arrogant,' he insisted, 'I was being sensible.'

What seemed to Best a decent line of argument – 'the team needs rebuilding and it should be rebuilt around me' – collapsed when Busby tersely told him: 'You're not responsible.' Nor was there a sliver of evidence in Best's recent past to suggest that the pledge he promptly made – 'make me captain and I will be responsible' – could have been consistently maintained. Best would look back on his ill-thought-out demand, as well as the invidious position in which he placed Busby, and admit: 'What I was saying was hard for him to accept.' It was also impossible for Busby to execute. He couldn't have embarrassed Charlton. There was no vacancy, and in urging the gerrymandering of one Best confirmed his unsuitability to lead in the first place. His negative reaction to Busby's firm refusal made him more unsuitable still.

He forgot the purity of his original intention, which was supposed to benefit United as much as himself. Best didn't interpret what Busby said to him – principally to be patient and to develop emotionally – as a piece of positive, wise advice. He took it as a slight and embarked on what he defended as an 'exercise in role fulfilment', citing the rejection as a legitimate reason to behave badly.

'Because I was being treated as if I was irresponsible I started behaving irresponsibly off the park,' he said. 'I was a rebel.'

He even likened himself – and foolishly said so – to an iconoclastic James Dean; though he never clearly defined the cause against which he was supposedly rebelling. Best admired Dean's 'adventurous spirit' and the fact he 'marched to his own beat', he said. He omitted the crucial detail that Dean chose to live fast and loose and died prematurely because of it, leaving only a series of brooding, beautiful images behind. Like Dean, however, Best saw himself as forever young. He spoke, especially early on, as if he was half in love with easeful death. 'I can't contemplate reaching forty,' he said. 'I think I'd rather die before being *that* old – peacefully in my sleep.'

He argued it was possible to 'play hard and live hard', never accepting that a candle burnt at both ends will never cast a lovely light for long. 'I went on going out every night and drinking. I thought it wouldn't catch up with me. . . I could get totally pissed and it didn't seem to matter . . . I could handle hangovers then.'

One of the distinguishing marks of George Best's career is the way in which for so long he managed to perform occasional magic on the pitch while disintegrating off it. However much he drank, however raggedly shambolic life became for him, Best was able to make a show of doing everything at once with a ball – and doing it better than anyone around him.

In Britain there was no one to match him. Among comparable figures elsewhere Pelé was already 31; he wouldn't play in another World Cup after winning his third in Mexico in 1970. Eusébio was nearing 30, his knees scarred and his international peak well over. Best saw his chief rival as Johan Cruyff, a year younger. Cruyff made his debut for Ajax only 15 months after Best's first appearance for Manchester United. He resembled Best, too: slight and thin-faced, with the slenderest of limbs. Cruyff possessed more skill than anyone – with the exception of Best and Pelé – could have expected God to have given them without considering Him to have been over-generous. Like Best, Cruyff established himself and rapidly won a domestic Championship, and then went on to win it again. In the same year as Best plundered six goals against Northampton, Cruyff matched him against AZ '67 Alkmaar. He paused in a game merely to tease, stopping the ball whenever it suited him. Best looked at Cruyff and saw a reflection of himself. At the end of 1971 Best, watching on television from a bar in Majorca, saw Cruyff claim the European Cup. Ajax overwhelmed the Greeks of Panathinaikos with Total Football at Wembley. Best was envious; though not of Cruyff's abundant abilities, which he admired, nor of Cruyff himself, whose company he liked. He spoke of his regret simply of not being there. It should have been United versus Ajax, and Best versus Cruyff. The inspiring Cruyff's reward after Wembley – just as Best's had been in 1968 – was the European Footballer of the Year award. Cruyff was being called the finest contemporary footballer; Best would have none of it. He wouldn't be subordinate to Cruyff. Whatever Cruyff could do, he would surpass with stand-out individualism achieved in spite of the poverty of the team around him. United couldn't compete with Ajax. But Best knew he could compete with Cruyff.

The modern player is fortunate. Every second of the Premiership is filmed, filed and saved. Each goal and incident is shown and re-shown from every conceivable angle because satellite broadcasters have the luxury of 24 cameras. Nothing goes unrecorded. Those who occupied Best's era had only the condensed *Match of the Day* or ITV's regional programming on Sunday afternoon, and the video recorder was still a prototype. Word of mouth or newspaper accounts alone preserved goals. It's said that in the press box, after another of Best's goals almost defied belief, a young reporter leaned across to a veteran neighbour to confirm the time of its scoring for his notebook. 'Never mind the time, son,' said the veteran. 'Just write down the date.' The story, attached to at least three different goals in at least two different places, emphasises that Best never seemed to score the same type of goal twice;

and that he seldom settled for easy ones. He was luckier than most because TV showcased some of the choicest. In the dying weeks of Wilf McGuinness's tenure, he got one of such majesty that it was screened across Europe.

A fashion photographer once gained access to Old Trafford specifically to take some action shots of Best to go alongside others of him modelling clothes. The photographer chose a game against Chelsea. A few days afterwards Best asked him whether he'd got what he wanted. 'Oh, I've got plenty of shots of you,' said the photographer. 'Hundreds, in fact. But on every one there's a bullet-headed fellow in a blue shirt with a number 6 on it standing at your side.' The photographer didn't recognise Ron Harris. The goal Best scored came during a League Cup tie. It counts as exceptional because of what he did to avoid Harris.

The move begins with John Aston, propelling the ball at speed out of defence and into midfield and finally releasing it to Best with a left-foot pass that splits Chelsea the way an axe splits wood. Best is almost 40 yards from goal. There are still two defenders flanking him and capable of closing off the chance. An ordinary player would have given up. But Best has too much pace in those legs and too much control in those feet. He takes only two touches before Harris attempts to cut diagonally across and take the ball with a trademark sliding lunge – the left boot tucked beneath the right leg, which reaches out for the ball. Harris expects to win this contest. Instead he is left on the turf, a felled failure who clips Best's heel. Best teeters slightly at the impact before steadying himself again, like a tightrope walker making a minuscule slip before regaining his poise. Peter Bonetti, the goalkeeper, is on his muddied six-yard box, unsure about whether to come or stay. He's waiting for Best to make the next move. When that move comes, it is classically Best. If you look at the frame a full second before his decisive step, the odds are still stacked against him. Bonetti is only three yards in front of Best. Another defender, Marvin Hinton, is hurtling in from the right. The space between them is narrowing quickly. Best is unperturbed, as if – amid the noise of the crowd, beneath the harshness of the floodlights and without the support of a solitary red shirt – he feels a supreme calmness. He will take the ball where he wants to; no one can stop him. With a feint, he forces Bonetti to lurch full length. Hinton is fooled, too. Like a train overshooting its platform, he runs past Best and also beyond his own keeper. He guards the goal – a lonely business – as Bonetti scrambles on all fours for a semblance of dignity. In two heartbeats Best goes from the penalty spot to the fringe of the six-yard area. He simply places the ball – side-footed – between the near post and Hinton, who watches it whoosh against the net. Harris watches this, too. He's seen this one-man performance on his knees. He straightens himself up only as Best takes the applause of the crowd. Of his attempt at a murderous tackle, Harris said: 'If I had caught him I would have been jailed for life.' Best's run and finish was spliced into the opening sequence of *Grandstand*, which Harris saw on television whenever Chelsea stayed in a hotel before an away game. 'Every Saturday lunchtime I thought I was going to get him,' he said.

The following season Best's play was more poetic still. There was a hat-trick against West Ham, who were skewered at Old Trafford. His second goal was good enough for laudatory notices in its own right. West Ham made an almighty, juvenile hash of clearing a corner at the Stretford End. Their weakly misdirected attempt scarcely got beyond the six-yard box, which was cluttered with ten players – six of them in blue and claret, including Bobby Moore, who looks an anguished spectator. The ball rises high in the air, before dropping close to Best, who first makes a three-quarter turn and then waits until it descends from chest to kickable height. Best is back-pedalling when he thumps it, left-footed, and a combination of hitting the ball and the awkward angle of the strike lifts him into the air. He falls backwards as the shot beats the goalkeeper and three defenders, motionless on the line, before pinging off the stanchion. His third goal is even better than this – a seven-second piece of destruction beginning at the corner flag. West Ham think Best cannot hurt them from there. Hurt them he does. He sets off as though he alone sees a brightly lit path. The first defender pumps his arms and legs in an attempt to get near him; he actually ends up further away. He's further away still when Best checks and, having beaten him on the outside, beats him on the inside, too, with a swish and a swerve. Best uses his left foot to go past him and his right to get into the heart of the box. From the six-yard area Moore takes five big strides to confront him. Best accelerates. He ducks out of Moore's way as easily as he'd go past a static cone in training. Best draws back his right foot, as deadly as a Lee Enfield, and shoots decisively from 12 yards.

Another declaration of class came at the Dell, where the stands were so tight to the pitch that it always seemed, like an Elizabethan theatre, as though the Southampton crowd could spill at any moment on to the grassy stage. Some of them queued from 9 a.m. to see Best. He claims another hat-trick. The first and third goals are opportunistic headers. The second is bliss in its execution. A low, swift cross cum through ball, delivered from wide on the left, reaches the crowded box. Fortuitously it finds Best, who has to both avoid a stud-showing tackle from John McGrath and retain possession. It's like watching Fred Astaire tap dance in a telephone box. He gets past the covering defender with a deft shimmy. The finish is about placement. He caresses the ball into the far corner.

There was also *the* goal – against Sheffield United – shown whenever highlights of Best's career appear. Researchers once gave chess grand masters a series of cognitive and perceptual tests. A study of their eye movements revealed that each looked at the edges of squares on the board much more than a lesser player. They saw a different board from their opponent. They were also capable of bringing to mind other games and situations, which enabled them to compute the correct move faster, too. Best was like this. But he also played freely and without licence; nothing was repressed.

You see the Sheffield United goal as a single moment – a sweep of action taking the ball from six-yard box to six-yard box. Break it down, however, and within are 16 small scenes.

The arching goal kick from Alex Stepney that, in the 84th minute, leaves his darkly shadowed penalty area and breaks into the autumn sunshine enveloping more than half the pitch.

Old Trafford as it used to be before tens of millions of pounds were lavished on it.

The white ball as it rises and then begins the curve of its descent.

The headed flick that an unmarked Alan Gowling deflects in the centre circle towards Best, who is ten yards in front of him.

The way Best controls the bounce, dragging the ball to him with a raised right foot.

The uncertainty of two defenders, who can't decide whether to attack or retreat. They're unsure about whether surrendering ground now will give them an advantage later.

The way both independently make the wrong choice. They head towards goal, each calculating that Best can't score from so far out.

The run Best begins, seeing the space – and the backs of those defenders – ahead of him.

The fabulous assurance of that run; Best beginning, almost slowly, and allowing everyone else to get into position, before he changes from first to top gear in only a pace and a half.

The low drive of his upper body as he takes the ball around one man and out-dashes a second.

The approach into the box – another two players beaten by his winged quickness.

The defenders' mistaken belief that Best has been pushed too wide to score now because the angle is too acute for him.

The fact that Best wants to be here; it's where, in fact, he has chosen to go.

The goalkeeper coming out, raising his hands as if giving up and going to his left as Best drives across him from the tip of the six-yard area.

The ball as it hammers against the far post and then into the net.

The look on Best's face – the head tilted back and the eyes tilted towards the sky, the fists clenched, the smile revealing perfect teeth.

As the ball crosses the line, there are *six* Sheffield United players in the camera shot. The only United player is Best.

In isolation all these goals are remarkable enough. The circumstances in which he scored them make each one almost a superhuman act. For between matches the depression and loneliness had considerably worsened, to the extent that Best had become a 'bloody wreck', he said. Further professional psychiatric counselling and a doctor's admonishment *might* have persuaded him to curtail his drinking now. For the need for alcohol had still not turned into full dependency on it. The groove he'd once been in nevertheless became a rut.

Manchester, which had originally seemed to him to be infinite in size, shrank to a few streets. He began to complain about the city, which he believed as stifling as 'your actual Peyton Place', the author Grace Metalious's depiction of a small town and the hypocrisies, gossiping and bitchy score-settling within it. Best knew all the clubs in Manchester. He knew all the women worth knowing in those clubs.

To get out of Manchester he would often go to London early and return – if he could be bothered – late at night. Once an avid news-paper reader, he stopped turning to the back page because 'all I'd find was bad news'. He'd hear people complain, 'I'm fed up with reading about George Best,' and he wanted to say to them, 'I'm fed up with reading about me, too . . . I know if I was reading day after day about someone else it would drive me mad. I'd end up hating him.' He couldn't watch himself on television. 'I don't recognise myself any more,' he said. Best also went as far as to admit, like someone wearing his central nervous system externally, 'I can't help but wonder who this strange public person called George Best is. Is it me? Or is it some third person that people claim as their own? Some two-dimensional cardboard cut-out who bears only a super-ficial resemblance to me?'

Best thought how differently things could have been for him if, like Denis Law, he'd married young and had a family. He'd seen how Law successfully separated his playing career from his private life. He'd watched him quietly leave after training, knowing home was where he wanted to be. 'I envied that,' said Best. 'Sometimes you hear the married men talking about their families and you feel out of things.' The ambiguity in those statements is nevertheless clear. Best couldn't be like Law. He told Michael Parkinson two stories that were typical of his brief relationships; some of them so brief as to qualify as only one-hour stands rather than one-night. In the first a woman knocks on the door at Che Sera and claims her car has broken down. Can she use the telephone to call the AA? The two of them have sex in the hallway before the mechanic arrives. In the second, he meets a woman on a Friday and goes back to her flat. He doesn't emerge from it until Monday morning. 'Three days just making love and eating while everybody outside went bloody spare trying to find me,' he said. Returning to Old Trafford, the club had to concoct a story to explain his vanishing. Best asks them to say he's had 'a touch of the 'flu'. Every paper runs a similar headline. 'Best Returns. Spent weekend in bed with touch of the 'flu'. That afternoon he received a telegram from the woman with whom he'd spent the weekend. What he read made him laugh aloud.

> *Roses are red*
> *Violets are blue*
> *I've never been called*
> *A touch of the 'flu*

He could no more settle down than he could flap his arms and fly to the moon. He wanted every woman who attracted him; he didn't want to be a humdrum, doting husband. To pretend otherwise was idealistic twaddle. 'I was trying to find myself,' he said. There didn't have to be much amatory heat for a liaison. Parkinson learned how one woman met Best at a party. 'She told me she was thinking about how to get George into bed. She spoke to him for about half an hour. Suddenly another woman came up and interrupted them. She introduced herself and simply said, "Would you like to fuck?" and he made his apologies and went off with her.'

Occasionally Best used Parkinson's Thames-side home as a bolthole. 'He'd ring up and ask if he could come down,' said Parkinson. 'I'd count to ten and then the phone would ring again. He'd say: "Forgot to ask. Can I bring a girl with me?" The girls were usually the same – blonde and long-legged.' Best never forgot to take a bag of footballs for Parkinson's sons. 'He'd always go out and play a game with them,' added Parkinson. At infant school, the youngest of the family was once asked by his teacher what he'd done over the weekend. 'I played football with George Best,' he replied. The teacher, assuming he was telling lies, ordered him to stand in the corner of the classroom.

It is an oversimplification to say that Best was bored with *being* Best. But he offered an articulate view of the awful state he was in by referring to himself in the third person. 'I was George Best, whether I liked it or not, and anywhere I went this creature called George Best, footballer superstar, went with me. . . I started hating my life. I started hating the hassle of being me. People would talk about me in front of me as if I was not there. It was like they were talking about someone else. About someone outside the door. Being the me I was supposed to be was an acting job; I was pretending to be me. I felt as if I was watching a monster on television who looked like me and talked like me but wasn't me at all.'

The hardest thing about being himself was living up to people's preconceptions. He began to hide behind a façade of his own creation, developing a split identity. He said there were two George Bests. The private Best was still shy, still sensitive, still unsure and sometimes nervy. That shyness was occasionally so inhibiting that he couldn't ring a restaurant to book a table. At a party Parkinson held at his home, the celebrities there, including the actor Michael Caine and the actress Sarah Miles, wanted to speak to Best. He retreated into the garden to kick a ball around with the children, which allowed him to avoid the adults. The 'other' Best was outgoing and confident – more like the figure portrayed in the gossip columns. 'Drink changed my personality,' said Best. 'Everybody, it seemed, was happy to drink with George Best, and who was I to disappoint them? It didn't take too many drinks to become the George Best they wanted to drink with. The other George Best wouldn't have interested them much.' He didn't stop there. One of his frankest admissions expanded that theme and proved also how part of his life was a show. 'What happens is that you get caught up in a myth,' he said. 'The private George Best is always going to be different from the public version. To some extent, there's always been a need to put on an act for people, if only to protect myself. I hate not being myself, but it was essential to get by. I learned very quickly that you have to be a good actor in public.' He did so like an automaton, the actions pre-programmed.

A cinema buff, one of his favourite films of the 1960s was *Charlie Bubbles*. He saw direct parallels with his own life in its script. Albert Finney, who was born in Salford, plays the eponymous lead, a fêted and famous writer returning to his home city, coincidentally Manchester. Bubbles – like Best – has come from an ordinary, humbly modest background to which he is sometimes reluctant to return. He – also like Best – now has what he's always desired: limitless pots of money, a Rolls-Royce, a stylishly contemporary home with closed-circuit TV and more rooms than he can ever live in, world enough and time to do as he pleases, a queue of women prepared to make themselves readily available to him. But – and this is where Best found the most troubling comparison – Bubbles isn't content; he isn't even remotely happy. As Best said of himself: 'You've got money. You've got fame. You've got beautiful women. What more do you want? What you want is someone to turn to.' In a crowd Bubbles still seems as if he's alone. The same could be said of Best. So could the fact that Bubbles' fame pains and bewilders him, precipitating a search for meaning and fulfilment. To fill the vacuum in it he looks for instant gratification. To stop himself from feeling bored he deliberately gets into chaotic situations or begins drinking. To try to simulate some enthusiasm he is constantly on the move.

In an early scene Bubbles switches off as his accountants and advisers talk to him about dividends and tax loopholes, the movement of monies between banks and get-rich, off-shore investments. He drifts into a half-trance in which the occasional upward or downward turn of his mouth or the sharp snap of his head makes it seem as if he's actually paying attention. Best used the same technique. 'I went to business conferences where they were talking about "exploiting my commercial potential" and all that bollocks,' he said. 'I used to fill my head with music and remember great games I'd played. They'd think I was listening, but I hadn't heard a word they'd said.'

At one stage Bubbles is told: 'It's time you grew up and faced reality' – a sentence (or a version of it) that Best heard from Busby and others time and again. At another a character responds to media harassment (a reporter's porcine face is pressed against a kitchen window and he begs to speak to Bubbles) with the question: 'Your life's not your own, is it?' – another line that Best could have composed about himself.

Best used to pine for normality. 'I can get almost anything done that I want,' he said. 'But I sometimes think I would like to be an ordinary bloke.' And he added: 'My life controls me. But I want to be in control of my life.'

Those quotations explain why his favourite moment in the film is the final one. Bubbles awakes, miserable and out of sorts and wanting to separate himself from everyone and everything. He tugs back the bedroom curtains in the remote cottage where he is staying and sees an unmanned balloon tethered in a nearby field. The ribbed skin of the balloon is bright, pumpkin-orange, which makes it appear as if two suns are rising that morning. Wordlessly Bubbles goes out of the cottage and strides purposefully towards the balloon, an idea of what he is about to do already fully formed in his mind. He steps into its wicker hamper and begins to untie its ropes and heave out the sandbags that are rooting it to the earth. Slowly the balloon rises against the hard blue of the sky, floating towards a few torn rags of clouds until it looks no bigger than a full stop. 'I used to think about escaping like that,' said Best, 'and going where no one could find me.'

There's a photograph of Best in Che Sera standing close to his lounge window. It was exposed in such a way that the light looks unnaturally strong, almost surrounding him, the way a corona burns around an eclipse. His arms are folded and his expression wistful, far away.

If you didn't know otherwise, you'd think he was scanning the horizon for an orange balloon.

12

A Just Man Falleth Seven Times

Ken Stanley had seen superstars of other eras sweeping floors, pulling pints and grubbing for handouts. He didn't want it to happen to George Best.

'Think about what football will be like when it's truly a world game,' he'd say to try to enthuse him. 'Think of the size of America. Think of every boy in Africa having a team shirt and a ball at his feet. Think about China and Japan and the rest of the Far East. There are billions of people out there, George. The game is still growing. They'll be watching you on television in Peking and Calcutta before long.'

Best didn't care and didn't listen. And anyway, if he couldn't get out of bed for an appointment in Stockport, how, for goodness sake, would he ever have got to China on time?

'Everyone still wanted him,' said Stanley. 'The offers were coming in.' Stanley had to stall prospective sponsors until Best had the inclination to discuss them, which wasn't often. 'He'd get a letter from 10 Downing Street and ignore it,' said Stanley. 'He couldn't even be bothered to reply to the prime minister.'

Best wasn't over-bothered about the start of the 1971–72 season either. He admitted he'd been 'spoilt' by success. 'If you said to a fifteen-year-old kid: "You're going to play for the club of your dreams, doing something that you'd always dreamed of doing and in seven years from now you'll have won two League Championships, a Youth Cup, the European Cup, been European Footballer of the Year and British Footballer of the Year", most of them will say: "That's all I want; that's the end of it". That's what I did.'

Sir Matt Busby told Best that Manchester United would appoint an 'older man' to replace Wilf McGuinness. Once more, Best expected a prestige name, such as Jock Stein, still six months short of his 49th birthday. Best's high opinion of Stein, as a man as well as a manager, was reciprocated. In a delightful phrase that underscored Best's unique-ness, Stein described him as 'another species', a player so outstandingly individual that he counted as incomparable; a player, moreover, who defied classification. If Stein came to Old Trafford, Best knew he and United would prosper again. Stein didn't need to chisel out a reputa-tion; he already had one. He wouldn't be daunted by United's recent history; he had already established a past for Celtic. His inventory of domestic trophies – six Scottish League titles, four Scottish Cups and five League Cups – surpassed United's in the same period. He'd not only won the European Cup – a year before United – but had taken Celtic to another final. He was exactly the sort of boss Best would have played for – 'the big man who is a big a man', he said of him. Stein would have walked into the dressing room or on to the training pitch with a kingly presence. 'He seemed as close as you could get to Sir Matt on all levels,' added Best. 'Not only in his love of football but also in the way he handled people and the way he wanted to play the game.'

Busby tried to recruit Stein. The two of them negotiated clandestinely in the rear seat of Busby's Mercedes at a petrol station equidistant between Manchester and Liverpool. But his allegiance to Glasgow – and his wife's reluctance to leave it – was always too firm to fracture, irrespective of the blandishments Busby gave him and the financial inducements United offered, which persuaded Celtic to increase their own to make sure he stayed. Busby, unconvinced by Stein's insistence that he wouldn't force the family to move against its wishes, complained afterwards that he had used the discussions as a lever to improve his salary there.

With Stein, how markedly different the next two and a half seasons – and the rest of his life – could have been for Best. Without him, the usual suspects were mentioned again. Since being considered and rejected in 1969, prior to Wilf McGuinness's appointment, Dave Sexton had won the FA Cup and the Cup Winners' Cup for Chelsea. Busby now made a grab for Sexton and found himself rebuffed by Chelsea's board. So instead he recruited a rank outsider, Frank O'Farrell, who scarcely figured on the bookmakers' radar. Only six years earlier he'd managed non-League Weymouth. Since then he'd taken Torquay from the Fourth Division to the Third and, afterwards, Leicester from the Second to the First and also to the 1969 FA Cup final, where squandered chances cost them the game against Manchester City. O'Farrell was 43, intelligent and politely pleasant. He had sharply parted hair, the colour of anthracite, and wore good wool suits and shiny shoes, which made him look like the prim manager of a smart town bank. The board deferred to Busby, allowing him to negotiate terms. He initially offered O'Farrell £12,000 per year, plus bonuses. In further talks O'Farrell discovered that Busby was attempting to hire him on the cheap. The board had authorised a salary of £15,000. 'I think our whole relationship was damaged from that moment onwards,' he said. 'I felt something wasn't right and Matt knew that I knew he had tried to cheat me.' This inauspicious start was compounded when O'Farrell discovered Busby still occupied the office that ought to have belonged to him. 'I told him, sorry, he had to move,' he said. As O'Farrell admitted, reflecting on Busby's crumbling court: 'There were people who shook their head in bewilderment when they heard I was to take the job.' There were others, he added, who 'urged me not to take it'.

The general state of disrepair perturbed him. The problems Wilf McGuinness inherited remained: an ageing team and the reluctance to accept change. 'The United players had a kind of mindset,' said O'Farrell. 'I can remember one particular phrase they used to say – "let's play the football" – which was a kind of vague concept. I also heard the comment that "if we get one, we'll get four". They weren't an easy side to bring up to speed with the modern game and tactics. They felt they were free spirits . . .'

Best said of McGuinness that he 'didn't have a bloody chance' of success. He felt identically about O'Farrell. The two of them were 'expected to work miracles', he said. O'Farrell was constantly aware of Busby's presence, which permeated every cranny and nook of Old Trafford. Best understood the dilemma facing both of Busby's successors. 'I called him boss,' he said of Busby. 'Everyone was the same. No matter who the manager is, who's coaching or who's taken over, he is still the boss.' Best said it was 'difficult to judge' whether he was still in charge and concluded: 'It wasn't helping.'

Early on O'Farrell lifted United to the top of the table. Near the half-way stage five points separated them from second-placed Derby, Manchester City and Leeds. O'Farrell didn't delude himself. He knew the position was flattering. Retaining it was entirely dependent on Best. 'We were probably a one-man team in some games,' said O'Farrell. 'If George wasn't a hundred per cent, it didn't always matter. He'd still get the attention from the opposition. He'd distract defences and that would leave space others could exploit.' He scored 11 League goals in ten matches between late August and late October; not bad for someone whose heart wasn't entirely in it. Already, O'Farrell was getting late-night calls delivering bleak news: Best was in a nightclub; Best had drunk too much; Best wouldn't go home. There were reasons for all this. Best knew he couldn't go on single-handedly propping up the side, which made him far gloomier. He was also in extreme pain on occasions. Haematoma of the shin afflicted him. His knees were so stiff and sore that sometimes cortisone injections alone got him on to the pitch. His right knee swelled because of excess fluid and he was unable to completely straighten it. His thighs and lower back ached. He played in matches despite swellings on both ankles. Another injection enabled him to roll on his socks without flinching.

Constant work is necessary to preserve art, but Best was beginning to recoil from it. He asked himself whether football was worth the hassle it brought and began to dread the thought of training or playing. 'I would say to myself I'm not going in, and stay in bed,' he said. Best employed Mary Fullaway's daughter-in-law, Olga, as Che Sera's house-keeper. Arriving to find him still in his room when he ought to have been preparing to train, Olga would ring Mrs Fullaway to ask her advice. 'He won't go to training. What shall I do?' However much he drank, Best was adamant on one thing. He wouldn't use hard or soft recreational drugs (he also hated smoking). He couldn't understand why anyone would snort or sniff them or stick a needle into a vein to get high. 'I just don't see why anyone would do that to themselves,' he said, oblivious to the irony of his moral indignation. He didn't particularly like taking a doctor's prescription to a chemist either. Best did so only because he wasn't sleeping. He found his insomnia couldn't be cured through medication anyway. Since none of the pills or powdered draughts – despite increasing doses – were effective, Best stayed out until the early hours because there was no point going home to lie awake in the pitch darkness.

And so it went on. A draining night. A reluctance to get out of bed once he got into it. 'A vicious circle,' said Best, who admitted he was drinking to 'forget' things; mostly his football.

'I felt the situation was hopeless,' he added. 'It was like being in a bad dream.'

* * *

The sight of Belfast during The Troubles – a 'city falling apart', he said – profoundly saddened George Best because he loved to meet and mix with its people. He'd accompany his father, Dickie, to an Ulster social club, which drew Protestants and Catholics alike. He said he'd look around him and see both denominations 'laughing and joking and singing and drinking together', and then he'd think of the scene outside. 'Ten yards from the entrance, [are] six or seven policemen with bullet-proof vests and machine guns [and] army patrols,' he explained. Inside the patrons of the social club 'show no fear at all', added Best, 'which is frightening in itself . . . You see how it affects people. They try to laugh it off. Deep down it's killing them.'

As a boy, living in predominantly Protestant East Belfast, it was impossible for Best to be ignorant of the religious schism or to pretend it didn't exist or wasn't important. It permeated everyday life. The Bests were Free Presbyterian. Dickie was a member of the Orange Order and a past Master and he also belonged to the Royal Black Preceptory, a Protestant fraternal society. On the anniversary of the Battle of the Boyne – 12 July – his son was given the distinction of the 'Holding of the Strings', which hung from the banners, and he strode beside the red-coated pipers and the drummers and the other marchers in sashes and collarets, white gloves and black bowler hats. What fascinated the young Best was the finery of the parade rather than its religious signifi-cance. He treated the Boyne celebrations like a street party with cake and biscuits at the end of it. He attended church because it fulfilled his parents' and grandparents' wish for Sunday observance. The deepest, starkest separations between Protestants and Catholics didn't interest him. His local football allegiance underlined this. He supported Glentoran because his paternal grandfather lived only a long throw-in from the turnstiles. He said he identified them as a 'Catholic team' because the club fielded players of both denominations.

His Protestant school, Grosvenor High, was on the edge of a Catholic

He was a footballer, a pin-up and a fashion-icon – and prepared to use the Old Trafford pitch as a backdrop.

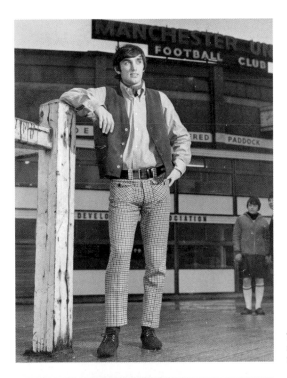

The cowboy at Old Trafford. He had more clothes in his wardrobe than the Great Gatsby.

Sometimes, though, he conveniently forgot to button up his shirt.

The most photographed footballer of the 1960s was always posing for the camera.

The photograph that captures the zenith of his career. He celebrates after scoring Manchester United's second goal against Benfica at Wembley.

And a view of the goal – he slides the ball into an empty net after going clear and taking it around the goalkeeper Henrique.

The fulfilment of a dream. Matt Busby, flanked by Paddy Crerand and George Best, take the trophy – plus a miniature replica – back to Manchester.

One year – 1968 – and two individual prizes. The Footballer of Year statuette and the European Footballer of the Year Ballon d'Or, which he receives beside Sir Matt Busby and Denis Law.

All smiles at a United photo-call. His relationship with Bobby Charlton, however, wasn't all sunshine.

Jackie Glass – his first serious girlfriend. 'I like women who are intelligent,' he said.

Showing off his new cine camera in Burren Way and walking through Madrid with his father, Dickie, in 1966.

'I was much closer to my mum,' he admitted, hugging her during his parents' silver wedding celebrations in 1970.

area, and Best was recognisable as one of its pupils from his blazer badge. Gangs of Catholic youths would chase him at the bus stop and try to filch his cap or scarf or books. He'd be called a 'Proddy bastard'. He would call them 'Fenians' in return. 'The most we ever threw at each other were names,' said Best. To play as a Protestant schoolboy footballer on a Catholic pitch meant being similarly cat-called. Some of the more zealous spectators brandished sticks or brought cooking pans, which were claimed to contain boiling water. A Catholic on a Protestant field would be verbally browbeaten and bullied equally in an attempt to frighten him. But the underlying tension between the faiths, and every small expression of it, didn't harden Best against Catholics. None of the hostility or the bickering turned him into a bigot. Nor did he pick and choose his friends because of religion. He didn't ask where someone worshipped; and he didn't care about anyone's beliefs. To act otherwise was inconceivable to him. 'I'm not hostile to anyone,' he said. 'I don't understand prejudice . . . I don't hate Catholics.' His religion was football.

What he described as the 'complete hatred' of the conflict dismayed him. He saw no sense in it – and no end to it – once the fighting began. He followed the escalation of riots, killings and bombings on television and also the assembling of barricades and barbed wire, the rumbling roll of armoured cars, the body searches and the sight of sectarian slogans spray-painted on to walls. His five-year-old sister Julie once said to him: 'George, please don't come home. They are shooting people here.' One of his cousins would later be shot dead, aged 16 – the innocent victim of crossfire – after leaving his girlfriend at a bus stop. An army bullet hit him in the back. Best thought The Troubles contributed to his mother's drinking. 'A lot drank to forget them in Belfast,' he said.

In the years that followed he would drive through the city and give a mournful commentary on what he'd witnessed. 'Homes boarded up. Bricks and planks nailed across the windows. A street of forty or fifty houses and maybe [only] one or two old people who've just been there so long there's no way they'll ever move. Stuck between the desolation, filth and squalor.' He said the city centre, which had once been 'a wonderland' to him, looked 'like Colditz'.

As The Troubles continued, he'd say: 'It's been going on for so long now a lot of people who are involved in it have forgotten what it even started about. I also think it's given rise to a lot of thuggery. People are getting away with things because of the situation. A lot of people just become gangsters with no interest at all in the political, and are using that as an excuse to get away with murder for gain or for the sake of violence. They use the situation to cover their badness, really. You could go on for ever about the atrocities.'

The Troubles forced some of his childhood friends to leave Belfast. 'I have lost touch completely with all of the pals I had when I was a kid,' he lamented. 'That's what I miss, actually. I would like to have someone who I could talk with about our school days and our early days.'

At every public event Best attended in Ireland – North or South – the crowds swamped him. He subsequently likened one appearance – the mundane opening of a village building society – to 'the coming of the Messiah . . . there were thousands there. A little village virtually closed down. Some of the kids had probably never even seen me play. I'm sure some of the old dears had never seen a football match in their lives except on TV.' The Irish people, Best said, 'almost feel they own me in a nice way. I'm a part of them and I always will be. That's what they feel, and that's the way I feel. I'm their son, really.'

Best said he didn't 'feel afraid' whenever he went to Belfast. He did so, however, on the mainland in October 1971. Greater Manchester police received a telephone call, purporting to come from the Irish Republican Army. The caller claimed Best would be shot if he played against Newcastle at St James' Park. 'The threat might be a hoax,' a policeman told him, trying to sound reassuring, 'but we can't take the chance.' The caller had been specific, the information passed on sounded reliable, and the geography of St James' Park was favourable for a marksman. There were vantage points opposite the Main Stand – Georgian sash windows and blue-tiled roofs – where a sniper could spot him from a distance. Best had read Frederick Forsyth's novel *The Day of the Jackal*, about the planned assassination of General de Gaulle. He imagined himself in the cross-hairs of a rifle.

His first thought wasn't for himself. 'My parents came immediately to my mind,' he said, knowing he couldn't protect them from the newspaper headlines. In particular he knew his mother would be distraught. He shielded her from as much upset as possible, never letting on about the amount of hate-mail he received, which would have been deeply troubling for her.

Best was familiar with anonymous letters, non-politically and non-religiously motivated, claiming one leg or both would be broken or that he'd be duffed up somewhere. These were couched in vague generalities, no precise date or place ever given. Best concluded the unknown authors were opposition fans, illiterate and unhinged. Only on one previous occasion had the police taken a declaration of intent seriously enough to provide advice and an escort home. Best went to watch a testimonial game at Bolton's Burnden Park, where officers told him someone had threatened to kill him afterwards. Best rang Malcolm Wagner and asked to be chauffeured back; he didn't explain the circumstances. Wagner arrived to find Best waiting for him in the foyer of the main entrance. 'He jumped in and we took off with police cars either side of us,' said Wagner. 'I said to him, "What's going on?" He just looked at me and smiled: "Don't worry – some bloke says he's going to kill me."'

Best couldn't be nonchalant about the possibility of IRA involvement. He was rumoured to have donated £3,000 to the Reverend Ian Paisley's

Democratic Unionist Party, then in the process of being formed and launched. The idea was unlikely to anyone who knew him well. Best insisted that he didn't dabble in politics; though, just a month before his death threat, he did try to provoke passport control in Moscow by asking 'Do you ban books here?' and then telling them he had two novels by Aleksandr Solzhenitsyn in his suitcase. He seldom spoke about The Troubles to avoid difficulties for himself and his family. Only in private did he ever express a cogent opinion about them – and he couldn't properly articulate it. 'You have to have some views one way or the other,' he said. 'I think if I'd stayed there and not left to make a livelihood somewhere else I'd have got more involved. I don't know if I'd been on a side. I'd maybe have tried to do more personally. But because of who I am – in a funny sort of way – I feel as if it's unfair to go back and take a stand.' Best appears to be saying his detachment from Belfast disqualified him from taking an active role in the peace-keeping process. He added nonetheless: 'I think of doing something to finish it. Or to cool it a little bit . . . If I was interested in politics I'm sure I could just go across there and do virtually what I wanted because of the sort of image I have among the Irish people.'

Best never envisaged himself as a target. For Catholic children didn't stop wanting to be George Best after discovering he was a Protestant. On parks or wasteland the Catholic aspiring footballers of the generation that came after Best pretended to be him, and chanted his name, and supported United because he played for them. As Teddy Jamieson writes in his book *Whose Side Are You On?*, a study of sport and The Troubles: 'In Northern Ireland you could be Orange or Green but you could still be a red.' Paddy Crerand once saw film of stone-throwing kids pelting one another across a wall sealing off Catholic and Protestant areas. On either side of the wall was the unmistakable flash of a United shirt and the club crest. Before going to Old Trafford Best was cautioned about his chances of making it there based on the mistaken belief that, since Busby was a devout Catholic, United would treat Protestants as second-class citizens. It was nonsensical. 'There was never the slightest act of discrimination,' he said. 'The boss was only interested in whether or not you could play football.' Whenever Best pulled on the emerald jersey, the people of Northern Ireland were only concerned with the football, too. Without Best the team was just another of those tiny nations aspiring to punch above its weight. With Best, it had respect.

He resented never being chosen at schoolboy level. A selector lived on the Cregagh Estate and, like so many others, wrote him off as too puny. The Northern Ireland FA hadn't considered him for a full cap until Jimmy Murphy got into a casual conversation with one of its committee members in a hotel lobby.

MURPHY: You ought to call up this lad. Almost eighteen and he's amazing.

COMMITTEE MEMBER: Thanks. Perhaps we could give him a game in our youth team to see how he goes.

MURPHY: Youth team! You're joking, aren't you? If he was Welsh, I'm telling you he'd have been in the first team now.

The committee member wasn't even aware that Best had already played for the youth team twice in 1962.

On a sodden pitch at Swansea's Vetch Field Best found himself – after only 16 First Division appearances – eventually capped against Wales in April 1964 during a transforming phase for the team. Only the remnants of the 1958 squad, which reached the World Cup finals in Sweden, remained.

With Best, Northern Ireland nearly qualified for the 16-team 1966 World Cup – a defeat in Switzerland proved fatal for them – and also the finals in Mexico four years later. So much expectation was heaped on Best that whether he would be fit or available to play dominated the pre-publicity and pre-planning of any fixture. His absences – particularly following defeat to Russia in a group game in Moscow at the end of 1969 – were treated like minor national disasters. There were long gaps between appearances, chiefly because United, driven by self-interest, were reluctant to release him at all for midweek matches. Excuses were made, injuries invented. Best became a half-willing collaborator in the pretence. Playing for them became 'recreational soccer', he said, because 'you were not really expected to get a result'. Sometimes Best arrived late and barely half-fit. 'Don't tackle him in training,' Billy Bingham, the manager, ordered during one team talk after learning about his delicate condition. 'No need to worry Billy,' replied Terry Neill, the captain, 'we can't get near him in training anyway.' The other players wanted Best on the team sheet irrespective of the compromises made to accommodate him. Dave Clements, who became Northern Ireland's boss for 11 matches in the mid-1970s, remembered: 'Often George wasn't there for the first training session. We didn't know if he'd turn up or not. Billy would call us together and say, "I can pick the team now or I can wait to see whether George is coming. What do you think?" We'd always tell him to give it another twenty-four hours. Everyone understood George was a special case.'

Northern Ireland had the consolation of seeing him at his absolute finest. At Windsor Park, in October 1967, Best produced a virtuoso performance against Scotland which was so exquisite that anyone who had a ticket regarded themselves as fantastically fortunate. A lot of those tickets were bought by teenage girls or fathers who, with no interest in football, had been talked into taking their daughters to see Best. 'We could just fill the ground with them,' said a Northern Ireland FA spokesman, speaking almost six months before the match.

The sparse moments of film of it confirm nothing said about Best or his contribution that afternoon was untrue. The stories neither fall into the category of taproom hyperbole – the companionable, rosy-hued glow of the tavern that nearly always leads to distortion and exaggeration – nor of excessive over-romanticism of an event because of the collective will to sustain a myth. Best enervated Scotland. As 1–0 defeats go, it was a hell of a beating. 'One-nil going on five,' said Celtic's Tommy Gemmell, the full-back directly opposing Best in the opening half. By the end the Scots were so disorientated and dizzy that you wonder how any of them walked in a straight line to the players' tunnel. The highlights are in black and white. Best bursts through them as if he's in burnished Technicolor. He reduces the role of everyone else – apart from the Scots' goalkeeper Ronnie Simpson – to the purely functional. 'It was him against me,' said Best, seen shooting from anywhere and from any angle.

Today's managers study ProZone's statistical data, which produces scientific shaped charts and a mountainous heap of statistics, like holy parchment. It can make the game seem a rigidly mechanical process in which numbers and percentages explain everything. ProZone would nonetheless usefully show how dominant Best became. Fed the raw data, the computer would probably overheat and spit it back as too implausible to process. Best had so much possession it was as though he'd brought his own ball along and wouldn't let anyone else have it. He retained it for so long that the Scots seemed to get only a couple of scuffling kicks every few minutes. They are mostly involved in a Tour de France of back-pedalling against him. 'I couldn't get close to him,' said Gemmell. 'It was like trying to catch the wind. I tried to body check him. Trip him. Kick him. Nothing worked.'

There's an apocryphal story that Gemmell pleaded with the other full-back, Eddie McCreadie, to swap sides at half-time. McCreadie is supposed to have replied 'Go fuck yourself.' In fact the Scots decided during the interval to try to nullify Best by suffocating his supply route to him; Gemmell would also man-mark him. Best made a tactical switch of his own. He changed flanks. Gemmell looked across the pitch and waved at McCreadie, hollering – no pun intended – 'best of fucking luck'. McCreadie was sliced up, too. There is one wonderful moment that makes you gasp. Best, on the far touchline, darts past one tackle, and cuts back in a jack-knife move to foil another before arrowing over a centre. All this is done at the speed of a thoroughbred racehorse on the flat. In another long-distance raid he collects the ball 40 yards out and jigs in between two midfielders, inside one defender and outside another, his stride languidly lengthening. He even created the winner, playing a one-two near the half-way flag, and running almost to the goal-line before putting in a cross, which was then hacked inelegantly to Clements, who scored from inside the box. 'He beat Scotland on his own,' said Clements. 'We joined in when he needed us, which wasn't often.' Afterwards in the Northern Ireland dressing room, everyone – apart from Best – was animated and exuberant. As if disappointed the game was over, he simply showered, towelled himself down and got changed with hardly a murmur. He didn't look especially pleased with his performance. Writing about Best in *The Scotsman*, John Rafferty said his display 'urges one to move out of the formal language of criticism and into the flowery sphere of poetry'. Danny Blanchflower gave a plainer verdict. 'The boy's play fills me with joy,' he said. 'I wish we'd had him in the '58 World Cup team.'

The ovation Best got made Windsor Park shake, as if the ground it stood on was shifting. It shook again during a Home International against England, a game remarkable for a 25-second segment which became Best versus Gordon Banks. The yellow-shirted Banks originally tried to heave the ball away from the edge of the area with his right hand. Best blocked that option. So Banks attempted to kick it, shuffling one way to give himself some space. He shadow-sparred, like a boxer trapped in the corner of a ring. Banks didn't know that Best had studied the method of his clearances. He'd noticed Banks tossed the ball higher than most other goalkeepers before thumping it downfield. Banks did so again. This was the invitation Best had been waiting for. He leaned backwards and his outstretched left boot flicked the airborne ball over the bamboozled Banks and towards the empty net. The two of them chased after it. There was never any doubt about who'd get to it first, however. Banks grasped vainly for it – and vainly for Best, too. A step and a half ahead, Best nodded the ball into the empty net on the bounce. Banks, overstretching, stumbled and fell and finished outside his left post before turning and waving at the referee in a desperate appeal. What constituted 'foot up' or interference was different then. But the referee, near the half-way line, had seen nothing like the incident before. For that reason he decided Best had infringed the game's laws and gave a foul against him – despite the fact Banks hadn't been tackled, pushed or manhandled in any way. Best was convinced of the goal's legitimacy, his sense of grievance made worse by England's solitary winner, which came with only ten minutes left. 'No one will ever persuade me that the goal shouldn't have counted,' he said. 'As Northern Ireland, we didn't tend to get decisions to go our way.'

Later in life, after reading extensively about the country's history, he'd come to believe a united Ireland was desirable. But as early as 1970, he'd urged the formation of an all-Irish side 'purely for football reasons' and to 'take on the world'. When he did it, FIFA allowed only 16 (and later 24) teams through the door and into its finals. Northern Ireland, despite coming close, never got there with him. Best said he found playing for them 'very emotional' nonetheless. The question he repeatedly heard was: 'Do you wish you had been born somewhere else?' The questioner usually meant England. The answer Best repeatedly gave was: 'No, I don't.'

So he couldn't understand now why some of his own countrymen apparently wanted him shot. He dismissed them as 'cranks', independent from any organisation, political or otherwise.

Frank O'Farrell gave Best the option of withdrawing from the team at Newcastle. He refused. 'No way do I want the person who's made the threat to beat me,' he said. 'What would happen anyway? If I didn't play, the threat would go on into the next and then the next again.'

The night before Best took his meals in his hotel room, guarded by two plain-clothes officers, who drew the curtains and ordered him to stay away from the window. Even the waiter, and his trolley of food, were checked before being allowed through the door. 'I was scared,' confessed Best. His nervousness increased considerably when detectives reported that the club coach had been broken into. He quite naturally connected it to the death threat without concrete proof. On the way to St James' Park he occupied an aisle seat and his minders sat either side of him. As he climbed the 12 stone steps from the coach to the entrance of the ground, two policemen in dark, buttoned mackintoshes went ahead; another two followed behind. A peak-capped, uniformed officer on a white horse held back a swaying, almost silent crowd straining for a glimpse of him from the car park. Those who had waited saw nothing more than his suited, bent back and the heels of his polished shoes. Already, nearly 40 police were stationed inside St James' on the cinder track perimeter of the pitch, near and along the tunnel and outside the dressing room. Undercover officers stood on the terraces. Strangely there were no bag or body searches for spectators who passed through the turnstiles.

On the field Best decided perpetual motion was the sensible option for him. 'I never stopped moving,' he said. 'Even when someone went down injured and the game stopped I carried on running. And I ran down the tunnel at half-time and full-time.' Neither the noise from the terracing nor the normal ebb and flow of the game gave him respite from the thought that a high-velocity bullet could have his name on it. No matter where he ran, Best felt exposed, which made absolute concentration impossible. In the 46th minute he still scored the only goal – from relatively close range – and claimed afterwards: 'It was the only time in my career when no one wanted to come across and hug me.'

The procedures that got him into St James' Park also got him out of it, and patrol cars escorted United's coach to Manchester, one force replacing another whenever a county boundary was crossed. The Troubles followed him into his own living room. Che Sera had to be protected, too. Police were parked in his driveway and detectives accompanied him to training at the beginning of the following week.

A further alert was raised after two men, both with Irish accents, aggressively badgered a woman walking in the area and asked for directions to the house. Neither acted nor sounded like sightseeing supporters. The woman claimed one of the men was carrying a long thin parcel, which she assumed contained a rifle. In the days after returning from St James' Park, Best frequently answered the ringing telephone to hear silence at the other end. For a while he took the phone off the hook, never sure how the caller had obtained his ex-directory number. Another dire warning came out of Belfast, where Best was due to play in a Nations Cup qualifying tie against Spain. To newspapers the game became 'The Fixture of Fear'. If Best went, it was said, he'd never see Manchester – or anywhere else – again because he'd be knifed in the back. The threat was contained in a letter sent to the *Manchester Evening News*. Best said he wanted to play because he thought that success could 'damp down the ashes of all that political-religious upheaval'. United pulled him out of the squad well before FIFA cancelled the match, which was finally staged at the beginning of the following year at a neutral venue. Windsor Park didn't host another international until 1975.

The idea of killing Best seems preposterous and counterproductive. He was a unifying presence across the country. Had the IRA, or any other political organisation, harmed him, it would have broken hearts beyond the borders of Protestant communities. The logistics of the threat make no sense either. It would have taken a skilled marksman to shoot Best from outside St James' Park, and then escape afterwards. In lacking a road map, plus the reconnaissance intelligence to know that the one-way glass wouldn't give them a view of whoever was inside, the men lurking near Che Sera were either the most unlikely assassins or particularly incompetent.

But the climate in Belfast and the mainland during those weeks made the prospect of an attempt on Best's life plausible. It was a particularly sensitive period in Northern Ireland. Internment had begun; 342 people were arrested. The first British soldier had been killed. The army had shot dead two Catholic civilians. Unrest forced the Irish League to postpone the beginning of its season. In the same month Best found himself walking in the shadow of the gunman, Edward Heath's Conservative government sent another 1,500 soldiers to Belfast. The army dismantled one bomb made of 351lb of gelignite, found in the foyer of the Europa Hotel, and another explosive device – a 501lb claymore mine containing shrapnel – jammed into a milk churn concealed on the border. CS gas had to be used to counter the Long Kesh riot. Only eight hours before Best reached St James' Park, troops shot three men dead in a gun battle in Newry.

Best's ghosted column appeared every Friday in the *Daily Express*. How unsettled and angry he felt after being dragged into The Troubles is emphasised in its edition of 12 November, 1971. He wrote the column himself, picking up a black Biro and using four sheets of a ring-bound, lined pad. Handing it to his ghostwriter, Best said: 'I don't know whether they'll think it's good enough to use.' There are six crossings out, but Best's handwriting – a looped I that resembles a number nine, the ruler-straight descending stroke of every y and p – is clear and certain. His punctuation and the construction of each of the 18 paragraphs is accurate and assuredly done, as if he'd been waiting to say it and this is a release for him. The *Express* made only two minor grammatical changes before Best's words were set in hot metal. 'Have you ever wondered,' he wrote, 'why anyone would dislike you enough to kill you? I've been thinking about it this week after a few cranks decided to finish me off.' Best didn't answer his own question. That he asked it in the first place, however, indicated how much the matter consumed him. The idea of his own mortality was churning around in his mind.

No one entirely appreciated the toll it was taking on him or recognised his clinical depression. 'The pressures of it all can become just too much,' he said. 'I'm not a machine.' Again describing himself as a 'loner', another obstacle in trying to untangle the complicated knot of his personality, Best felt nobody – certainly not at Old Trafford – fully comprehended what he was thinking and feeling, or how difficult normal life was becoming for him.

Best had once left a note for Jackie Glass in which he wrote 'Nobody Knows Me', a statement he would claim was composed flippantly, while also insisting contradictorily: 'In some ways it was true.' A variation appeared in the American magazine *Sports Illustrated*, which then rarely covered 'soccer' because the editors regarded it as a minority interest for its readership. What attracted *Sports Illustrated* was the story of the sportsman sucked into a political and religious dispute and also the perception the public had of him from his image. The writer it dispatched to Manchester trawled through the recent history before Best, as accommodating as ever, allowed him into Che Sera. One line in the published piece stands out: 'No one knows how it feels to be me,' said Best. Contained in those nine words is the ever-increasing isolation he felt.

This is Your Life alluded to almost none of this when Best became its subject a few weeks after the death threats (nor did it mention those either). Planned months in advance, the programme was a celebration. The pages of its Big Red Book were turned quickly and out came the people from his past: Bob Bishop, Bud McFarlane, Mary Fullaway, Eric McMordie. Best, legs crossed, sat impassively through it, as if already thinking something he would admit ten years later.

'The title was wrong,' he said of the programme. 'It should have been This Was Your Life.'

To his credit Frank O'Farrell – like Sir Matt Busby and Wilf McGuinness before him – tried to understand George Best.

In January 1972, Best told O'Farrell: 'I'm worried about my family's safety in Belfast.' O'Farrell unhesitatingly promised to go to the directors and explore the possibility of buying a house in Manchester, which his father and mother could rent from the club. O'Farrell thought Best would live with them, an arrangement he foresaw as solving two problems: the family's vulnerability in Belfast and Best's lack of stability in Che Sera. As he always did, Best agreed because, when put on the spot, he tended to pacify and placate. Wanting the plan to remain secret, O'Farrell went to Dublin – under the pretext of watching a match – and caught a train from there to speak to Dickie and Ann, who were agreeable, but noncommittal, about the idea.

O'Farrell arrived back at Old Trafford to discover Best had missed almost a week's training. He'd rung United, claiming to be dealing with 'a family matter' at his parents'. A clever lie contains at least a modicum of believability. The club, aware of his mother's issues with alcohol, didn't ask him to explain further. Even Best hadn't known of O'Farrell's journey to Burren Way; and he hadn't the sense to contact his parents to either let them in on his dodge or to check whether United had rumbled it.

The headlines were 'George Best Vanishes', and 'Best Goes Missing Again' and 'Where's George Gone Now?' Implying that he'd disappeared so successfully as to be untraceable was stretching the facts. He hadn't left Che Sera, declining to get out of bed. Every evening he resolved to go to training the following morning. When morning came, Best said he 'couldn't face it'. Ken Stanley tried to talk to him through a half-open door; Best closed it and refused to budge. 'I didn't want help. I wanted understanding,' he maintained. Best repeated what he'd said after his episode in Sinead Cusack's flat. He was forcing O'Farrell to drop him from the side so his plight and mental condition could become public. He wanted to be rescued, a fact he half-conceded. 'Maybe I was putting myself into difficult situations so that someone would make the decision for me rather than me having to do it,' he said, investing tremendous explanatory power into that opinion.

One of O'Farrell's beliefs was: 'You do what is morally right – even if you have to suffer the consequences.' He didn't want to leave Best out of his team. United were playing Wolves at Old Trafford and, without a win for more than a month, sorely needed to beat them. But O'Farrell couldn't allow Best's absence to go unpunished – and so he punished him and also himself. For without Best United lost again – 3–1. Best wasn't even sitting in the stands. He flew to London and went to a nightclub. He came back on a train, hiding in a first-class compartment with the curtains drawn.

On his appointment as manager O'Farrell asked for a list of the players' salaries. He found Bobby Charlton and Denis Law were still being paid more than Best. Considering it unfair, he made him the club's highest earner. His wage was increased to £225 per week. But Best – deciding he didn't want to disclose his depression after all – announced that a dispute over money was behind his non-appearance at training and his subsequent absence from the team. United were 'taking advantage' of him, he said, sounding like a striking worker who had downed tools. Best said he was worth £1,000 per week. O'Farrell didn't want to embarrass Best. He didn't snap at the bait or defend himself by letting slip the hike in wages already implemented on Best's behalf. The board didn't want to alienate their number one asset, and

Sir Matt Busby agreed to be lenient towards the truant again. Best was fined £350, ordered to forfeit his day off for five weeks and made to train during the afternoon as well as in the morning. A specious compromise was reached, giving the tale a twist and guaranteeing front-page coverage. Best was told to leave Che Sera and go back to his digs at Mary Fullaway's. O'Farrell spoke of Best as a 'lonely boy' and took the Christian view of forgiveness, quoting Proverbs – chapter 24, verse 16 – from the Bible:

For a just man falleth seven times and rises up again.

The very cynical said Best fell seven times every Saturday night because of his drinking.

The idea of making him sleep in Mrs Fullaway's front bedroom again was eccentric and unworkable; but Mrs Fullaway was sincerely pleased to see him. She'd found it impossible to live with idle hands. After Best left Aycliffe Avenue, she'd taken a part-time job in a newsagent's to keep herself busy. The change of routine had been difficult for her. 'It was so quiet,' she said. 'The phone wasn't ringing every ten minutes.'

Best was photographed sitting on his old bed – a red-patterned tea cup in hand – with a smiling Mrs Fullaway beside him. 'To me he is still a little boy – still the shy, painfully introverted schoolboy I knew at fifteen,' she said. 'Because he's had quite an easy sort of life – with everything going for him – he hasn't really had time to mature. So when he comes up against a problem he often lets it get him down. I can always tell when George is depressed. He just goes quiet and retires into his shell.' She talked, too, about why he'd failed to go to training. 'Having missed the first day, I know he would find it difficult to turn up and face the music,' she said, correctly, before promising: 'I shall kick him out myself each morning.' For she was only ever angry with Best when he didn't report for training – or when he wouldn't get up to go on time. Mrs Fullaway added something crucial: 'He has very few real friends – but lots of hangers-on. Sometimes I can't distinguish between the real ones and the fair weather ones.' The insights she gave into her lodger's mannerisms and moods, and the giveaway signs of his introspection, showed she knew more about Best than any of his managers did – including Busby.

Best was concerned for Mrs Fullaway and angry on her behalf. She now began receiving letters accusing her of exploitatively living off his reputation and earnings. He described the content of them as 'obscene' and apologised for inflicting them on her.

While placidly going along with the public facade United created for him – a Potemkin village of pretence and deception – he still continued to go wherever he liked and returned to Che Sera whenever it suited him. His insistence that 'now I'm back in my old digs I aim to get home around six o'clock for a meal' would never have withstood investigation. 'I was sleeping all over the place . . . I didn't really know where I wanted to be,' said Best. His drinking had escalated over the previous six months. He'd become a 'bout' or binge drinker; someone, he explained, who would 'drink solidly' over a period. 'It was the easy way out,' he added. In this state half a glass is never enough. It is always a swallow or two away from empty. Best finished one drink to start another. For a minuscule while, it brought a couldn't-care-bloody-less, fantastic feeling of contentment. The playwright Tennessee Williams, awash with booze, called this exhilarating high 'The Click', a sensation of abandon – the moment when enough alcohol has been shipped to make everything else seem immaterial. In the hour after The Click occurs the drinker believes he sees – and judges – everything with a vibrant clarity, as if God had just tweaked the lens of the eyes, the way an optician adjusts the magnification of a pair of glasses during a test, to allow him precious insights into the meaning of life. Several negatives accompanied the fleeting pleasure The Click provided. To attain it a certain level of alcohol needed to be absorbed into the system. As the body taught itself to tolerate that amount, so more was needed to achieve the same effect – and then more still. One consequence of The Click was always the same – an awful downhill slither into morose disappointment. Another was the stupid temptation to go in pursuit of it again, which only made the drunk drunker still. 'When you're drinking,' said Best, 'nothing else but that matters.'

Nor did Best have to pay for his own drinks. There was no shortage of fellow drinkers willing to buy one for him. Best's need to be the champion of everything was apparent at the bar. He drank as if there was a gold medal for the feat. 'I don't like the idea of people drinking more than me,' he said. 'So I am usually the last man standing. It's not easy for me to walk away. Sometimes it is not easy for me to walk. If my pals drank twenty pints, I'd have to have twenty-one. If they went home at four a.m., I went home at four-thirty.' He drank a bottle of vodka for a bet. At his most dire he stuck his fingers down his throat, making sure he threw up in the toilet basin to get rid of what he'd already consumed so he could drink again. Best would regularly wake up the following morning still wearing the previous night's clothes. His blackouts were worsening. Entire weekends were sometimes lost to him, the drink drilling wide, deep holes into his memory. He would ask, almost jocularly: 'Where did I go? Who did I meet? What happened?' Like everyone around him, Best presumed it was no big deal. 'We all laughed and joked about it. You can't remember where you parked your car and it seems funny at the time,' he said.

One witless session begat another and he always seemed on the precipice of an awful mistake. 'Drink became my company instead of people,' he said. 'Physically and mentally, I went beyond my limits.' The drinking continued into the early hours – 'until four or five in the morning', he said. He remembered David Sadler, a former lodger at Mrs Fullaway's, asking: 'What are you doing to yourself? Think of your health.' There was no convincing reply he could give to assuage him.

Best bumped along in a losing team, as though the player in the shirt he wore was a look-alike substitute, and went 11 games without scoring, the imbalance in his season demonstrated by another statistic: 14 First Division goals between August and late November and only four afterwards. United finished eighth in the table, ten points behind the new champions, Brian Clough's Derby. Clough, resentful of the fact Busby hadn't approached him about Old Trafford's managerial vacancy instead of O'Farrell, saw it as a vindication of his own methods and arrogance, both of which led to Busby scratching him off the candidates' list. 'When I won that title I said to myself, "I wonder what the bugger thinks now,"' said Clough.

Three months before the end of the 1971–72 season Best announced he was 'sick of United'. He was even 'sick enough', he added, to 'ask for a move', and continued: 'I'd go anywhere I thought there could be success.' The reason he gave was the standard of the team. 'It's just not good enough. It's just not going anywhere. I could go right through the team and find things wrong. People knock me when I'm not doing it. But when I'm not doing it, who is?' In what he said was a 'funny sort of way' Best accepted he might be selfish. 'Why should it be one success after another?' he asked. The answer he gave to his own question still suggested he believed any selfishness was legitimate. 'They had everything going for them,' he said of United. 'It should have been success year after year.'

Best missed informal chats over a pot of tea with Jimmy Murphy, who used to listen to him as comfortingly and non-judgementally as a trained Samaritan. 'What's the matter with you?' Murphy would ask, leaving a gap for Best to fill. Gentle catechism was always Murphy's method of easing information out of Best, as if using a pair of tweezers to slowly pull the words free. Murphy had retirement pressed upon him in 1971 – shamefully he was given only £20,000 and a £25 per week scouting job – and Best felt his absence severely and thought it created a hole in the heart of the club.

Without having the courtesy to tell O'Farrell in advance – and so insulting a manager who had been good to him – he sought out Busby privately, outlining each personal grievance and the distress it was causing him: the urgent need for quality players, fresh tactics and the futility he felt. 'I feel like giving up,' he said. There was no assurance of jam tomorrow from Busby. All Best got was a smile and the inference Busby agreed with him wholeheartedly. He waited for radical change, which never came. From afar it looked as though, wanton and dervishly self-destructive, he was neglecting his football because he no longer cared about it. The opposite was true. Best was a picture of unbalance because he cared about it too much. He drank on irrationally nonetheless, knowing it would only make matters worse for him and United, because drink represented his only coping strategy. When drunk, he could at least kid himself that things would get better. When sober, he realised it was a delusion, and so drank again. 'I'd get fed up trying to explain what was going wrong and felt that nothing had been done about it. That would start it off,' he said.

He went to speak to O'Farrell, repeating his request for £1,000 a week and asking for United to buy Che Sera. On the one hand, he had ambitions of living in a penthouse apartment with his own lift in a yet to be designed, let alone built, tower block in Manchester's city centre. On the other, he didn't want to kick another ball. Exhaustion was distorting the way an enfeebled Best saw everything, including himself. He mistook the debilitating effects of his drinking as an indication of professional burnout. Best couldn't bring himself to go back to Busby to tell him directly because he said he found it 'hard to confront those I love'.

The traits and habits we develop and exhibit early in life can follow us into adulthood. It was certainly so for Best. What he did as a boy and in his youth foreshadowed and bore the same pattern as the behaviour he demonstrated in his most troubled years at United.

The 11-year-old Best had responded to miserable experiences at the authoritarian Grosvenor High School by regularly truanting, ingeniously hiding his school bag at an aunt's house in the morning and secretly reclaiming it at the end of the afternoon. The 15-year-old Best had run back to Belfast from Manchester on only the second day of his trial, which was another form of truancy. The 24-year-old Best had hidden in Sinead Cusack's flat. The 26-year-old Best – feeling as desolate now as he'd done on each of those previous occasions – decided to flee, too. In this way running off became one of the motifs of his life.

As to his reluctance to face problems directly, even as an adult, Best readily acknowledged it as a flaw. 'I tend to run away and think about sorting them out somewhere else – usually in another country,' he said.

The country he chose now was Spain.

13

Trying to Sleep Eight Hours a Night

Two days before his 26th birthday George Best was due to play for Northern Ireland against Scotland at Hampden Park in the Home International Championship. But, alone in Che Sera, he was on the brink of a complete mental and physical breakdown. The world seemed to be dropping away from him on all sides. 'I believed I was slowly killing myself,' he said. Best began to juggle three scenarios in his mind.

1. He could go to Scotland to play for Northern Ireland.

2. He could stay in Manchester and continue 'to drink myself stupid'.

3. He could get 'the hell out of it all' by buying an aeroplane ticket.

Best, so flustered, couldn't see the fourth option. He could have owned up to the fact he needed a complete rest and counselling, which Manchester United would have arranged for him.

Another sleepless night ratified a decision Best had already made. After an evening out, he returned to Che Sera at 2.30 a.m. By 5.30 a.m., he was still awake. At 6 a.m., after throwing a few clothes and toiletries into a bag, he was in a taxi heading for Manchester airport. He asked the driver to get him a ticket 'on the first plane out to anywhere'. He flew to London and then, he said, 'drifted in a daze' to a five-star hotel in Marbella. By mid-afternoon the bare-chested Best, wearing a pair of aviator sunglasses, was lounging beside the ultramarine blue of a swimming pool and sipping iced beer. Several empty bottles were clustered on the table in front of him; a couple more sat at his feet. 'All I wanted to do was escape,' he added. Escape was a chimera for Best, and the Utopia he sought – a place where he could be famous and anonymous simultaneously – existed on no map.

There are two images of Best which linger from the first week of his abdication on the Costa del Sol. The first is a monochrome photograph. He is sitting on a wooden-backed, metal-framed chair beside the window of his hotel room. He is in a vest and a pair of brief, flowery patterned shorts. His left foot rests on a cheap panelled football. His right hand holds a champagne flute in which only the dregs remain. The light falls across him, and Best looks dishevelled, as though he's wandered in, half-cut, from another session on the booze and decided to swill a last drink of fizz as a pick-me-up. The second is in a colour snippet of film, which was shown on the television news. He wears clothes that are of varying shades of pink. He stands on the hotel patio, spinning a football between his hands. The sun is directly above him, throwing only minimal shadow. The point at which the sky meets the sea is indistinguishable in the far distance. The sea shines like tinplate. The horizon is wrapped in heat haze. Boats and yachts are anchored in the harbour and a motor cruiser leaves a narrow, V-shaped wake behind it in the flat water. In this paradise Best drops the ball and begins flicking it from one, tanned shoeless foot to the other and then on to his right thigh for the benefit of the photographers. He finally catches the ball before tossing it into the air and heading it four times, the last effort sliding off his forehead. The amount drunk throughout the past year has given him a small paunch, visible against the tight, stretched fabric of his vest.

There's something inherently sorrowful about both the photograph and the piece of film. A platoon of Fleet Street reporters had followed Best to Marbella to gain confirmation of the well-spread rumour that he was about to retire. But the imminent announcement isn't what gives the film and the photograph a doleful, downcast edge. What does is his face. His expression never fully conveys the relief and liberation he claims to feel. Best looks like an unwilling participant in an event that he precipitated but no longer controls. Even the content of the 'I QUIT' newspaper article he later signed is unconvincing. It's as if he is demanding the reader to believe him.

'Nobody knows what has been going on behind the glamorous image of George Best . . . For the last year all I've done is drink . . . I can't cope any more . . . I'm going to get out before the game kills me . . . It [football] has become work instead of the sport I always enjoyed . . . I was in a void of despair . . . My decision is irrevocable . . . I have passed my peak. . . . I never intend to watch a match again, not even on TV . . . I've played my last game . . . Nothing will change my mind . . . I hope to find myself again . . . When I can sleep eight hours at night I know I will be getting better.'

So it went on.

He 'dare not go home' to Northern Ireland because of The Troubles, he said. He was going to sell Che Sera and live in London. He was going to wander aimlessly around the world for six months beforehand. He was going to design clothes. He was going to open another business. He was going to survive financially on his investments – even though his decision would cost him at least £12,500 a year in wages and bonuses. He wasn't going to miss the pressure of the game. 'I won't change my mind,' he insisted. 'I know a lot of people aren't going to believe me. They will only accept it when I don't turn up at the start of the season.'

The more he reiterated all this, the less credible he sounded. He was speaking his mind in the wrong way at the wrong time. For these were the lame-brained statements of someone too bone-tired to think rationally. Best surely heard the puerility in them, and yet he kept on talking anyway. Those who were stupefied by it tried to interpret his riddling speech. The most incisive assessment came from Ken Stanley, whose office telephone rang until the bell almost broke. Best hadn't told Stanley about his intentions in advance. Nor had he considered the commercial repercussions. Sponsors, current and future, took their wrath against Best out on his agent. Contracts were dependent on Best continuing to be a footballer. Stanley found himself fending off or attempting to mollify companies – their warehouses brimful with Best-branded merchandise – who were threatening him with a court appearance or demanding to be repaid. A writ was served as soon as Best publicly declared he was quitting because the newspaper to which he sold his story – the *Sunday Mirror* paid £5,000 for it – wasn't the one that owned his byline. His agreement was with the Express Group. Amid this tumult, which threatened his reputation as well as his livelihood, Stanley was charitable towards his errant client. 'Once again George did things the wrong way,' he said. 'But you don't select the time when you have severe mental depression.' The last three words dug to the bare root of why Best had behaved abnormally. This wasn't an arrogant flouncing out or a stroppy tantrum. It wasn't a temporary slump into the doldrums. Stanley thought what ailed Best required medical attention.

Best got a chocolate cake with candles on his birthday. As he blew those candles out he made his wish public: never to walk on to a football pitch again. The wicks were still warm when he began to change his mind. From carefree he soon went to careworn. Every day in the holiday resort seemed to last a year. It was monotony under the sun. The reality of a beach existence was simply the swapping of one routine for another, which proved less satisfactory and less stimulating for him. Without football, there was no foundation to his life. Out of boredom he drank. Out of boredom he ate – tapas, hamburger and fries, steak sandwiches.

Out of boredom he'd take the same walks, the view and the heat no consolation. He'd wake in the middle of the morning and drink a shandy or three to rid his dry mouth of the sour aftertaste of the night before. Best was always 'topping up'. For lunch there'd be beer and chilled white wine – 'I like a cold glass,' he said to the barman – and then he'd move from his hotel to a local bar before going into town in the evening and starting on the vodka.

Early on Sir Matt Busby and Frank O'Farrell stuck to a public policy of non-intervention. Busby knew that pursuing Best would be counterproductive. You needed to be patient. You didn't chase someone as elusive and evasive as Best in case you drove him further underground. You waited until he was ready to come back of his own accord. In the boardroom United calculated Best's market value. The club couldn't afford to sack him or cancel his contract. The British transfer record stood at £220,000 – the amount Arsenal paid Everton for Alan Ball in the closing weeks of 1971 – and Best was worth almost double that sum. The catch was this: no sane club would allow its manager to gamble so much on damaged goods; especially since the full extent of that damage had still to be established. And no one at United thought Best was finished with them anyway. The initial question was how he could come back to Old Trafford without looking like a chump. The followups were all about getting Best fit, making him reliable and productive again and the restoration of trust. Best pretended otherwise, but the same thoughts – and the dilemma each one posed – were occupying him, too. Football gave him something alcohol never did. 'The buzz for me was thinking how I could get fifty thousand people on their feet, chanting my name. The best feeling in the world was knowing I had the crowd in my pocket,' he said. He'd admit that his 'biggest problem' was replacing that buzz – 'anything to give me back that sense of excitement'. Best knew it wasn't hiding somewhere in Spain, just waiting to be found, which is why he soon made his peace with United.

What drove him away from football – boredom and dissatisfaction – also drew him back there. After some more ballyhoo of the 'Will-He-Won't-He' variety, Best U-turned and returned to Old Trafford following a six-week sojourn that had been half circus, half tempest and which he alone instigated.

Best was docked two weeks' wages and suspended for a fortnight, which didn't rank as a bread and water punishment. Asked if this was Best's final chance, O'Farrell replied non-specifically: 'You know me. An eternal optimist.' He said it with a smile, which is all he could have done. The caution implicit in those two short sentences, however, suggested that he suspected any protestation of devotion from the prodigal son would be followed by another separation from United eventually; and O'Farrell was running low on fatted calves. The relationship between them now revolved around O'Farrell's patronage, and Best's dependence upon it. These were flimsy things on which to build. He was beholden to someone with whom he found it difficult to communicate. O'Farrell was philosophic. 'If Busby couldn't handle George, how could I?' he later asked.

Busby had nothing new to say about solving the Best Problem. He knew spells of calm were the briefest of punctuations – always semi-colons rather than full stops. Pledges to start afresh from Best were so frequent that constant repetition stripped them of any meaning. Busby said of him: 'I am sure that he wanted to be different and that he always intended to keep his promises. But he lacked self-control. With him it was a promise today broken tomorrow . . . There was always a next time, another disaster.' He did make a practical suggestion. Busby offered Best a room in his own home, an invitation declined with delicacy by the prospective boarder. 'I told him he would have the freedom of the house and as much privacy as he wanted,' said Busby. While appreciating the magnanimous gesture, Best saw such an arrangement as the equivalent of entombment. He'd always be on tiptoe – cautious about causing offence, guarded in what he said, uneasy in an atmosphere he was certain would be too constrictive for him. The outcome would have pained both him and his benefactor. He'd have to mind his Ps and Qs, which would only have made conflict with Busby inevitable. What if he came home late and ever so slightly the worse for drink? What would Busby think of him then? What if he decided to stay in bed one morning and avoid training? Would Busby pull off the covers and frog-march him there? How could he ever come down to breakfast in his underwear and unshaved in front of Lady Busby?

O'Farrell wrestled with two questions of his own: Where should Best live? How should he be policed? As the first was inseparable from the second O'Farrell's suggestion, an ostensibly sound piece of 'tough love', was to choose a completely new 'safe' house for him. Best couldn't – publicly at least – be seen to slip permanently through the door of Che Sera again. Nor could he go back to Mary Fullaway's to do as he pleased. For appearance's sake O'Farrell had to convince his critics that Best was being properly tethered, the rein on him much tighter than before. He had to demonstrate Best's return was dependent on terms and conditions the club, rather than Best himself, had laid down.

The big idea was to lodge Best in Paddy Crerand's semi-detached home in Chorlton. The percentage chance of success was so low that, by forcing it through, O'Farrell handed the newspapers two juicy stories: the first when Best moved in and the second when he moved out again. Best arrived in his E-type Jaguar, which he parked on the road, and took one suitcase and his washbag out of the boot. He was put into the boxroom previously occupied by Crerand's eldest son. Noreen Crerand was already looking after three children under eight; now she had a fourth, aged 26 and two and a quarter months. Best had to take his washing back to Mrs Fullaway's. He wasn't given a key for historical reasons. Babysitting for the Crerands in the mid-1960s, he'd invited a girlfriend into the house after the couple had gone out. He was also expected to do his own basic cooking. He ordered a breakfast of eggs and bacon and found it waiting for him next morning. But there was a snag. 'I didn't realise I'd have to put them into the frying pan myself,' said Best, incredulously. The small incident underscored how much Mrs Fullaway cosseted him and the way in which Best automatically assumed everyone else would do likewise. He lasted less than 72 hours at the Crerands'. O'Farrell let him return to Mrs Fullaway's, where normal service regarding breakfast was resumed.

A sportsman can read his own body. He can tell by the way his heart and lungs respond how far he can push them; and also how much mileage his legs will allow him to cover before he's run the energy out of them. Best was in a poor way. He was no longer the perfect specimen. The muscles in his torso had lost their tautness, and his belly sagged and bowed a little. 'I was tubby,' he said. His calves and thighs, once like iron, were flabby, too, through neglect.

When he got on to the scales in mid-July United found his weight had increased from 10½st, which it had been in May, to 12st, 4lb. 'I'd really let myself go,' he said, ashamed about it. Except for a few token barefoot kicks of that plastic ball on the beach, Best said he'd taken 'no exercise at all' and was 'horrified to find out how unfit I was'. A daunting slog lay ahead of him and initially he trained with the youth team, which was like regressing ten years. There were sprints and long runs, which made him feel like throwing up, and sessions in the gym to get his muscles into basic shape and try to give him some stamina. The man who used to adore the toil and sweat of training – and who prided himself on his appearance when stripped – found the programme tediously repetitive. On occasions he looked blank-eyed at the end of a session, as if the soul had flown from the body. The suspension United imposed was necessary to dispense the smack of firm government to the miscreant. But putting the naughty boy in the corner proved counterproductive. Best missed four warm-up matches, depriving him of competitive hours on the field. Far from match-fit on the League's opening Saturday, Best breathed hard through a 2–1 defeat to Ipswich. It set the tone for the months to come.

'I'd worked hard to get ready for the season,' he said. 'I soon wished I hadn't bothered.'

When George Best went on the record to say that 'if someone has a talent or a gift or is different . . . they have to be treated differently', he was referring to himself. When he added that 'if I was in charge of a team and I had the greatest player in the world and he chose on days to turn up without socks on I would let him do it if he was performing on the field', he was pleading for preferential treatment as an individualist. But, at the end of his exile in Spain, there were no triumphant anthems to greet him at Old Trafford.

The atmosphere in the dressing room had been bad enough before his disappearance. One defeat after another in the closing months of the old season had, like the effect of constant days of hard rain, turned the mood melancholic. Best said no one spoke much after matches, the silence worse for him than stand-up rows or shouted accusations because it underscored the helplessness he saw within the team. Best was reluctant to get changed following a game Manchester United had lost. He'd yank off his boots and socks and then sit in the rest of his kit without speaking, contemplating the uselessness of another performance and how he planned to obliterate it from his memory with drink. 'I felt this terrible emptiness,' he said.

Best was apprehensive about the reception he might receive and went as far as to say that his 'greatest worry' was facing the other players again. He specifically meant facing Bobby Charlton.

Asked, point-blank, about how the team had responded in the aftermath of his failure to turn up for a week's training the previous January, Best gave a slashing reply, which was quite untypical of him.

'They've been great,' he said. 'All except one. I'm not saying who he is but his name is Bobby Charlton.' In the summer Charlton was cornered at Heathrow Airport en route to his holiday in Bermuda. The newspapermen, wanting to know Charlton's thoughts on Best's future, got a tetchy response. 'If it wasn't for him we wouldn't be going on holiday to Bermuda. It's impossible to go anywhere in Europe because you get pounded by British tourists asking what's happening to George Best.'

Things had once been different between them. As Best blossomed in the Championship seasons of the mid-1960s, Best and Charlton were cordial and admiring of one another without ever being bosom buddies. Each created chances for the other, and the thanks and congratulations between them when it brought a goal were bona fide illustrations of mutual respect. Charlton spoke warmly of Best, amazed by his capabilities and his goals, which he regarded as classics of improvisation. Everything Best did was 'heroic', he said. In 1969 Charlton even wrote an article entitled 'My Pal George', likening his personal relationship with Best as paternal. 'Put George and me side by side and I suppose we could pass as father and son. I'd be proud of him if he were.' Best reciprocated, describing Charlton as 'a brilliant passer' and saying his ability to land the ball where he wanted was 'like radar picking you out from half a field away'. To Best, he was 'a god' and 'a joy to play with'.

By the beginning of the 1972–73 season that joy had long since drained away for Best.

The deterioration of his relationship with Charlton is one of the most important sub-plots – a drama within a drama – at Old Trafford in those years following the European Cup win. Like so many feuds and disagreements, it was deadly serious at the time for Best and seems staggeringly trivial when examined now.

Best and Charlton had only two fundamental things in common: the colours of United and a working-class upbringing. In nearly every other regard this was a pairing of polar opposites. 'We lived in different worlds,' said Best. The reasons for it were generational and temperamental. In age nearly a decade separated them. Charlton, born in 1937, was a teenager of the early 1950s, the years of austerity and reconstruction, and also of Bill Haley's 'Rock Around The Clock'. He became one of United's Babes in 1956, well before Best and the post-war baby boomers began carving out a vibrantly distinctive culture of their own. A lot of the devil-may-care attitude within Charlton was ripped out on that airfield at Munich, where he survived and thereafter asked himself the unanswerable question: Why? For Charlton the normal processes of maturity, especially the realisation that a man's life is finite, were accelerated in one of the most horrible ways imaginable. On impact, the Elizabethan aircraft snapping in half, he'd been thrown 100 yards across the runway. Those who died were sitting near the tail. Charlton was in a front seat, his back to the nose of the plane. He recovered from relatively minor injuries – concussion, a gashed head, a strained neck – to play again within a month of the crash. But the mental wounds of Munich could never heal. 'It still reaches down and touches me every day,' he said, almost half a century after the catastrophe.

Beneath the silken armour of his shirt there was no question that Charlton counted as muscular. Here was someone who kept himself in top athletic shape. He also had that shot, fierce enough from either foot to stop a train. But, even before he played alongside him, Charlton appeared to Best to be far older than the others. There was the pinched face and the baldness, hardly hidden with long, combed-over strands of hair and a parting only two inches from his left ear. A zephyr could send it into disarray. The clothes he chose were so different from those Best hung in his wardrobe. With his sober collection of jackets and slacks, plus the white shirt and tie, Charlton dressed like Best's father. Best wore llama coats; Charlton wore sheepskin. Best drove sports models with sleek bonnets; Charlton drove business-like or family cars and looked as if he might do so in a pair of those fretted, shammy leather gloves beloved of Sunday afternoon motorists. Best was the epitome of glamour with a sexy edge; Charlton represented the cosiness of middle-class respectability to him.

Away from Old Trafford, their lives had no reason to intersect. Charlton was married with two young daughters. Best, the bachelor, watched him head off to the world of domesticity after every game and then went in search of his own idea of what he called 'a good time'. He and Charlton seemed to have shared a semi-confidence only once. Charlton invited Best to his house after the two of them played in a friendly in 1969 – Wales versus the Rest of the United Kingdom at Cardiff – and then travelled back to the North West together. The rail journey was uneventful and the conversation didn't catch alight. 'Never having much to say to one another, we'd hardly spoken,' said Charlton, who was 'astonished' when Best agreed to get off the train at Crewe and accompany him home by car for dinner. Charlton's wife and daughters were away, and Best settled on the settee in the lounge, feet up, watching TV, flicking through magazines. Charlton took a bag of frozen scampi out of the fridge and cooked it. After the meal Best began to ask domestic questions that were entirely out of character. Who does your garden? Do you have a cleaner? How much did the carpet cost? 'I was baffled. Then it came to me. George was thinking of getting married,' he said. Charlton was right. The unlikely conversation, which Charlton remembered as both 'strange' and 'poignant', took place shortly before Best's courtship of Eva Haraldsted became known. But the exchange didn't foster a friendship of traded secrets. Never again did Best seek out Charlton to glean further insight into matrimony, nest-building or finance. Instead there was an incremental building up of small resentments and grudges, which ought to have been easily resolved through a few words of judicious arbitration.

Charlton, a stickler for professional protocol, was dismayed whenever Best missed training or arrived late, nursing another hangover. The wrist slaps and mild rebukes he got from successive managers bewildered him, too. Charlton said he watched Best blunder 'from one outrageous escapade to another' without being 'exposed to the discipline I experienced during my early days', a fact he ascribed to Munich. Sir Matt Busby was more forgiving of personal mistakes after the catastrophe than he'd been before it. 'Three or four times Frank O'Farrell let him off when the rest of the players were looking for a lead,' added Charlton. 'The players were all for the club, even if they'd lost faith in O'Farrell. But the Best business was an embarrassment to them. It seemed at times that George was the club. The atmosphere was terrible.' As captain, senior pro and the figurehead of the club, Charlton considered it his duty to voice disapproval of what he described as Best's 'uncontrollable impulses'. Charlton was clear on this point: other players came to him to complain about Best's drinking and the effect on morale. 'It was then my job to speak to the manager about it, which I did on several occasions.'

O'Farrell was caught in the crossfire. 'I understood why Bobby was upset. He came in and worked every day and kept his end up. George didn't. But the team wasn't good enough without him. I had to keep on picking him. I told Bobby that and he didn't necessarily agree with me. Perhaps he thought differently a little while later when he became a manager himself and saw that sometimes in that position you have do things that others find hard to accept.'

Best regarded running to O'Farrell as telling tales. He claimed 'one or two other players' weren't enamoured with Charlton either. 'They didn't get the sort of publicity I did,' he explained. He dismissed him with personal put-downs, which included 'he's a bit dour' and 'a bloody misery'. In a television interview Best was asked about who had influenced his football. 'Cissie Charlton,' he said sarcastically, fed up with hearing how Charlton's mother had coached her son as a lad in Ashington's back streets and wanting to ridicule him for it. He grew weary, too, of what he saw as Charlton's nannying. 'I do what I want – not what Bobby Charlton wants,' he said. However he chose to live, Best went on, he maintained it was none of Charlton's 'fucking business'. Best believed he was solely carrying United, and accused Charlton of never saying 'well done' to him for that contribution. He was also tired of being told by others 'you should be more like Bobby Charlton', which made him critical of what he believed was Charlton's 'holier-than-thou attitude'.

'I wish I could hear him say fuck just once,' said Best, deliberately using brassy language within his earshot.

He also expressed an alternative view to Charlton's about how the deaths at Munich continued to have a bearing on United's thinking. He believed Busby was over-loyal to Charlton, which got in the way of rebuilding United after the European Cup win. Best said Charlton was 'able to play on a little longer than he should have done' and argued: 'As he became less effective United became less effective.' Playing cards, he would chide anyone who gambled badly with the line: 'You're making more mistakes than Bobby Charlton.'

Best thought Charlton ought to have accepted that he was 'part of the problem' rather than the solution. 'I represented the future of Manchester United – or should have done. Charlton represented the past,' he said; and then went on to claim that Charlton 'resented' that fact. Charlton's retort to the charge was just as robust. Best displayed a 'definite sourness' towards him because he, rather than Best, was closer to the club.

What also grated on Best was his perception of Charlton's attitude during United's slump. 'He first of all started trying to put the blame on himself. It was all his fault, which tended to make him a little worse. Little things used to annoy me about him. I always thought that he thought he was better than us. Not as a player, but as a person. I suppose

I was the only one that said too much about it.' Best said Charlton wasn't 'one of the boys' and never could be. He thought Charlton would 'rather stand and have a drink with the directors than with the other players', as if he belonged to the upper classes at Old Trafford. 'He regarded himself as a member of the upstairs team – and everyone else was downstairs,' he added.

Disagreement between them worsened. Antipathy turned to enmity for Best. A cold war developed, dominated by silence. They were like Oscar Wilde's ships passing in a storm. They made no sign. They said no word. They had no word to say – at least largely to one another. According to Alex Stepney, Charlton would go straight to his peg in the dressing room. 'Without as much as a nod to anyone he would stare straight at the wall . . . change into his kit and leave the room. There was never any conversation. Often, behind his back, you would see Denis [Law] or George making gestures as if to say: "What's got into him?"' Stepney added that he thought Best's 'complete lack of concern for the club' threw Charlton into this 'desperately black mood'. Best, he went on, 'suddenly had a coldness in his heart'.

It reached the stage where Best conceded that off the field 'we never spoke except to say good morning – if we were in a good mood'. On it he strived not to pass to Charlton if there was another ball he could play. Out of annoyance, after a move broke down, Best admitted he'd sometimes call Law 'a prick'. Charlton would be similarly insulted – but there was one difference. 'I didn't mean what I said to Denis . . . in Bobby's case I was understating my feelings,' he said.

Best could be maddening himself because of his hogging of the ball. 'I was probably responsible for him losing his hair,' he said. In one game – there are at least three varying accounts, each identifying the opposition differently – Charlton resolved to teach him a lesson. He saw Best in possession on the left touchline and refused to move into space to support him. Best came infield, running directly across Charlton, who continued to stand still, as if his feet were cemented to the grass. With his route blocked by defenders Best checked back – again galloping past Charlton, who watched him return to almost the exact spot where he'd started 15 seconds earlier. For a third time Best, undeterred and taking no notice of anyone in a United shirt, set off and went ahead of his stationary team-mate, who by now thought his retention of the ball had gone 'beyond a joke'. He was about to call him greedy when Best lashed his shot into the roof of the net. 'What a goal,' said Charlton. Best observed that he and Charlton had begun to share the same faults in the 1970s. Best said Charlton played as if wearing blinkers. 'When I first got in the team I used to frustrate him with some of the things I did with the ball. When he got to the end of his career, he used to frustrate me. It turned a complete circle – we'd swapped places, almost. Making mistakes. Trying to do things that weren't coming off any more.'

Best felt dejection over his conflict with Charlton. He'd even talk about it to Philomena Lynott in the Biz. 'He was terribly upset about the friction at the club,' she said. The irony is that Best and Charlton should have been in harmony when United needed them most. They were equally as upset over the team's inadequacies – and felt equally as powerless when it came to tackling them. The crisis at Old Trafford, which ought to have brought Best and Charlton closer together, actually made the split between them cavernously wider. It then became wider still in mid-September when United staged Charlton's testimonial against Celtic. Best claimed an injury to his right ankle meant he was unfit to play, a convenient excuse which didn't disguise the calculated snub behind it. Best didn't want to support Charlton. His friends had already joshed him about double standards. He was seen in a photograph congratulating Charlton for scoring a goal. Best had embraced him, his left hand patting Charlton's breast bone. 'You did that when we know what you really think of him,' was the sort of ribbing he got. Best said taking the field in the testimonial would have been 'hypocritical', given their lack of empathy and the animosity he felt towards him. Best watched the first five minutes of the match before leaving Old Trafford and going to the Brown Bull, where he threw beer and hurled two dozen eggs at Charlton's portrait, which hung on a wall. News of what Best had done, and why, sped like a lit fuse. He did nothing to stop it or contradict the accounts. He wanted the public to know and he also wanted Charlton to squirm. 'In those days I just didn't have too much time for him as a person,' he said.

The undignified episode was a prequel to a handful more – each one worse than the last – in three months of anguish that followed for Best.

Manchester United assumed that once Best had run off the fat, and played sufficient games, he'd be as devastating as ever for them. At first, he thought so, too. But the Best who had gone to Spain was not the same Best who had come back to Old Trafford.

In *Golden Boy*, Clifford Odets's play about a boxer, the principal character announces: 'Speed, speed, everything is speed – nobody gets me!' It had always been like this for Best. His speed had meant no one could get him either. He moved as fast as an eyelid's soundless blink then. Two years earlier the German director Hellmuth Costard had positioned eight 16mm cameras around Old Trafford, each focused exclusively on Best. The one-hour-40-minute film he made from the footage, *Football As Never Before*, tracked every step Best took and every tackle, header and shot he attempted. Among the noticeable aspects is Best's pace. From a standing start he breezes past defenders. In full stride it is like watching an Olympic sprinter. Now some of that speed – Best's elastic snap – had gone. It was as if it had been spirited away almost overnight. Years later Best would hear Bobby Moore tell him, 'You can only do what your legs do,' and he'd think back to his comeback and properly understand the wisdom of it. His legs would no longer take him where his brain told him to go. He could still dart past defenders. What he lacked was the ability to go well beyond them, burning off his marker. Bobby Charlton immediately noticed that Best was struggling to recapture what had been commonplace in every previous performance – an exceptional change in pace whenever he chose to use it. That 'killer' weapon had vanished for ever, and Best admitted as much. 'All the skills were there,' he said, stressing that his close control and ability to body swerve remained intact. 'There was simply no way I could get my old speed back. No amount of training made any difference.' He could be overtaken, caught and restrained now; and the realisation of that was troubling for him. Best was suddenly mortal. It was like Superman finding out that he didn't have his super-strength any more. Sir Matt Busby noted it, too. 'I saw the change in him,' he said.

Frustration piled upon frustration for Best. He'd dismissed Ken Stanley without explanation, jeopardising the agency itself. 'My father was devastated,' says David Stanley. 'He couldn't understand it. There was a long, difficult period for him before he sorted out the business and stabilised it. Contracts were waiting to be signed. Other negotiations were complete or half-complete. George just walked away from them. My father was an honourable man. He felt personally responsible for every deal he did, which made matters worse for him.' Best, so wrapped up in himself, chose not to think about the storms he inflicted on others, such as Stanley. For in not thinking about them, he could pretend they hadn't happened. Only well after the fact did Best accept, somewhat sheepishly: 'I think I sent Ken towards a nervous breakdown.'

The red top tabloids were beginning to rile Best. 'They say I'm over-weight,' he said. 'Have you ever seen your average journalist? They must be one of the unfittest bunch of people on the planet. They write the most hurtful things.' And United were abysmal. Their attacks were as ineffective as fixed bayonet charges against defences packing artillery. Three successive defeats were followed by four consecutive draws, and then another two defeats were piled on top of them. Best scored only the odd goal: one against Leicester, another at West Ham. The team were in the bottom three in the table and looking like relegation fodder. Even Charlton was dropped. Frank O'Farrell had bought Wyn 'The Leap' Davies from Manchester City for £60,000 and added Ted MacDougall for £200,000 from Bournemouth. Neither impressed Best. With the exception of Martin Buchan, the players O'Farrell recruited weren't worth the fees he paid for them, he claimed. Best said Davies was 'too old'; MacDougall was 'just another bad buy'; a third, Ian Storey-Moore, who had come from Nottingham Forest for £200,000 six months earlier, was 'terribly injury prone'. Best continued: 'The team was bad and getting worse . . . They were buying players that didn't have the right to wear the red shirt . . . I got totally disillusioned playing with amateurs after playing with some of the greatest players in the world . . . the bad players started making me look bad and that made me worse.'

In late October Spurs beat United 4–1 at Old Trafford and, a month later, the Manchester derby at Maine Road was a doddle for City, who won 3–0.

The thought of being unable to influence a match as commandingly as he'd once done made Best feel inadequate and mediocre – even though his definition of a mediocre contribution would have counted as a very good one for almost anyone else. 'I couldn't face simply being a very good player,' he said. 'I was the best player the world has ever seen.' The quotation sounds arrogant, as if he's following the dictum Flaubert set down – 'live like a bourgeois, think like a demigod' – but it illuminates the inner struggle Best was having with himself. He looked peculiarly isolated, an extreme goer-alone. His life was one of not so quiet desperation – a ramshackle existence. Prodigal with his days and nights, some which passed without him knowing it, he fell into a malaise of his own making and sought his own cure in more alcohol.

He'd be woozy – or worse – at ten in the morning. 'I'd have got smashed the night before and I was still pissed. I'd hear Paddy Crerand say that I stank like a brewery.' Some days, he said, 'I was getting home when [United] were reporting for training. It got to the stage where I couldn't get up to go . . . I was too embarrassed to let the lads smell drink on me. So then I wouldn't go in and that, of course, made it ten times worse. The longer it went on, the more embarrassing and difficult I found it.' There'd be gaps of two days and then three days when he didn't train. O'Farrell would ring Malcolm Wagner and ask plaintively: 'Where's George?'

Best had taken a small, ground-floor office in the centre of Manchester. He began camping there overnight, turning on the gas fire and sleeping on the floor. The heat of the fire made his face glow and its fumes made his head pound. He indulged in some retail therapy, too, buying another Rolls-Royce, second-hand for £10,750, a sum which would have bought two small family cars for every household in Aycliffe Avenue.

Best saw no future for United unless new and better players arrived. He saw no future for himself if it meant turning up to go through the motions of another defeat. 'They'd never have improved to the level I'd have wanted . . . Maybe I was setting my sights too high. Maybe I was a perfectionist.' The outcome for him – as well as for United – looks so obvious now that you wonder why two decisions the club's board made weren't reached sooner. The team couldn't go on losing. Best couldn't go on doing as he liked. There was bound to be a breaking point, unpleasant but unavoidable.

For Best, it began after police charged him with actual bodily harm for slapping a woman in a Manchester nightclub at 2 a.m. (a magistrate later accepted Best had experienced 'a great deal of provocation' but found him guilty anyway). O'Farrell fined him £200, suspended him for 14 days and put him on the transfer list. There was a bungled attempt to tell Best officially of the decision. A letter was hand-delivered to Mary Fullaway's. Her lodger wasn't there, and O'Farrell sounded hapless when he conceded 'we don't know where he is', and then helpless as he added: 'We have done all we could . . . He has not behaved like a full-time professional . . . I do not pretend to know what goes on inside his head.'

Nor, it has to be said, did Best.

What the next four weeks brought was calamity on a grand scale. Best fell apart. He first went on a bender in London and missed two successive days' training. He failed, too, to turn up for a meeting with the directors to discuss his conduct. His Rolls was vandalised; someone raked a knife across the white paintwork of the driver and passenger doors. The company that had assumed control of his boutiques removed his name from the shops. He lost his boot deal with Stylo. The manufacturer gave the contract to Kevin Keegan, a player described by one critic as 'not fit to lace Best's drinks'. To add to the plethora of second chances Best had been given, United announced he'd be training with them again as soon it was practicable, which was tantamount to both removing him from the transfer list and lifting his suspension at warp speed. No one informed O'Farrell, who was incandescent, and Best paid only lip service to the announcement, staying away from Old Trafford. 'They'd never have transferred me,' he said.

United, minus Best, were humiliated 5–0 at Crystal Palace, who were bottom then and would be relegated at the season's end. The club, as it had done with Wilf McGuinness, subsequently treated O'Farrell in a way that was both clumsily ham-fisted and callous. He was summoned to a board meeting the night after a testimonial banquet for Charlton. O'Farrell got an inkling of the turmoil ahead when he saw the seating plan for the dinner. 'I wasn't on the top table,' he said. The following morning the directors sacked him and Best in a one-stop purge. O'Farrell asked for a reason for his dismissal. None was forthcoming. Busby made no eye-contact and also made no attempt to speak during the meeting. O'Farrell had to take legal action to get the monies the club had promised him and to which he was entitled. Only the imminent prospect of a court case – in which Busby would have been called to give evidence – later persuaded United to pay up. O'Farrell, starved of cash, had even been forced to sign on at the labour exchange, entering it through the back door to avoid being seen.

And Best?

'We've finally had enough,' said Busby, photographed stepping over a carpet of ripped up team pictures thrown by a disgruntled fan.

Best had a premonition of his own fate. So he, like O'Farrell, steeled himself for it. He wrote a 271-word letter of resignation. His friend Frank Evans, now in charge of paperwork that Ken Stanley had once handled, got his father to type it out with one finger on Best's own headed notepaper – his name spread over two lines in a 56 point font of modern capitals – to keep it confidential as long as possible. Best didn't want any newspaper to get hold of it in advance. 'The news would have gone around Manchester like fire,' said Evans. Best addressed the board as 'Dear Sirs'.

I had thought seriously of coming personally and asking for a chance to speak at the board meeting, but once again I am afraid when it comes to saying things face to face, and I might not have been completely honest. I am afraid through my somewhat unorthodox ways of trying to sort my own problems out I have caused Manchester United even bigger problems.

I wanted you to read this letter before the board meeting commenced, so as to let you know my feelings before any decision or statements are issued following the meeting. When I said last summer I was going to quit football, contrary to what many people said or thought, I seriously meant it, because I had lost interest in the game for various reasons. While in Spain I received a lot of letters from both friends and well-wishers, quite a few asking me to reconsider. I did so, and after weeks of thinking it over, I decided to give it another try. I came back hoping my appetite for the game would return, and even though I like to think I gave 100 per cent in every game, there was something missing. Even now, I am not quite sure what. Therefore, I have decided not to play football again, and this time no one will change my mind.

In conclusion I would like to wish the club the best of luck for the remainder of the season, and for the future. Because even though I personally have tarnished the club's name in recent times, to me, and thousands of others, Manchester United still means something special.

The pre-emptive strike of this letter was a waste of time because the board made the decision to rid themselves of Best before reading it. Shakespeare could have put all his wit and bite and insight and poetry into it and still failed to shift the opinion of those for whom it was intended. No one wanted to listen.

What Best sent them is a peculiar, maladroit composition: a *mea culpa*, an attempt to clarify and explain that ends with the finality of a fond but maudlin goodbye. The choice of language and the structure of the letter get in the way of what Best is trying to say. You have to read it more than once to understand his essential message and register the admissions he is making. He's scared of talking one-on-one. He won't necessarily tell you the truth. He doesn't know how he lost his spark for the game. He doesn't know why he can't regain it. As he makes the point that 'no one' will change his mind about quitting, you get the distinct impression he is waiting for the board to do exactly that. To call him back into the room. To forgive and to forget. To understand him.

On this piece of paper Best is as he is – confused, disturbed, unsure of everything, especially himself, and estranged from United.

He had no idea what to do next.

14

The Nuisance of Being a Genius

The future has a habit of never turning out exactly the way we expect. So it proved for George Best.

The teenage Best gave a reasoned account of how he viewed his career progression. He would establish himself, unquestionably, as the world's premier player, harvesting every club honour in the process, well before his vintage period began between 1973 and 1978. 'That's when I'll be at my peak,' he said, forecasting that Manchester United, without break or blemish, would win League Championships regularly and dominate Europe. Best also insisted he would never retire completely. The idea of quitting didn't figure in the plan. He adored football too much to willingly abandon it. 'I'm sure I'll still be playing at some level or other when I'm a sixty-year-old grandaddy,' he claimed, adding that he'd 'play for anyone' once United decided he wasn't good enough for them. 'When my professional career is over, I'll probably be kicking a ball around on a park pitch for a Sunday pub team just to get a game somewhere.'

Best even extrapolated about the type of elder statesman he'd become at Old Trafford at the end of the 1970s. When Father Time took half a yard of pace out of his legs, he would cope successfully with the loss because there was so much else on which he could draw as compensation. Visionary passing from midfield would still allow him to dictate games. Close control and creativity around the area would still allow him to claim his goals. He might become a much better team player because a lack of zip and nip would encourage him to beat only two or three defenders rather than half a dozen. He'd be more generous about sharing the ball and content to be seen as the manipulative schemer, who at will would govern the pattern and tempo of play. He promised to train hard and study harder. He believed a comprehensive knowledge of other teams' tactics and also their weaknesses would enable him to beat them through cunning. Best was convinced he could imitate the long-serving greats. Didn't Puskas and Di Stefano allow Real Madrid to conquer Europe when the former was portly and 33 years old and the latter balding and a year older? Didn't Stanley Matthews finally triumph in the FA Cup at 38? Didn't Pelé, only three months away from a birthday with 30 candles on the cake, look at his leaping, athletic zenith in the broiling heat of Mexico in 1970? Wanting to be just like them, Best saw no reason why he couldn't be the classy veteran, the respected senior pro who'd lead through shining example and instruct those around him. Novices could watch him train and learn something. His tutorials would be a School of Excellence for them.

Pleasure from playing, plus the acclaim of the crowd, weren't Best's only motivations. Conscious of what others thought, he talked of never allowing his career to 'slump into something like an anti-climax'. He'd played alongside and against those who he considered had laboured on one or two seasons too long, either deluding themselves – or trying to delude others – about the extent of their decline. The reluctance to give up was perfectly understandable to Best. Money was one factor. Pride was another. Being unable to face – or wanting to defer – the question of what to do after football was a third. Ex-players of the late 1960s and early 1970s regularly swapped boots for bar work, using their testimonial takings to buy pubs in the hope supporters would pay for the privilege of sharing a pint with them, however drab or remote the pub or however unsuitable the life of a licensed victualler proved to be. Few other options existed. Some went into sales, again relying on their name alone to clear the stock being sold. Some opened sports shops. Some never got over the fact the cheering had stopped, were quickly broke and went on the dole. Best said that there was 'something sad at the sight of former world-class stars, who cling on and on and end up showing their fading skills to crowds of just a few hundred'. Not wanting to be what he termed 'some has-been who gets a place because of who he used to be', Best promised he wouldn't become one.

Every prediction he made didn't come with the obvious caveat, which was this: he would have to change if he wanted to flourish into foot-balling old age.

The year George Best pinpointed as the beginning of his grand vintage – 1973 – brought only questioning self-doubt and clinching evidence that the serious part of his career was already over and irreclaimable.

For four years Best's waxwork had sat in the Hall of Famous Entertainers in Madame Tussauds, a golden ball stuck to his left boot. The curators now decided to replace him with Johan Cruyff. The decapitated torso was carried into the attic by two workmen in buttoned-up brown overalls. The head was placed on a shelf beside other heads also deemed to be yesterday's men and women. It was an eclectic collection: the former Prime Minister Clement Attlee, the former American President Herbert Hoover, George III, Jackie Kennedy (then Mrs Onassis), Stanley Matthews, someone who no one could remember from the Chamber of Horrors and a lady who had once run Tussauds' gift stall. The replacement of Best with Cruyff seemed symbolic, like a torch passed. 'If Best merits it, he could be put back on display,' said a spokeswoman, who didn't sound as if she meant or expected it.

He called it his sanctuary and his refuge. But Che Sera quickly made George Best feel like a specimen in a glass case.

The problem of being a genius is that you're seldom left alone; especially when you make yourself so visible in a white Rolls Royce.

Despite the presence of the ball, George Best has just announced his retirement and is already regretting it.

A player and his managers. Sir Matt Busby escapes from the Football Association's headquarters at Lancaster Gate, where Best has been given a £250 fine for ill-discipline.

Wilf McGuinness poses with him after training.

Frank O'Farrell chats to Bobby Charlton. And Tommy Docherty welcomes Best back into fold.

A perfect physical specimen. 'I used to love training,' said George Best. And this is the proof of it.

No need to guess what will happen to the ball. He will control it with aplomb.

Asked about the most valuable trait a footballer could possess, George Best answered with a single word – balance.

He had a dancer's poise. And he could head the ball too.

Prisoner 76245 is home and relishing his first hours of freedom.

This is how George Best came home. This is how Belfast said goodbye to its son. His funeral procession drives along Prince of Wales Avenue in the grounds of Stormont.

TOILETS

DISABLED TOILETS

Typical of the tributes that were left for George Best in both Belfast and Manchester.

BEST

THANKS FOR THE MEMORIES GEORGIE

RED STAR SPORTS

ANGELO

HRS BEST

RED STAR THE BEST

At the height of his fame. The epitome of 1960s cool.

Neither did Best. The limb he most exercised was his drinking arm. The amount Best drank meant the weight shed in the autumn was piled back on in winter; and a few extra pounds were added, too. 'I lazed around all day,' he said, never regaining his super slimness of the 1960s and early 70s. His pallor turned an unhealthy grey, and he let his pirate's beard grow. Best looked like the male on the cover of Dr Alex Comfort's *The Joy of Sex*, another recreation in which he indulged with unstinting vigour. Whenever Best appeared on the news pages of the tabloid newspapers, he was nearly always featured with a woman or a group of women. After one of those heart-to-hearts with Sir Matt Busby, supposedly fundamental to his playing future, he was seen blithely judging a beauty contest in a Manchester nightclub. He was pictured doing a high-kick in Paris beside cabaret troupe the Bluebell Girls, who wore jewelled, skimpy costumes and brandished more feathers than a peacock in full plumage. He was photographed entering or leaving neon-signed doors with someone whom the standard, bright and breezy accompanying caption regularly identified in classic tabloidese as vivacious or flirty. This language, once translated, meant 'cor blimey, what-a-stunner'. She would then be described as being one or a combination of the following: model/dancer/beauty queen/bunny girl/socialite/woman-about-town. Fascination with Best gathered more steam after his second retirement which shows how trouble is guaranteed to create headlines in battalions. No footballer had gone through this before. There was an intense, crazy clamour to follow every move he made. To the *Sun*, which devoted a two-page spread to Best and called him 'The Body Beautiful', he was 'superstar, jet-set playboy . . . and self-confessed bird-happy Casanova' now in search of a fresh purpose. While easy to lampoon, the thumbnail portrayal of him as a fallen idol, wayward soccer star and artist as a randy dog reflected the readership's perception. It proved that fame means having a lot of nonsense talked about you and is the aggregate of misunderstandings. The public's idea of Best was of someone wallowing in the contentment of wine and women. He was actually trying to recalibrate his whole life.

Che Sera was put on the market. He also saw the sense of unloading another millstone. He cut his losses and traded in the Rolls-Royce, which was still attracting leering yobs and vandals to whom it was a target. What Best couldn't do, however, was separate himself from rabble-rousers, who saw him as a target as well. In Manchester he got embroiled in a minor pub scuffle after reacting to the insult that he was 'crap'. Following another half-scrap on a street corner – comprising of two traded punches and a bit of girly hair pulling – he ended up with a bruised eye, which he hid behind dark glasses. He'd stopped at traffic lights and found a pedestrian, snarling in anger at him, staring through the windscreen. The man began to shout 'call yourself a fucking footballer' and then shallowly dented the car's bodywork with a kick. Best got out of the driver's seat and the two of them began to wrestle before the blows were struck.

Best told friends his interest in football was nil. He was 'pissed off' with the game and 'absolutely pissed off' with those who ran it.

Gallons of ink were still used to speculate about where he might go after Old Trafford. Chelsea were installed as the bookmakers' favourites on the basis that London's West End was a drinking haven for Best. Malcolm Allison considered reviving an audacious attempt to take him from the red to the blue half of Manchester. Allison was adamant that Best wanted to work with him as dearly as he wanted to work with Best. His directors had slapped down an earlier request to table a bid. 'There is no board support for it,' said Allison's chairman brusquely, probably calculating that two drinkers under the same roof would lead each other into temptation and benefit no one but the trade of journalism. Brian Clough thought about making an approach, too. 'I'd sort George out in a week,' he said. 'I'd hide the key to the drinks cabinet and I'd make sure he was tucked up with nothing stronger than cocoa for the first six months. Women? I'd let him home to see his mum and his sisters. No one else in a skirt is getting within a million miles of him.'

The obscure World Indoor Football League, based in Canada, offered him an £800-per-match comeback. Its six-a-side fixtures were to be played on carpet behind a three-foot-tall perimeter wall. Best went to Toronto only because he said he 'needed to be somewhere I could open a newspaper and not find my name in the headlines' and because the Canadians were prepared to give him a cheque with lots of noughts on it. He didn't stay there. The fact the organisation wasn't affiliated to FIFA offered a handy escape for Best, who used it as his public excuse to disguise private concerns about the dubiousness of the overall operation, which he found shady, as if trapped in the first *Godfather* film. When Best made one of his quick exits – without saying goodbye – he discovered two suited men as wide as linebackers tailing him out of Canada and into California.

More inexplicable was his refusal to sign for New York Cosmos, owned by the mega-rich, film and entertainment-dominating Warner Corporation. Best originally agreed to the move. Cosmos general manager, Clive Toye, worked out a pay-as-you-play arrangement to secure his resignation from Manchester United, who would reap £10,000 whenever Best took the field during his first season in the North American Soccer League. Toye came to Manchester with Best's contract in his luggage. 'There was only one problem,' he said. 'No one could find the bugger to sign it. We searched every bar, every club, every place where he might be.' Best, like the elusive McCavity, wasn't there.

Best knew Cosmos wanted him for far more than his football. He would be used as an ambassador for the game in the New World. As a Fleet Street journalist Toye had covered Northern Ireland's World Cup qualifier in Albania in 1965. On the flight home he'd witnessed American travellers hoodwinked into believing George Best was really George Harrison. 'He even signed autographs as George Harrison for hours,' said Toye. 'You need a bit of cheek and charisma to pull that off on an aeroplane. And we wanted that cheek and charisma in New York. He was going to be a billboard face. Through him we could sell Cosmos to women, anyone with Irish blood in them and also to the fans of *any* country.' America hadn't embraced the NASL. One columnist dismissed it as 'just a game played by Commies and fairies in short pants'. Banks of empty seats prompted the Cosmos goalkeeper to admit that his team were drawing fewer people than the skin flicks on Eighth Avenue. Match tickets were given away with purchases at Burger King. Best was being lined up to revive the franchise and become the poster boy of the NASL. He'd be a cover story for *Sports Illustrated* and the Grey Lady of the *New York Times* – like every other lady in New York – would fall for him. Some reports said he would earn £1 million annually and get the same starry, red-carpet treatment afforded to Warner's movie actors and recording artists – a high-rise apartment in Uptown Manhattan, a stretch limousine and a peak-capped chauffeur. The basic deal from Cosmos was more modest – £400 per week and £1 million in image rights. It still constituted the highest sum Best had ever been offered as a player. He still wouldn't take it. Eventually Toye recruited someone in Best's place; his name was Edson Arantes do Nascimento.

Every life is plagued by the thought of roads not taken. Best's contains a Spaghetti Junction of over and under-lapping routes like that. Not becoming a Cosmonaut counts as one of his most egregious. But New York in the early and mid-70s was crumbling into anarchy. It was a dirty, litter-strewn and dangerous city waiting to be cleansed. Times Square was choked with prostitutes and their pimps. The streets around it, full of beggars, became known for daylight muggings and shootings. The nights there were worse. Although Best would have been cocooned from the sleaze, the gunshots and the poverty, the level of social unrest made him understandably nervy. If New York could have been relocated to California or Florida, he would have regarded the deal differently and taken up Toye's invitation to play in it. Best stayed away, describing the city as 'good to visit but not to live in'.

What Best lost because of his attitude became apparent when Pelé, at 34, assumed the role of Cosmos and NASL standard-bearer, his colour photograph appearing immediately beneath *Sports Illustrated*'s masthead. Even if Best had raked in only a quarter of Pelé's sponsorship and advertising deals – Pepsi-Cola among them – the commercial pickings would still have been rich indeed. Even if he hadn't proved to be as popular as Pelé, he would still have been popular enough to secure name recognition and then loyalty among Cosmos virgin-to-soccer, consumer-orientated audience. And even if he'd accepted that the NASL was an inadequate substitute for the Football League – the Yankees' or Giants' stadiums never replicating the fevered atmosphere of Old Trafford, Anfield, Stamford Bridge – he would still have been at the epicentre of something worthwhile and memorable. For a small spot in time, a Cosmos game with Pelé in it became the thing to see and to be seen at. Sold-out signs were hung on the gates. Those inside included Hollywood actors, such as Robert Redford, and pop icons, such as Mick Jagger, and politicians, such as Henry Kissinger. Americans ignorant of the finer or tactical elements of the sport came to watch Pelé perform a bicycle-kick the way patrons of the circus file into the big tent because there's a trapeze artist, a lion tamer, a contortionist. Pelé didn't let them down. Nor would Best have done. What Pelé did he could have matched and surpassed because his competitiveness derived from always wanting to prove a point. When, after bringing Pelé to New York, Toye was asked about missing out on Best, he deflected the question by waggishly asking one in reply: 'Why sign George Best when you can sign *the* best?' Toye knew nonetheless what Best could have achieved for Cosmos and for himself. 'He'd have been an idol too,' he said.

Best later turned down the prospect of a contract as a gridiron kicker with the New York Giants in the National Football League. That role would have made Cosmos salary look minuscule. As a publicity stunt he went to Shea Stadium to pose for photographers. He took off his dark, double-breasted coat and kicked ten successive field goals off a kicking tee while wearing a flowered shirt, flared trousers with enough material in them to have made a yacht's sail and a pair of tan, Cuban-heeled shoes with slim toes. Best was pulled aside and asked: 'Why are you bothering with the NASL? Why don't you join the NFL?' The thought of wearing a helmet and strapping on shoulder-guards to come off a bench for a few minutes a week was boredom writ large for Best. The rigid structure of the game itself – and all those statistics about rushing yardage – held about as much appeal as watching a tea towel dry on a radiator. A third negative – and also the deal-breaker – was New York's climate. 'It's just too cold here,' said Best, casually forgoing a chance that others would have murdered twice for.

Best liked being somebody, and fretted about becoming nobody. 'Sometimes I feel I'd like to be left alone for a few hours,' he said. 'Then you get to realise that the time to start worrying is when no one is interested in you or what you're doing.' But, paradoxically, in the months after leaving United he appreciated the anonymity America gave him. It's said that if you want to watch your own country disappear, the place to go is the States, where the insularity of its media and the people's preoccupation only with what's happening coast to coast means the rest of the world's business seldom rates a mention. Despite the odd article about him in *Time* and *Sports Illustrated*, and short agency reports in big city newspapers, Best was unknown to the American audience. He could shop normally. He could stroll along a sidewalk and never be stopped for an autograph. He could go into a downtown bar and sit there without worrying whether a drunk might suddenly appear to stab a finger in his face. Best had met an American mega-millionaire businessman and entrepreneur in Spain. He made the arrangements and laid on hospitality for him in San Francisco and Los Angeles and Palm Springs. Best chased the sun like an exhausted executive on a recuperating sabbatical and did things which were both typical and untypical of him. In San Francisco he was the everyman sightseeing tourist, visiting the Golden Gate Bridge and taking the boat to Alcatraz. In Palm Springs he skinny-dipped – despite an aversion to swimming – with Californian models and would-be movie starlets, who thereafter walked and drank and gossiped naked around the poolside. And in Los Angeles he queued with goggle-eyed children to go on the Disney resort submarine ride. Accompanying him throughout was Malcolm Wagner. 'George forgot about everything back home,' he said. 'He was smiling all the time. He was totally relaxed. He didn't drink much at all. I think it counted as one of the happiest few weeks of his life. Only one thing worried him. He didn't want *anyone* to know he'd been on the Disney ride in case it cost him his street cred, so he wouldn't let me take a photograph.'

Acapulco was the last stop before returning to Manchester. Mexico, football-obsessed, knew all about Best. His photograph appeared regularly in its newspapers and sports magazines. The checking-in clerk at the hotel immediately recognised him. The manager arrived to roll out the red carpet, upgrading his apartment to a villa with its own pool. The staff took it as an honour to spoil and treat him royally. Nothing was too much trouble for them. Best was the sort of person who would repay kindnesses done to him; that's the way his parents had brought him up. He agreed to play for the hotel waiters' football team. A golf cart transported him up on a mountain path to the pitch – solid clay with only spikes of grass – on which he played in a pair of borrowed boots in front of a crowd of 150 or so, who'd come to see the ringer make an appearance. Best, unaccustomed to the altitude, found it difficult to breathe. The unfit former European Footballer of the Year came off after less than half an hour.

It's true you can travel 10,000 miles and stay exactly where you are; for this is what happened to George Best. He came back to Manchester – and home to Mrs Fullaway's pots of tea and wholesome cooking – and discovered his old dilemmas lingered, unresolved.

By the end of April the novelty of not playing had become tarnished. Best began to train again, running and kicking a ball on his own and lifting weights in his bedroom in Chorlton-cum-Hardy. By the beginning of May, already fed up with it, he'd flown to Marbella.

It might have gone on this way: Best half-heartedly making an attempt to get fit before catching a plane somewhere warm and dry. What saved him was a near-death experience. Sitting in a Marbella bar, Best felt the inside of his right leg go numb near the top of the groin. He dismissed it initially as a harmless strain or a trapped nerve, which would soon pass. As he tried to walk off the discomfort, the leg began to swell and throb. A doctor, summoned to Best's hotel, failed to recognise deep vein thrombosis. He prescribed antibiotics and the application of an anaesthetising spray, rubbed into the flesh. He reassured his patient, wrongly diagnosing that he'd be fine and fiddle-fit again inside a day or two. In the early hours Best's leg was blotchy, badly discoloured, appreciably swollen and tender to the touch. He looked as if he'd been kicked by a horse. Having no confidence in the Spanish doctor, he gambled on going back to Manchester for treatment. In all likelihood the decision saved his life.

Best was always jittery about flying. He felt safe boarding a plane with Manchester United's team only because he didn't think one club could possibly experience two air catastrophes. The constant, excruciating pain in his leg obliterated his aerophobia now. Best never forgot this three-and-a-half-hour flight. He sweated so heavily that his shirt stuck to his skin. He couldn't put on his right shoe because his foot had ballooned in size. He slumped in his seat because he couldn't sit upright. And, though desperate for sleep, he couldn't actually go to sleep because the antibiotics had no effect on his worsening condition. Malcolm Wagner arranged for another doctor, who was already aware of the symptoms and read them correctly, to be waiting for him at the airport. 'He took me straight to hospital and had me on a drip within twenty minutes of touchdown,' said Best. 'I was very lucky.' The thrombosis travelled down the body rather than up. 'If it had hit my heart or brain I would have been dead.' Best was told he required complete rest. He learned the thrombosis had probably occurred because he had stopped training and also because of the amount of alcohol he'd been consuming. The hospital suggested an abstemious two months were necessary to allow his liver to recover from the soaking he had given it. 'It scared me because it made me realise how I'd punished my body,' he said.

Best remained under hospital sheets, staring at the walls of his room. In a fortnight he'd be 27. What was there to celebrate? He was jobless, currently confined to bed and a huge proportion of the public – fans and non-fans alike – were writing him off as a waster; someone concerned only with playing a merry fiddle and expecting everyone else to dance around him. As someone who had barely considered God, religion or the psalms and books of the Bible since he was a boy, Best was surprised where one strand of thinking took him as he ruminated on life. He said he began to ask himself whether his illness was a form of 'divine intervention'. Had he been carried to the brink deliberately? Was this His way of forcing him to mend his ways and get himself sorted out and into shape again?

An early visitor was Sir Matt Busby, who arrived without advance notice and brought a big basket of fruit. He'd grown increasingly fearful for Best. Busby had already confided to Michael Parkinson that he thought Best could conceivably commit suicide in the future. Busby was fearful that whatever route Best took would carry him back to the same rocky place eventually; and when he looked at things dispassionately, Busby didn't know how Best could overcome his problems unscathed.

He drew a chair alongside the bed and listened as Best explained the week's sequence of events. Once the polite preliminaries were over, the conversation – at Busby's instigation – became a linking chain of reminiscences, as if the two of them hadn't seen one another for a generation. Memory Lane is where Busby, in that Scottish burr, a creased smile on narrow lips, took Best. He spoke about him as a sapling talent . . . about the Championships United had won . . . about the European Cup win . . . about the goals Best had scored. It was an attempt to make Best feel better about himself and to forget, if only for half an hour, his predicament. But, along with his compassion, which was genuine, the psychologically savvy Busby's ulterior motive was apparent, too. With his degree in people, he judged what Best was thinking. Busby knew he was emotionally in pieces. He knew he was feeling disconnected from his past. He knew, too, that at this moment of personal crisis he didn't know where to turn next and whether a return to the game – and United – was feasible. Busby couldn't have been more emollient, diplomatic or solicitous towards Best. Nor, unless he'd stuck the olive branch in a red pot, could he have been much clearer about his purpose. Merely by visiting, Busby was demonstrating to Best that reconciliation was possible if he wanted it. By concentrating on the nostalgia of the 1960s, rather than interrogating Best on his latest misfortune or berating him for it, he was attempting to renew his interest in football again. Only fools rush in; and Busby was no fool. He waited before delivering the short speech he'd specifically come to make. Everything he said in advance of it was preparatory work for the following words.

'It's about time you were back playing again, isn't it?'

The construction and timing of the phrase and its dead-pan delivery were critical. Busby had already left Best's room and so turned on his heel to startle him. He craned his head around the half-open door, so only it and his shoulders were visible before speaking the sentence. However rusty the device, by framing it as a question *to* him, instead of issuing a statement *at* him, Busby demonstrated how well he knew Best's sensitivities over such matters. If he'd made it sound like a demand or a put-down Best wouldn't have taken any notice. In making it seem like a casual aside, an afterthought that had only now occurred to him because the rest of their talk had planted the seed of this idea in his mind, Busby was allowing Best to dwell on a suggestion full of good intentions. At some stage Best could even say he'd independently reached the same conclusion, which wouldn't make him seem as desperate as Busby knew him to be. It also avoided the direct enquiry, which could have been misconstrued on Best's part as pleading and on Busby's as being needy on behalf of United.

Best listened as Busby's footsteps echoed down the corridor, knowing his former boss was right and knowing also that he'd been courted. 'I realised what a fool I'd been,' he said.

Going on behind the scenes, unbeknown to Busby, were other transfer manoeuvrings for Best. Discreet approaches were made directly to Best to bypass Old Trafford. He reacted favourably to this 'tapping up', flattered by it. Real Madrid offered to pay him £250,000 a year – tax free – and buy his registration from United. The go-between in negotiations was Alfredo Di Stefano, then manager of Valencia. Since his own employers couldn't afford Best, he saw no conflict of interest in working as a fixer for his former club. Aston Villa, a distant third to the promoted clubs in Division Two the previous season, wanted Best just as much. Its chairman, Doug Ellis, owned the travel company that organised most of Best's holidays. Ellis told Best he would double the salary United were paying him and also cut him into a lucrative commission deal over the sale of newly built holiday apartments in Fuengirola. Ellis invited Best to Birmingham to 'see if you like our set-up and then make a decision'. Di Stefano invited him to Valencia to finalise arrangements for his move to Madrid. The Bull Ring versus Puerta del Sol? It wasn't going to be much of a contest. Frank Evans arrived at Mary Fullaway's to collect Best. Ellis agreed to fly him to Majorca on his private jet after a tour of Villa Park. From Majorca, Evans had arranged a further flight to Valencia to dust over Best's tracks as clandestinely as possible. Inside Aycliffe Avenue he discovered Best had a plan of his own. He was going to talk to Busby instead. Evans assumed all along Best would sign for Real. He likened United's intervention to a 'kidnapping' and added: 'He could have set himself up for life in Madrid. He just wouldn't leave Old Trafford.' Evans watched Best on the television news later the same day and heard him use a line he'd repeat for the next 30 years.

'This is the only club I have ever really wanted to play for.'

On the day after George Best had transformed himself from mere footballer into new superstar – coming back triumphantly from Manchester United's European Cup quarter-final against Benfica in March 1966 – he found a familiar face coming towards him through the crowd at the airport. Tommy Docherty, then in charge of Chelsea, was about to fly off on a scouting assignment. Docherty had watched the game in Lisbon on television, enchanted like everyone else by what Best had done, and wanted to congratulate him. Best was wearing that oversized sombrero, and Docherty shouted 'Hello Pancho' to get his attention before waving at him like an old friend. He shook hands with Best and slapped him on the back, talking effusively about his performance. 'It was another sign of the impact I'd made,' said Best.

He regarded Docherty as a 'decent bloke', someone who could tell and take a joke and winked at life's vicissitudes. Something of a scallywag's brashness about him appealed to Best from the start. That favourable impression was reinforced, shortly afterwards, when chance brought them together in Spain. Best shared an agreeable holiday beer with Docherty after discovering him in the same resort. Again, he considered him to be a hail-fellow-well-met type, approachably matey and unpretentiously down to earth. He thought he'd be a good boss to work for. Now Docherty was Manchester United's third manager in three and a half years.

He'd been smoothly installed after the dismissal of Frank O'Farrell following that five-goal humbling at Crystal Palace. To conspiracy theorists the circumstances surrounding his appointment reeked of premeditation. If that had not been the case, only one of two further conclusions could be reached: either Sir Matt Busby, usually so meticulous and methodical in choosing his successors, had acted out of character, suffering a Niagara Falls rush of blood to the head and making the decision to hire Docherty instantly and in rage because of United's ineptitude; or he'd chosen him privately beforehand and nothing but the timing and the terms of his appointment needed to be determined. Docherty was at Selhurst Park, sitting not far from Busby in the directors' box. He said he'd gone there because the game was 'an intriguing one'; because, as Scotland boss, he wanted to check the progress of a Palace defender who had been recommended to him; and because he thought O'Farrell, a former team-mate at Preston in the 1950s, might be 'in need of a friendly face'. Within half an hour of United's defeat – four days before O'Farrell's sacking became breaking news – the post was Docherty's. He was sitting in the tea-room when Busby asked to speak to him. In an exchange lasting barely a minute Busby made his pitch – 'fancy the job?' he asked – and warned Docherty that United were so shambolic 'you might find yourself having to take a step back in order to take a leap forward'. As blunt offers of betrothal go, it was reminiscent of the writer Thomas Hardy's proposal to the woman who'd become the second Mrs Hardy. He took her to the grave of his first wife and pointed to the vacant burial plot alongside it. 'That's for you,' he said.

Docherty wasn't deterred. Not only had he always wanted to manage United – it was a 'lifetime ambition', he said – but he guessed, accurately, that O'Farrell's and Wilf McGuinness' failures would allow him more autonomy and latitude than either of them got from Busby or the rest of the board. He'd be protected against a quick dismissal, too, because United wouldn't want Old Trafford to look like a managerial abattoir. And he'd have a better chance of being able to sell or usher into retirement those players who his immediate predecessors couldn't shift for fear of volcanic repercussions. In tastelessly inappropriate language Docherty once described the club as being 'riddled with cancer', which he defined as 'old players, skivers, players who were more concerned with getting rid of the next manager, whoever he may be'. Docherty said he'd been brought in to 'do the dirty work', which meant 'chop, chop, chop'.

He was 44 years old. Unlike O'Farrell and McGuinness, he had won a significant domestic trophy – the League Cup for Chelsea in the competition's pre-Wembley era. He'd taken them to the FA Cup final in 1967, too, before resigning less than five months later. 'We had a mutual understanding,' he said of his relationship with the Chelsea chairman who got rid of him. 'We disliked each other.' Since then Docherty had gone into a tailspin as a club manager, seldom staying anywhere long enough to know where to wash his hands or hang his coat. He lasted a year at Rotherham; only 29 days at Queens Park Rangers; 13 months at Aston Villa; 16 months at Porto. But Scotland brought him stability and – totalling seven wins and two draws from a dozen internationals – he brought them respectability and built the foundations for World Cup qualification, which would follow in 1974 under his successor, Willie Ormond. Another factor separating Docherty from the strait-laced public personas of O'Farrell and McGuinness was his vaudevillian performances in front of the media. He spoke with exclamation marks and aimed to entertain, regularly producing a gag to spice up the sports pages in the manner of W. C. Fields delivering sarcasm with a po face. A collection of Docherty's choicest quotations, which were sometimes short-cuts to express awkward truths, would have run to several dozen pages.

'I talk a lot. On any subject. Which is always football.'

'Football management is like nuclear war. No winners, just survivors.'

'I promised Rotherham I would take them out of the Second Division, and I did – into the Third Division.'

Best admired the fact Docherty could be so drolly self-deprecating. 'You got the idea it would be fun to play for him,' he said. But fun and Docherty were never words Best would use positively in the same sentence again after going back to Old Trafford. Their relationship lasted only 15 weeks, stretching from September to early January, and almost nothing – apart from the beginning and the break-up – is remembered now.

The beginning was all about entwined harmony, the two of them together in a photograph like a couple who have just announced their engagement. In a chequered jacket loud enough to be cut into a pair of golfer's plus-fours, Docherty has his hand around Best's shoulder, as if about to pull him even closer and plant a kiss on his cheek. Best's hair is much longer and more unkempt than it has been before. His beard is stragglier and denser, too. He isn't looking at his new manager. What's most revealing about the picture, however, is the mauve shirt Best is wearing. It looks at least half a size too small for him – too tight around chest and midriff, the cotton pulled into firm horizontal pleats around the buttons, which seem likely to burst if Best moves sharply or breathes out. He is a stone overweight.

It's easy to conclude now that his willingness to come out of retirement and Docherty's willingness to embrace him was always going to be a doomed arrangement. The central basis for striking such an agreement was wildly delusional because each believed in something impossible. Best wrongly thought he could turn back time. Docherty was wrongly persuaded that he could control him more successfully than Busby had ever done. To think these things in the first place invited incredulity; immediate bets were taken about how long it would be before the first 'Best misses training' headline appeared. To go on thinking them was persistence in folly. It's nonetheless equally easy to see why both Best and Docherty were willing accomplices to the notion; and why it led to irreconcilable division, what Best saw as a poisonous parting from the club. From the outset the onus on each of them was to justify the move. But in trying to convince others of its sanity both found themselves overstating the case for it and inflating promises of success.

Four months earlier Docherty courted Best with megaphone diplomacy. In a signed newspaper article he announced: 'I want him to play again. I would love to be the manager helping him and guiding him.' He added a caveat, which the general emphasis of the piece suggested was not insurmountable. 'That will never be because United – rightly – have committed themselves to a future without him.' Docherty was in the process of steering United away from relegation. Losing only six of 20 matches – and finishing 18th in the table – looks an unspectacular record until placed beside O'Farrell's. Comparison made what Docherty had done shine like a divine miracle. He'd drawn from the bank to achieve it, including £200,000 spent on Lou Macari from Celtic and £130,000 to bring George Graham from Arsenal. Docherty was still perilously short of good players, let alone great ones. Even in a semi-dilapidated state, and however much United insisted he wouldn't be recalled, Best was sorely needed. Or so Busby in particular argued. 'I never really thought it would work,' said Docherty. 'I was asked to give it a go by Sir Matt. So I did.'

In the right environment Docherty said Best could go on 'playing at the top into his thirties'. An effort of 70 per cent from him would be worth more than 110 per cent from almost anyone else at United. While there was no way around the risks – Best might abandon them in less than a month – Docherty sought to minimise them. What he did seems misguided, given his scorn towards United's lack of control over Best in the 1960s. His assessment was cutting: 'He was subject to no real discipline, and by that I mean sensible discipline. He did what he wanted, and got away with murder.'

The clear implication was that Docherty wouldn't have been so benevolent. His previous responses to anyone messing him about suggested that beneath his iron glove was also an iron fist. In 1965 Docherty fined and gave rail tickets home to eight Chelsea players for breaking a hotel curfew in Blackpool. He banned them from the season's last two matches – and hurriedly bussed in reserves as replacements – when there was still a mathematical chance of taking the League title. His decimated side lost 6–2 at Burnley, conceding their first goal in under 30 seconds and two more in the opening 20 minutes. 'I suppose one could say that I forsook what chance we had of winning the Championship on a matter of principle,' he said. 'However, I felt I had to make a stand.' Who'd have thought someone capable of doing that would come to such a generous understanding with Best, whose charge sheet for larking about was A3 size? An unwritten sub-clause in the contract was loaded in Best's favour as well.

'He understood that once in a while I had a late night or got involved in this and that,' said Best, almost coyly. 'If I missed training, but came back in the afternoon, he'd be fine with that.' Best said another solemn promise was that the newspapers wouldn't find out if he didn't train when he should have done. Best claimed Docherty's words were: 'It will be between you and me – that's the way we'll work it out.' He described it as a 'gentlemen's agreement'. Others saw it as his get out of jail card. Allowing him such licence demonstrated trust on Docherty's part and what he hoped would be responsibility on Best's. But the whole agreement contained a fatal flaw, which was its vulnerability to abuse, exploitation or misunderstanding. Best was always going to be a hard dog to tether to the porch. If anything, Best had too much freedom.

Ignoring the clichéd newspapers' responses, such as the return of the prodigal son and the label of being predictably unpredictable, Best chose his sentences carefully. Each was meant as a mark of seriousness. 'I'm here to stay . . . United are the only club I want to be with . . . This time I mean it . . . if I don't stick to it no one will believe me again . . . I've realised how much football means to me and I've missed it.' A confession he made subsequently to Michael Parkinson disclosed how quickly that optimism was stripped away and replaced by dread. 'I think I knew when I went back to the ground for the first time that I had made an awful mistake,' said Best. 'There used to be a special feel about that ground . . . Not any more. It felt different, depressed, doomed . . . I remember distinctly thinking Oh Christ, it's different, as I went through the door on my comeback.'

Docherty's coach was Tommy Cavanagh, a Scouser with a flop fringe of silver hair. He was an aggressive disciplinarian; some thought he bullied them. Best was frank enough to tell Cavanagh that the only game he'd figured in for seven months was the kick-about with those Mexican waiters in Acapulco. Cavanagh asked what Best had been eating and drinking as well as what he did during an average week. Like a doctor, knowing what he's being told is a half-truth to camouflage embarrassment, Cavanagh calculated Best's alcohol intake upwards. He made Best slog repetitively up and down empty terracing, his rapid footsteps on the concrete echoing beneath the roof of the stand.

Cavanagh instigated a programme of army-style shuttle sprints and lapping of the pitch in which Best competed against the stopwatch to the background noise of bawled, swearing threats designed to ensure he didn't slow or slacken. He checked Best's diet and weight and, surreptitiously, got close enough to smell his breath and scan his eyes, which would betray lack of sleep or early morning shenanigans. Five years earlier Cavanagh had been through an identical regime with another inveterate drinker, 'Slim' Jim Baxter, at Nottingham Forest. Baxter, like Best, was boozing away his talent in bars. He was staying out late, arriving for work hungover, getting mixed up in ugly pavement brawling. He didn't deserve the 'Slim' sobriquet earned during his halcyon seasons at Glasgow Rangers because alcohol and laziness had made him corpulent. He'd begun to develop a double chin and pronounced jowls, which wobbled in a moon-round face when he ran. Baxter, only 28 then, looked like a lacklustre middle-aged man who'd allowed himself to go to seed. 'There was a difference between Best and Baxter,' said Cavanagh. 'Baxter knew his career was on the slide and he couldn't do much about it. Best wanted to prove he could still play. He worked his balls off and didn't complain.'

Best's right leg continued to ache after the thrombosis and he didn't think Docherty could safely call on him until Christmas. Docherty had earlier calculated it would take Best five months to get ready for the First Division and eight to ten games to be properly match-sharp. Best's plea to Docherty from the start was: 'Don't rush me . . . I'll play with the reserves just to get fit.'

Expediency forced him back much sooner than either of them antici-pated. United were in free-fall – only one win from the previous eight matches – when Docherty, demanding too much of him, picked Best against Birmingham City in mid-October. 'It was a mistake,' said Best.

In the 19th century cricket's administrators would often place a sign on the gate that read: 'Admission 6d. If W. G. Grace plays Admission

1s.' United could have legitimately increased the prices at Old Trafford for Best's much awaited reappearance. The 49,000 crowd was nearly 3,000 higher than the average home gate so far that season. Almost all of them booed and hissed and cat-called when Docherty, as an act of mercy, brought him off with a quarter of an hour left; Best's legs were about to give way beneath him. Much to Docherty's relief, United clung on to win 1–0 – because of Alex Stepney, who, incongruously, had become the team's penalty-taker. That Stepney was now joint top scorer – on two goals – meant nothing more needed to be said about how desperately United required Best's services.

It was plain then that there was more of him than anyone had seen before. He'd gone from resembling Fred Astaire to looking like a young Oliver Hardy. The presumption nonetheless was that he'd lose his bulk and the spare tyre over the coming months, harden his calf and thigh muscles and one afternoon emerge from the tunnel as if it was 1968 again. Already Cavanagh saw it differently. 'Nothing he did made much difference. He couldn't get his weight down.' Best became disheartened, slowly slipping into another disabling depression, which resembled those which had precipitated his two previous partings from Old Trafford. Docherty, as helpless as O'Farrell and McGuinness had been, attempted to counsel him. Best continued to think of himself as the world's number one; Docherty tried to get him to concentrate on being Britain's number one. The drop in status made Best more depressed still.

The prospect of Division Two, which is where United were heading, made him think of bailing out. The team was off-kilter, wins were elusive and he was a passenger. He was too broad across the waist, too big around the arse and moved with a scuttling step. There were a few nice passes, the odd shimmy and the occasional few seconds when from a distance, foot on the ball or a shoulder dipped against a full-back, it was possible to see him as he used to be. But then he would stumble or be robbed of possession and the image evaporated and you'd see instead the Best he'd become. There was another confession to Parkinson: 'I started cheating in training. I started cheating on the field. I couldn't do it any more. I didn't want any part of it.' In December he made a different kind of admission, which set off the warning sirens at United. 'I still long to drive to the airport, jump on a plane and have dinner in Rome,' he said, his wanderlust unsated. Best led Docherty to believe he would commit himself exclusively to his football. So the manager was less than enamoured to discover he was opening a club in Manchester called Slack Alice, a night job which didn't seem to Docherty to be compatible with the day one. Best was dressed in a well-cut dinner suit and an oversized black bow tie, as if about to greet his customers in the manner of a master Maître d'. What he said was meant to reassure United of his commitment to them as much as the business: 'I'm settled – calmer than I have ever been. I am so relaxed I can hardly believe it. I'll spend maybe three nights a week in the club, being respectable, walking around in my dinner suit, being nice to people – and going nowhere near the place before a match.'

No one at United – least of all Docherty – was convinced of that.

The two Tommys, Docherty and Cavanagh, christened George Best 'The Quare Fellow', a reference to the title character in Brendan Behan's 1954 stage play. The word 'quare' is Hiberno-English. It means 'queer' in the original definition – someone who is 'strange', 'unusual' or 'peculiarly funny' – rather than referring to sexual orientation. Behan's 'Quare Fellow' is the axis on which his whole drama turns; but he is neither seen nor heard. Best was a bit like this at Old Trafford. So much went on around him – especially conjecture about his future and his fitness – even when he wasn't there. Instead of being the dominant force, which Busby had forecast, he became a distracting presence. No one – including Best – knew from one day to the next whether he would turn up, never mind at the appointed hour. Too much time was being spent either waiting for or worrying about Best.

It couldn't go on; something had to give. The inevitable break-up between Docherty and Best turned into one of those plate-throwing divorces in which each partner spits bile at the other as the china smashes against the kitchen wall. At its messy end Best branded Docherty 'a very dishonest man', and Docherty said of Best: 'We're better off without him.'

An account of any event depends on the perspective from which you view it, which explains why Docherty's and Best's versions of what occurred and why, and also the things said during it, were diametrically opposed.

Docherty and Best only ever agreed on minor points. Two of them were purely factual and therefore irrefutable. On New Year's Day Queens Park Rangers thumped United 3–0 at Loftus Road. Their next game was a third-round FA Cup tie against Plymouth Argyle at Old Trafford. What happened in between the end of that first match and the kick-off of the second is intensely disputed.

Docherty said Best, along with everyone else, was given a day off on 2 January. He missed the resumption of training on 3 January, reporting back the following morning with an excuse about having had a 24-hour bug. On match day – 5 January – Docherty was adamant Best didn't turn up for the pre-match lunch at noon. With a team to hand in to the referee, he scratched him off the sheet at 2.15 p.m. According to Docherty, he then saw Best 'around' 2.35 p.m., and he was unmistakably drunk. Docherty claimed he sent him on his way with the rebuke: 'Rather than thinking about playing football, you should be thinking about being breathalysed'. Almost 40 years afterwards Docherty supplements that quotation with another, which is: 'If you come in here now I'll have to breathalyse the whole team.' He insisted Best was 'paralytic' and also had brought a woman with him. 'Tommy Cavanagh answered a knock on the dressing-room door,' says Docherty. 'He said: "It's the Quare Fellow." He'd brought a woman with him. A blonde. She was a stunner. I told him he wasn't playing because he wasn't in a fit state to play.'

Best was utterly contemptuous both of the substance of the charges and the sequence of incidents that Docherty said had taken place. He conceded the 24-hour bug was an invention to hide his partying at Slack Alice. The corks were still popping well into a second night of festivities arranged to wet the head of 1974. The drink must have made him confused because dates and days were jumbled in an initial attempt to recall them. In one telling Best maintained he'd missed training on both 2 January (when no one else was training anyway) and again on 3 January. In another he said he'd taken advantage of Docherty's permission to train in the afternoon on 3 January before training, as normal, on 4 January. But the story he gave of arriving at Old Trafford before the Cup tie contained no inconsistencies, and he never wavered from it. 'Had lunch,' he said. 'Back one and a half hours before kick-off. I was usually the last to get ready. Today I wanted to be early. The team had not yet been put up.'

Best said he was removing his jacket when Docherty asked to see him privately. The gist of the conversation, as Best remembered it, went like this.

DOCHERTY: I'm not playing you today.
BEST: Why?
DOCHERTY: You didn't come in for training (on) Thursday morning, so as an example I'm leaving you out.

Best protested, imploring Docherty to believe he'd clocked on during the Thursday afternoon. He was stupefied by what he insisted Docherty said next: 'I can't let it be seen that you are bigger than me.' Best was now close to tears.

The follow-up to all this was blindingly obvious to him: if he wasn't good enough to play against Third Division minnows, such as Plymouth, then he wasn't good enough to play against anyone. 'I knew that was it for me . . . I wasn't coming back.'

Best strongly refuted each allegation Docherty made against him. He hadn't been drunk. He hadn't brought a woman to Old Trafford. He hadn't missed the pre-match meal. He said Docherty had 'lied' to him and 'should put his hands up and say he was wrong'. Damning him as the sort of manager who 'would make a promise and then he would break it', Best was emphatic about 'not working with someone like that'.

Docherty could have made four legitimate counter-claims to portray himself more flatteringly. On the question of broken promises Best's behaviour disbarred him from casting the first stone; that, after doing everything within reason to accommodate Best's addictions, he'd been let down; that, without acknowledging it, Best had squandered what he'd asked for – a third chance at Old Trafford; and, finally, he could have relied on a quote he'd once read from Cicero – 'Trust, like the soul, shall never return once it has departed' – and let others read between the lines. In the final analysis, there was nothing Docherty could have done; Best was unmanageable.

Docherty still chose another tack. In between the warm welcome and stony goodbye Best had made 12 appearances, scoring only two goals, one of them the consequence of a deflection. In reviewing the games Docherty spoke with regret of Best's 'journeyman' displays, which he labelled as 'sad to see' and concluded: 'Bringing him back was a disaster. He was more trouble than he was worth.' Those sentences, uttered in regret rather than anger, sound like an adaptation of Joe Mercer's thoughts about genius, which he said is 'great when it's on song' and 'more than a nuisance when it goes bad because it contaminates and destroys what is around it'.

In casting himself as the victim, and Docherty as the black-hearted scoundrel, Best was able to call decisively on the only other witness to the meeting. Docherty's assistant, Paddy Crerand, defended Best wholeheartedly. No, he wasn't drunk, said Crerand. No, he didn't bring female company with him. No, Docherty couldn't have taken Best off the team sheet because his name was never on it. Crerand attempted to placate Best. 'Come in on Monday morning and we'll forget it,' he advised. 'He's just showing you who is boss.' Because he was a friend of Best's, it could be argued that loyalty allied Crerand staunchly to him; more so because Crerand would later admit his trust in Docherty 'completely evaporated' after his marginalisation at Old Trafford in the seasons to come. But one of United's team against Plymouth corroborated another aspect of Best's evidence; Brian Kidd said he 'definitely' remembered Best telling him of his omission 'well before' 2.30 p.m.

Best believed Docherty had been waiting for an excuse to provoke and embarrass him. Why avoid him, putting off an inevitable confrontation, when news of his absence from training had broken across the back pages the day before the Cup tie? Best read it as proof of crude Machiavellianism. Docherty's ex-wife, Agnes, categorically stated in her 2008 autobiography, *Married to a Man of Two Halves*, that her husband had decided to cut his losses on Best. She said his New Year resolution for 1974 was 'the permanent removal of another Old Trafford legend'. She wasn't speaking about Bobby Charlton, who, probably sensing that the optimum time to quit is before the boss advises you to do it, had gone of his own volition nine months earlier. And she didn't mean Denis Law, given a free transfer the previous summer. Docherty strenuously denies the accusation.

Less than a week after he and Docherty agreed to disagree, Best was put on the transfer list and suspended for two weeks. The suspension was gratuitous. Docherty's Old Trafford was the last place on the planet where Best wanted to go.

There should be something grand about the end to a career. Bobby Charlton's passage into retirement in April 1973 had lacked nothing except a brass band and coloured bunting and a white-gloved handshake from the Queen. It was a celebration of his achievements, the highlights flashed across television screens and recorded in newspaper supplements, which paid him full homage.

This was a long goodbye of gratitude and reminiscence. There were debates about which goal counted as his greatest and which match constituted his finest. Erudite articles were written about his ambassadorial contribution to the game and addressed the question of whether or not his going drew the curtain on the era of the gentleman professional. The consensus view was yes, it did.

Before his last game at Old Trafford, Charlton got a guard of honour as he emerged alone from the tunnel. He bowed his head, as if afraid he would break down lachrymosely if he glanced up and looked around him. Both Manchester United and their opposition, Sheffield United, gave him silver for the sideboard and afterwards the crowd refused to go home until he appeared in the directors' box.

Before the final farewell, against Chelsea at Stamford Bridge, there was well-meaning chaos. The teams stood facing one another on the centre circle. Inside it the scrum of photographers and TV cameramen obscured the ceremonial presentation. Charlton received a silver cigarette box, a gift no club would give and almost no player would want nowadays; but the sincerity of the thought counted. A club with whom he had no connection – either emotionally or geographically – felt it was principled and proper to regard him with esteem and to say thank you for the services he'd given elsewhere. At the end Charlton clasped both hands above his head, saluting those who were saluting him. He got an ovation rapturous enough to suggest those clapping and shouting for him would wake with sore hands and sorer throats next morning.

George Best's parting from United ought to have been like Charlton's, too – a procession from one cheering ground to another, the handing over of engraved silver.

What Best had done for United warranted it. What he'd contributed to the game as a whole justified it. What he'd meant to those who had seen the breathtaking scope of his football would have validated it and any flashy, bells-and-whistles parade. When Tommy Docherty left him out, Best said: 'A lump came into my throat. The whole thing I'd built up seemed to die in that split second. The bottom had just dropped out of everything.' Alone, hearing the familiar cacophony of a match day going on around him, Best began to sob. He had to rinse his face in cold water to get the redness out of his eyes before going into the players' lounge. People were used to seeing Best shortly before kick-off; most weren't aware he'd been dropped. He heard, but couldn't bring himself to acknowledge, the good luck greetings he got. 'I didn't have the guts to say I wasn't playing. I was in a daze.'

Best couldn't bring himself to watch the Cup tie; but neither could he bring himself to leave Old Trafford. He watched the three o'clock race from Haydock Park and drank tea. He followed the game from the crowd's reactions to it, which he heard indistinctly, as if lodged at the back of a cave. He knew United had won 1–0, the result immaterial to him. Afterwards anyone who asked 'what the hell is going on' heard him say: 'I'm finished' or 'It's over' or 'I'm never coming back', each of which was supplemented with a downcast glance or a shake of the head.

As the clock ticked on, he went on his own into the now empty stands. Like someone about to embark on a long journey, who wants to absorb the sights he won't see for some time, Best sat in the shadows and stared across the pitch; *his pitch*. The floodlights were still on, the ground staff working beneath them, forking the turf and flattening divots and smoothing down the scuffed surface. The only sounds were the rattle of tip-up wooden seats and the drag and sweep of brushes clearing litter. Best was thinking of other days and other nights. What he saw in front of him was his past, rolling by. What he heard was the crowd noise; Old Trafford filled to capacity and everyone yelling and chanting and screaming for him.

He was 17 again, making his debut against Graham Williams.

He was playing in a European Cup semi-final and feeling that Busby's Babes, the players who had perished on that Munich runway, had returned from the dark town of the dead and were running beside him, urging him and United on.

He was flummoxing Bobby Moore, sending him one way and then the other.

He was embarrassing Eddie McCreadie near the touchline.

He was evading Ron Harris outside the box.

He was scoring a goal against Burnley while wearing only one boot.

He was outrunning Sheffield United's defenders before sending that slanting shot against the net.

He was in command of a ball no one can take from him.

He was being George Best.

'The thoughts and memories blurred together into one feeling of utter, incredible sadness and I started to cry again,' said Best, knowing now he'd never make more memories there to match them.

He couldn't remember how long he sat in that stand. 'Could have been twenty minutes,' he said. 'Could have been an hour.' He walked to the edge of the pitch and along the touchline before leaving Old Trafford in early evening darkness. A knot of autograph hunters, wearing United scarves, thrust a blank page of their book or a photograph in front of him and asked for a signature, which he gave wordlessly. Here was a man of sorrows, acquainted with fresh grief and trying not to show he'd been sobbing. He got into his car and drove away.

No one waved him off.

15

The Sun Always Shines in Margaritaville

George Best would wear the shirt and the badge of plenty of other clubs; modest names such as Stockport County and Bournemouth. He'd make guest appearances in scrubby-looking places like Creasey Park, Dunstable, a Southern League ground beside a disused gas works and scrapyard where the main stand had burnt down and another was blown sideways in a gale. He'd go far afield, too, taking off to South Africa and Australia and to both the east and west coasts of America. He'd play in the Scottish First Division for Hibernian. He'd turn out in the League of Ireland for Cork Celtic.

And briefly – oh, so briefly – he'd entertain wonderfully for Fulham in Division Two, where he said his purpose was 'to make football fun again'. He did it, too, alongside Rodney Marsh and Bobby Moore. Best and his *amigo* Marsh – temperamentally suited and sharing the same aesthetic principles – were like a two-man circus, pitching their tent to perform Big Top tricks. As someone perspicuously observed, Best in particular generated the kind of 'oohs and aahs' from the crowd at Fulham that 'people make at fireworks displays'. He and Marsh would even tackle one another to pep-up a League match if interest in it flagged. 'We did it to put a smile on people's faces,' explained Best. The sight-gag always worked because the participants took it seriously. In training he was more showy still. He struck a £10 bet with Peter Mellor, Fulham's goalkeeper, that he could score a penalty against him without looking. Mellor was beaten by a back heel into the bottom corner, which came after a two-step backwards run.

Best stayed nowhere for long except Fulham – 42 appearances over two seasons – and America, where he played in 139 matches for three NASL teams: Los Angeles Aztecs, Fort Lauderdale Strikers and San Jose Earthquakes. Elsewhere Best's arrival and departure were almost simultaneous; no more than a sleep-over. Clubs were always keen to recruit him nonetheless because he drew sizeable crowds and brought them the razzmatazz and a drum-roll of publicity. The Jewish Guild in Johannesburg willingly paid him £11,000 for 360 minutes, a sum equal to the salary he would have earned for 35 First Division appearances.

Wherever Best went the cameras and photographers followed. Those who queued at the turnstiles were there to see him and gawped from the terraces, as if some physical freak were being paraded in front of them. Fulham's usual home gate – under 10,000 – swelled to 21,000 for his debut. A week later there were over 25,000 inside Craven Cottage. Stockport's average gate barely touched 2,000. There were more than 8,000 to watch Best in a fund-raising friendly, and 9,000 came to his first League match. Bournemouth agreed to play Best primarily in home matches, which led them into subterfuge. Football League rules stipulated that clubs had to pick their strongest team. 'I kept making up excuses for him – a dodgy knee or I'd say he wasn't feeling well,' said Bournemouth's manager, Don Megson. Again, the crowds came: 9,000 – double the usual attendance – saw his debut at Dean Court. Bournemouth thought there was a moral obligation to let the customer know whenever Best wasn't appearing. Simple posters – red and black lettering on a bilious green background – were produced for the purpose, comprising the club's crest, a pen and ink drawing of two footballers challenging one another under a high ball and the following words in capital letters:

GEORGE BEST WILL NOT BE PLAYING TO DAY

Either the designer or the printer hadn't noticed the space between the two syllables of the word 'today' or they didn't know how to spell. The souvenir hunters didn't mind. The posters, pinned or pasted on to boards outside the ground, were filched and became collector's items. Everyone still wanted something from Best – even if it was a piece of ephemera.

His wandering made him look like someone itinerantly jobbing to pay the rent, which also happened to be partly true. But Best was doing something much more, too. He was trying to fill in any way he could what he described as the 'terrible void' which enveloped him after leaving Manchester United. 'I didn't want to play with them the way it was,' he said. 'I didn't also want to play for another team.'

The manner of his leaving initially did him crippling harm. The threat to retire loses its shock value when you use it as often as Best had done. The public, tired of such posturing, hardened its mood against him. Those rooting for Best were outnumbered by others shouting disapproval, saying good riddance. The criticisms were that he'd had a vain and fancy opinion of himself; that he'd been a malcontent, disruptive and ungrateful; and that he'd shown disdain towards the rest of the team, as if those players were beneath him – second XI sort of chaps. It distorted how he and his accomplishments were viewed. The tendency was to dwell on what Best had given up instead of what he'd given.

Sacks of mail were forwarded from Old Trafford to Mary Fullaway's and then ignored. The handful of letters Best did slit open were abusive.

Newspaper reports of his leaving read like an obituary stripped of those polite euphemisms, so often used to conceal, or soften, misdeeds and mistakes in respect for the dead. Tommy Docherty was rebuked for daring to think he could reform him and for failing to reach for the whip more often. But most of the opprobrium and the contempt, as well as the blame, fell on Best. When United finished second from bottom at the end of the season, slipping ignominiously into the Second Division, Best was held partly responsible for it, a convenient scapegoat. 'I had bugger all to do with it,' he protested, the accusation swelling his sense of personal outrage towards Docherty all over again. 'All I ever wanted,' he said, 'was for United to be the top team in the country.'

United cancelled his contract in May 1974 and then held his registration for another 17 months until the board gave him a free transfer. There was a terrible finality about signing the documents, like completing divorce papers when you don't really want to part from your spouse. Best had daydreamed about Docherty leaving or being sacked, enabling him to make a glorious comeback in that crimson shirt. Now it was impossible. Sir Matt Busby had once remarked of football: 'Once you are in this game you are in it for life. Life without it is a vacuum – a vacuum that can't be filled by any substitute. You die a thousand deaths in the game. You die a thousand deaths without it.' This applied also to the way Best felt after his estrangement from Old Trafford. Busby added another lament: 'Every manager goes through life looking for one great player, praying he'll find one. *Just one*,' he said. 'I was more lucky than most. I found two – Big Duncan and George. I suppose in their own ways, they both died, didn't they?'

When he said it, Best was only 28.

The loss of United from his life unbalanced Best, tilting him towards all sorts of calamities over the next ten years. Nearly all were self-inflicted. It affected his career, his reputation, his physical well-being and his mental health, which brought about a further kind of breakdown. He found no lasting peace; nor any place he could truly call home for long. While there were weeks or sometimes months at a stretch when Best thought he'd discovered a lasting contentment, he saw these moments afterwards as only interludes in a struggle he was always losing to control his drinking.

In the late 1960s and early 70s he drank to compensate for United's loss of stature. In 1974 and 1975 he did it to cope with his parting from them. It precipitated bouts of what Best said was 'serious', chronic drinking. He traced the beginning of his full-blown alcoholism to this point. 'When I was playing, I wasn't going out deliberately to drink myself into oblivion,' he confessed. 'After I stopped playing, I did.'

He said he began 'to get a little bit bored' and started gambling as well. 'I was looking for something to pass the time,' he added. He began with horse racing. 'If you'd said to me five years earlier I was going to put a fiver on a horse, I'd have shit myself.' Now he had a bookmaker who accepted his calls on credit. 'I remember one statement. I thought, maybe, I'd made half a dozen bets [and] the total was three or four hundred pounds. I got a bill for two and a half grand.' Best moved on to dice – almost always choosing his United shirt numbers of 7 or 11 – and also roulette. In one session of dice Best and a gambling cum business partner were £17,000 down at 2.20 a.m. Best asked for the house limit to be doubled to £2000 to recoup his losses. He imagined having to sell his car or take a loan or give away a portion of his shares in Slack Alice to settle his debts. He hummed the tune of *Let Luck Be A Lady* and the gentleman finally saw how nice a dame luck could be. By 4 a.m. the two of them were cashing in winnings of £26,000 – a £43,000 turnaround in less than an hour and a half. 'There'd be other nights when you'd walk away virtually penniless,' recalled Best, who would tuck a couple of ten pound notes into his top pocket as insurance in case he got cleaned out in the casino and couldn't afford to hail a taxi home. 'I was putting all this money on because it didn't mean anything to me,' he said, as if indulging in a game of Monopoly.

In drinking and gambling Best said he thought he'd discover 'the highs' that playing for United had given him. But the gambling provided 'almost no excitement', he said, and so the drink dominated more than it had before. 'I foolishly kept searching for it in another glass, another bottle. And the harder I looked the worse I became.'

He'd go to a pub before arriving at Slack Alice – 'a drink with the lads early, say six p.m. or seven p.m., and I'd get to the club about ten p.m.,' he said of his itinerary. Best estimated he drank four or five bottles of wine easily during that spell before continuing elsewhere. 'While I was in the club I didn't really consider it drinking. It was part of life.' He'd go to bed between 4 a.m. and 6 a.m., sleep throughout the morning and afternoon and then get up, bathe and start his day in the early evening. 'Sounds a great life,' said Best. 'You've got your pick of any girl you want, almost. Good food. Plenty to drink. Gambling money in your pocket. I suppose I was trying to kid myself that it was what I wanted to do.'

Only someone of Best's abilities could have continued playing – and impressed a crowd – when life was anarchical. He even did enough to be recalled by Northern Ireland's manager, Danny Blanchflower, for a World Cup qualifier against the Total Football of Holland in October 1976. Best hadn't appeared for his country for three years and didn't think he would add to his collection of caps. 'I appealed to him and he accepted the invitation without hesitation,' said Blanchflower. 'He wanted to play for us. He also wanted to make a point.' The point in question was a piece of one-upmanship against Johan Cruyff. Best still tracked the rises and the falls in the game's pecking order. His stock had fallen; Cruyff's was in the ascendancy. Best wanted to make a categorical statement about who, between them, counted as the finest footballer.

He hadn't forgotten how staff at Madame Tussauds had replaced his waxwork with Cruyff's, as if declaring 'The King is Dead. Long Live the King'. Whenever Cruyff was described as the world's best player, Best felt the need to show it wasn't so. The match in Rotterdam was expected to be a pushover, no more than a gentle flexing of their muscles for the Dutch, who'd lost the 1974 World Cup final to Germany in Munich and would go on to lose the 1978 final controversially to Argentina in Buenos Aires, too. In those days newspapermen were trusted to travel on the team bus. The *Daily Express*'s Bill Elliott sat next to Best on the way to the stadium. The two of them slipped into a conversation about Cruyff.

'Is he better than you?' asked Elliott. Best laughed at him. 'You're kidding, aren't you? I'll tell you what I'll do . . . I'll nutmeg Cruyff first chance I get.' After only five minutes Best received a ball wide on the left. He went crossfield purely to get to Cruyff, who was on the opposite flank. 'He took the ball to his opponent, dipped a shoulder twice and slipped it beneath Cruyff's feet,' said Elliott. 'As he ran round to collect it and run on he raised his right fist into the air. Only a few of us knew what this bravado act really meant.' Best inspired a 2–2 draw, an achievement no one had thought possible beforehand. Afterwards the concierge at the team hotel had to bring the house telephone into the lounge bar, where Best was sitting, because of the number of callers asking to speak to him. A plethora of European clubs, mostly from Italy and Spain, rang to enquire about his availability. Best couldn't take the offers seriously. 'You'd think I was an unknown,' he said. What he really wanted to do, even then, was to play for United. He saw himself strictly as a one-club man. While Best always admitted multiple infidelities with women – he found it 'impossible', he said, to be faithful to one partner – he didn't want to cheat on United with anyone and he had no passion to return to Old Trafford on someone else's team sheet. So he selected clubs where the climate suited what he wanted to wear – shorts and flip-flops. And he chose the North American Soccer League because the money was better than the First Division's. 'Most of the players who stay will be paupers,' said Best of the Football League before leaving it. He was conscious of the difference between the way 'stars' were treated on either side of the Atlantic. 'They put you on a pedestal,' he said of Britain, 'and then first thing they want to do is knock you off it. Once you're through they forget all about you. You're finished. Look at Bobby Moore.' In America he switched on the television to find Jesse Owens, four-time Olympic gold medallist at the 1936 Berlin Games, plugging products during prime-time advertising slots, and old-time baseball players – heroes when Truman was president – also able to earn a living through billboard endorsements. The sunny climate, the availability of alcohol and suntanned women, the laid-back atmosphere and the relatively undemanding standard of the 'soccer' in America was seductive. 'There was no point in hanging around. I wasn't going to win another European Cup. I wasn't going back to United,' he said.

Michael Parkinson opened a door in the States for him. Mark McCormack, a lawyer, writer and commentator, established himself as the godfather of sports marketing. With an A-star clientele, which included Jack Nicklaus and Arnold Palmer and, later on, Bjorn Borg as well, McCormack counted as the premier sports agent in the world. He'd always wanted to represent Best and had approached Ken Stanley about cutting a deal on several occasions in the 1960s and early 70s. Stanley said no, believing McCormack wouldn't provide the individual attention Best required. Now McCormack promised to make Best a dollar millionaire quickly. He asked Parkinson, another of his clients, to set up a meeting. As he always did, Best pretended to listen intently and agreed with everything McCormack said to him. The instructions weren't complicated. McCormack would arrange his transfer to a team in the NASL. Best should wait until he received a phone call from him to confirm it. He mustn't speak to anyone else. Best just ignored him. Shortly afterwards Parkinson received a midnight telephone call from McCormack. Was the rumour true? Had Best gone off on his own accord and signed a contract with a club? Parkinson immediately rang Best at Slack Alice. In his usual come-day, go-day fashion, Best confirmed it. McCormack had guaranteed him financial security. He'd also guaranteed him further fame through association with his company and the household names integral to its success. Parkinson asked Best what someone else could offer that McCormack, the absolute expert, could not.

'Twenty grand in readies,' said Best, again casually certain that tomorrow would take care of itself.

Unless you were a part of the NASL, or established a niche interest in it, you won't remember who won what during its heyday. In any game of word association the NASL is instantly coupled with Pelé and the New York Cosmos, plastic pitches and shoot-outs. George Best had always seen sport, especially football, as an extension of showbusiness. He couldn't understand why, performing for a crowd of 50,000, he didn't earn as much as Frank Sinatra or Tom Jones, who made 1 million or more dollars for singing in front of 1,000 people in Las Vegas. 'I could get injured and my career could be over. The worst Tom Jones will get is a sore throat or a pair of women's knickers thrown in his face,' he said. So he never minded the blaring music and horns of the NASL. Or the kits of many colours. Or the manufactured names of the teams. Or the tinkering with FIFA's rules to make the game more appealing to Americans.

America was going to become Best's home because he believed he could reform himself there. What he saw was the possibility of paradise. What he got was purgatory because he couldn't ration his drinking. 'I thought I was getting away from a nightmare when, in fact, I was taking it across the Atlantic with me,' he said.

A drinker who buys a bar is always going to be his own number one customer. After signing for Los Angeles Aztecs, Best used his 'readies' to open 'Bestie's' on Hermosa Beach, where sometimes, beside the Pacific rollers, he would pull pints of Watneys ale for customers. More often, he'd pour a drink for himself. He'd listen to the chorus of what became one of his favourite songs, Jimmy Buffett's 'Margaritaville'. The song is all about the delights of chilling in a hot climate over that cocktail, the words suggesting that the protagonist is reflecting on his past – regretting some of it and wondering how his life has reached its present point. He looks at the sunbathing tourists. He thinks about his friends, wondering what each of them makes of his situation and his old entanglements and misadventures, particularly with women. He ponders on the lovely comfort that a swiftly swallowed back margarita brings him. He finally concludes that the man responsible for the situation he's in is, of course, himself. Best began to see himself as the character in Buffett's lyric, living in his own version of Margaritaville where the sun always shone.

As if trying to replicate the impact of putting on that sombrero a decade earlier, he'd arrived in America wearing a T-shirt emblazoned with the message 'Who the Hell's George?' to send up the fact that in the mid-to-late 1970s the readership of most American newspapers knew next to nothing about him or the game. Reporters there frequently asked Best nonetheless whether he saw himself as the 'Joe Namath of soccer', a comparison which suited the teams employing him because it stripped them of the need to explain his huge appeal in Britain, the broadness of his talent and his gossip-column, cosmopolitan lifestyle. Linking Best to Namath, the New York Jets quarterback and Super Bowl III winner, sprinkled glitter on to him.

The two men were contemporaries. Namath, born in 1943 and nick-named 'Broadway Joe', took the Jets to the Super Bowl only eight months after Best won the European Cup at United. Similarities abounded, and nothing in either life went unreported. Had Best and Namath met then the conversation would have revolved around swapped stories about the virtues and vices of fame, plus money, tax, agents, fashion, sex, coaching, the definition of genius and high achievement. Namath owned a $5,000 black mink coat, which he wore on the sidelines during games. His version of Best's Che Sera was a $25,000 Manhattan apartment in which he placed an oval bed, a leather-decked bar, a fitted llama carpet and Siberian snow leopard pillows. His Slack Alice was a bar called Bachelors III, which he owned on the Upper East Side. At one stage Best and Namath, as if wanting to appear like brothers, both had a gaucho moustache and long sideburns. The only difference was that Best had blue eyes and Namath's were green. Namath always seemed to have a different woman on his arm and *Playboy* commented with surprising demureness about his 'off the field activities', and said these had 'assumed the dimensions of modern myth'. Namath, like Best, preferred blondes, too. He also complained about the 'bullshit' written about him in newspapers and reminded everyone – as Best frequently did – that 'I'm young and single'.

The two men were photogenic and instantly recognisable symbols of their team, their sport, their adopted cities and much else besides. But to those who saw the 1950s as an atoll of placid, conservative bliss and grey flannel suits Best and Namath were also anti-establishment anti-heroes purely on the basis that their clothes, their hair and their priorities marked them out as different. What the *New York Times* said about Namath, the London *Times* could have also said about Best: 'He defied all the old-fashioned rules. He didn't work with the team. He reported late for practice. He was not like the old moral sports heroes.'

Best saw the connection between them and the significance within it. To all intents and purposes Best was Namath; and Namath was Best. No sportsman in Britain really knew what it was like to be Best every day and go through the hoops of his celebrity. Only Namath, a continent away, would have understood exactly because everyone wanted a pound of his flesh, too. Namath said he was a 'product of my time, a product of the sixties', and spoke of his 'different restraints and different liberties', which is how Best saw himself. Namath, like Best, was news with a capital N. He'd received hate mail and death threats, the FBI guarding him the way the British constabulary had guarded Best. Also like him, he'd become bigger than the game he played and won lucrative advertising contracts because of it. The difference was that Namath rated as an earnings superpower. He'd signed for the Jets in 1964 for $240,000. The possibility of a $5 million contract to promote a Fabergé fragrance for men prompted Namath to tell his agent: 'For that amount I'd drink the stuff.' Best didn't give away much against any opponent because he hated finishing second. But he conceded that Namath was 'everything and more than I was in terms of a jet-setting playboy'. What also linked them was first alcohol and then alcoholism. Namath admitted he 'drank to get drunk', confessing that booze eventually 'consumed him'. He began drinking in his youth and, during his rookie year with the Jets, self-medicated on Johnnie Walker Red to numb the pain of an injury. Namath was indiscriminate about what he drank: brandy, rum, wine, Black Russians, beer and then vodka. He became more choosy only because his doctor told him: 'If you have to drink, drink the clear stuff and not the brown stuff.' Namath said of alcoholism: 'One of the first things you learn is that you're powerless.' He could have been speaking for his spiritual twin from Belfast.

There were many occasions when Best took no enjoyment from drinking; but, sadly, there were plenty more when drink alone made him feel alive and good. He still classed drinkers as 'liars' and 'the biggest conmen in the world', and said boldly of himself: 'At my worst I was the biggest conman.'

The irony is Best found it difficult to get drunk quickly. He said he could drink 'day after day', behaving as if all he'd imbibed was a glass or two of dry sherry. Concealed was the chaos beneath – more blackouts, insomnia and amnesia.

When the wine goes in, strange things come out and words are mistaken for thought. So, predictably, the drinking led to minor mishaps, misunderstandings, rows in restaurants with men he didn't know, the threat of fisticuffs and confrontation. In a comically *Carry On*-like scene, Best stumbled on a flight to Australia and inadvertently sent the drinks trolley wheeling unattended through Economy from the aisle in First Class. In London he'd almost killed himself after the borrowed car he was driving clipped a kerb outside Harrods and smashed against a lamp-post. Because he wasn't wearing a seatbelt, the collision catapulted him through the windscreen. He fractured a shoulder blade, numbed the nerves in his left cheek and the shattered glass lacerated his face so severely that he needed 57 stitches. He looked like Lon Chaney in horror make-up. Best said he felt as if his head was being 'held together by Sellotape'. There were also repellent and inexcusable acts, some of which – incidents of violence against women – happened when the alcohol took such utter and ugly possession of him that he ceased to be himself at all. He was more beast than Best. Nothing is so painful to the human mind and heart as a great and sudden change in someone. The drink went to work and twisted Best's personality malignantly, turning him into something hateful, vengeful and short tempered, which was as far from his real nature as it was possible to get. It was as if Stevenson's description of the Mr Hyde within Dr Jekyll – that a 'man is not truly one, but truly two' – had been proved in some awful experiment. When it happened there was a shudder of distaste. Best became a stranger to his friends and the greedy gulps of alcohol made him a fiend, which afterwards brought the hell of intense remorse. That remorse would have been unbearable for Best if he hadn't developed a psychological trick to deal with it. Life did indeed imitate Stevenson's art. Best's earlier concession that there were, indeed, two George Bests – the private and the public, which were markedly different from one another – allowed him to separate the first from the second.

The private Best represented his good side. The public Best represented the bad. He was able to rationalise the most repellent aspects of his behaviour with the deception that, whatever the act, it had been committed by the bad Best, which wasn't really him. To err is human, but it is easier to handle if you think someone else is accountable.

Those who don't know how anyone can get addicted to drink are rare now. What we haven't resolved is the debate about whether or not alcoholism is a disease. This has been on-going since Rush and Trotter were writing about drink and inebriation in the early 19th century. Best was sure it should be classed as such, and equally certain of the genetic causes. He asked himself the simplest of questions:

How can some people drink only moderately or even regularly, but then abstain for days or weeks or months without missing it, whereas others, such as himself, become alcoholics?

In doing so he remembered his mother's alcoholism as well as his own. Mary Fullaway recognised Ann had a drinking problem well before she understood Best had one. Ann and Dickie would stay at Aycliffe Avenue. Afterwards, during cleaning, she discovered empty bottles hidden around the house. His mother drank secretly, said Best, 'because she didn't want people to see her drinking'. As a lot of drinkers do, she became abusive and severely critical of those around her, picking fights with people she loved. Her family used to look through the front window before going into the house. If she was sitting in her chair, it usually meant she'd been drinking. If there was no smell of food inside, it meant she'd been doing so for hours. Sometimes she'd go into the city centre, drink there and return bruised. Once, she broke her leg. Her husband, Dickie, would get back from work and then reach for his coat and walk the streets to avoid bickering. He begged her to seek medical help for her addiction. He tried to take her to a hypnotist. He went into pubs and the shops nearby, which sold alcohol, and asked them not to serve her. He said he wanted to take a match and burn down the closest off-licence. But Ann didn't see herself as an alcoholic. 'I was doing the same things myself at that stage, and I couldn't see it either,' admitted Best. In the mid-1970s – he couldn't pinpoint the exact year – he went to Belfast and tried to speak to her about drink just as Sir Matt Busby had once spoken to him. His mother welcomed him as mothers do – with a kiss, an embrace and a tear or two after a long absence. Initially he thought nothing of it. Surely, he thought, the flood of affection – including those tears – was her way of letting him know how pleased she was to see him and also what he meant to her. The extent of her drinking became apparent only as the hours passed. She expressed her concern for him – about the dissolution of his career – and he tried to be reassuring in return. 'Don't worry,' he said. 'I can handle everything. I always have done.' He watched her go off on her own – as she'd done during her silver wedding anniversary – to surreptitiously seek a drink and then a top up. The drinking made her steadily more depressed. There was nothing he could say to get her to stop. 'Everything would worry her,' he explained. 'Even little things would become too much.' By the end of the evening she sat beside him silently, holding his hand or rubbing his arm. She wept a lot. Best didn't know how to respond. 'I offered what help I could. I wasn't getting through.'

His mother reacted as he had done with Busby. She nodded, said yes to whatever he said. Best travelled back to Manchester and drank a bottle of wine on his own before heading into a bar to drink some more. 'I couldn't really sort myself out, let alone my family,' he said. 'Whenever I called my father, he'd say: "We were arguing last night." It was just becoming worse. She was in a terrible state.'

Ann Best died in her sleep in October 1978. She was 54 years old. Her death certificate recorded natural causes. A heavy smoker, she'd had two previous heart attacks before the one that killed her. After the second of them Best had travelled to Burren Way, finding the change in her 'drastic'. This time he didn't know how to respond constructively to her condition. 'I told her she looked fine,' he said. She and Dickie were sleeping apart during the week before she died; Dickie occupied the sofa downstairs. He took her morning tea and left it on the bedside table. Returning to find it untouched, he laid his hand on her shoulder. The coldness of her skin told him she was dead.

Seldom are children prepared for the death of a parent – irrespective of the circumstances in which it occurs. The suddenness of her passing exacerbated Best's ineffable grief. It is the custom in Belfast for the coffin to leave for the church ceremony directly from the house. As is also the custom, the coffin was left open for a period. Best said he found the experience 'harrowing'. 'I couldn't go and see her,' he explained, remembering the vigil his eldest sister, Carol, kept beside the casket. 'I just couldn't bring myself to go anywhere near. I could go and look at someone else [but] I couldn't bring myself to even look across because it was my mother.'

Ann never complained about his fame. She never gave it – or anything else – as the reason why she began drinking and continued to drink. Nor, despite missing him awfully and inconsolably, did she blame him for not visiting her regularly enough. His trips home were always celebratory, grand occasions for her. 'When he's here he'll only go to places where he won't be bothered. If me and his daddy didn't take him, he'd never go out. He'll sit in the house and never stir,' she'd said, simply glad to see him. In the beginning Best came back to the family once a fortnight. Then once a month. Then once every three months. And then once every six. 'As the visits became less regular,' he said, 'it became more difficult to return.' He forgot to telephone. He stopped writing. He seldom sent cards. 'I could never remember birthdays,' he confessed. 'You don't realise at the time how important it can be to people to do things like that.' Best never forgave himself for doing so. He thought he'd shamed her because of some of his behaviour; and so he felt shame himself. The grief seemed unsurvivable. He came to regard his mother's death as 'all my fault' and said: 'For years and years afterwards I felt terribly guilty about it.' Even the phrase 'terribly guilty' underplayed what Best went through. Wherever he went he towed an enormous cargo of guilt around with him. There was the guilt of not being there. Of not seeing her often enough. Of not saying some healing words – though Best never knew what – that might have cured her. 'I can remember months afterwards, either one or other of my sisters having terrible times because they'd be looking through old photographs or stuff belonging to my mother and they'd come across an empty bottle she'd tried to hide. It would shatter them. That's when it hit me hardest of all.'

His father tried to offer him solace, Best remembered: 'The funny thing was [he] said to me . . . "We've actually become so much closer now since it happened. We've become like pals rather than father and son."' Dickie began to think, added Best, that 'the sort of life she was leading, the way she was going, she was better off getting out of it, getting some peace of mind'. But Best sank into moroseness that was beyond black. 'I wished it had been me that had gone instead of her,' he said.

Still he couldn't stop drinking.

Always, the first step towards solving any problem is to accept you have one. But it was 1981 before George Best properly admitted his alcoholism to others as well as to himself. He was nearly 35 years old. Only two years earlier he'd insisted: 'I've never considered myself an alcoholic. I don't wake up gasping for a drink.' Best even claimed he wasn't drinking heavily. Yes, he liked a drink – perhaps one too many. No, it didn't require treatment because he didn't 'need to drink every day', he said. Best thought he would overcome his drinking on his own, slowing down as he aged. The eventual confession came as a reluctant last resort and was spoken only after he'd slid through the descending stages of compulsion and dependence, each depth leading to a lower depth still. Prescribed

Antabuse tablets, Best tested how much he could drink before the medication made him physically sick. Gradually he developed his tolerance to them. So a few sips became a full swallow. So a small glass became a big one. In the end he would only pretend to take a tablet, concealing it under his tongue or behind his top teeth before spitting the thing out.

Not even the responsibility of marriage and the subsequent birth of his son, Calum, made a difference to Best's drinking.

In January 1978 he wed Angela McDonald Janes. He was 31 going on 32. She was 25, a personal assistant to Cher. She'd first met Best – he was 'tipsy', she said – during a modelling assignment at Earls Court in 1970. Five years later she spoke to him again at a party in Beverly Hills. A few weeks afterwards she went to another party at Hermosa Beach. What failed to go off, she said, were 'the alarm bells that ring when you meet a man who likes to hang out in bars'. The wedding took place at the Candlelight Wedding Chapel in Las Vegas, which was as gaudy as it sounds. The groom wore an American checked jacket with collars that spread towards his shoulders like a pair of wings, a white shirt and black trousers. He said he looked 'horrendous'. The bride wore a white jacket and a pale shirt and skirt. She said the outfit 'made me look like a schoolmarm'. The new Mrs Best also described the wedding as 'a complete fiasco' and went on: 'I defy anyone to come forward and tell me they had a worse wedding day than mine.' Mr Best said the only good thing about the service was 'that it lasted only three minutes'. George didn't recognise Angela because her straight hair had been curled. Angela noticed that George, who confessed to being 'a little drunk', hadn't washed his hair, which was greasy. There was a mix-up over obtaining the marriage licence. The priest was dressed in a lime green suit and read the vows over taped music. George had to borrow a ring, which didn't fit Angela's wedding finger. At the reception, a waitress spilt Coca-Cola and stained Angela's jacket. The food was inedible. George took his wife to the casino at Caesar's Palace, where he lost his money. And there was a two-hour chase around Vegas to avoid newspapers that were trying to out-scoop the rival that had bought exclusive rights to the nuptials. Later that evening, back in Los Angeles, George changed and went out for a drink alone. 'Don't wait up,' he said before leaving. In his own words, he then got 'stinking drunk for several days'. What he called the 'deadly dragon of booze' made him a 'very bad' husband. 'No matter where we went, the bottle went with us,' he added.

Their first Christmas and New Year as a married couple were spent apart because Best went missing for a fortnight. He'd stayed with another woman and later admitted: 'I was unfaithful everywhere.' When he returned, and a row began, his wife ended up stabbing him in the rump with a kitchen knife. He threw an onyx ashtray at her. On another occasion she hit him over the head with a two-inch plank of wood after he barged, drunkenly and aggressively, into a hotel room.

If Best couldn't find his car keys, he would walk up to eight miles to reach a bar. He also fell off a bicycle on to the road and badly cut and bruised his arms and legs. He frequently got lost or forgot where he lived and had to be taken home. He'd disappear on benders that lasted for days; sometimes another of those 'lost' weeks would pass. He once went almost a calendar month when alcohol was his main sustenance. The only food he ate were bowls of nibbles – peanuts and crisps and pretzels, which sat in glass dishes on the bar. He said these were 'periods of sheer madness'. Best didn't like to have drink in the house because of what had happened to his mother. But he began to store beer in his fridge after developing the morning-after shakes. A can or two was a cure for the trembling in his hands, which would otherwise have been noticeable whenever he signed autographs.

He remembered making Angela 'ill with worry and nerves' and how, nevertheless, she tried to support him as well as she could. She crushed sleeping pills and tipped the powder into his coffee and stirred it in an effort to prevent the binges. She tried to ration the amount of money in his pocket to prevent him from buying a drink. So Best began to steal. He took the cents and quarters out of a bottle used to store their loose change. He stole from her purse. He stole from a stranger's purse, too, taking $10 after she left the bar to go to the toilet without taking her bag. 'She was just an ordinary working woman,' he said, ashamed. The following afternoon he returned the money to her because his conscience dictated it. Everything was a jumble, including his football. 'I played for so many bad teams,' said Best. 'I showed them one or two things that kept them happy. But it wasn't keeping me happy . . . I always wanted to do something worthwhile.'

From Los Angeles Aztecs he moved to Fort Lauderdale Strikers. His rows with their coach, Ron Newman, a former winger for clubs such as Portsmouth and Gillingham, Leyton Orient and Crystal Palace, made his disagreements with Tommy Docherty look like a polite kerfuffle over the Earl Grey at a Victorian garden party. Newman made two substitutions against New York Cosmos, throwing on inexperienced players to replace seasoned ones. Then leading 2–1, Best's team eventually lost 3–2. Afterwards Best slung his shirt at Newman, telling him 'you're just another bloody Alf Ramsey', before adding, disgustedly, that 'he knew so little about football he probably took that as a compliment'. Breaking point came after a wrangle over his registration, which led, disproportionately, to a world-wide FIFA ban and five months of inactivity for him. To ease into his return Best asked for a few games to get match-fit. Within an hour of the first, he was brought off. On his way to the dressing room he peeled off his shirt and, once more, used Newman as a target for his throw. 'To my way of thinking it was simply a repeat of the same old story,' he said. 'Coaches who didn't understand what I was about. It was easier to drink and forget it all.'

Next stop was San Jose Earthquakes. He considered the team 'mediocre and getting worse'. The refereeing, he said, was 'soul-destroying'.

The coaching was 'second rate'. The plastic pitches of the NASL jarred his knee joints and his right leg began to swell, which allowed him to insist he was drinking purely for medicinal purposes. Earthquakes' general manager, John Carbray, regularly tried to persuade him to seek help. Best didn't want to talk about it at all. When Carbray eventually got him into a room to discuss his drinking, Best accepted the offer of a cup of tea before the conversation began. He then insisted on brewing the pot himself. Carbray thought nothing of it; he had the key to the front door, after all. Five minutes later the kettle still hadn't boiled. Carbray went into the kitchen to discover Best had sneaked out through a window minuscule enough to have defeated a cat burglar.

At the beginning of 1981 Best was arrested for drink-driving and held overnight in the cells. He finally went into counselling because of it and, two months later, moved into a live-in rehab centre, the Vespers Hospital in California.

Best hadn't liked his original counselling. Those he met there, sitting in a bare room on chairs arranged in a semi-circle, were like him. He didn't like the rehab centre either: the dozens of questions he filled in on various coloured forms; the fact he was woken at 7 a.m.; the duty to make his own bed – or lose his sheets as a punishment – and return his plate and tray back to the kitchen after every meal. He referred to it as 'The Prison'. There was an obligation to share his feelings, which for someone so emotionally restricted was akin to opening an ulnar vein and letting everyone watch him bleed. How vulnerable he felt is evident in two instances. In the first, Best sits in the communal television room watching *The Hustler*, the film about 'Fast Eddie' Felson and his ambition to beat the legendary champ 'Minnesota Fats' on the pool table. Paul Newman is Felson. The lantern-jawed George C. Scott plays his unscrupulously ruthless manager, who spells out to his client what it takes to win. 'Talent isn't enough,' he says with a demonic glare. 'You've got to have character.' When Best heard those words on screen he was sure every pair of eyes in the room was burning a hole through him. He assumed the others were comparing the fictional sportsman to the real one. A bearded Hell's Angel responded as if Best's thoughts had appeared in a cartoon-like bubble above his head. He laid his big biker's hand on Best's shoulder and said: 'You came in here on your own, man. You've got character.' In the second, Best is occupying the clinic's 'Love Seat' – a high-back, leather swivel chair. What he went through appeared to him like a no-holds-barred inquisition. It was actually an adaptation of the Twelve Steps of Alcoholics Anonymous. Step one is the realisation that your life is unmanageable. Other steps include making a moral inventory of the hurt you've caused to yourself and others, an admission of your wrongs and the attempt to make amends. Best was encouraged to write down ten examples of where and when he'd let himself down through drink; his six worst traits (using his fame to glean drinks and also procrastination, he said); and six examples of how drinking had affected his friends, family and finances. 'Only six examples?' he said. 'Well, at least I got off lightly there.'

The session in the Love Seat took place with 27 fellow patients clustered around it. A row began because Best was wearing a short leather jacket that another patient didn't like. A counsellor then distributed a piece of paper that catalogued almost three dozen of his worst faults. The others put a tick beside which of them he or she perceived as being true. Each person in the room then read them aloud as Best turned the Love Seat to face them. He thought he was popular and collegiate; someone tackling the programme in the correct spirit. The Love Seat disabused him of those notions. The majority of his peers believed Best regarded himself as a cut above them; that he didn't want to collaborate; that he treated the sessions as 'a joke'; that he was primarily concerned with pretence, which meant covering up and trivialising his problems; that he was entirely preoccupied with getting away from the hospital; that he was afraid of opening up; and that he hadn't talked enough about his mother. 'I started crying,' said Best, who also felt physically sick. 'Really crying. I cried my eyes out. It was hurtful and humiliating and I wanted to hide.'

The point about his mother was valid. When doctors learned about the circumstances of her death, Best was told: 'It's not your fault.' He was encouraged to write a letter to her, and dictated an apology cum explanation cum expression of remorse that asked for her forgiveness. 'It certainly helped me come to terms with the death of my mother,' he said. What it didn't do was allow him to talk about it fully and frankly.

Best believed the doctors 'couldn't quite figure me out'. A lot of patients, he explained, had 'lost homes, marriages, kids – there was nothing left for them'. He added these were ordinary but highly intelligent people – lawyers, bankers, business executives. 'They weren't winos who slept in the gutter,' he stressed. Unlike them Best hadn't hit what he termed 'rock bottom'. He did admit he was a 'complete disaster'; and also that he'd come to think drink was obligatory to 'have a laugh' or 'to do anything' else. He said he 'didn't know' when he was likely to go on one of his weekend or full-week benders or what led him in that direction. After talking to him at length the doctors diagnosed something about Best which he'd only half-realised himself. 'They were frightened for me because I usually did it [the bender] when things were going well for me,' he said. There were reference points from his past to underscore that theory, such as the Footballer of the Year dinner and his inability to recall the European Cup final celebrations. Another example of it would follow within a year. At a banquet in California for the New York Cosmos – due to play San Jose in a pre-season friendly – first the Cosmos coach, Professor Julio Mazzei, and then Pelé toasted Best as the world's greatest player. During the preamble Best, sitting at the back of the hall, presumed Mazzei was about to ask for a standing ovation for Pelé. He was ready to rise from his chair and applaud him like everyone else. To hear his own name attached to the accolade instead was overwhelming. But the way Best responded to it was another example of that self-sabotage and self-abasement, which doctors at the Vespers had recognised and interpreted correctly. He began drinking and didn't stop for 12 days, missing the match against the Cosmos. He reacted to success as though he didn't deserve it, wasn't entitled to it and felt some need to reproach himself for the good things his talent had brought him.

The Love Seat sceptics were also right. Best confessed later that he 'conned' the doctors into discharging him after only 18 of the 30 days he was supposed to stay there. 'I was a fraud,' he said. 'I faked it.' As he left, an Irish-American orderly called his bluff. 'George, you ain't conning me,' he said, knowing Best would be in rehab again soon. The thing is Best knew it, too. In saying to himself 'I won't drink for a year', which is what Best did on his release, he admitted his intention to resume drinking once that year had ended. During his introduction to Vespers Best had been sitting between two other patients when a doctor looked at them and predicted: 'In five years' time one out of the three of you is going to be dead. One's got a slight chance of making it. One of you will be back here within a year.' He was right on two counts. Best returned voluntarily to the Vespers Hospital, finally completed its course and left with an Alcoholics Anonymous medallion in his luggage as a reward. The man who had sat to Best's right was already dead by then. 'The shock of finding that out made me stay and see it through,' he said.

What turned him dry – the treatments and the doctors' warnings – could, alas, never keep him dry.

George Best was forever promising that sobriety was on the way. He went to health clubs and ran and kicked a ball around in a park in an effort to regain fitness and reform. 'I'm ready to get back to where the trophies are being won, where the big games are, where I belong,' he said, pledging to live frugally and monastically and always sounding sincere and determined. But there was only ever a hiatus before the temptation to drink overpowered him again.

Some of his misfortunes were the result of a very bright man doing very dim things. For someone who had seen the world, Best was surprisingly unworldly about the nuts and bolts of business and practicalities of basic housekeeping. A gardener cum handy man who he'd employed at Che Sera used to find screwed-up banknotes on the floor, strewn across the tables or left on the sofa and chairs. Best would return from a night out, simply empty his pockets of cash wherever he stood and not bother to pick up the money again. He never paid sufficient attention to his investments or the amounts that were coming in and going out of his accounts. He banked with Irish Trust, which went into liquidation in 1976, closing its offices in Dublin and Manchester. Best lost savings totalling £27,000. 'I knew I'd never be broke,' he said. 'I could always pick up a few quid somewhere. What I couldn't be bothered to do was work out what I should do with it.' Best explained that he didn't know how to buy a postal order or deal with a teller at a bank. 'The one time I went to the post office to buy a stamp I ended up at the wrong counter.' He thought the mollycoddling footballers received didn't prepare them for such mundane tasks. On any overseas trip, each of which he likened to 'one long school outing', the clubs booked his airline ticket, his hotel room, his transportation and paid for his meals. All Best had to do was hand in his passport; he did nothing for himself. 'I was a kid when I arrived at United and I was a kid when I left them,' he said. Mathematics was Best's choice subject as a boy. He still couldn't make sense of his income, and considered himself to be a 'piece of high price meat' for financial advisers to pick over. When those financiers, eager for his attention, spoke about endowments, Best conceded that he 'didn't have a clue' what such policies entailed and also was disinclined to learn. He said he did no more than dabble in his businesses, regarding them as 'just hobbies', which explains why, in November 1982, he was declared bankrupt after his failure to pay £17,996 in back taxes on his earnings at Fulham. Best offered £10,000 immediately and said he would clear the remainder of the debt within six months. The Revenue refused. 'They thought I had money stashed away everywhere,' said Best. 'I didn't.'

In the decade that passed before his bankruptcy was discharged, making him legally solvent again, there were two more black dates Best would never forget: the degradation of jail and his self-demeaning appearance on *Wogan*. He called prison 'dehumanising'. He called the chat show – in front of an audience of 4 million – 'five minutes of making a fool of myself'.

Prison came first. In December 1983 he was sentenced to three months for drink-driving and assaulting a policeman. His car was stopped shortly before 2 a.m. on The Mall. The breathalyser showed he had 112 milligrams of alcohol in 100 millilitres of breath after a Friday night and Saturday morning session. There was no disputing his guilt; he was 77 points over the limit. And there was no disputing the idiocy of his decision to drive home instead of hailing a taxi. He did so because it was raining. Best then compounded the felony by failing to appear at Bow Street Magistrates' Court later that same morning. Not realising the judicial system worked on a Saturday, he assumed his case would be heard on the Monday. Police, including two Special Patrol Group units, were dispatched to arrest him. He looked out of his window and saw three police cars, two police motorcyclists and two constables on foot. Best thought it would be a clever idea to lock himself in his flat and then attempt to out-run the officers by making a 20-yard sprint across the road, where he planned to hide in the apartment of an acquaintance. In the struggle that followed, he said he 'stuck the nut' on one constable. The stipendiary magistrate described the assault as 'extremely grave'. Best received bail nonetheless and applied successfully for an appeal, which was heard at Southwark Crown Court. His counsel believed character witnesses would be useful, and chose two journalists, Hugh McIlvanney of the *Observer* and Jeff Powell of the *Daily Mail*. Sitting in the court canteen beforehand McIlvanney remembers telling Best that the recruitment of Powell and himself to the cause might 'make you the first man to be hanged for a driving offence'. The judge dismissed the appeal and Best was handcuffed and taken to Pentonville Prison, where the cells had once held murderous men such as Dr Crippen and John Christie. 'Thanks boys,' he said, leaving McIlvanney and Powell with some gallows humour. 'If it hadn't been for you two I'd have got fourteen days.'

He was prisoner 76245. The number was scrawled on a square cardboard box, in which he placed his clothes after stripping off and putting on a uniform of blue denims, a striped shirt and a navy, V-neck sweater. His cell on A-wing measured 12 x 8 feet and contained nothing but a bed, a chair, a basin and a slops bucket. Inmates asked for his autograph. One prisoner tried to solicit sex from him in the shower. Another compiled a list of dos and don'ts for his benefit, which included the names of wardens to trust. A pair of prisoners protected him from persecution, like hired bodyguards.

As a cathartic exercise Best set to work on a diary, written on wide loose sheets of unlined paper. In ball-point pen he wrote of the tears he shed on his first night, the cacophonous din of prison as it awoke, the vile smell of shit and piss during slopping out, the overflowing sluice and the cockroaches, the fear of losing any remission just by not knowing the rules, the porridge that was only one grade up from pigswill, the 48 hours of Christmas Eve and Christmas Day of which 46 were spent alone thinking of his son unwrapping presents. Best received more than 2,000 cards, including the seasonal wishes and support of managers such as Lawrie McMenemy and Jim Smith, ex-players, among them Gordon Banks and Eddie Gray, and his old youth coach at Manchester United, Jack Crompton. Julian Lennon, son of John, urged him to 'master the sadness and loss'. The player-boss of Tranmere Rovers, Bryan Hamilton, a former team-mate for Northern Ireland, scribbled a note that made Best grin, which was rare then. 'As you can see,' Hamilton wrote, 'I'm the present manager of Tranmere – so you think you've got problems!'; a few days later Hamilton was sacked. Michael Parkinson visited Best in Pentonville. 'George was a sorry and wretched sight,' he said. 'He looked crushed, sad. He'd always stood out in a room before. Now he looked like everyone else.'

The sentence brought Best closer to his father, Dickie, who wrote what he told his son was the 'hardest letter I've ever written'. He considered not posting it. 'It brings a lump to my throat every time I read it,' said Best. 'He didn't spare me anything. He told me what he thought I'd done with my life. But he stressed I must ignore the people who say I am a "fallen idol" – because I'm not fallen.'

Best always believed the severity of his punishment was 'unjust'. The length of it owed more to his celebrity than his crimes, he said. An editorial in the *Guardian* agreed with him. 'There is a whiff of sanctimoniousness about it,' said the newspaper. Soon transferred to Ford Open Prison in Sussex – the van taking him there drove tantalisingly within 300 yards of his flat – Best took the awful memory of Pentonville with him. 'Once you've been through it, you don't forget it and you don't want to go there again,' he said. At Ford, Best refused to join the football team because he didn't want newspapers to publish long-lens photographs of him shuffling after the ball on a park pitch when uniformed wardens were guarding the touchline. The team he saw were beaten 6–1, and Ford's goalscorer absconded at half-time. The following day the lag on the run was sporting enough to ring the prison to apologise for scarpering. The story went unreported only because the newspapermen sent to cover the match gave up on it after discovering that Best wasn't playing. He was working on what Ford classed as one of its 'red band' jobs – light duties comprising cleaning and tidying, tea making and message running, for which he was paid £2.40 a week.

During the 56 days he spent in Pentonville and Ford – the Home Office released him a month early – Best calculated he'd read 44 books, written more than 200 letters and lost almost a stone in weight. 'I felt fitter than I'd done in ages,' he said. He was pictured in a foamy bath, his legs lolling over its edge. His head was tilted backwards and his eyes were staring at the ceiling. He looked content, and also half-surprised, as if unable to believe his ordeal was over. Best claimed to have no desire to drink again. 'I intend to get even fitter,' he swore. The vow of abstinence lasted only a further ten days before two beers led to two more, and then took him on to the optics. So it went on. 'Once a drinker gets a taste, the old weakness resurfaces,' he said.

No one was ignorant of Best's drinking. He was photographed all too frequently emerging out of bars and nightclubs as if he'd taken up residence inside them. He could even walk into any pub and get drunk without paying for a drink. Some would call it killing with kindness. Best was able to sit at a table with half a dozen or more glasses of white wine lined up beside him. When one of his friends asked a barman why he didn't freshen Best's existing drink, instead of giving him another one, he was told: 'Everyone who buys a drink for George likes to see it poured into a glass.'

The indignation Best aroused during the broadcast of *Wogan* in September 1990, however, made it seem as if his habit had previously been classified information, the disclosure of which now counted as a revelation. Each year the YouTube segment of the interview still attracts thousands of hits. There's Best in his hideous olive green suit and a paisley shirt, buttoned at the collar, emerging from the wings to clasp his host, Terry Wogan, in both hands. Wogan has already registered that, as he put it later, 'the worst had happened' and knows that his first interviewee is 'as drunk as a skunk'. Best's hair is long and lank and dirty-looking. His stubble looks more than a day old. His eyes are glazed and the eyelids flutter. It's as though, after flopping down on the sofa in front of Wogan, he's about to lean back and doze off after being overwhelmed by a longing for sleep. While answering questions, he repeatedly leans across and attempts to touch Wogan's knee. Wogan is professionally straight-backed. It's as if he thinks his own formal posture might encourage Best to do likewise. He glances at Best with increasing apprehension, sometimes looking downwards and willing his flushed-faced and sweating guest to be miraculously sober when he stares directly at him again. In the interview Best asks whether the programme is live and also whether it is permissible to use the word 'shit'. He goes on to lambast Tommy Docherty. Nothing Wogan does or says will make any difference to Best. The measure of his complete desperation is encapsulated in the superfluousness of one question, which is broken into two parts. Wogan says: 'What about the booze? Is that still important to you?' Best confirms it is, unsurprisingly. This is car crash television, a combination of tragicomedy and what-will-happen-next suspense, and the millions watching it, who tuned in from the beginning, are now calling others, originally uninterested, to hurry around the set as the programme proceeds. The nadir of the exchange – the lines which will be quoted most often – is still to come. Best interrupts and blurts out, as though it, too, was a secret until he shared it: 'Terry, I like screwing, all right?' Whatever Wogan asks next – and however blandly he expresses it – can only lead to more trouble. He unwisely chooses: 'So what do you do with your time these days?'

'Screw,' replies Best, his mind still locked on his earlier statement.

Smug outrage was everywhere afterwards. That sanctimonious busy-body Mary Whitehouse, head of the National Viewers' and Listeners' Association, was capable of seeing filth in a basket of freshly laundered linen. She shot off a letter to the BBC complaining that Best had been allowed to remain on the set even after Wogan shortened the interview. Why wasn't he banished from it, she demanded to know. Wogan did try to usher him away off camera. Either Best didn't understand what Wogan was telling him to do or he deliberately chose to ignore him. The newspapers spoke of his 'shame'.

An internal BBC memo said that Best didn't seem to be drinking an 'undue amount' in the hospitality Green Room. But, crucially, it added that '*up until 18.58 p.m.* [my italics] there was no suspicion by anyone that the imminent interview would be anything but normal'. It continued that what happened subsequently 'is anyone's guess'. The BBC didn't know that Best had been drinking during the afternoon, so every small sip he took in their presence supplemented his earlier consumption. Nor were the studio staff aware of his ability to look sober and communicate normally when he was actually close to the edge of drunkenness. But if – as the memo implies – his unfitness became apparent at 18.58, then why was he allowed to go on at all? The opening credits of the programme didn't roll until 7 p.m. Reappearing on *Wogan* in 1992, Best relied on humour to try to explain away the change in his demeanour between 18.58 and 19.01 – and to make himself, rather than the BBC, wholly culpable for his appearance. 'You'd be amazed,' he said, 'what an Irishman can drink in three minutes.'

The darkest part was still to come for George Best, the conclusion forecast long before it occurred. In an unfolding tragedy, he drank on. 'Just pouring alcohol into my blood,' he said.

What Best had accomplished for Manchester United and his status in 1960s culture meant he was never going to disappear into the obscurity of the small print. He had a permanent home in the tabloids, which followed a life that was like a fever. It had highs and lows. 'I began to realise I would always be in the papers,' he said.

Best became an on-stage memoirist. Every episode from his past or present became material for a performance of cosy reminiscences, which he gave in theatres and sportsman's clubs and at black tie dinners. His friendly interrogators were predominantly men who were part of the 60s and wanted to relive either their boyhood or early adulthood and share it with him in 'I saw you play' moments of all our yesterdays. The point of coming was to be able to say afterwards that you'd spoken to Best from the stalls. Best knew what was on the way and learned his replies by rote. How much was Sir Matt Busby a father figure to him? Why didn't he get along with Bobby Charlton? Did Denis Law complain when Best didn't pass the ball to him? Should his 'goal' against Gordon Banks have counted? Who was his hardest opponent? What did he think ranked as his greatest performance? Would he like to have been born English rather than Irish? Was he jealous of the salaries paid in the Premiership?

He'd take a drink to settle his nerves beforehand and preferred to answer questions rather than speak either from a script or off the cuff. Usually Best began with a reference to his unreliability, asking the crowd 'Hands up all those who didn't think I'd turn up tonight?' and then his drink problem: 'It's a pleasure to be standing here. It's a pleasure to be standing up,' he said, a line cribbed from *Raging Bull*, Martin Scorsese's biopic of the boxer Jake LaMotta. The tone was droll and self-deprecating and much of the dialogue became popularly established in books of quotations and has since been repeated to the point of becoming clichéd.

If I'd been born ugly, you'd never have heard of Pelé.

In 1969 I gave up women and alcohol. It was the worst twenty minutes of my life.

I spent a lot of money on booze, birds and fast cars. The rest I just squandered.

I've stopped drinking . . . but only when I'm asleep.

Nothing was off limits to Best. He talked about his health and his hospitalisations, his arrest and his trial and being awash with money and being without it. He spoke about his first marriage, which ended in divorce in 1986. He spoke about the 'bliss' of his second to 23-year-old Alex Pursey in 1995, which would later end in divorce, too. Women came into his life and then left again. 'They say I went out with seven Miss Worlds,' he said. 'It was only four. I didn't turn up for the other three.' The real figure was two. The first, the American Marjorie Wallace, accused him of stealing a fur coat and some jewellery from her flat. Best was subsequently cleared. The magistrate announced that he was leaving court 'without a stain on his character' after Wallace chose not to appear to give evidence, which left the prosecution minus its case. A reporter rang him to claim Wallace kept a little black book in which she rated her lovers out of ten. 'You only got four,' he said to Best, who replied like a comedian putting down a heckler: 'Well, that's three more than she got.' The second was Mary Stavin, the subject of his most celebrated anecdote, which is still told and retold because its punch-line is loaded with meaning.

The story succeeds on several levels, which is why it endures. On the first, it is genuinely funny. On the second, Best recited it both against himself – which was disarming – and with a jack-the-lad nod and a wink that told you he was boasting inside. On the third, it confirmed that Best – despite everything bad that had happened to him – would always remain the sort of man that other men aspired to be.

You will have heard it before.

In the early hours of the morning Best is in a luxury hotel room drinking a bottle of champagne. Several thousand pounds of gambling winnings are scattered across the bed, the high-denomination notes looking like discarded ticker-tape. Stavin comes out of the bathroom clad only in a see-through, short black negligée. Her perfumed emergence coincides exactly with the arrival of an Irish waiter, who is bringing more champagne into the room and whose eyes are sticking out on stalks, like a cartoon character who has been struck on the head with a mallet. He looks at Best. He looks at the money. He can't help but look at the ex-Miss World in her transparent nightwear. As he leaves the trolley and claims his tip, he turns to Best and says:

'George, I've got to ask you . . . Where did it all go wrong?'

There was no need for Best to self-mythologise or fabricate elements of his life. The true events were compelling enough to hold the attention. But he invented the hotel, made up the circumstances, created the Irish waiter and put them together in one pithy account to give whoever was listening an idea of his fame and the benefits it had brought him. There are several versions of 'Where Did It All Go Wrong?'. Sometimes Best claimed the hotel was in Manchester. On others he shifted its location to London or Birmingham. Adding a further few threads of embroidery, the waiter wheeled in caviar or smoked salmon and lobster along with the champagne. The value of the money strewn on the bed wildly differed, too, fluctuating between £25,000 and £50,000 in the telling. But who cared about mere details? The legend became fact and was printed as such. And, because it sounded like the sort of thing that could plausibly have happened to Best, the public accepted it willingly as gospel. The only consistent part of the tale is Stavin, a Swedish model whom Best always identified as the woman in the negligée. Stavin didn't understand the joke after hearing it, calling the harmless white lie 'cute' nonetheless. 'I would never wear a negligée,' she said, adding firmly and irrefutably: 'I wasn't there.' Much in the same way Frank Sinatra always had to sing 'My Way', so Best was expected to tell 'Where Did It All Go Wrong?' which became his signature routine.

He was never far from the public gaze. He put his name to ghosted books, columns and newspaper articles. Three of his four autobiographies have a common thread that bind the closing chapters. Best is in a relationship, which he confidently says has put his life in order at last. He says he's 'on the straight and narrow'. He's also 'very happy'. He's sure, too, that 'everything is so great'. But presentiment really is that long shadow on the lawn. You sense, even as you read those sentiments, that the contentment contained within them won't last.

Sometimes, looking back on his life, Best had to rely on memories of memories because those alcoholic stupors of the mid-to-late 1970s and early 80s meant he couldn't always recall events with any exactness. A few he couldn't recall at all. He would occasionally ring friends and ask them to recount certain episodes to him. He did studio punditry for Sky Sports on a Saturday. The company prepared for those afternoons when he didn't arrive for his noon appointment and couldn't be found; an understudy was on stand-by. A taxi, booked for mid-morning, would arrive at his Chelsea flat. Often Best would tell the driver he had unfinished business or had left something inside his local, the Phene Arms, which he needed to collect urgently. He'd go inside for a drink, occasionally failing to re-emerge.

Best had become more wary than ever of strangers since a drunken man hit him on the head with a pint pot after he'd gone into a pub to order a Chinese takeaway over the phone. The attack happened because the man, a Liverpool supporter, was angry that Best had never played for his team. Half a dozen bar towels couldn't staunch the bleeding. In a separate incident Best was attacked by a group of men in the street because he'd defeated them in several games of pool a few days earlier.

He'd usually sit in the Phene, where Dylan Thomas had drunk when he lived only ten minutes' walk away in the 1940s. Just as Thomas had done, Best read the newspapers and did the crosswords. If he got stuck on a clue, he'd ring his father in Belfast and the two of them would find the solution together.

Were it not for the drinking, and the fact that the barometer of his emotional nature was always set for a spell of riot, Best's semi-retirement would have been sedately paced and idyllic. Of the 1970s, he accepted that only the training kept him alive because of the amount he drank. It was like a safety net. Now there was nothing to break his fall. He used to insist his general health was good, convincing himself – though no one else – that his body would survive whatever punishment alcohol inflicted on it.

By April 2000, jaundiced, vomiting and coughing up blood, he was taken into hospital with suspected liver failure. The organ was functioning at barely 20 per cent. Best claimed the pain, which he likened to a knife being thrust into his gut and twisted, made him contemplate suicide. He was going to fly to Jamaica or the Bahamas, and swallow sleeping pills washed down with bottles of Louis XIII brandy and Dom Perignon. Those who really knew him never believed it. Best's motto had always seemed to be 'live all you can – it's a mistake not to' and he loved life too much to leave voluntarily. Almost two and a half years later he underwent a liver transplant, a ten-hour operation during which he almost died after internal bleeding. His blood was so thin it failed to clot properly. He required transfusions totalling 40 pints of blood. Without the transplant, the doctors calculated he'd have been dead within three months. Afterwards Best swore – as he always had done – to forsake the drink, a promise that was soon broken because he thought his new liver would allow him to live his old life again.

Words were running out then. Time was running out, too.

It's said there is no need to visit the dead, for they visit us whenever we speak or think about them. It was true for George Best. The people responsible for shaping his Manchester United career always came back to him that way.

His boyhood mentor Bud McFarlane died in 1977 while on holiday in Spain. He'd retired just four years earlier after giving a quarter of a century's service to Glentoran. Mary Fullaway died in 1983 – three weeks after her 74th birthday. Best did not attend her funeral. In life she'd been pestered in public because of him. In death she was entitled to her privacy, which is the reason he stayed away. Her family understood why. 'He didn't want press and photographers there,' said Steve Fullaway. 'We knew how much he loved my mother, which is the only thing that counts.' Jimmy Murphy, at 79, died in 1989. To the very end he preached the simplicity of football. 'I wonder,' he once said, 'how many George Bests are being destroyed at this very minute by coaches who fail to appreciate that a pennyworth of skill is worth a pound of theory any day.' Bob Bishop received £8 net from United for finding Best. His £100 cheque didn't arrive until 1970. 'Ninety-two pounds went on tax,' he said, without bitterness, thinking it a 'nice gesture' and insisting, 'I didn't expect anything extra.' He'd go on to discover Sammy McIlroy and Norman Whiteside. He'd tell United to sign Pat Jennings and then discover that the scout dispatched to look at him had gone to the wrong match. Tottenham stole Jennings away. 'Twenty players of mine made it out of hundreds,' said Bishop, aware early on of the one he'd be proudest of and remembered for. Bishop, aged 90, died in 1990.

Even giants grow old and die.

Sir Matt Busby, almost 85, was buried in Chorlton-cum-Hardy's municipal Southern Cemetery in 1994. Only 18 months earlier he and his European Cup winners of '68 had gathered together again to make a souvenir film ahead of the final's Silver Jubilee. United were reunited at Wembley. 'How are you, son?' Busby asked Best in a creaky voice, the words sounding like a statement from a parent rather than a plain greeting. The stadium was empty, forlorn-looking and in need of improvement. The turf, once impeccably smooth, grew in shallow tufts in some places and was sparsely brown in others. Those who had played on it against Benfica now had paunches and crow's feet and grey or receding hair. They walked across it like veteran soldiers recalling the geography of a distant battle; proud of the victory medal it had brought them. Busby wore a white shirt and his club tie and blazer, the badge embroidered on to the top pocket. He carried a pipe. He stared around him like the rest of them. After a while, the early recollections exhausted, Best announced to the others 'the boss wants to go' and he and Busby strolled off the pitch together. Best shortened his stride to match his manager's, who looked as fragile as glass. Best still didn't imagine the world without him. He was as unready for Busby's death as he had been for his own mother's. 'You know he loved you?' Busby's son, Sandy, asked him at the graveside. 'I could hardly speak,' said Best.

When someone close to us dies we consider our own life. Best said his 'flashed' in front of him on the day of Busby's burial. The smallest thing – a word, a scent, the way one person or place can resemble another – is capable of triggering the biggest memory. The route of the cortège took Best past the bus stop where Busby used to pull up his car to collect him – and where Best used to hide from him at the rump end of the queue. Everything came back to him then in a swarm of bright detail. Watching the coffin being lowered into the ground, fine rain beading his coat, Best went back to the beginning. He saw his arrival in Manchester. His immediate return to Belfast. The compassion and forgiveness both his parents and United showed in regard to his homesickness. The progress he began to make and then his Old Trafford debut against West Bromwich Albion, which still seemed to him to have happened only yesterday. So did the Championships, the European Cup, the fame and the money and the sight of Busby, with a beetled brow, always striving to wrest order from chaos after some transgression or misunderstanding which Best had got him involved in.

Best never believed that what came later counted as a tragedy for him. The memory of the heart, after all, does tend to magnify the good. 'On balance I came out on top,' he would say. He regarded himself as lucky. Lucky to have signed for United. Lucky to have arrived when the club's rebuilding after Munich had already gone beyond its first phases. Lucky to have played alongside Law and Charlton when both, like him, got to a peak. And lucky, above all, to have had Busby on his side. He'd regularly insist he had 'no regrets' professionally, having the phrase ready, like a shield, to deflect further questions. Something did nag at Best nonetheless. He never knew how much further his gift could have taken him. He did know, however, where that gift always ought to have been plied.

Near the end of his life Best was asked which decision he would most like to change. 'Leaving Manchester United,' he replied, unhesitatingly. In saying so Best also imagined an alternative scenario for himself at Old Trafford, far sweeter than the reality he experienced. In it he played on there for 'another five years' at least, he said. He was the fulcrum of the team and its organising brain, the teacher to up-and-coming youngsters and one of the game's true chevaliers. In this parallel football universe – perfect in every way for him – Busby was still his manager; United were still the champions; the European Cup was still within his reach. 'And I broke every record going,' he said. No one who saw him play doubts he could have done exactly that – and more.

If only things had been different. If only he had been different.

AFTERWORD

Always Wearing That Red Shirt

3 December 2012, Manchester

Of course, he never left Manchester United.

George Best is still there today; cast in bronze on a 5ft 6in-high granite plinth, waiting for anyone who wants to find him. His right hand rests on his slim waist, as though he's expecting a game to restart at any moment and is ready for it.

It is a doleful Monday in Manchester and bursts of rain have rinsed the city clean, and a gusting wind has chased off the clouds that came earlier, dressed as drably as peasants. Now there is a huge, canvas sky and a low sun that offers almost no warmth but gives a sheen, like a spray of polish, to the still wet glass façade of the East Stand. The gleam of the distant scene, beyond Sir Matt Busby Way, is reflected in its tinted green-grey panes, which faintly capture the movement of traffic and people and the dark shapes of buildings. The East Stand is the natural gathering point for anyone making the pilgrim's journey to Old Trafford. This is the spot where past and present align for United.

You can judge a place – just as you can judge a country – by the statues it erects. In sculptured likenesses debts are paid and an appreciation of history is acknowledged. What United thinks about its boys and its boss of the 1960s is evident in how lavishly it commemorates them. Busby's grand statue looks across the damp forecourt. He is depicted holding a ball languidly against his hip. Best's – part of the club's Holy Trinity – looks across at him, which is as it should be. Standing alongside him, Denis Law salutes a goal and Bobby Charlton cradles another ball, as if about to make a presentation of it. Admirers, dwarfed by the stadium's architectural scale, wander from the first monument to the next and then back again. Photographs are taken; snaps as souvenirs.

Someone, far too young to have ever seen him play, tries to touch Best's left boot with the flat of an outstretched hand. He wears a vintage United shirt beneath an oily-looking parka and almost loses the red and white scarf draped loosely around his neck as he makes his leap, which is like an exaggerated hop. Someone else, at least a generation and a half older, looks up at the statue with such a respectful expression that you'd think he was studying the stained glass behind an altar. He yanks a badged woollen hat from his pocket and pulls it over his ears, which the cold has reddened. You can eavesdrop conversations about Best as you walk around Old Trafford or go into its museum, which is an enormous treasure chest of medals and silver, or into its shop, which is a riot of red, some of it kitsch. He comes alive again – brimful of running, elevating matches above the ordinary on his own. Time collapses. The clock stops at 1969. The decade, which vanished around him, is summoned once more. One recollection releases another and then another still, each coming out in sparkling bits.

What goes unmentioned is the significance of the date. No one seems aware it is the anniversary of that day when his home city sombrely stopped to pay its respects and say its last goodbyes to him. It doesn't really matter. Nothing is lost to us if we remember it; and so the very act of remembering him is sufficient in itself. Months and years accrue quickly, speeding by, and so it can seem as though Best left us an age ago. But the intensity of the memories that remain of him conveys the effect he had and continues to have.

He is everywhere.

You can fly into Belfast and arrive at George Best Airport, its five-foot signage the flourish of his signature. You can holiday-rent the house at Burren Way and sleep in the tiny rectangular room that once belonged to him. You can go to the end of the road – as Best always did when he went back there – and look across the field where those childhood games counted as the be all and end all of everything for him. You can kick a football against the pale brick of the wall where he endlessly practised – though only if you ignore the wooden sign, black capitals on a white background, which warns sternly: NO BALL GAMES ALLOWED. You can stand on the kerbside in Donard Street and point to the spot where Dickie took that Kodak photograph of his infant son with a baby ball at his feet. And you can travel along the Ballygowan Road to the tree-decorated, 160 acres of Roselawn Cemetery where Best was buried in the same plot as his mother and where his father, who died in 2008, now lies with them. The headstone is modest because the family wanted it that way. It's no more prominent than those on the same row or on the other rows that run alongside it, stretching far towards the hills in one direction and to the horizon in the other. Visitors come daily. It isn't uncommon for mourners, attending a service or a burial at Roselawn, to seek out Best's grave afterwards. The metal marker labelling it – S 295 – has been stolen, replaced and stolen again on umpteen occasions.

The inscription on black marble refers to him solely as 'Dear Son, Brother and Father'. Nothing on it highlights his heroics as a foot-baller. But those who go there – or to Old Trafford and gather below the statue – do so because of his football. 'The only thing that mattered to me *was* my football,' he'd said, shortly before his death. The only thing that matters to his admirers is his football, too – and the preservation of him foremost as a footballer. He appealed to be remembered for that alone, knowing well enough that 'the rubbish', the euphemism he used to refer to his drinking and the personal disasters it precipitated, would never be detached from future inter-pretations of his career. How could it be? Because of its insidious effect on everything, the piquant fact of his alcoholism can neither be rubbed out nor taken in isolation. He was aware that the melo-dramatic swirl of his life and complications of it – more 'rubbish', he said – needed to be cleared away and carted off before anyone got a clear view of him as a player again, allowing serious judgements to be made.

Since fame came at the very start of that life, and the long struggle came afterwards – reversing the usual sequence of events – he always seemed to be living it backwards, which is the first thing to be overcome in taking the full measure of someone we think we already know from old assumptions. The second is this. While what he achieved as a player is considerable, he still seemed to be only on the verge of accomplishing what was in him. Seen in its entirety, it looks as if his career was only half-realised and incomplete. Even when BBC2 devoted a full night's programming to him, screened to coincide with his 50th birthday, the idea persisted that what he had he threw away and those most maudlin of sentences, beginning 'What if' or 'What might have been' surfaced in critical analysis. This had a lot to do with others' high expectation of him; for it is common to constantly demand more from someone who has already given so much. While he played for United, he carried that pressure around with him, which was testing enough. When he stopped playing for them, he said he had to cope with the sense of deprivation others felt at 'not being able to see me play'. He was asked regularly, even by those who adored him: 'Don't you know you're a fool?' For all these reasons, it has taken a while to see him afresh. But, as he once forecast, posterity is finally putting greater emphasis on the artistry rather than the affliction.

What it reaffirms is his greatness and also the emotional sweep of his story in which reality usurps invention.

Danny Blanchflower eloquently expressed the philosophy of the footballer as the rarefied aesthete. 'The game is about glory,' said Blanchflower. 'It is about doing things in style, with a flourish, about going out and beating the other lot, not waiting for them to die of boredom.' Best thought like that, too. Mind you, he seemed to regard the avoidance of boredom as the entire purpose of life. To play ordinarily and without spontaneity counted as a failure of the imagination as far as he was concerned.

One pro always knows the worth of another. In Best's case Blanchflower was poetic about 'the grander surprises' he – more than anyone else – made on 'the mind and the eye'. Those who played against him appreciated his rarity. At West Ham Bobby Moore said he played a few yards 'further off' Best than anyone else because 'he could have headed in one of ten directions or done twenty different things with a ball'. At Spurs Alan Mullery made stopping him sound virtually impossible. 'I didn't know whether he's going left, over my head or through my legs,' he said. 'I tried to guess which way he was going. Nine times out of ten I guessed wrongly.' At Chelsea Ron Harris simply said, as if to apply an emphatic full stop to any debate about who counted as his most serious opponent, that he 'was the best'. At Liverpool Emlyn Hughes retained the memory of losing heavily to United at Anfield. He confessed: 'I had not got near him. Neither had his marker or anyone else. He skinned us.' Hughes went into the dressing room expecting the most awful bollocking from Bill Shankly. In the mortuary silence of the losers' dressing room Hughes heard the sound of Shankly's shoes as he strode along the corridor and then the click of the door as it opened. Hughes glanced up to study Shankly, who in turn was studying his own team, their heads hung in tiredness and fright. He heard Shankly use only seven words in one of the most concise post-match verdicts he ever gave. 'Boys,' he said, 'you have just seen a genius.' Shankly's acclamation stayed with Hughes. He'd never known his manager talk about *any* non-Liverpool player as a genius – apart from Tom Finney, 'The Preston Plumber', whom Shankly always spoke about as though saying prayers for a deity. Hughes paid his own tribute. 'He was like no one else I ever played against,' he said. Even Sir Alf Ramsey, not known for preferring flamboyance over fortitude, wished he could have picked him for England. During a practice session Ramsey attempted to refine a set-piece. No one could accomplish what was needed to his satisfaction. He looked around him, finally saying quietly and to no one in particular, 'I wish I had George Best.'

Nearly 25 years after he and Graham Williams duelled at Old Trafford on his debut, the two of them sat on a beach in Majorca as pals. 'I've still got your stud marks down the back of my legs,' said Best jokingly. In response Williams paid him a compliment that became one of the quintessential Best stories. 'Well,' he replied, 'it's nice to see your face for a change instead of your arse dashing away from me.' Every full-back knew what he meant.

There is no battle to be fought over Best's talent. The only debate is the subjective one of his ranking in an elite table comprising predecessors, contemporaries and successors.

In attempting to establish one, the homemade message written in black felt-tip pen across each quarter of the flag of Ulster, hung on low metal railings at the end of Burren Way on the morning of his funeral, did the job as well as anything could. The most successful advertising slogans arrest the intelligence with wit and catchy brevity, lodging immediately in the mind. You're reciting the words back only a second after absorbing them. Everyone can recite this one.

MARADONA GOOD
PELÉ BETTER
GEORGE BEST

The sadness is that he had to die before it got written. He would have relished its composition and content not only, and naturally enough, because of the superior status it affords him, but also because it chimes with his competitive instincts, which, like the lion's, were all about dominating the pack. Maradona, born in 1960, was in a pushchair and short pants when Best made his debut at Old Trafford. Best saw him nonetheless as a rival because Maradona's reputation threatened to usurp his own during the mid-1980s. His favourite photograph, which he framed, caught Pelé trying to trip him in a North American League match. 'No one paid me a greater compliment,' he said, using it also as prima facie evidence of his ability to out-genius the genius.

He didn't want to grant equality to anyone.

The question of whether he'd dominate today is easily answerable. The better pitches, the bend on the ball, the abolition of the tackle from behind and the interpretation of who is and isn't interfering with play would be Elysian for him. The Ulster flag that gave him the nod over Maradona and Pelé pre-dates the arrival of Lionel Messi, who, like Best, warrants nothing but superlatives. Also, like Best, you'd pay at the gate to see him alone. Indeed, on the attack Messi and Best are footballing brothers, alike in stature and skill and attitude. Were Best in La Liga and dressed in Barcelona's Catalonian colours, however, you wouldn't be able to take the ball off him. As Mike Summerbee says: 'Great players can't be caught when their pace over ten yards is awesome. His pace over *fifteen* yards was awesome. When we played we had markers up our arse. You couldn't move. You wouldn't be able to allow him the space the modern player gets. He would destroy you.'

Best mapped the co-ordinates of football celebrity in Britain. Footballers became commercially aware because of him and the wages he earned, however slim compared to the weekly platinum standard of the current Premiership, encouraged others to ask for more. His legacy is evidenced in another important way, too. Out of his myriad troubles came a change in attitude among all clubs, some of whom previously didn't think it was necessary to give the game's equivalent of pastoral care to players or did it only tokenly. Too many directors still thought of footballers the way mill owners had regarded machine-workers a century earlier. Their welfare was immaterial to them once the factory gates shut.

Whatever custom and practice was prevalent and considered the norm in the 60s, it still counts as a dereliction of duty. The lack of protection and guidance on offer was detrimental to both parties. Best wanted those who followed him to be taught how to handle money matters and media attention, the strains of being a professional and the dangers of drugs and alcohol, spivs and hangers-on. He didn't want anyone else to go through what he'd endured and end up like him because of it. From his day to the present one more than a generation of players has benefited from the enlightened lessons his plight taught them. Very commendably the Professional Footballers' Association has seen to that. So have managers such as Sir Alex Ferguson, whose swaddling of Ryan Giggs stemmed specifically from his awareness of the mistakes United made over Best and his determination to avoid the repetition of history at Old Trafford. Ferguson didn't abandon Giggs to his own devices. Giggs didn't give a newspaper interview until he was almost 20. He didn't have an agent to forage for merchandising contracts on his behalf until Ferguson deemed it appropriate. 'He handled it perfectly,' said Best, who eschewed handing Giggs over-elaborate advice about his future. He never interfered in anyone else's business since he'd disliked others interfering in his own.

That he preferred not to be preachy or poke his nose in presumptuously says a lot about sides of his personality that tend to get overlooked. Yes, everyone knew him as the public performer, the entertainer of evocative power. Yes, we're familiar with him as the womaniser and the addict, ripe for scandal and controversy. But there were other Bests more representative of his true self.

He never ignored the players he'd played against.

One late afternoon in Leeds Best was eating a meal in a pizza parlour when he spied Albert Johanneson. The South African-born Johanneson was 'The Black Flash' of Don Revie's Leeds. At the end of the 1964–65 season, became the first black player to appear in an FA Cup final. Following his retirement in 1971 Johanneson, like so many footballers before and since, found himself unprepared for life without his profession. He took drugs. He became an alcoholic, drinking rough cider from litre bottles. As his health and memory gradually deteriorated, Johanneson washed dishes in a Chinese restaurant, the only work he could find. Best didn't know him well. He did, however, regard him with esteem both as a performer and as a person. Best considered him to be 'brave' for even going on to the pitch because racists went unpunished and the language of racism was common usage then and actually defended as being either inoffensive or as legitimate banter.

When Best met him again, Johanneson was in a bad way. His face was puffy and the sclera of each eye was red-yellow instead of white. He shuffled along. He and his clothes needed a good clean. He was all but penniless. That night Best was supposed to be appearing beside Jimmy Greaves at a city theatre. He decided to give Johanneson a treat instead; Greaves had to go on stage alone. The stark retelling of that event can make the act of abandoning Greaves look selfish and Best seem irresponsible. But he didn't use Johanneson as an excuse to bunk off. What Best recognised was a man who, like him, hadn't survived the admiration the 60s had brought him. Johanneson had fallen further and faster, and in his bloated, downcast face Best saw the awful desperation he'd once seen in his own. Johanneson needed someone to listen to him and be there for him; if only for a few hours. Best took Johanneson into a posh hotel, where the waiters initially balked at fetching and carrying for someone who appeared to live each night on the streets. Only a quiet word from Best got them some service. The two of them talked until around midnight, reliving matches. Johanneson died in 1995, aged only 53. His body lay undiscovered for almost a week in his tower-block flat. When Best heard of the death and its circumstances he was more certain than ever that he'd done the right thing. He urged anyone who'd seen Johanneson play to think of him in the full flush and flight of those days, thus affording him the respect his work warranted. No doubt thinking of himself too, Best said he hated the tendency to sanctimoniously tut-tut at those who, once successful, had fallen on hard times, as if they were always to blame. And he couldn't understand why anyone would sneer and gloat at another's misfortune.

He tried to be altruistic. He often gave money to those in need of it, including street beggars. He made hospital and charity visits and sought no publicity for them. He'd turn up at a school and kick a ball around with its pupils for hours. He donated international shirts and caps for charitable auctions. In his days as a boutique owner he readily and regularly gave hard-up reserve and youth team players lifts in his Jaguar and offered them clothes on the never-never, which he then 'forgot' to get paid for. After leaving United, he played in 93 testimonials, benefits, friendlies or fund-raisers. Again, he sometimes 'forgot' to claim his fee or expenses. He'd also turn out in friends' five-a-side teams to avoid a side being a man short. Always the soft touch, he autographed photographs and memorabilia placed in front of him by people who pretended to be genuine fans or collectors. He knew it was a form of exploitation as soon as he heard two sentences. 'Just sign your name. I don't want it dedicated to anyone.' The item, its value instantly increased, would be offloaded quickly to make a few bob for the rapacious seller. Seldom did he say no to such requests.

For much less than Best achieved, a platoon of celebrities – sporting and non-sporting alike – have been given an invitation to Buckingham Palace and gone away with a ribboned MBE or better. Best never did. Before being imprisoned in 1984 he'd joked: 'Well, that's the knighthood fucked.' But, during the autumn of 2002, he was considered – at last – for the forthcoming New Year's Honours. The early recommendations made to the Honours Committee weren't particularly populist. Best's name was put forward to add some razzle-dazzle to the list. The move got no further than being discussed around a table; Best never knew a thing about it. Had he done so, we know he'd have shrugged in response, accepting what he couldn't change, because that's how he reacted in the end to almost everything that went against him.

'What's the point in staying disappointed?' he'd ask.

It's said suffering is the staple of life. We differ only in our capacity to endure it.

One of the remarkable things about Best is that, even when his suffering was at its worst, he could still do something unmatchable on the pitch.

At 35, when Best's performances ought to have been subdued echoes of what he'd done in his heyday, one of the most talked about goals of his career – a masterpiece among a collection of masterpieces – came at a crisis point for him. He was an alcoholic in and out of counselling and rehabilitation and aware that his body was beginning to break down because of drink. But, if you didn't know the back-story, you would reject as insane the very idea that there was anything amiss in Best's life. He ran as he did during the 1960s – giving the slip to one defender after another. Magnetism seemed to hold the ball to his feet. The goal, which had a vehemence and monumentality about it, was scored for San Jose Earthquakes against Fort Lauderdale Strikers in July 1981.

When a short, innocuous pass is played to him from the near touch-line Best is more than 30 yards from goal. Freeze the picture and you see every Strikers player, except the goalkeeper, in the rectangular frame. Seven of them are in front of – or level with – Best. What he does next is superlative. You watch it first in admiration, then mounting stupefaction and finally – unless you lack a pulse – you feel a sense of awe. You are very grateful that cameras were there to record it.

Strident American commentators are prone to hyperventilate over nothing; partly because it takes a lot to hold the attention of the average viewer in the USA. The commentator fears his armchair audience might be about to nod off or, worse still, yawn and switch to another channel. But because the microphone is used like a megaphone, through which the ordinary or the common are always sold as being unique, there is nowhere to go on the vocal register when something extraordinary really happens. Nor are there fresh ways of saluting it since all the fine words have already been used up trying to breathe life into banality. The co-commentators on Earthquakes versus Strikers got lucky in being in the right place at the right time. Their response to it was the trading of gut emotions. 'I don't believe this move . . . This is truly a great, great goal . . . You talk about individual effort [and] that's the greatest soccer goal I have ever seen.' The speaker never tells us how many goals he's actually seen; though you can extrapolate and conclude it can't possibly be a lot in comparison to his contemporaries in Europe or South America. The statement is heartfelt nonetheless. There's a sincerity about the pitch and timbre of his voice, which also contains an edge of trembling incredulity. It's as if he's just watched someone spontaneously levitate from a standing position.

Best allows the ball to cover the early ground for him, letting a pass run a yard and a half before finally seizing on it. The Strikers' defenders, thinking there is no threat, initially make no more than a token approach to steal possession. He is still well adrift of the box and one marker assumes the other will prevent him from getting into it. The first doesn't read where he is going. The second is instantly out of the game, left flat-footed like a sprinter whose spikes have got stuck in his blocks. Best heads rapidly to the right, fooling his closest pursuer into going the other way and then riding the recovery tackle, which is a sliding lunge. He's on the brink of the area. The defenders are still convinced he'll be shut down or run out of room and be forced to backtrack; for Best has lulled them into believing it. He shapes to go wide a little – another two white shirts are closing around him – and then abruptly changes direction by bringing his right foot down on the ball and taking it on with his left. The next stage sees him operate in no more than three square feet near the penalty spot. He holds off one raid by going sideways before he reverses marginally – just enough, in fact, to throw someone else off balance. The hunted here is always smarter than the hunter. The defender regains composure and tries to block him; Best brushes him aside. There's only one man between him and the goal now and Best isn't going to let anyone else capitalise on the position he's made for himself. Again, he moves the ball sharply across the last defender, who – like everyone before him – is pulled into a panicky half-turn, guessing incorrectly the direction Best is heading. The defender can't get close to him and knows he's beaten. The game's up. The run is over. The dribble, mostly accomplished with the right foot, is finished with the left. The shot from eight yards is low and hard, ending up in the bottom corner of the net.

That last defender is Ken Fogarty, who played alongside Best at

Stockport County. He remembers staring at Best and thinking to himself: 'He's in the zone.' 'The zone' is that transfixed state in which the participant's focus and concentration are so intense that whatever flows from them comes spontaneously and without self-conscious effort. Nothing extraneous can divert or distract, and to be finally wrenched out of it is like emerging from a hypnotic trance. 'You just couldn't stop him when he was like that,' says Fogarty. 'I thought I was going to get the ball and then he glided away from me. I went one way and he went the other. He made me look like a drunken penguin on a wobbly skateboard.' No one said much in the dressing room afterwards, he added. 'What could we say? We'd just conceded one of the greatest goals you'll ever see – and that wasn't his best run of the match.' Fogarty describes another, from the far touchline, as being superior. 'He beat about seven players before he got into the area where we brought him down. If he'd scored then, I'm telling you, no one would talk about the other goal.' Fogarty was right about the zone. Best said it felt to him as if he and everyone else were moving in super-slow motion. He could 'see everything' so clearly, he said, and knew where to go and when. It was as if he and all those around him were dancers in a ballet, who had rehearsed these moves for weeks. Seeing it again on film was bedazzling for him. 'It was like watching someone else, rather than me, get that goal,' he said.

His only regret?

That he hadn't scored it for Manchester United in front of the Stretford End. 'Imagine the reaction if I'd done that,' he said.

Certain events ripple through a life, continuing to have an effect long after the event itself has passed. For Best everything came back to Manchester United and those happy years. He regarded himself as an honorary Mancunian, believing he'd been born to play and stay at Old Trafford. He said he never got over – and didn't like to think about

– his splintering departure from the club because of the 'disappoint-ment' it brought back. His choice of such an anodyne word was delib-erate. It masked the extent of his hurt. He was incapable of successfully analysing the emotional turmoil of the estrangement as he experienced it, but being called an ex-United player – which is how profiles and programme notes and TV commentators referred to him – was a convulsing shock to his system, like being repeatedly told something you just don't want to believe. Only later on did he recognise what he'd undergone as a state of mourning and four stages of grief: disbelief, denial, vague hope, depression.

The further he got from the 60s, the closer he felt to United and the people who launched and sustained his career. Some of his attitudes changed, too. He'd be forever Busby's son; everyone knew that. But he said he came to respect 'for different reasons' two of the 'tremendous' men who succeeded Busby.

He remembered Wilf McGuinness graciously telling him: 'If I'd known then what I know now I'd have just left you on your own. I was chasing you around, following you. I know now I'd have been better off just letting you do what you wanted . . . and only been concerned about what you did on the field.' And he was grateful for the kindnesses of Frank O'Farrell. 'If I've ever been in trouble or in a situation, he's always called or written,' he said. 'When my mother died, he rang. He made a point of finding my number in Belfast and said he was sorry and asked how I was. Lovely man.'

Best met up again with Ken Stanley, who he took to the Phene Arms. He and Stanley, then in his late 70s, spent hours reliving the good days and even some of the bad ones. 'George recognised how much my father had done for him,' said David Stanley.

Best was also reconciled with Bobby Charlton. He conceded pernickety disputes between them were 'childish' and then added: 'We were like school-kids and it was daft.' As well as the rancour itself, Best even forgot its original source. 'I probably had the hump with him having the hump with me,' he explained. When United gathered to mark that Silver Jubilee of Wembley '68, he and Charlton sat together at a small round table as the match was replayed for the team. Best patted Charlton lightly on the back as his captain's first goal flew into the net. And when Best neared death – lying in the Intensive Care Unit behind pale, concertina curtains – Charlton went to the hospital. So upset by Best's ever-weakening condition and so emotional when facing up to the premature end of his colleague's life, he was heard to say quietly at the bedside 'this is bollocks', which expressed his pain and frustration and also the sense of helplessness he felt.

Best even chose to overlook a shameful decision, blocking attempts to award him a testimonial. In the autumn of 1979 friends asked United to award him one for services rendered. Best was still reeling financially after the loss of his savings in Irish Trust. 'At one point I had almost nothing,' he said. United rejected the request, informing Best's supporters that he hadn't played the requisite number of years to qualify for such benevolence. Harry Gregg's appeal for a testimonial had been similarly rejected. United's board thought that granting Best's would allow Gregg to restate his own case. Best simply assumed United were 'pissed off' with his conduct in the early 1970s and were now dishing out revenge, served cold. The club compounded the pettiness of its first denial with another. Best was refused permission to hire Old Trafford so he could arrange his own match there. He'd helped them win two Championships and a European Cup. He'd earned them hundreds of thousands of pounds, the money handed over at the turnstiles by those men and women who had gone to Old Trafford only to watch him. He'd made 474 appearances, claimed 181 goals between 1963 and 1974 and finished top scorer for five successive seasons. This was no mayfly career. Whatever the letter of United's own rules said, on figures alone Best deserved a testimonial. On reputation and accomplishments he deserved it twice. He didn't protest publicly or make a fresh appeal. Pride wouldn't allow him to beg. The club, as wrong as wrong could be, never relented.

Best forgave them all the same.

His forgiveness didn't stretch as far as Tommy Docherty. In the months immediately following his departure, he pretended to be ambivalent about United because he didn't want to give Docherty the satisfaction of knowing how much it meant to him. In the years that followed it, his antagonism towards Docherty hardened. He held him – and no one else – responsible for his exit. When the club gave Best his registration papers, he insisted the documents were signed and collected from Old Trafford the following day, which was a Sunday, because he needed them urgently and also because he said he wanted to inconvenience Docherty.

'I hated him so much I didn't even want to go there,' said Best. 'The only reason I did was because I knew it was killing him to have to get up on a Sunday morning to go in.'

For symbolic purposes Best had left a pair of his boots hanging on a hook at Old Trafford in 1974. There was something both heroic and hopeless about it. Best said 'anyone' was welcome to borrow them. The discarded boots were there to remind everyone of his absence. In his 50s, Best said, he had a recurring dream, the grieving and guilt and wish-fulfilment contained within it so obvious as to make Freudian interpretation unnecessary the following morning. In the Old Trafford he had first known – before its trendsetting cantilever stand was constructed – Best would find himself being called up to play for the United of Beckham and Cantona and Keane. But he couldn't find his boots. 'I had to play in some carpet slippers,' he said. In these dreams the years fell away. He was as good as he'd ever been.

He regretted walking away from United. And he regretted not being able to go back when the chance finally came – less than six months after scoring that goal for the Earthquakes. Best, appearing on a Manchester radio station, said he'd 'love' to go and play for United again. Within an hour of the broadcast United's manager, Ron Atkinson, was asked whether he would be interested in signing him. 'If he wants it, I'll willingly talk to him,' he replied. An appointment was arranged for the two of them to meet at 8 a.m. in a London hotel before United's next match – against Arsenal at Highbury. At 8.05 a.m. Best hadn't appeared. 'I got up and left,' said Atkinson, certain Best wouldn't be coming. Atkinson thought then – and does now – that Best used United as a publicity stunt. But Best was one of those people capable of creating a headline simply by doing nothing if that was his purpose. What actually happened was that Best gave an instinctively truthful reply to an interviewer's question – yes, he did want to play for United again – and only thought afterwards what making a comeback would mean. Irrespective of what he did or didn't do in someone else's kit, it was never going to disturb the images of his career at Old Trafford, a slide-show travelling in front of the eyes whenever his name was mentioned. But to play for United again would ruin all that. The new images would impinge on the old; and perhaps not flatteringly for him. Best was in no condition for the First Division. 'I would have been cheating myself,' he said. 'When I played I was the best of all time. If I'd gone back I wouldn't have been the best. I'd have got away with it. But it wouldn't have been up to my standards. My standards are high.'

In his mind he remained United's player nonetheless – no matter where he was in the world and no matter how many seasons had passed. 'I always looked for their results first,' he said of his decades without them. 'I felt I was part of the club . . . I hoped to spend my whole career there.'

Those three short sentences demonstrate how much United meant to Best. They were everything to him.

There was no one else he really wanted to play for. There was nowhere else he ever wanted to go. There was no true football love for him other than that first love. The bond of man to club was imperishable then and is imperishable still. Best knew that; and he wanted us to know it, too. Now, we do.

Even the least of us lives in the hope of being remembered. Best – a football immortal – will be.

He'll survive in all those dribbles and goals and in all those feints and swerves and cheeky-sod party pieces that no one else could do. He'll be young and beautiful and framed within the 1960s. And we'll always see him just as he always saw himself.

Wearing that red shirt.

Author's Notes and Acknowledgements

It is late June. It is also one of those rare days in our so-called 'summer' unspoilt by rain. Only wispy clouds hang over Belfast, each like a strip of torn rag.

I am standing on one of the roads that run through the vast grounds of Roselawn Cemetery, where George Best is buried.

This is the end of a personal tour, which George's sister, Barbara, and her husband, Norman, are giving me.

Already, we've been to Donard Street where, barely 18 months old, George was photographed by his father kicking a ball near the kerbside outside his grandparents' home. We've been to his red-brick school. We've been inside the Best family home in Burren Way. I've seen the field where he played endlessly as a boy, the wall against which he practised and polished his skills, the wide, high murals painted in his honour.

At Roselawn, I'm about to appreciate how much he meant – and still means – to Belfast.

When we arrive, there are already four black-clad figures clustered in front of the headstone. They form a ragged semi-circle, heads bowed.

They scan the inscription contemplatively. We hold back for a moment or two before starting our slow walk towards them. As we turn into the row, and begin to draw closer, one of the group recognises Barbara. He comes forward, ever so courteously introducing himself and the others. Hands are shaken. Polite hellos are exchanged. The good weather is mentioned.

They'd been to another funeral, he says, as if there is a need to explain why we've found them there. They'd wanted to see George's grave. They felt it was appropriate to pay their respects to him.

Much later I learn how common this is. There are no signposts to the plot and so Roselawn's staff are frequently asked for directions. 'People attend family or friends' funerals first before going to see George,' I am told.

I think 'Going to see George' is a lovely phrase in the circumstances.

During the writing of *Immortal* I've thought often about that small scene at the graveside and the serendipity of the moment.

In particular I remember that the man began to extol George's abilities and then stopped, switching himself off in mid-sentence. It resonated because I'd done the same thing earlier that day.

I'd met Barbara and Norman at the Stormont Hotel, which sits near the gates of the Stormont Estate. On the morning of George's funeral one of the hotel's exterior walls was decorated with *Big Lily*, a 100ft x 60ft fans' flag that has followed Manchester United across the globe.

We sat beneath the glass canopy of the big reception area, where I explained that his zenith and the beginning of my devotion to football occurred simultaneously. Indeed, he was responsible for my boyhood obsession with it. The game seemed even more glamorous to me purely because he was the pulse of it. He was repeatedly on the front cover of magazines and on the back pages of newspapers. He was the prize card in each season's collection of stickers, which I bought in paper packets at the corner shop and assiduously put into albums. He was always the player everyone wanted to be in the playground and in the park.

I could have gone on. I stopped there, however, because my story is common to my age; those of us for whom the 1960s represent infancy and childhood, which meant we were blissfully ignorant of the fact that our arrival into the world had coincided with the heavy upheaval of change. We didn't know the 60s were a bit of a carnival; we merely took it as we found it. Moreover – and even if you're tightly conservative in your calculations – whatever I could say to Barbara and Norman had already been said to them by others on a million and twenty-one previous occasions. They created and run the George Best Foundation and, after his death, replied to every letter or card of condolence – many of which included personal vignettes similar to mine.

What I could tell them was this: *why* I was compelled to write about him.

I spoke about an evening I'd spent in Manchester, where five of Sir Matt Busby's European Cup winners – Paddy Crerand, Alex Stepney, Nobby Stiles, David Sadler and John Aston – gathered to reminisce and reflect. Beforehand the boys of '68 chatted genially to any of us who approached them, signed autographs and posed for photographs. When the formal Q&A began, the early questions were almost exclusively George-related. Eventually there was an obligation to move on before he dominated the event. Few there were in doubt about his place in the pantheon; you were in the presence of the converted, mostly middle-aged or of pensionable age.

It reaffirmed one of my motivating factors: to tell those too young to have seen George play about his fantastic talents and the visceral thrill of watching him on pitches that were like torn-up battlefields.

Quoting someone else saves you from the burden of original thought. Quoting yourself is even lazier, but you can just about justify the repetition by claiming that you don't see the need to dress up an old point – still valid, still worth re-emphasising – in new clothes. So here's one I made earlier.

'It can take a lot of persuasion to convince a new generation – raised on Ryan Giggs, Cristiano Ronaldo and Wayne Rooney – about the claims of a decade of which it bore no witness; especially without supporting evidence comprising several miles of cine film.'

It's worth remembering that *Match of the Day* didn't exist when George made his debut for United and that the Sunday afternoon highlights programmes on commercial television's regional stations were launched only in belated response to it. So we are both lucky and unlucky in regard to what's on the library shelves. We're unlucky because we'd get George Best whole and uncut if he was playing nowadays – every flick and feint and pass and goal. We're lucky because at least – owing to who he was and who he played for – we've got enough to provide evidence of his genius. But time moves on apace and parts of the past subsequently get hollowed out and half-forgotten.

What interested me was capturing George in his prime; and also placing that prime in the context of 'his' decade so I could explain what fame really meant back then and why he was so vulnerable to the consequences of it.

Biography is damn hard graft. You relive your subject's life as you continue to live your own and the division of energy can be draining. That subject is beside you every morning, noon and night for several years. It's like sharing a small room with them. For this reason I choose to write about people that I like. For who can share a small room interminably with someone they *don't*? That for me would be akin to Sartre's *No Exit*. I told Barbara and Norman all this. I added, however, that I'd be writing about George's drinking, too – and the madness, depressions and unpleasantness that drinking caused.

They couldn't have been more helpful or supportive. They took me into their home, where I looked at keepsakes, souvenirs and memorabilia, newspaper cuttings (which George's father Dickie had saved) and photographs. A box, which included the books George had been reading shortly before his final illness, was brought out so I could go through it. They answered everything I asked them. And, if Barbara didn't have a memory of something specific, she contacted her older sister Carol to fill in the gap on her behalf.

I am immensely grateful for their trust and constant kindness during our meetings, phone calls and emails and for their ready willingness to formally approve and support the book.

I owe a host of other debts.

For I wouldn't have met Barbara and Norman without Malcolm Wagner. And I wouldn't have met Malcolm without Sir Michael Parkinson.

I'll start with Malcolm, of whom George said of their unbroken 40-year friendship: 'He was the only one I ever trusted to look after me.' He added that Malcolm was a 'bloody nuisance', too. Of course, George was joking. But I fear I was a bloody nuisance to Malcolm, who responded at all times nonetheless with extraordinary patience and equanimity despite the constant pestering to check this or clear up that for me. He was always available and made enquiring phone calls to George's other friends and former team-mates on my behalf. I warned him in advance that I'd ask questions of pernickety detail – the way a room looked, the colour of a pair of curtains – that might appear trivial or stupid to him until he read the book. If he thought I was mad, he didn't show it. George said he 'loved Waggy to death'. How highly I regard him can be found on page 104.

Sir Michael gave his backing unhesitatingly and wholeheartedly. He shared memories and views of his friend and spoke beautifully and honestly about him. His son, Michael, then sent me the DVDs of the interviews his father had done with George in this country and Australia. I grew up with 'Parky' almost as much as I grew up with George. When

I was a boy, our late Saturday-night viewing was a ritual: *Match of the Day*, then *Parkinson* and then the *Midnight Movie* (on BBC2). I only wish my parents were alive so I could tell them what I've just told you. They wouldn't believe me.

David Stanley shadowed George during those days when his father, Ken, handled the roaring industry that 'the Fifth Beatle' became and lived through the sheer unfathomable rush of it. David's home is in a far-flung part of the British Isles. Fortunately for me one of his close friends lives a mile and a half from my front door. We met on my patch and, from the outset, he was an incredible champion of the book. As well as plunging into the 1960s and early 1970s for me, he sent documentation about his father's agency and its work with George and also allowed the use of that agency's photographs. As a witness, he was invaluable. As a man, he is someone I like and respect enormously.

Hand on heart, I can say exactly the same of Steve Fullaway and Jackie Glass.

Like Malcolm, Steve answered questions that must have appeared bizarre to him. Also like Malcolm, he didn't raise an eyebrow about it. My first session mining Steve's memory marked my reintroduction to Guinness, for which I am very grateful, too. Even after we'd finished talking about George, we carried on talking about football in general. So I'd also like to say thank you to Jean, Steve's wife, for her understanding. Her shopping trip to Manchester lasted far longer than she'd planned because of me.

Jackie is now known as Ani Richen Khandro since her ordination in 1994 as a nun of the Tibetan Buddhist tradition. She hadn't spoken about George for more than 40 years. I can tell you she is very intelligent and very articulate – two facts that become apparent within a minute of meeting her. She is also a Manchester United fan who knows her football.

That's the upside of biography. You meet some wonderful people.

I'll never forget Eric McMordie, talking so enthusiastically and generously in his kitchen about Bob Bishop and that day when he and George arrived in Manchester and fled home again. Or Philomena Lynott recalling the Biz. Or even Sinead Cusack, who said she was sorry not to be able to add anything to much publicised accounts of her long weekend with George, but did so in the politest and most charming manner possible. On meeting him, I realised immediately that Mike Summerbee is a gentleman of the highest rank. I also know how sincere he is when he discusses his friendship with George. When we spoke in an executive box overlooking Manchester City's pitch, Mike's love for him was *that* transparent.

It's not an exaggeration to say that George wrote as much about his life as Winston Churchill did about the Second World War and the English Speaking Peoples. Reading it all you become aware that the same event can differ – sometimes in minor ways, sometimes significantly – from one retelling to the next. This is complicated further by variations in newspaper articles and columns that he signed. To all the aforementioned I say a particular thank you for helping me clear them up.

Another particular thank you goes to Graeme Wright for his fabulous generosity. Graeme was George's ghost for one of his autobiographies. It was written at a stage when George's fortunes were – to say the least – ebbing. A lot of the publicity surrounding him was rotten. And, when it wasn't, a kind of 'oh no, not him again' indifference permeated much of the coverage. We didn't know it then, but George was already approaching the half-way mark of his life. He was looking back on his glory, glory years and uncertain about what lay ahead. Graeme did a brilliant job. When we chatted about George, he was thoughtfully precise and perceptive in analysing him as a man and also examining the complicated mechanism of his personality. 'I've kept the full transcripts of our talks,' he said. 'I knew if I hung on to them long enough someone would come along and be able to make good use of them.' As with all such books, an author hears or records material that can't be used contemporaneously for myriad, but obvious, reasons that include sensitivity, taste and legality. Allowing me to read that material gave me a much fuller understanding of George and his thinking.

I'd also like to acknowledge the contributions – in various ways – of the following: Willie Anderson, John Angus, Ron Atkinson, Paul Bew, Graham Budd, Alex Butler, Paul Carson, Steve Chapels, Dave Clements, Patrick Collins, Campbell Crawford, Johan Cruyff, Jaap de Groot, Tommy Docherty, Martin Edwards, Bill Elliott, Frank Evans, Keith Farnsworth, David Farrar, Ken Fogarty, Jackie Fullerton, Tommy Gemmell, Brian Glanville, Peter Hain, Ron Harris, Nick Hencher, Derek Hodgson, Bob Holmes, Brian Hughes, Norman Hunter, Philip Jackson, Leo McKinstry, Mark Kram Jr, Iain McCartney, Graham McColl, Frank McGuinness, Wilf McGuinness, Hugh McIlvanney, Sammy McMillan, David Meek, Don Megson, Peter Mellor, John Motson, Jimmy Murphy Jr, Frank O'Farrell, Hugh Peck, Jeff Powell, Tom Richmond, John Roberts, Phil Rostron, Sefton Samuels, Colin Shaw, Ken Shellito, Colin Shindler, Arnie Sidebottom, Veronica Simpson, Tommy Smith, Geoff Snape, Peter Stewart, Ian Storey-Moore, Clive Toye, Graham Williams.

My earlier life, which revolved around sitting in football press boxes, proved to be a boon. As I told Tommy Docherty, I'd originally spoken to him informally about George three decades before the conversation we had for the book. In the days when Denis Law worked regularly on BBC Radio, I once bored him at the City Ground before – no doubt gratefully – he made his escape. (I did the same to Dave Mackay, Ian St John and Jimmy Hill.) So I've been able to incorporate the thoughts of those who are sadly no longer with us: Malcolm Allison, Danny Blanchflower, Billy Bremner, Malcolm Brodie, Noel Cantwell, Tommy Cavanagh, John Charles, Brian Clough, John Connelly, Tommy Lawton, Joe Mercer, Bobby Moore, Brian Moore, Don Revie, Peter Taylor.

AUTHOR'S NOTES AND ACKNOWLEDGEMENTS

Staff at Roselawn Cemetery, plus the following libraries, were exemplary: Manchester, Belfast (especially the newspaper section which is outstandingly efficient), Leeds, Newcastle, the London Library, the British Library at Collingdale, Sheffield University, the British Film Institute.

My appreciation goes to Andy Smart and Viv Richardson for their toil for the cause. In the pubs and shops, at the bus stops and on the pavements at Belfast, I'd like to thank the people who spoke to me about George's funeral. Some of them must have thought they'd been button-holed by a lunatic.

At Century, my editor, Ben Dunn, was there whenever I needed advice and made sensible, clear suggestions at all times. Francesca Pathak's work was also precious to me – as was her patience. The fine eye of line editor Bella Cunha's insights were important to say the least. And I relied – as I perpetually do – on the ever-wise counsel of my agent, Grainne Fox, who steers me in the right direction with the sort of common sense I wish I possessed.

Those of you who have read any of my previous books will know I always end this sort of thing in the same way. Debts? I owe more than a few to my wife, Mandy – for her love, support and editing skills and also her ability to tolerate me on a daily basis, which requires the sort of forbearance that the Nobel committee ought to give a prize for. She is a Manchester United fan and George – chiefly at his handsome peak – has lived in our house since early 2010. Mandy says she still prefers the short, baggy-eyed, portly bloke she married. I trust her – and her judgement – implicitly, of course. But I think in this case she may be indulging in something I once heard the writer Keith Waterhouse say: 'I lie only when it would be rude to tell the truth.'

And there you have it. The secret of a happy marriage.

Picture Acknowledgements

©Bob Thomas/Getty Images; ©Popperfoto/Getty Images; ©Getty Images; ©Mirrorpix; ©Peter Robinson/EMPICS Sport; ©PA/PA Archive/Press Association Images; ©AP/Press Association Images; ©Peter Robinson/ EMPICS Sport; © The Sun / News Syndication; ©Belfast Telegraph; ©Solo Syndication

Timeline

George Best

Born: Belfast, 22 May 1946
Died: London, 25 November 2005

1961

August: Signs amateur contract for Manchester United and moves permanently into Mary Fullaway's home in Chorlton-cum-Hardy.

1963

May: Signs professional contract for Manchester United.

September: First Division debut v West Bromwich Albion at Old Trafford.

1964

April: Northern Ireland senior debut v Wales at Swansea.

1966

March: Bewilders Benfica in a rampaging 5–1 European Cup quarter-final win in Lisbon. Scores two goals and is christened 'El Beatle'.

Opens boutique with his friend Mike Summerbee.

1967

October: Exemplary individual display – probably his finest – in a 1–0 win over Scotland at Windsor Park.

1968

May: Named Footballer of the Year.

His extra-time goal sends Manchester United on their way to a 4–1 win over Benfica in the European Cup final at Wembley.

June: Matt Busby knighted.

October: Sent off in the World Club Championship against Estudiantes at Old Trafford.

December: Named European Footballer of the Year.

1969

January: Sir Matt Busby announces he will retire at the end of the season.

June: Wilf McGuinness appointed as Busby's successor.

August: Announces he is considering marrying Eva Haraldsted.

October: Splits from Eva Haraldsted (which leads to a breach of promise suit, which is settled out of court).

1970

January: Gets four-week FA suspension – and £100 fine – for dissent at the end of a League Cup semi-final against Manchester City the previous month.

February: Returns to Manchester United's team and scores six goals against Northampton in a fifth-round FA Cup tie.

April: Sent off for spitting and hurling mud at the referee during Northern Ireland's game against Scotland.

July: Moves out of Mrs Fullaway's home and into his own in Bramhall. It is named Che Sera.

December: Wilf McGuinness sacked as Manchester United manager. Sir Matt Busby becomes caretaker boss.

1971

January: FA fine him £250 and give him a six-week suspended sentence for accruing three cautions in a 12-month period. Misses train to match at Chelsea. Travels to London and stays with actress Sinead Cusack. Manchester United suspend him for two weeks for failing to report for Stamford Bridge fixture.

June: Frank O'Farrell appointed as manager.

October: Receives death threats – both in Northern Ireland and Manchester. One says he will be shot if he plays against Newcastle at St James' Park. He plays – and scores.

November: Subject of *This is Your Life* TV programme.

1972

January: Dropped after missing a week's training. Ordered to return to live with his former landlady, Mrs Fullaway.

February: Says he would be willing to leave Manchester United.

May: Flees to Spain and announces his retirement. Admits to a drinking problem.

July: Does a U-turn. Agrees to return to Old Trafford. The club suspend him for two weeks.

November: Misses training repeatedly and is dropped.

December: Again, misses training and Manchester United suspend him for two weeks and put him on the transfer list. Several teams are interested in him, including Derby, Manchester City and the New York Cosmos. Frank O'Farrell and Best are both sacked on the same day – though Best, ignorant of his own fate, simultaneously writes to the club to announce his retirement for the second time. Tommy Docherty replaces O'Farrell.

1973

January: Considers signing for the World Indoor Soccer League in Canada before changing his mind as soon as he arrives there.

May: Suffers thrombosis in a leg while on holiday in Spain. Sir Matt Busby encourages him to return to Old Trafford.

August: Agrees to go back to Manchester United.

October: Makes his first-team comeback v Birmingham City at Old Trafford and is substituted.

November: Opens a nightclub in Manchester called Slack Alice.

1974

January: Plays his final game for Manchester United v Queens Park Rangers at Loftus Road. He subsequently fails to turn up for training and is left out of an FA Cup tie against Plymouth at Old Trafford. He quits the club, which suspends him for two weeks anyway and transfer-lists him.

February: Charged with stealing a fur coat and other items from Miss World Marjorie Wallace. Hands over £6,000 for bail to secure his release.

April: Cleared of all charges relating to the case.

May: Goes to South Africa to play for the Jewish Guild.

1975

November: Manchester United release Best from his contract.

Plays for Stockport County in home games.

December: Signs for North American Soccer League side Los Angeles Aztecs.

1976

August: Signs for Fulham, then in Division Two.

September: Makes his League debut for Fulham, scoring a goal after just 71 seconds.

October: Plays first Northern Ireland game for three years v Holland in Rotterdam.

1977

July: Bud McFarlane dies while on holiday in Spain.

November: Plays final game for Fulham.

1978

January: Marries Angela MacDonald Janes in Las Vegas.

June: Transferred from Los Angeles Aztecs to Fort Lauderdale Strikers.

October: His mother, Ann, dies.

1979

July: Suspended by Fort Lauderdale Strikers for going AWOL – from games as well as training.

November: Signs for Hibernian and makes his debut v St Mirren.

Manchester United turn down an appeal – made by his friends – to grant Best a testimonial.

1980

February: Hibernian suspend Best after he fails to turn up for a game and is later briefly sacked – before being reinstated – after being in no fit state to play in another.

April: Signs for San Jose Earthquakes.

1981

February: His son, Calum, is born in San Jose.

March: Checks into a rehab centre in San Jose to tackle his alcoholism. He leaves it at the end of that month.

July: Scores a truly exceptional goal – demonstrating remarkable close control – for San Jose against Fort Lauderdale.

August: Plays his last NASL game.

September: Claims he wants to play for Manchester United again. Ron Atkinson, the club's manager, arranges to meet him in London to discuss the possibility. Best does not appear.

1982

January: Readmitted to the rehab centre.

February: Released from rehab centre.

March: Is awarded Goal of the Year prize for his solo effort against Fort Lauderdale.

November: Declared bankrupt.

1983

March: Signs for Bournemouth – another fleeting arrangement.

Mrs Fullaway dies, aged 74.

July: Plays for Brisbane Lions in Australia.

November: Charged with drink-driving and subsequently arrested after failing to appear in court. During his arrest he assaults a policeman.

December: Given a three-month jail sentence for those two offences. After his appeal fails, he is sent to Pentonville and then Ford Open Prison.

1984

February: Released after serving eight weeks of his sentence.

1986

July: Divorced from his wife, Angela.

1995

July: Marries Alex Pursey.

2002

July: Admitted to hospital for liver transplant.

2004

February: Divorced from Alex Pursey.

Match by Match Manchester United and Northern Ireland record

1961–62

Lancashire League Division 1: Games 5, Goals 2
Lancashire League Division 2: Games 22, Goals 10

1962–63

FA Youth Cup: Games 2, Goals 0
Lancashire League Division 1: Games 10, Goals 7
Lancashire League Division 2: Games 18, Goals 19

1963–64

DIVISION ONE
14 Sept: v WBA (H) 1–0
28 Dec: v Burnley (H) 5–1 (one goal)
11 Jan: v Birmingham City (H) 1–2
18 Jan: v WBA (A) 4–1 (one goal)
1 Feb: v Arsenal (H) 3–1

8 Feb: v Leicester City (A) 2–3

19 Feb: v Bolton (H) 5–0 (two goals)

22 Feb: v Blackburn (A) 3–1

21 March: v Tottenham (A) 3–2

23 March: v Chelsea (H) 1–1

27 March: v Fulham (A) 2–2

28 March: v Wolves (H) 2–2

4 April: v Liverpool (A) 0–3

6 April: v Aston Villa (H) 1–0

13 April: v Sheffield United (H) 2–1

18 April: v Stoke (A) 1–3

25 April: v Nottingham Forest (H) 3–1

EUROPEAN CUP WINNERS' CUP

25 Feb: Quarter-final, first leg: v Sporting Lisbon (H) 4–1

18 March: Quarter-final, second leg: v Sporting Lisbon (A) 0–5 (4–6 on aggregate)

FA CUP

4 Jan: Third-round: v Southampton (A) 3–2

25 Jan: Fourth-round: v Bristol Rovers (H) 4–1

15 Feb: Fifth-round: v Barnsley (A) 4–0 (one goal)

29 Feb: Sixth-round: v Sunderland (H) 3–3 (one goal)

4 March: Sixth-round replay: v Sunderland (A) 2–2

6 March: Sixth-round second replay: v Sunderland (at Leeds Road, Huddersfield) 5–1

14 March: Semi-final: v West Ham (at Hillsborough) 1–3

OTHERS

Central League: Games 8, Goals 3

FA Youth Cup: Games 4, Goals 5

Lancashire League Division 1: Games 5, Goals 7

1964–65

DIVISION ONE

22 Aug: v WBA (H) 2–2

24 Aug: v West Ham (A) 1–3

29 Aug: v Leicester City (A) 2–2

2 Sept: v West Ham (H) 3–1 (one goal)

5 Sept: v Fulham (A) 1–2

8 Sept: v Everton (A) 3–3

12 Sept: v Nottingham Forest (H) 3–0

16 Sept: v Everton (H) 2–1 (one goal)

19 Sept: v Stoke City (A) 2–1

26 Sept: v Tottenham (H) 4–1

30 Sept: v Chelsea (A) 2–0 (one goal)

6 Oct: v Burnley (A) 0–0

10 Oct: v Sunderland (H) 1–0

17 Oct: v Wolves (A) 4–2

24 Oct: v Aston Villa (H) 7–0

31 Oct: v Liverpool (A) 2–0

7 Nov: v Sheffield Wednesday (H) 1–0

21 Nov: v Blackburn (H) 3–0 (one goal)

28 Nov: v Arsenal (A) 3–2

5 Dec: v Leeds (H) 0–1

12 Dec: v WBA (A) 1–1

16 Dec: v Birmingham City (H) 1–1

26 Dec: v Sheffield United (A) 1–0 (one goal)

28 Dec: v Sheffield United (H) 1–1

16 Jan: v Nottingham Forest (A) 2–2

23 Jan: v Stoke City (H) 1–1

6 Feb: v Tottenham (A) 0–1

13 Feb: v Burnley (H) 3–2 (one goal)

24 Feb: v Sunderland (A) 0–1

27 Feb: v Wolves (H) 3–0

13 March: v Chelsea (H) 4–0 (one goal)

15 March: v Fulham (H) 4–1

20 March: v Sheffield Wednesday (A) 0–1

22 March: v Blackpool (H) 2–0

3 April: v Blackburn (A) 5–0

12 April: v Leicester City (H) 1–0

17 April: v Leeds (A) 1–0

19 April: v Birmingham City (A) 4–2 (two goals)

24 April: v Liverpool (H) 3–0

26 April: v Arsenal (H) 3–1 (one goal)

28 April: v Aston Villa (A) 1–2

FA CUP

9 Jan: Third-round: v Chester (H) 2–1 (one goal)

30 Jan: Fourth-round: v Stoke City (A) 0–0

3 Feb: Fourth-round replay: v Stoke City (H) 1–0

20 Feb: Fifth-round: v Burnley (H) 2–1

10 March: Sixth-round: v Wolves (A) 5–3 (one goal)

27 March: Semi-final: v Leeds (at Hillsborough) 0–0

31 March: Semi-final replay: v Leeds (at the City Ground Nottingham) 0–1

INTER-CITIES FAIRS CUP

23 Sept: Round-one, first leg: v Djurgaarden (A) 1–1

27 Oct: Round-one, second leg: v Djurgaarden (H) 6–1 (one goal)

11 Nov: Round-two, first leg: v Borussia Dortmund (A) 6–1 (one goal)

2 Dec: Round-two, second leg: v Borussia Dortmund (H) 4–0

20 Jan: Round-three, first leg: v Everton (H) 1–1

9 Feb: Round-three, second leg: v Everton (A) 2–1

12 May: Quarter-final, first leg: v Racing Strasbourg (A) 5–0

19 May: Quarter-final, second leg: v Racing Strasbourg (H) 0–0

31 May: Semi-final, first leg: v Ferencvaros (H) 3–2
6 June: Semi-final, second leg: v Ferencvaros (A) 0–1
16 June: Semi-final, play-off: v Ferencvaros (A) 1–2

1965–66

DIVISION ONE

21 Aug: v Sheffield Wednesday (H) 1–0
24 Aug: v Nottingham Forest (A) 2–4 (one goal)
28 Aug: v Northampton Town (A) 1–1
1 Sept: v Nottingham Forest (H) 0–0
4 Sept: v Stoke City (H) 1–1
8 Sept: v Newcastle (A) 2–1
11 Sept: v Burnley (A) 0–3
15 Sept: v Newcastle (H) 1–1
15 Oct 9: v Liverpool (H) 2–0 (one goal)
16 Oct: v Tottenham (A) 1–5
23 Oct: v Fulham (H) 4–1
30 Oct: v Blackpool (A) 2–1
6 Nov: v Blackburn (H) 2–2
13 Nov: v Leicester City (A) 5–0 (one goal)
20 Nov: v Sheffield Utd (H) 3–1 (two goals)
4 Dec: v West Ham (H) 0–0
11 Dec: v Sunderland (A) 3–2 (two goals)
15 Dec: v Everton (H) 3–0 (one goal)
18 Dec: v Tottenham (H) 5–1
27 Dec: v WBA (H) 1–1
1 Jan: v Liverpool (A) 1–2
8 Jan: v Sunderland (H) 1–1 (one goal)
12 Jan: v Leeds (A) 1–1
15 Jan: v Fulham (A) 1–0

29 Jan: v Sheffield Wednesday (A) 0–0

5 Feb: v Northampton Town (H) 6–2

19 Feb: v Stoke City (A) 2–2

26 Feb: v Burnley (H) 4–2

12 March: v Chelsea (A) 0–2

19 March: v Arsenal (H) 2–1

9 April: v Leicester City (H) 1–2

FA CHARITY SHIELD

14 Aug: v Liverpool (H) 2–2 (one goal)

FA CUP

22 Jan: Third-round: v Derby (A) 5–2 (two goals)

12 Feb: Fourth-round: v Rotherham (H) 0–0

15 Feb: Fourth-round replay: v Rotherham (A) 1–0

5 March: Fifth-round: v Wolves (A) 4–2 (one goal)

26 March: Sixth-round: v Preston (A) 1–1

EUROPEAN CUP

6 Oct: Preliminary-round, second leg: v HJK Helsinki (H) 6–0
  (two goals)

17 Nov: First-round, first leg: v ASK Vorwaerts (A) 2–0

1 Dec: First-round, second leg: v ASK Vorwaerts (H) 3–1

2 Feb: Quarter-final, first leg: v Benfica (H) 3–2

9 March: Quarter-final, second leg: v Benfica (A) 5–1 (two goals)

13 April: Semi-final, first leg: v Partizan Belgrade (A) 0–2

1966–67

DIVISION ONE

20 Aug: v WBA (H) 5–3 (one goal)

23 Aug: v Everton (A) 2–1

27 Aug: v Leeds (A) 1–3 (one goal)

31 Aug: v Everton (H) 3–0

3 Sept: v Newcastle (H) 3–2

7 Sept: v Stoke City (A) 0–3

10 Sept: v Tottenham (A) 1–2

17 Sept: v Manchester City (H) 1–0

24 Sept: v Burnley (H) 4–1

1 Oct: v Nottingham Forest (A) 1–4

8 Oct: v Blackpool (A) 2–1

15 Oct: v Chelsea (H) 1–1

29 Oct: v Arsenal (H) 1–0

5 Nov: v Chelsea (A) 3–1 (one goal)

12 Nov: v Sheffield Wednesday (H) 2–0

19 Nov: v Southampton (A) 2–1

26 Nov: v Sunderland (H) 5–0

30 Nov: v Leicester City (A) 2–1 (one goal)

3 Dec: v Aston Villa (A) 1–2

10 Dec: v Liverpool (H) 2–2 (two goals)

17 Dec: v WBA (A) 4–3

26 Dec: v Sheffield United (A) 1–2

27 Dec: v Sheffield United (H) 2–0

31 Dec: v Leeds (H) 0–0

14 Jan: v Tottenham (H) 1–0

21 Jan: v Manchester City (A) 1–1

4 Feb: v Burnley (A) 1–1

11 Feb: v Nottingham Forest (H) 1–0

25 Feb: v Blackpool (H) 4–0

3 March: v Arsenal (A) 1–1

11 March: v Newcastle (A) 0–0

18 March: v Leicester City (H) 5–2

25 March: v Liverpool (A) 0–0

27 March: v Fulham (A) 2–2 (one goal)

28 March: v Fulham (H) 2–1

1 April: v West Ham (H) 3–0 (one goal)

10 April: v Sheffield Wednesday (A) 2–2

18 April: v Southampton (H) 3–0

22 April: v Sunderland (A) 0–0

29 April: v Aston Villa (H) 3–1 (one goal)

6 May: v West Ham (A) 6–1 (one goal)

13 May: v Stoke City (H) 0–0

FA CUP

28 Jan: Third-round: Stoke City (H) 2–0

18 Feb: Fourth-round: Norwich (H) 1–2

LEAGUE CUP

14 Sept: Second-round: v Blackpool (A) 1–5

1967–68

DIVISION ONE

19 Aug: v Everton (A) 1–3

26 Aug: v Leicester City (H) 1–1

2 Sept: v West Ham (A) 3–1

6 Sept: v Sunderland (A) 1–1

9 Sept: v Burnley (H) 2–2

16 Sept: v Sheffield Wednesday (A) 1–1 (one goal)

23 Sept: v Tottenham (H) 3–1 (two goals)

30 Sept: v Manchester City (A) 2–1

7 Oct: v Arsenal (H) 1–0

14 Oct: v Sheffield United (A) 3–0

25 Oct: v Coventry City (H) 4–0 (one goal)

28 Oct: v Nottingham Forest (A) 1–3 (one goal)

4 Nov: v Stoke City (H) 1–0

8 Nov: v Leeds (A) 0–1

11 Nov: v Liverpool (A) 2–1 (two goals)

18 Nov: v Southampton (H) 3–2

25 Nov: v Chelsea (A) 1–1

2 Dec: v WBA (H) 2–1 (two goals)

9 Dec: v Newcastle (A) 2–2

16 Dec: v Everton (H) 3–1

23 Dec: v Leicester City (A) 2–2

26 Dec: v Wolves (H) 4–0 (two goals)

30 Dec: v Wolves (A) 3–2

6 Jan: v West Ham (H) 3–1 (one goal)

20 Jan: v Sheffield Wednesday (H) 4–2 (two goals)

3 Feb: v Tottenham (A) 2–1 (one goal)

17 Feb: v Burnley (A) 1–2 (one goal)

24 Feb: v Arsenal (A) 2–0 (one goal)

2 March: v Chelsea (H) 1–3

16 March: v Coventry City (A) 0–2

23 March: v Nottingham Forest (H) 3–0

27 March: v Manchester City (H) 1–3 (one goal)

30 March: v Stoke City (A) 4–2 (one goal)

6 April: v Liverpool (H) 1–2 (one goal)

12 April: v Fulham (A) 4–0 (two goals)

13 April: v Southampton (A) 2–2 (one goal)

15 April: v Fulham (H) 3–0 (one goal)

20 April: v Sheffield United (H) 1–0

27 April: v WBA (A) 3–6

4 May: v Newcastle (H) 6–0 (three goals)

11 May: v Sunderland (H) 1–2 (one goal)

FA CHARITY SHIELD:

12 Aug: v Tottenham (H) 3–3

FA CUP

27 Jan: Third-round: v Tottenham (H) 2–2 (one goal)

31 Jan: Third-round replay: v Tottenham (A) 0–1

EUROPEAN CUP

20 Sept: First-round, first leg: v Hibernians (Malta) (H) 4–0

27 Sept: First-round, second leg: v Hibernians (Malta) (A) 0–0

15 Nov: Second-round, first leg: v FK Sarajevo (A) 0–0

29 Nov: Second-round, second leg: v FK Sarajevo (H) 2–1 (one goal)

28 Feb: Quarter-final, first leg: v Gornik Zabrze (H) 2–0

13 March: Quarter-final, second leg: v Gornik Zabrze (A) 0–1

24 April: Semi-final, first leg: v Real Madrid (H) 1–0 (one goal)

15 May: Semi-final, second leg: v Real Madrid (A) 3–3

29 May: Final: v Benfica (Wembley) 4–1 (one goal)

1968–69

DIVISION ONE

10 Aug: v Everton (H) 2–1 (one goal)

14 Aug: v WBA (A) 1–3

17 Aug: v Manchester City (A) 0–0

21 Aug: v Coventry City (H) 1–0

24 Aug: v Chelsea (H) 0–4

28 Aug: v Tottenham (H) 3–1

31 Aug: v Sheffield Wednesday (A) 4–5 (one goal)

7 Sept: v West Ham (H) 1–1

14 Sept: v Burnley (A) 0–1

21 Sept: v Newcastle (H) 3–1 (two goals)

5 Oct: v Arsenal (H) 0–0

9 Oct: v Tottenham (A) 2–2

19 Oct: v Southampton (H) 1–2 (one goal)

26 Oct: v QPR (A) 3–2 (two goals)

2 Nov: v Leeds (H) 0–0

9 Nov: v Sunderland (A) 1–1

16 Nov: v Ipswich (H) 0–0

23 Nov: v Stoke City (A) 0–0

30 Nov: v Wolves (H) 2–0 (one goal)

7 Dec: v Leicester City (A) 1–2

14 Dec: v Liverpool (H) 1–0

21 Dec: v Southampton (A) 0–2

26 Dec: v Arsenal (A) 0–3

11 Jan: v Leeds (A) 1–2

18 Jan: v Sunderland (H) 4–1 (one goal)

1 Feb: v Ipswich (A) 0–1

15 Feb: v Wolves (A) 2–2 (one goal)

8 March: v Manchester City (H) 0–1

10 March: v Everton (A) 0–0

15 March: v Chelsea (A) 2–3

19 March: v QPR (H) 8–1 (two goals)

22 March: v Sheffield Wednesday (H) 1–0 (one goal)

24 March: v Stoke City (H) 1–1

29 March: v West Ham (A) 0–0

31 March: v Nottingham Forest (A) 1–0 (one goal)

2 April: v WBA (H) 2–1 (two goals)

5 April: v Nottingham Forest (H) 3–1 (one goal)

8 April: v Coventry City (A) 1–2

12 April: v Newcastle (A) 0–2

19 April: v Burnley (H) 2–0 (one goal)

17 May: v Leicester City (H) 3–2 (one goal)

FA CUP

4 Jan: Third-round: v Exeter City (A) 3–1

25 Jan: Fourth-round: v Watford (H) 1–1

3 Feb: Fourth-round replay: v Watford (A) 2–0

8 Feb: Fifth-round: v Birmingham City (A) 2–2 (one goal)

24 Feb: Fifth-round replay: v Birmingham City (H) 6–2

1 March: Sixth-round: v Everton (A) 0–1

EUROPEAN CUP

18 Sept: First-round, first leg: v Waterford (A) 3–1

2 Oct: First-round, second leg: v Waterford (H) 7–1

26 Feb: Quarter-final, first leg: v Rapid Vienna (H) 3–0 (two goals)

5 March: Quarter-final, second leg: v Rapid Vienna (A) 0–0

23 April: Semi-final, first leg: v AC Milan (A) 0–2

15 May: Semi-final, second leg: v AC Milan (H) 1–0

WORLD CLUB CHAMPIONSHIP

25 Sept: First leg: v Estudiantes (A) 0–1

16 Oct: Second leg: v Estudiantes (H) 1–1

1969–70

DIVISION ONE

9 Aug: v Crystal Palace (A) 2–2

13 Aug: v Everton (H) 0–2

16 Aug: v Southampton (H) 1–4

19 Aug: v Everton (A) 0–3

23 Aug: v Wolves (A) 0–0

27 Aug: v Newcastle (H) 0–0

30 Aug: v Sunderland (H) 3–1 (one goal)

6 Sept: v Leeds (A) 2–2 (two goals)

13 Sept: v Liverpool (H) 1–0

17 Sept: v Sheffield Wednesday (A) 3–1 (two goals)

20 Sept: v Arsenal (A) 2–2 (one goal)

27 Sept: v West Ham (H) 5–2 (two goals)

4 Oct: v Derby (A) 0–2

8 Oct: v Southampton (A) 3–0 (one goal)

11 Oct: Ipswich (H) 2–1 (one goal)

18 Oct: v Nottingham Forest (H) 1–1 (one goal)

25 Oct: v WBA (A) 1–2

1 Nov: v Stoke City (H) 1–1

8 Nov: v Coventry City (A) 2–1

15 Nov: v Manchester City (A) 0–4

22 Nov: v Tottenham (H) 3–1

29 Nov: v Burnley (A) 1–1 (one goal)

6 Dec: v Chelsea (H) 0–2

13 Dec: v Liverpool (A) 4–1

26 Dec: v Wolves (H) 0–0

27 Dec: v Sunderland (A) 1–1

10 Feb: v Ipswich (A) 1–0

14 Feb: v Crystal Palace (H) 1–1

28 Feb: v Stoke City (A) 2–2

17 March: v Burnley (H) 3–3 (one goal)

21 March: v Chelsea (A) 1–2

28 March: v Manchester City (H) 1–2

30 March: v Coventry City (H) 1–1

31: March v Nottingham Forest (A) 2–1

8 April: v WBA (H) 7–0 (one goal)

13 April: v Tottenham (A) 1–2

15 April: v Sheffield Wednesday (H) 2–2 (one goal)

FA CUP

3 Jan: Third-round: v Ipswich (A) 1–0

7 Feb: Fifth-round: v Northampton (A) 8–2 (six goals)

21 Feb: Sixth-round: v Middlesbrough (A) 1–1

25 Feb: Sixth-round replay: v Middlesbrough (H) 2–1

14 March: Semi-final: v Leeds 0–0 (at Hillsborough)

23 March: Semi-final replay: v Leeds 0–0 (at Villa Park)

26 March: Semi-final second replay: v Leeds 0–1 (at Burnden Park)

10 April: Third Place Play-off: v Watford 2–0 (at Highbury)

LEAGUE CUP

3 Sept: Second-round: v Middlesbrough (H) 1–0

23 Sept: Third-round: v Wrexham (H) 2–0 (one goal)

14 Oct: Fourth-round: v Burnley (A) 0–0

20 Oct: Fourth-round replay: v Burnley (H) 1–0 (one goal)

12 Nov: Fifth-round: v Derby (A) 0–0

Nov 19: Fifth-round replay: v Derby (H) 1–0

3 Dec: Semi-final, first leg: v Manchester City (A) 1–2

17 Dec: Semi-final, second leg: v Manchester City (H) 2–2

1970–71

DIVISION ONE

15 Aug: v Leeds (H) 0–1

19 Aug: v Chelsea (H) 0–0

22 Aug: v Arsenal (A) 0–4

25 Aug: v Burnley (A) 2–0

29 Aug: v West Ham (H) 1–1

2 Sept: v Everton (H) 2–0 (one goal)

5 Sept: v Liverpool (A) 1–1

12 Sept: v Coventry City (H) 2–0 (one goal)

19 Sept: v Ipswich (A) 0–4

26 Sept: v Blackpool (H) 1–1 (one goal)

3 Oct: v Wolves (A) 2–3

10 Oct: v Crystal Palace (H) 0–1

17 Oct: v Leeds (A) 2–2

24 Oct: v WBA (H) 2–1

31 Oct: v Newcastle (A) 0–1

7 Nov: v Stoke City (H) 2–2

14 Nov: v Nottingham Forest (A) 2–1

21 Nov: v Southampton (A) 0–1

28 Nov: v Huddersfield (H) 1–1 (one goal)

5 Dec: v Tottenham (A) 2–2 (one goal)

12 Dec: v Manchester City (H) 1–4

19 Dec: v Arsenal (H) 1–3

26 Dec: v Derby (A) 4–4 (one goal)

30 Jan: v Huddersfield (A) 2–1

6 Feb: v Tottenham (H) 2–1 (one goal)

20 Feb: v Southampton (H) 5–1

23 Feb: v Everton (A) 0–1

27 Feb: v Newcastle (H) 1–0

6 March: v WBA (A) 3–4 (one goal)

13 March: v Nottingham Forest (H) 2–0 (one goal)

20 March: v Stoke City (A) 2–1 (two goals)

3 April: v West Ham (A) 1–2 (one goal)

10 April: v Derby (H) 1–2

12 April: v Wolves (H) 1–0

13 April: v Coventry City (A) 1–2 (one goal)

17 April: v Crystal Palace (A) 5–3 (two goals)

19 April: v Liverpool (H) 0–2

24 April: v Ipswich (H) 3–2 (one goal)

1 May: v Blackpool (A) 1–1

5 May: v Manchester City (A) 4–3 (two goals)

FA CUP

2 Jan: Third-round: v Middlesbrough (H) 0–0

5 Jan: Third-round replay: v Middlesbrough (A) 1–2 (one goal)

LEAGUE CUP

9 Sept: Second-round: v Aldershot (A) 3–1 (one goal)

7 Oct: Third-round: v Portsmouth (H) 1–0

28 Oct: Fourth-round: v Chelsea (H) 2–1 (one goal)

18 Nov: Fifth-round: v Crystal Palace (H) 4–2

16 Dec: Semi-final, first leg: v Aston Villa (H) 1–1

23 Dec: Semi-final, second leg: v Aston Villa (A) 1–2

WATNEY CUP

1 Aug: First-round: v Reading (A) 3–2

5 Aug: Semi-final: v Hull (A) 1–1

8 Aug: Final: v Derby (A) 1–4 (one goal)

1971–72

DIVISION ONE

14 Aug: v Derby (A) 2–2

18 Aug: v Chelsea (A) 3–2

20 Aug: v Arsenal (H) 3–1 (at Anfield after OT is closed)

23 Aug: v WBA (H) 3–1 (two goals) (at the Victoria Ground)

28 Aug: v Wolves (A) 1–1 (one goal)

31 Aug: v Everton (A) 0–1

4 Sept: v Ipswich (H) 1–0 (one goal)

11 Sept: v Crystal Palace (A) 3–1

18 Sept: v West Ham (H) 4–2 (three goals)

25 Sept: v Liverpool (A) 2–2

2 Oct: v Sheffield United (H) 2–0 (one goal)

9 Oct: v Huddersfield (A) 3–0 (one goal)

16 Oct: v Derby (H) 1–0 (one goal)

23 Oct: v Newcastle (A) 1–0 (one goal)

30 Oct: v Leeds (H) 0–1

6 Nov: v Manchester City (A) 3–3

13 Nov: v Tottenham (H) 3–1

20 Nov: v Leicester City (H) 3–2

27 Nov: v Southampton (A) 5–2 (three goals)

4 Dec: v Nottingham Forest (H) 3–2

11 Dec: v Stoke City (A) 1–1

18 Dec: v Ipswich (A) 0–0

27 Dec: v Coventry City (H) 2–2

1 Jan: v West Ham (A) 0–3

22 Jan: v Chelsea (H) 0–1

29 Jan: v WBA (A) 1–2

12 Feb: v Newcastle (H) 0–2

19 Feb: v Leeds (A) 1–5

4 March: v Tottenham (A) 0–2

8 March: v Everton (H) 0–0

11 March: v Huddersfield (H) 2–0 (one goal)

25 March: v Crystal Palace (H) 4–0

1 April: v Coventry City (A) 3–2 (one goal)

3 April: v Liverpool (H) 0–3

4 April: v Sheffield United (A) 1–1

8 April: v Leicester City (A) 0–2

12 April: v Manchester City (H) 1–3

15 April: v Southampton (H) 3–2 (one goal)

25 April: v Arsenal (A) 0–3

29 April: v Stoke City (H) 3–0 (one goal)

FA CUP

15 Jan: Third-round: v Southampton (A) 1–1

19 Jan: Third-round replay: v Southampton (H) 4–1 (two goals)

5 Feb: Fourth-round: v Preston (A) 2–0

26 Feb: Fifth-round: v Middlesbrough (H) 0–0

29 Feb: Fifth-round replay: v Middlesbrough (A) 3–0 (one goal)

18 March: Sixth-round: v Stoke (H) 1–1 (one goal)

22 March: Sixth-round replay: v Stoke (A) 1–2 (one goal)

LEAGUE CUP

7 Sept: Second-round: v Ipswich (A) 3–1 (two goals)

6 Oct: Third-round: v Burnley (H) 1–1

18 Oct: Third-round replay: v Burnley (A) 1–0

27 Oct: Fourth-round: v Stoke City (H) 1–1

8 Nov: Fourth-round replay: v Stoke City (A) 0–0

15 Nov: Fourth-round second replay: v Stoke City (A) 1–2 (one goal)

WATNEY CUP

21 July: First-round: v Halifax (A) 1–2 (one goal)

1972–73

DIVISION ONE

12 Aug: v Ipswich (H) 1–2

15 Aug: v Liverpool (A) 0–2

19 Aug: v Everton (A) 0–2

23 Aug: v Leicester City (H) 1–1 (one goal)

26 Aug: v Arsenal (H) 0–0

30 Aug: v Chelsea (H) 0–0

2 Sept: v West Ham (A) 2–2 (one goal)

9 Sept: v Coventry City (H) 0–1

16 Sept: v Wolves (A) 0–2

23 Sept: v Derby (H) 3–0

30 Sept: v Sheffield United (A) 0–1

7 Oct: v WBA (A) 2–2 (one goal)

14 Oct: v Birmingham City (H) 1–0

21 Oct: v Newcastle (A) 1–-2

28 Oct: v Tottenham (H) 1–4

4 Nov: v Leicester City (A) 2–2 (one goal)

11 Nov: v Liverpool (H) 2–0

18 Nov: v Manchester City (A) 0–3

25 Nov: v Southampton (H) 2–1

LEAGUE CUP
6 Sept: Second-round: v Oxford (A) 2–2
12 Sept: Second-round replay: v Oxford (H) 3–1 (two goals)
3 Oct: Third-round: v Bristol Rovers (A) 1–1
11 Oct: Third-round replay: v Bristol Rovers (H) 1–2

1973–74

DIVISION ONE
20 Oct: v Birmingham City (H) 1–0
27 Oct: v Burnley (A) 0–0
3 Nov: v Chelsea (H) 2–2
10 Nov: v Tottenham (A) 1–2 (one goal)
17 Nov: v Newcastle (A) 2–3
24 Nov: v Norwich City (H) 0–0
8 Dec: v Southampton (H) 0–0
15 Dec: v Coventry City (H) 2–3 (one goal)
22 Dec: v Liverpool (A) 0–2
26 Dec: v Sheffield United (H) 1–2
29 Dec: v Ipswich (H) 2–0
1 Jan: v QPR (A) 0–3

OTHERS
Central League: Games 1, Goals 0

SENIOR GAMES FOR MANCHESTER UNITED 474, GOALS 181*

---

* Almost every statistical record of his appearances and goals for United differs depending
on whether or not the following matches are included: World Club Championship,
Charity Shield, Watney Cup.

OTHER CLUBS

1974

BP League: Jewish Guild: Games 4, Goals 1

1975

Division Four: Stockport County: Games 3, Goals 0

1975–76

League of Ireland: Cork Celtic: Games 3, Goals 0.

1976

NASL: Los Angeles Aztecs: Games 24, Goals 15

1976–77

Division Two: Fulham: Games 32, Goals 6
FA Cup: Games 2, Goals 0
League Cup: Games 3, Goals 1
Football Combination: Games 1, Goals 0

1977

NASL: Los Angeles Aztecs: Games 25, Goals 13

1977–78

Division Two: Fulham: Games 10, Goals 2
Anglo Scottish Cup: Games 1, Goals 1

1978

NASL: Los Angeles Aztecs: Games 12, Goals 0
Fort Lauderdale Strikers: Games 14, Goals 5

1979

NASL: Fort Lauderdale Strikers: Games 19, Goals 2

1979–80

Scottish Premier Division: Hibernian: Games 13, Goals 4
SFA Cup: Games 3, Goals 0

1980

NASL: San Jose Earthquakes: Games 26, Goals 8

1980–81

Scottish Division One: Hibernian: Games 4, Goals 0
Scottish League Cup: Games 2, Goals 0

1981

NASL: San Jose Earthquakes: Games 30, Goals 13

1982–83

Division Three: Bournemouth: Games 5, Goals 0

1983

Brisbane Lions: Games 4, Goals 0
Northern Ireland

NORTHERN IRELAND

1963–64

15 April: v Wales (A) 3–2
29 April: v Uruguay (H) 3–0 F

1964-65

3 Oct: v England (H) 3–4
14 Oct: v Switzerland (H) 1–0*
14 Nov: v Switzerland (A) 1–2 (one goal)*
25 Nov: v Scotland (A) 2–3 (one goal)
17 March: v Holland (H) 2–1*
7 April: v Holland (A) 0–0*
7 May: v Albania (H) 4–1* (one goal)

1965–66

2 Oct: v Scotland (H) 3–2
10 Nov: v England (A) 1–2
24 Nov: v Albania (A) 1–1*

1966–67

22 Oct: v England (H) 0–2**

1967–68

21 Oct: v Scotland (H) 1–0

1968–69

23 Oct: v Turkey (H) 4–1 (one goal)*
3 May: v England (H) 1–1
6 May: v Scotland (A) 1–1
10 May: v Wales (H) 0–0

1969–70

10 Sept: v USSR (H) 0-0*
18 April: v Scotland (H) 0-1
21 April: v England (A) 1-3 (one goal)
25 April: v Wales (A) 0-1

1970–71

11 Nov: v Spain (A) 0–3**
3 Feb: v Cyprus (A) 3–0 (one goal)**
21 April: v Cyprus (H) 5–0 (three goals)**
15 May: v England (H) 0–1
18 May: v Scotland (A) 1–0
22 May: v Wales (H) 1–0

1971–72

22 Sept: v USSR (A) 0–1**
16 Feb: v Spain (H) 1–1** (played on neutral ground – Hull)

1972–73

18 Oct: v Bulgaria (A) 0–3*

1973–74

14 Nov: v Portugal (A) 1–1*

1976–77

13 Oct: v Holland (A) 2–2*
10 Nov: v Belgium (A) 0–2*
27 April: v West Germany (A) 0–5 F

1977–78

21 Sept: v Iceland (H) 2–0*
12 Oct: v Holland (H) 0–1*
SENIOR CAPS 37, GOALS 9

*World Cup qualifier
**European Nations Cup qualifier
F – Friendly
All other games are Home International Championship

OTHERS

1961–62

Youth Internationals: Games 2, Goals 1

Selected Sources

Videos, Television programmes, DVDs, CDs and Cassettes

George Best's Funeral; BBC, Sky News, RTI
Best: The Most Glamorous Sporstman of All Time
Best: His Mother's Son (BBC)
George Best: Football's Greatest (Sky)
The Best of the Mrs Merton Show
George Best: In his Own Words (BBC)
George Best and Rodney Marsh: Drugs, Mugs and Thugs?
Best and Marsh: On Stage and Uncut
Best and Marsh: The Perfect Match
Best and Marsh
Best and Marsh 2
Brought Up by Booze: Calum Best (BBC)
Carnaby Street Uncovered (The Arts Channel)
The George Best Story, Ulster TV
George Best and Jimmy Greaves in Unscripted Conversation,
  Tower Bridge, 1983
George Best Genius, CBS Fox
George Best Remembered, IMC Vision
George Best: The Final Interview (TalkSPORT)
George Best: Genius, Maverick, Legend, The Official Story, MUFC
Best Intentions and Best's View, IMC Vision
George Best: A Genius and a Legend, Duke

There's Only One George Best (BBC)

Charlie Bubbles

In the Shadow of Busby, Zoogon

Manchester United Legends: Charlton, Best, Law (BBC)

George Best: This is Your Life, 1971 (ITV)

Imagine: Vidal Sassoon (BBC)

Official History: Manchester United Football Club (two VHS)

The Saturday Men: West Bromwich Albion

The Time of Our Lives: Manchester United Under Matt Busby (Sky)

Sporting Lives: Tommy Docherty (TalkSPORT)

The Busby Era: Manchester United 1918–1958–1968

A Tribute to Busby (Telstar)

Bobby Charlton: This is Your Life (ITV)

Frost on Saturday (ITV)

Reunited: Manchester United's Heroes of '68

The Irish Connection: Manchester United's Players Past and Present from both sides of the Border

The Official History of Manchester United (BBC)

George Best on the Parkinson Show BBC and ABC in Australia

Wagner, M: Podcast, *Daily Mirror*, 2010

Selected Bibliography

Arthur, M; *The Busby Babes, Men of Magic*, Mainstream, 2008

Bagchi, R. and Rogerson, P; *The Unforgiven: The Story of Don Revie's Leeds United*, Aurum, 2002 and 2009

Barnes, J; Bostock, A; Butler, C; Wylie, M; Ganguly, A. and McColl, G; *The Manchester United Official History*, Manchester United and Carlton Books, 2001

Best, B. and McDowell, L; *Our George: A Family Memoir of George Best*, Sidgwick & Jackson, 2007

—, *George Best Will Not Be Playing Today*, GFH HBF, 2011

Best, G; *George Best's Football Annuals 1–7*, Pelham Books, 1966 onwards

—, *Best of Both Worlds*, Pelham Books, 1968 and 1969 (updated edition)

—, *On the Ball*, Pelham Books, 1970

—, *Hard Tackles and Dirty Baths: The Inside Story of Football's Golden Era*, Ebury Press 2005

Best, G. and Benson, R; *The Good, the Bad and the Bubbly*, Simon & Schuster, 1990

Best, G. and Collins, R; *Blessed*, Ebury Press, 2001 and 2003 (updated edition)

Best, G. and Knight, M; *Scoring at Half-Time: Adventures on and off the Pitch*, Ebury Press, 2003

Best, G. and Scott, L; *The Best of Times, My Favourite Football Stories*, Simon & Schuster, 1994

Best, G. and Wright, G; *Where Do I Go from Here?*, Queen Anne Press, 1981

Booker, C; *The Seventies, Portrait of a Decade*, Allen Lane, 1980

Bowler, D; *Danny Blanchflower: Biography of a Visionary*, Victor Gollancz, 1997

Buchan, C; *Soccer Gift Book*, CB, 1968

Burn, G; *Best and Edwards: Football Fame and Oblivion*, Faber, 2006

Burtenshaw, N; *Whose Side Are You on Ref?*, Arthur Baker, 1973

Busby, M; *My Story*, SBC, 1959

—, *Soccer at the Top, My Life in Football*, Weidenfeld, 1973

—, *Manchester United Scrapbook*, Souvenir Press, 1989

Butler, B; *The Football League, 1888–1988*, Queen Anne Press, 1988

Carman, D; *No Ordinary Man: A Life of George Carman*, Hodder, 2002

Charlton, B; *Bobby Charlton's Book of European Football*, Souvenir Press, 1969

—, *Most Memorable Matches* (with Jones, K.), Stanley Paul, 1984

—, *My Manchester United Years*, Headline, 2007

—, *My Life in Football*, Headline, 2009

Charlton, C; *Cissie*, Bridge Studios, 1988

Clarke, B; *Docherty: Living Legend of Football*, Mandarin, 1992

Clarke, P; *Hope and Glory, Britain 1900–1990*, Allen Lane, 1996

Collins, P; *The Sports Writer*, Virgin, 1996

Connor, J; *The Lost Babes: Manchester United and the Forgotten Victims of Munich*, Harper Sport, 2006

Crerand, P; *Never Turn the Other Cheek*, Harper Sport, 2007

Crick, M. and Smith, D; *Manchester United: Betrayal of a Legend*, Pelham Books, 1989

Crompton, J. and Butler, C; *From Goal Line to Touchline*, Empire, 2008

Davies, H; *Boots, Balls and Haircuts*, Cassell, 2003

—, *The Bumper Book of Football*, Quercus, 2007

Dewhurst, K; *When You Put on a Red Shirt*, Yellow Jersey, 2009

Docherty, A; *Married to a Man of Two Halves*, John Blake, 2008

Docherty, T; *Call the Doc*, Hamlyn, 1981

—, *The Doc, Hallowed Be Thy Game*, Headline, 2006

Docherty, T. and Roberts, B; *An Invitation to Dinner with the Doc*, Media World, 1988

Doogan, D; *Doog*, All Seasons, 1980

Dunphy, E; *A Strange Kind of Glory: Sir Matt Busby & Manchester United*, Aurum, 1991

Edwards, A; *The Northern Ireland Troubles*, Osprey, 2011

Egan, S; *The Doc's Devils*, Cherry Red Books, 2010

Ellis, G. and Taylor, R; *Ruth Ellis, My Mother*, Smith Gryphon, 1995

Engel, M; *Tickle the Public*, Victor Gollancz, 1996

Evans, F; *The Last British Bullfighter*, Macmillan, 2009

Evans, P; *The 1960s Home*, Shire Library, 2010

Falkiner, K; *Green Devils; The Irish and Manchester United*, Hachette, 2008

Ferris, K; *Manchester United in Europe*, Mainstream, 2004

Foer, J; *Moonwalking with Einstein*, Penguin, 2011

Foot, M; *The Politics of Paradise: A Vindication of Byron*, Collins,

Foulkes, B; *Back at the Top*, SBC, 1965

—, *United in Triumph and Tragedy*, Know the Score, 2008

Fullerton, J; *I Did It My Way*, Mainstream, 2007

Fry, B; *Big Fry*, Harpercollins, 2001

Gascoigne, P; *Being Gazza*, Headline, 2006

Gemmell, T. and McColl, G; *Lion Heart*, Virgin, 2007

Giles, J; *A Football Man*, Hodder, 2010

Giller, N; *Footballing Fifties*, JR Books, 2007

Glanvill, R; *Sir Matt Busby, A Tribute*, Virgin, 1994

Glanville, B; *People in Sport*, SBC, 1967

—, *Soccer: A Panorama*, Eyre & Spottiswoode, 1968

—, *Football Memories*, Virgin, 1999

—, *Footballers Don't Cry*, Virgin, 1999

—, *For Club and Country*, GB, 2008

Green, G; *Great Moments in Soccer*, Pelham Books, 1972

— *There's Only One United*, Hodder, 1978

Gold, J; *Tramp's Gold*, Robson, 2001

Greaves, J; *This One's on Me*, Arthur Baker, 1979

—, *The Heart of the Game*, Time Warner, 2006

Godsell, A; *Europe United: A History of the European Cup/Champions League*, Sports Books, 2005

—, *Pardon Me for Living*, George Allen & Unwin, 1984

Gregg, H. and Anderson, R; *Harry's Game*, Mainstream, 2002

Hall, D; *Manchester's Finest: How the Munich Air Disaster Broke the Heart of a Great City*, Bantam Press, 2008

Harding, J; *For the Good of the Game: the Official History of The Professional Footballers' Association*, Robson, 1991

Harris, H; *Hold the Back Page: Football's Tabloid Tales*, Know the Score, 2006

Harris, N; *The Charlton Brothers*, Stanley Paul, 1971

Haslam, D; *Manchester, England, Story of the Pop Cult City*, Fourth Estate, 1999

Henderson, M; *50 People Who Fouled Up Football*, Constable, 2009

Herd, M. (ed.); *The Guardian Book of Football: Fifty Years of Classic Reporting*, GB, 2008

Hewitt, P. and Baxter, P; *The Fashion of Football: From Best to Beckham, from Mod to Label Slave*, Mainstream, 2004

Highlights from the National Press: Best, G. 1946–2005, Historic Newspapers, undated

Hill, G. and Thomas, J; *Give a Little Whistle*, Souvenir Press, 1975

Hill, J; *Soccer '69*, Stepheyns Ltd, 1969

Hill, T. (ed.); *George Best Unseen Archive*, Parragon, 2001

Hilton, C. and Cole, I; *Memories of George Best*, Sports Books, 2007

Hodgson, D; *The Manchester United Story*, Arthur Baker, 1977

Holmes, B; *The Match of My Life*, Kingswood Press, 1991

—, *My Greatest Game*, Mainstream, 1993

Holt, O; *If You're Second You're Nothing: Ferguson and Shankly*, Macmillan, 2006

Hopcraft, A; *The Football Man: People and Passions in Soccer*, Collins, 1968

Hopkins, G; *Star-Spangled Soccer: The Selling, Marketing and Management of Soccer in the USA*, Palgrave, 2010

Hughes, B; *Starmaker: The Untold Story of Jimmy Murphy*, Empire, 2002

Hughes, E; *My Great Britons*, Partridge Press, 1988

Hugman, B; *Rothmans Football League Players Records, The Complete A-Z 1946–1981*, Rothmans, 1981

Inglis, S. (ed.); *The Football Grounds of Great Britain*, Willow Books, 1987

—, *Charles Buchan's Manchester United Soccer Gift Book*, CB 2007

James, C; *Fame in the 20th Century*, BBC Books, 1993

Jamieson, T; *Whose Side Are You On? Sport, the Troubles and Me*, Yellow Jersey, 2011

Kriegel, M; *Namath: A Biography*, Penguin, 2004

Laschke, I; *Rothmans Book of League Records, 1888–89 to 1978–79*, Macdonald, 1980

Law, D; *Living for Kicks*, Stanley Paul, 1963

—, *Denis Law's Book of Soccer 1–6*, Pelham Books, 1966 onwards

—, *The Lawman*, Deutsch, 1999

—, *The King*, Bantam Press, 2003

Law, D. and Crerand, P; *United: The Legendary Years, 1958–1968*, Virgin, 1997

Levin, B; *The Pendulum Years: Britian and the Sixties*, Cape, 1970

Lewis, P; *The 50s*, Heinemann, 1978

Lovejoy, J; *Bestie, Portrait of a Legend*, Macmillan, 1998

Lovesey, J; Mason, N. and Turner, E; *The Sunday Times Sports Book*, World's Work, 1979

Ludden, J; *A Tale of Two Cities, Manchester and Madrid, 1957–1968*, Empire, 2012

Lynott, P; *My Boy*, Hot Press Books, 2001

Keesel, N. and Walton, H; *Alcoholism*, Penguin, 1969

Kelly, S. F; *Back Page United*, Queen Anne Press, 1995

Kennedy, M; *Portrait of Manchester*, Robert Hale, 1970

Liversedge, S; *Busby: Epitaph to a Legend*, Soccer Book Publishing, 1994

Luscombe, W. (ed.); *The Park Drive Book of Football, 1968/69 season*, Pelham Books 1969

Macari, L; *Football, My Life*, Bantam Books, 2008

MacCarthy, F; *Byron: Life and Legend*, John Murray, 2002

McCartney, I; *Irish Reds*, Britespot, 2002

McColl, G; *Manchester United in the Sixties*, Manchester United Books, 1997

— (ed.); *United We Stand* Manchester United and, Carlton Books, 2002

McGuinness, W. and Ponting, I; *Manchester United – Man and Babe*, Know the Score, 2008

McIlroy, S; *Manchester United: My Team*, Souvenir Press, 1980

McIlvanney, H; *On Football*, Mainstream, 1994

McKinstry, L; *Jack & Bobby: A Story of Brothers in Conflict*, Harpercollins, 2002

McKittrick, D. and McVea, D; *Making Sense of the Troubles: A History of the Northern Ireland Conflict*, Penguin, 2001

Marsh, R; *Priceless*, Headline, 2001

Marsh, R. and Woolnough, B; *I Was Born a Loose Cannon*, Optimum, 2010

Marshall, I; *Old Trafford; 100 Years at the Home of Manchester United*, Simon & Schuster, 2010

Matthews, S; *The Way it Was*, Headline, 2000

Marvick, A; *The Sixties*, Oxford University Press, 1998

Meek, D; *The Manchester United Football Book 1–9*, Stanley Paul, 1966 onwards

—, *Anatomy of a Football Star, George Best*, Arthur Baker, 1970

—, *Manchester United's Greats*, Sportsprint, 1989

—, *George Best: Tribute to a Legend*, Weidenfeld & Nicolson, 2005

—, *Legends of United*, Orion, 2006

Miller, D; *Cup Magic*, Sidgwick & Jackson, 1981

Minnis, I; *The Troubles in Northern Ireland*, Heinemann, 2001

Moore, C; *United Irishman*, Mainstream, 1999

Moore, T; *Bobby Moore by the Person Who Knew Him Best*, Harper Sport, 2006

Morrison, I. and Shury, A; *Manchester United: A Complete Record, 1878–1992*, Breedon, 1992

Motson, J; *Match of the Day: The Complete Record Since 1964*, BBC Books, 1992

Mullery, A; *In Defence of Spurs*, Stanley Paul, 1969

Munro, J. N; *When George Came to Edinburgh: George Best at Hibs*, Birlinn, 2010

Murphy, J; *Matt . . . United . . . and Me*, Souvenir Press, 1968

Myers, K; *Watching the Door: Cheating Death in 1970s Belfast*, Atlantic, 2009

Nawrat, C. and Hutchings, S; *The Sunday Times Illustrated History of Football*, Ted Smart, 1998

Neill, T; *Revelations of a Football Manager*, Sidgwick & Jackson, 1985

Nolan, D; *Tony Wilson, You're Entitled to an Opinion*, John Blake, 2010

O'Farrell, F; *All Change at Old Trafford*, Jellyfish, 2011

O'Reilly, O; *The Book of Best*, The Collins Press, 2006

Palmer, J. (ed.); *George Best: His Greatest Matches*, Anthem, 2006

Parkinson, M; *Sporting Fever*, Hutchinson, 1974

—, *Best: An Intimate Biography*, Hutchinson, 1975

—, *Sporting Profiles: Sixty Heroes of Sport*, Pavilion, 1995

—, *On Football*, Hodder, 2001

—, *Parky: My Autobiography*, Hodder, 2008

—, *Parky's People*, Hodder, 2010

Partridge, P. and Gibson, J; *Oh Ref*, Souvenir Press, 1979

Pawson, T. (ed.); *The Goalscorers*, Cassell, 1978

—, *The Observer on Soccer*, Hyman, 1989

Pelé: *The Autobiography*, Simon & Schuster, 2006

Phillips, D; *The Complete George Best: Every Game – Every Goal*, Empire, 2008

Ponting, I; *George Best: The Extraordinary Story of a Football Genius*, Simon & Schuster, 2012

Potter, D; *When Football Was Fun*, Empire, 2010

Powell, J; *Bobby Moore: The Life and Times of a Sporting Hero*, Robson, 2002

Randall, S; *They Played the Game: The Playboy Interviews*, M Press, 2006

Rankin, P. (ed.); *Stormont*, Ulster Architectural Heritage Society, 1999

Roberts, J; *Sod This, I'm off to Marbella*, Sport Media, 2010

Robinson, P; Cheeseman, D; and Pearson, H; *1966 Uncovered: The Unseen Story of the World Cup in England*, Mitchell Beazley, 2006

Rollin, J; *Rothmans Football Yearbook* (various years), Queen Anne Press

Samuels, S; *Northerners: Portrait of a No-Nonsense People*, Ebury Press, 2011

Sandbrook, D; *White Heat: A History of Britain in the Swinging Sixties*, Little, Brown, 2006

Scovell, B; *Bill Nicholson, Football's Perfectionist*, John Blake, 2011

Shaw, P; *The Book of Football Quotations*, Ebury Press, 2008

Shindler, C; *Fathers, Sons and Football*, Headline, 2001

—, *George Best and 21 Others*, 2004

Singy, D; *A Pictorial History of Soccer*, Hamlyn, 1968

Smailes, G; *The Breedon Book of Football League Records*, Breedon, 1991

Smith, B. and Hunt, M; *George Best: A Celebration*, John Blake, 2007

Smith, D; *The Boys Book of Soccer*, Evans Brothers, 1968

—, *The Boys Book of Soccer*, Evans Brothers, 1969

Smith, M; *40 Years of Match of the Day*, BBC Books, 2004

Smith, S; *The International Football Book No. 9*, Souvenir Press, 1967

—, *The International Football Book No. 10*, Souvenir Press, 1968

Steen, R; *The Mavericks*, Mainstream, 1994

Stelling, J; *Jellyman's Thrown a Wobbly*, Harper Sport, 2009

Stepney, A; *In Safe Keeping*, Pelham Books, 1969

—, *Alex Stepney*, Arthur Baker, 1978

—, *Tooting Common to the Stretford End*, Vertical Editions, 2010

Stiles, N; *Soccer My Battlefield*, Stanley Paul, 1968

—, *After the Ball*, Hodder, 2003

Stock, A; *A Little Thing Called Pride*, Pelham Books, 1982

Summerbee, M; *The Story of a True City Legend*, Optimum, 2010

Sutcliffe, R; *Revie: Revered and Reviled*, Great Northern, 2010

Sutherland, J; *Last Drink to LA*, Short Books, 2001

Taylor, P; *The Provos: The IRA and Sinn Fein*, Bloomsbury, 1998

—, *Loyalists*, Bloomsbury, 2000

—, *Brits: War against the IRA*, Bloomsbury, 2002

Taylor, R. and Ward, A; *Kicking and Screaming: An Oral History of Football in England*, Robson Books 1995

Tennant, J; *Football: The Golden Age*, Cassell, 2001

Thomas, C; *By the Book*, Willow Books, 1984

Thornton, D; *Leeds United and Don Revie*, Robert Hale, 1970

Tossell, D; *Playing for Uncle Sam: The Brits' Story of the North American Soccer League*, Mainstream, 2003

Tyler, M; *The Professional Book of Football Skills and Tactics*, Marshall Cavendish, 1973

Wagner, M. and Page, T; *George Best and Me, Waggy's Tale*, Empire, 2010

Walden, C; *Babysitting George*, Bloomsbury, 2011

Wangerin, D; *Soccer in a Football World: The Story of America's Forgotten Game*, WSC, 2006

Ward, A. and Williams, J; *Football Nation: Sixty Years of the Beautiful Game*, Bloomsbury, 2009

Whitehead, P; *The Writing on the Wall: Britain in the Seventies*, Michael Joseph, 1985

Whiteside, N; *Determined*, Headline, 2007

Williams, R. (ed.); *George Best: A Life in the News*, Aurum, 2006

Wilson, J; *Inverting the Pyramid: A History of Football Tactics*, Orion, 2008

Wooldridge, I. (intro); *Great Sporting Headlines*, Collins, 1984

—, *Searching for Heroes*, Hodder, 2007

Newspaper Articles

SUNDAY PEOPLE

1971, 10 Jan: On the mat!

1971, 17 Jan: Georgie the real untold story: Best – and his birds

1971, 17 Jan: George Best in takeover surprise

1971, 24 Jan : Best – My boy George

1971, 31 Jan: Best – the future he fears

1972, 9 Jan: Come home, Georgie

1972, 16 Jan : George Best the lover by the girl he planned to wed

1972, 30 Jan: Georgie finds a way for love

1972, 28 May: Hey, they're Georgie's Girls!

1973, 14 Jan: George and me – by the girl he hit

1973, 8 April: The Doc: I'd gamble – and handle George

1974, 20 Jan: Cheerio, George

1974, 28 April: I *did* take Marji's diary, says Best

1974, 28 April: What I found out about Marji in her little black book

1974, 5 May: I was framed – was it the mystery man at Miss World's flat?

1974, 12 May: Georgie's nights out with 1,000 birds

1976, 4 April: Bestie, USA

1976, 10 April: George Best – by his hot Gospelling sister

1977, 11 Dec: Best: Why I'm quitting Britain

1979, 21 Jan: Georgie Best mends marriage bust-up

1979, 27 May: Georgie on his best behaviour

1979, 22 July: Best: how I'll beat the booze

1981, 11 Oct: Best is Past It

1982, 14 Feb: Dried-out Best will lecture the drunks

1982, 21 Feb: Deplorable, obnoxious, sarcastic, ignorant and horrible!

1982, 18 July: Divorce blow for Best

1982, 25 July: Love rival thumps Best

1982, 25 July: Miss World, the barmaid and all those other women in George's life

1982, 1 Aug: I grabbed the kitchen knife and stuck it in his bottom

1983, 9 Jan: Best drove me barmy

1983, 3 July: George caught between love of two women

1984, 20 May: Why Mary said 'no' to Best twice

1984, 10 June: Angie takes in George as lodger

1984, 9 Sept: Why I wanted to kill Best, by wife Angie

1984, 23 Dec: Radio shock for George Best's son

1991, 27 Jan: At home with George Best

NEWS OF THE WORLD

1966, 13 March: Chelsea Fizz

1968, 2 June: Busby United – the greatest

1969, 24 Aug: Love at first sight say George and Eva

1969, 23 Nov: The truth about Eva and me – by George Best

1970, 8 Feb: By George – six of the Best!

1970, 15 March: Georgie Best's dad on dole

1970, 30 Aug: Georgie's new place

1970, 25 Oct: She's George Best's new housekeeper

1971, 28 Feb: THE BIRDS won't believe he isn't really GEORGIE

1972, 9 Jan: Best row: It's over pay not birds

1972, 11 June: Best says I will play for anyone

1972, 16 July: Nightmare!

1976, 22 Aug: George: It's a match

1979, 10 June: Me and Mister Heineken by George Best

1982, 25 July: My Best days are over for good

1983, 1 May: George Best Exclusive: Confessions of an alcoholic

1983, 8 May: Give me another chance says Best

1983, Oct 9: G-E-O-R-G-I-E!

1984, 23 Dec: George sealed our love with a kiss and vowed: I'll never have a drink again

2000, 16 April: I kept on drinking brandy

2000, 23 July: Soccer legend George tells of moment 5-month booze ban ended in bender

2005, 27 Nov: Alex kissed him then whispered a final goodbye . . .

2005, 27 Nov: If you really want to know what George was like, listen to Helter Skelter by the Beatles . . . and play it very loud

2005, 4 Dec: Genius broke down divisions. Farewell to a legend

2005, 4 Dec: United for Best / Schoolboy pal says farewell

2005, 4 Dec: Best's final secret

2005, 4 Dec: Best bows out a hero

DAILY MAIL

1966, 10 March: United's greatest

1966, 12 Nov: Idol with no illusions – and a million pounds in mind

1967, 23 Oct: Best much too good for Scots

1968, 25 April: United miss the two-goal target

1968, 12 Oct: I don't like girls who smoke, says George Best

1969, 31 May: Me and my 1,000 dollies

1969, 25 Aug: George Best's girl tells boyfriend 'It's all off'

1969, 10 Nov: England get an agent

1969, 12 Dec: George Best sued by ex-girlfriend

1970, 2 Feb: That's show-biz says six-goal George

1970, 5 June: Guess who could sell stair-rods in a bungalow

1970, 29 Oct: Best's best ends a Chelsea myth / Shankly salutes that goal

1971, 5 Jan: Best the incredible

1971, 13 Jan: 'Suddenly, it all started to go sour'

1971, 4 May: How I learned to live with myself

1971, 1 Nov: George Best dropped after death threats

1971, 15 Nov: Now Scots may follow Best out of Ireland

1971, 29 Nov: The trial of George Best

1972, 10 Jan: A quick kiss for George from Carolyn

1972, 11 Jan: The George Best story: A house is not a home / The mixed-up god – a classic case of status problems

1972, 20 Jan: That old Best magic is back

1972, 20 Sept: Best misses it / It's 'the Best car in the world'

1972, 19 Oct: Best is sent off in cup rumpus

1972, 6 Dec: Now George may go for good

1972, 6 Dec: At last – Best gets the boot

1973, 23 June: George Best gets black eye in street fight

1973, 11 Sept: It's hard going, admits Best

1974, 2 Jan: I'm depressed explains Best

1974, 25 July: Best plans return for 50-fan club

1975, 8 Nov: George Best can go for nothing

1975, 10 Nov: Best pleads for time

1975, 18 Nov: If George wants to be left alone, why does he insist on selling Best so hard?

1978, 26 Jan: Georgie – by his new mother-in-law

1979, 1 Nov: Macho of the Day!

1981, 7 Feb: Best baby boy!

1981, 18 Sept: How Angela has brought the best out of Best

1982, 31 March: Bye, Best!

1983, 15 Feb: My husband upstairs . . .

1983, 25 March: Cheers! George celebrates his Bournemouth move

1983, 12 May: GOODBYE! Mary walks out of George Best's life with regrets

1984, 4 Dec: Jailed Best wins bail plea after his 'shock' sentence

1984, 13 Dec: I want to try drink cure again, says anxious Best

1984, 22 Dec: A moment with Angie for jailed soccer star

1986, 4 June: Best walks out on his World Cup TV job

1990, 1 Sept: Why I feel afraid for Gascoigne

1990, 21 Sept: Best, drink and some sobering truths

1996, 18 May: Greatness stands the test of time

1996, 21 May: Is George really the best hero we have?

1996, 22 May: Raise a glass to the cribbage king of the Phene Arms; a round with George Best

1996, 21 Sept: Missing, but still Best

1998, 23–26 May: The George Best Story – in 3 parts

1998, 23 Dec: I simply don't go to clubs now . . .

2000, 11 March: The girls he could handle. But he let the drink seep into his soul

2000, 23 March: Women and booze – if only I could save my son George . . . but I can't

2003, 14 July: It's the lost glory that is driving George to drink again

2003, 12 Aug: Selfish, puerile and utterly disloyal. So why do we treat him as a hero?

2003, 26 Sept: George was a true great. Without the booze he'd have been the best

2005, 8 Oct: I won't cry when George goes

2005, 19 Nov: New infection puts Best back in intensive care

2005, 26 Nov: George Best 1946–2005. Farewell to a football legend. Tribute edition

2005, 26 Nov: Genius whose easy Irish charm was irresistible

2005, 26 Nov: He tormented the finest defenders but could not conquer his own demons

2005, 26 Nov: No flowers, please, just remember his genius

2005, 26 Nov: Was George the Best of all time? My verdict on his place in football's hall of fame

2005, 26 Nov: Do not mourn, celebrate him

2005, 28 Nov: What a perfect tribute to our fallen genius

2005, 29 Nov: If George Best is our hero, God help us

2005, 1 Dec: Old Trafford's tribute to George

2005, 3 Dec: Saturday essay: To some, he was a selfish alcoholic who threw away a second chance of life . . .

2005, 5 Dec: A rebuke to the elite as Best unites Belfast in a symbol of hope

2005, 8 Dec: (*Femail* magazine): First interview with Alex Best after his death

2005, 27 Dec: George's last blonde

2007, 27 Jan: Best feared son would blow legacy

2010, 21 Oct: Best's legacy is sold for £250,000

2011, 27 May: Fergie's born-again Babes

SUNDAY MAIL

1967, 22 Oct: The Windsor Wisp

1984, 16 Dec: A team unites to defend its leader

MAIL ON SUNDAY

1992, 6 Sept: The works outing of the Gods

1996, 12 May: George had the best of both worlds

1996, 19 May: No regrets, only best wishes to a boy genius charming us still at fifty

1999, 20 June: (*Review*): The truth about George Best being drunk on Wogan

2000, 12 March: The doctors have warned me – just one more drink and I'll be dead

2000, 23 July: George Best was my first love

2001, 23 Sept: Sadness of king George

2002, 13 Jan: I refuse to let death threats rule my life

2002, 11 Aug: People say I do not deserve this liver. I'd never tell anyone: You deserve to die

2002, 15 Sept: I know I look like someone from Belsen . . .

2002, 1 Dec: This tribute means everything to me

2003, 20 July: I'm so ashamed

2003, 3 Aug: Prozac will give me a new personality

2003, 24 Aug: As Best days of glory fade his last trophies go for sale

2005, 13 Feb: The Best is yet to come

2005, 20 Nov: Best on life support with family at bedside; new infection leaves soccer legend battling to survive 24 critical hours

2005, 27 Nov: The day Best said I'm going to murder you / George's organs 'aren't suitable' for transplant

2005, 4 Dec: We won't forget our Belfast Boy

2005, 4 Dec: We mourn you . . . but we're proud to have you home

2006, 19 Feb (*Property on Sunday*): Alex Best: Why I'm selling the house George so loved

2011, 30 Oct: 1.16 million a year

DAILY TELEGRAPH

1966, 10 March: Manchester U. Storm into Semi-final

1968, 8 Nov: Sir Matt doesn't have to sweep the pitch

1970, 17 April: George Best 'involved in comic dispute'

1971, 15 Jan: Best apologises in reconciliation with Sir Matt

1971, 12 Nov: What a bad lad I am

1973, 12 Jan: George Best guilty of nightclub assault

1974, 25 April: Best cleared of robbing Miss World

1975, 28 Nov: Best missing

1979, 22 March: George Best challenge to FIFA's life ban

1979, 27 March: Best's soccer ban plea rejected by judge

1979, 29 March: Best's ban lifted says club

1981, 3 Oct: Best misses tax hearing

1981, 28 Nov: George Best still owes £17,000 tax

1983, 20 April: Cars and drink ate up George Best's fortune

1983, 27 July: Best could be debtor for life

1990, 24 Sept: Elusive winger swaying a way to Skid Row

1996, 20 April: Best the hardened drinker softens with passing years

1999, 1 May: The house that George built

1999, 24 May: Of Best, Bacchus and Busby

2005, 26 March: Paying homage at the court of King George

2005, 19 Nov: Best's condition worsens

2005, 24 Nov: Your view: Best a true legend of football

2005, 25 Nov: George Best – The Life of a Legend

2005, 25 Nov: George Best – 12-page tribute

2005, 25 Nov: His genius offered a footballing immortality. His weakness would kill him

2005, 26 Nov: Flashback: George Best at Manchester United's training ground, the Cliff, 1964

2005, 26 Nov: Obituary of George Best. Flawed genius of Manchester United and Northern Ireland who was football's first superstar

2005, 26 Nov: 'Bagsy George Best' – the playground sound of the 1960s

2005, 1 Dec: Fans unite to relive Best of memories

2005, 3 Dec: United by grief, Ulster honours George Best

2005, 3 Dec: George Best 1946–2005: A gift to football beyond imagination. On the day of his funeral in Belfast, David Miller pays tribute to a genius

2005, 5 Dec: Public glory of Best's farewell

2008, 2 Feb: How Busby's philosophy became the stuff of legend / The Munich story 6 Feb 1958

DAILY MIRROR

1965, 22 Feb: Best breaks the law with only one boot

1965, 27 April: Manchester United Champs

1966, 10 March: Best blasts Benfica

1967, 25 Nov: Matt: Success beyond my wildest hopes

1968, 25 April: United dream is fading

1968, 28 May: Benfica's £1,000 cup bait

1968, 30 May: From brink of disaster

1968, 4 June: Men who earn fame at £11 a minute

1968, 6 July: 'Marked Man' Best gets third red card. . .

1968, 26 July: . . . just one of Matt's millionaires / Busby triple bid – without spending

1968, 9 Sept: Ireland not getting the best of George

1968, 23 Sept: Into the furnace of football. . .

1968, 26 Sept: United rocked by 'no goal' decision

1969, 16 May: Fans bring shame to United as they flatten Europe keeper

1969, 22 Oct: Irish rage over Best body-blow

1969, 15 Nov: George Best calls off romance

1970, 3 Jan 3: The trouble with Eva . . .

1970, 9 Feb: 'I wish Best had got 4 months instead of four weeks'

1970, 27 April: FA call for probe on Best 'free pardon'

1970, 1 July: George faces a weighty problem

1970, 6 July: George Best flies off to his new bird

1970, 7 July: George Best says: I proposed to Siv – now I'll wait for her

1970, 19 Aug: Georgie-mania!

1970, 30 Oct: Gorgeous, Georgie!

1970, 14 Dec: 'Pardoe nearly lost leg' / 'Fair tackle by Best' – Sir Matt

1971, 9 Jan: Busby blasts George Best

1971, 11 Jan: £250,000 of skill with nowhere to go . . .

1971, 11 Jan: The problems of George Best – by his girl friend

1971, 13 Jan: The secret I share with the boss

1971, 13 Jan: Munich was quite a worry too, George

1971, 9 Feb: The little people save Best

1971, 5 March: Police probe story of panda car's trip to a pub for
   George Best's party drinks

1971, 14 May: I want a hat-trick against England

1971: 10 June: 'I want to carry on in the Busby style'

1971, 16 July: Keen? We've already had to put the brake on

1971, 26 July: Not the best of George . . .

1971, 20 Aug: George . . . He is such a spirited lad

1971, 10 Sept: Missing again

1971, 15 Dec: Not my puppet!

1972, 11 Jan: 'Mum' knows Best!

1972, 20 May: Has Best walked out of soccer? / Film star Georgie?

1972, 22 May: I don't want to be a bum

1972, 22 July: Just think about the kids!

1972, 7 Aug: Genius on the brink! It's up to you

1972, 4 Sept: Goal sparks zest of the wayward United star

1972, 19 Oct: Sad George is sent off

1972, 8 Dec: Three Loves of George Best, by Fiona

1972, 20 Dec: George Best's letter to Manchester United

1972, 20 Dec: Booted Out!

1973, 12 Jan: The taunt that made George Best hit out

1973, 12 Jan: Why George Best hit Stevie the nightclub girl in the face

1973, 19 Feb: George Best in Death Threat

1973, 7 Sept: Best back to stay

1974, 22 Feb: Night they met

1974, 22 Feb: The case of George Best and Miss World's fur coat

1975, 10 March: The Best and the Worst

1975, 13 Nov: Georgie Porgie pudding and pie, kisses the girls and the booze goodbye

1976, 23 July: The Best yet

1976, 14 Aug: Gorgeous George – by the girl he wants to marry

1976, 15 Dec: The worst of Best by girl who left his love-nest All Washed Up! The star's big match is over

1977, 25 May: Happy Birthday dear Georgie!

1977, 9 Sept: Best quits

1978, 24 Jan: Meet the Best bride

1978, 25 Jan: Best toasts his bride

1978, 26 Jan: All the very Best – picture exclusive on a kick-off to marriage

1978, 8 Feb: My Best eleven / The Virgin Scorer /

1979, 8 June: Wife gives boozy Best yellow card

1979, 30 July: Best is booted out

1979, 2 Aug: Georgie foots the bill

1979, 13 Aug: Soccer's fallen star

1979, 14 Nov: I'm the boss now says Best's wife

1979, 14 Dec: When the playboy had to stop

1980, 18 Feb: Don't buy George a drink

1980, 19 Feb: Last of the big benders

1980, 29 April: George turns to poetry for the love of Angie

1981, 4 March: Best dries out after bender

1981, 31 Oct: George Best keeps the taxman waiting

1981, 11 Dec: I'm back to book World Cup spot

1981, 15 Dec: Best walks out again!

1981, 16 Dec: The Best of George (by his missus)

1982, 13 Jan: George's Best

1982, 6 July: Divorce riddle of George Best

1982, 1 Sept: 'George was so broke he had his watch melted down to make my wedding ring'

1982, 2 Sept: Now . . . the George and Mary show

1982, 7 Sept: Just the Best of co-stars

1983, 10 April: 'Jealous' Best in nightclub punch-up

1983, 20 April: I'm a drunk and I'm broke

1983, 22 April: 'George isn't an emotional invalid. If he were, I wouldn't be around'

1983, 8 June: Mary's Best after all

1983 16 July: The worst of Best

1983, 23 Dec: Hello son – it's Santa George

1984, 5 Nov: Best's night on the town ends with a night in the cells

1984, 6 Nov: Best draws the crowds to court

1984, 8 Nov: Double shock for Angie Best

1984, 5 Dec: Best pays the price

1984, 5 Dec: The bottle always comes off Best

1984, 18 Dec: Prison nightmare of George Best

1984, 19 Dec: Wish you were here!

1996, 22 May: A quick drink with Bestie; lasted . . . 14 hours!

2000, 11 March: I've been to the edge; Best vows to quit the booze after liver scare

2000, 17 May: Mine's a pinta; Ex-boozer Best's £500,000 deal to promote milk

2000, 17 July: It was a mistake / I only had 2 glasses of champagne

2001, 15 June: Bestie on booze and his body

2001, 26 June: Last night's view: Why Best was worse for wear

2004, 6 July: Where did it go wrong . . . no Best time to answer

2005, 22 Nov: Critical days for sick Best

2005, 22 Nov: Darren Fullerton: Remember Best as the balletic idol who danced with genius

2005, 24 Nov: Sick Best faces new problems

2005, 25 Nov: Georgie BEST – a tribute to a legend

2005, 28 Nov: George Best 1946–2005. We were just skinny boys . . . but Best grew to be great

2005, 30 Nov: 30,000 can go to Best's funeral

2005, 1 Dec: Tears for the greatest / George Best 1946–2005: A silent tribute

2005, 2 Dec: Welcome home George – Son Calum brings legend back to Belfast today by private jet

2005, 2 Dec: George Best: 1946–2005: Getting to the funeral

2005, 2 Dec: George Best: 1946–2005: Bestie flies back home

2005, 3 Dec: George Best: 1946–2005: Calum's smile for loving fans

2005, 3 Dec: A kiss goodbye; Son's loving tribute as hero George's body is carried home to Belfast

2005, 5 Dec: George Best: 1946–2005: The final journey

2005, 5 Dec: In death, he achieved dignity which often eluded him in life

2005, 5 Dec: Thank you: Bestie's heartbroken father pays tribute to Ulster for show of grief

2005, 8 Dec: No regrets; George's last interview . . . weeks before he died

2005, 27 Dec: 1,000 people visiting Best grave every day. Plans for city memorial to soccer icon

2006, 11 March: Manchester gets ready to honour Best

2007, 25 May: When we were at his bedside I was saying: George, let go. Exclusive TV show reveals Best's last hours

2008, 5 June: Best days of his life

2008, 2 Oct: 'Depressed George was incredibly self-centred, selfish and completely focused on himself'. Angie Best on life with troubled soccer legend

2009, 10 July: Georgie, Georgie, they call him the . . . Billy Boy

SUNDAY TELEGRAPH

1970, 19 April: George Best sent off

1994, 23 Jan: Sir Matt pointed way to the top in golden age of
management / United rise to occasion with fitting act of
remembrance

1995, 17 Sept: With the Best will in the world

2001, 27 May: Why Ferguson should sever all ties with Old Trafford

2001, 23 Sept (*Magazine*): The Best of all worlds

2002, 4 Aug: The boy done bad

2005, 9 Oct: When his troubles seemed so far away

2005, 27 Nov: Glass always half full in Best's wonderful world

2005, 27 Nov: Memories too rich to be lost in a bottle

SUNDAY MIRROR

1965, Jan 10: The man I am happy to call The Boss

1966, Sept 4: NOBBY: I love to hear fans boo me – it means I'm
doing my job

1967, 15 Jan: The Best family is joining George

1967, 22 Oct: The Best of Georgie Boy

1970, 8 Feb: Cup Greed! Six of the Best Goals by George

1970, 22 Nov: I cannot change myself says George Best

1971, 10 Jan: Best: I'm ready for showdown

1971, 17 Jan: George is back – for a night out in style

1971, 11 July: George Best's super holiday – with a girl for every day

1971, 3 Aug: Best Bedford Clay

1971, 3 Oct: George's Best

1971, 24 Oct: Best has his own defenders

1971, 21 Nov: Georgie's Girl

1971, 28 Nov: Clockwork Casanova

1971, 5 Dec: George's dream of marriage

1972, 30 April: Where will George Best Go?

1972, 21 May: 'For the last year all I've done is drink'

1972, 21 May: I quit by George Best

1973, 7 Jan: George Best Shocker / Scuffle in pub as United fans jeer

1974, 28 April: George Best, Miss World, Tom Jones – The Facts

1974, 19 May: Secret of George's princess

1975, 16 Nov: Six years to live

1976, 26 Sept: George's Love nest

1980, 24 Feb: Booze and Me

1980, 9 March: George Best – The *real* truth – I've been drinking for eight years

1980, 16 March: George Best – The *real* truth – Our dream second Best!

1980, 22 June: Best babe on the way

1981, 12 July: Only now can I face it . . . I broke my mother's heart

1981, 26 July: Beginning of the end

1982, 25 July: Best left me broke says Angie

1982, 1 Aug: Best brought down a rung

1982, 19 Sept: Best girls keep their distance

1983, 17 July: My 22 lost days by George Best

1983, 9 Oct: Best beats the booze

1984, 4 March: My life and hard times with George by Angie Best

1984, 18 March: Spend, spend, Angie

1984, 27 May: Best Body: Angie shapes up for life after George

1984, 3 June: All the Best: 'The booze cure that saved my life'

1984, 10 June: Best: Why I'll not play for Ron / How I could buy up United – now

1984, 2 Sept: 'Cured' Best back on the booze

1984, 4 Nov: Warrant for Best on drink charge

1984, 9 Dec: Day Best wept

1984, 23 Dec: Making the Best of porridge

1984, 30 Dec: Best: I missed my son so very much

2000, 7 May: George Best trim, fit, and back at work

2000, 16 July: From Best to worst

2003, 12 Oct: Stotty on Sunday: sleazy money & seedy spivs

2005, 6 Nov: Angie stunned by skeleton Best

2005, 27 Nov: Voice of the Irish Sunday Mirror: The best days of our lives

2005, 27 Nov: His skills were mesmerising. George in full flight was simply the best. George Best 1946–2005

2005, 11 Dec: Divorce bill left star penniless: Bestie was broke

2007, 9 Sept: George fancied a quiet home life

DAILY STAR

1979, 7 June: Best's wife walks out

1979, 18 Aug: Best is killing himself

1979, 26 Sept: So sexy! So virile!

1980, 22 Feb: Best's better half

1981, 4 Feb: A new life for George

1982, 15 Jan: Booze spree shatters his Angie

1982, 19 July: My Mary / My new love

1982, 20 July: How I told Angie about Mary

1982, 22 July: I'll be back vows Best!

1982, 10 Sept: Best of friends

1983, 14 Jan: Best's girl slams 'soft' jailing for pub attack

1984, 5 Nov: Best in hospital drama

1984, 4 Dec: My Fear Of Prison

DAILY EXPRESS

1959, 14 Feb: Matt Busby: living proof of unbreakable spirit

1961, 5 Dec: The faith that forced this man to fly again

1964, 2 March: The boy who kept United in the Cup

1965, 4 May: Matt Busby: Team dictator I said I would be – so they gave me a contract

1965, 6 May: Matt Busby: Wanted, a genius – and I knew just the man

1965, 7 May: Matt Busby: I cannot see life without my team

1965, 1 Nov: By 25 I'd like £60,000

1966, 10 March: Busby boys book for Europe final

1966, 11 March: Ole! I am El Beatle

1971, 11 Jan: George's girl tells of 'our ruined evening'

1971, 18 Feb: It's all finished with Sinead, says George Best

1971, 30 April: George Best in Savile Row

1971, 3 Sept: Let's salute 'Big Heads' who end up winners

1971, 8 Oct: Brother, it's a fine life

1971, 15 Oct: I will dine with the Prince – if Ireland let me

1971, 22 Oct: Drugs? Not for me at any price

1971, 19 Nov: Why I envy the life of Law

1971, 3 Dec: 'Di Stefano – he could do the lot'

1971, 10 Dec: Just like Jackie

1971, 17 Dec: Yes, maybe I HAVE changed

1971, 24 Dec: Presents for Olga and Fred

1971, 31 Dec: Yes, I'm off form, but late-night charge is just rubbish

1972, 11 Jan: George – back to Chorlton-cum-Homely / The Best sentence

1972, 14 Jan: Saints? This is where I came in

1972, 28 Jan: Eastham – you've earned all this

1972, 19 May: Best goes missing – Yes, again

1972, 23 May: Best: If I had a son . . .

1974, 4 Jan: George Best turns up – at his own night club

1974, 6 Aug: Best comes to Dunstable

1975, 11 Nov: Best bounces back . . . and he scores

1975, 29 Nov: Best booms in but gone is old skill

1978, 28 April: The taming of Georgie

1979, 13 Sept: Home's Best

1979, 27 Oct: He's like a baby – his heart can be broken so easily

1980, 18 Feb: Cup of despair

1980, 25 Feb: Ireland's greatest dribbler, George Best, has muffed it again.

1980, 30 May: She's the Best

1981, 7 Sept: Best's wife theft probe

1982, 24 Sept: I'm having more fun with George now we're apart says Angie Best

1982, 18 Oct: Going it alone . . .

1983, 13 Jan: Man who attacked Best is jailed for 60 days

1983, 22 April: Mark is Angie's best pal

1983, 19 May: It's the Best way to keep in shape

1983, 23 Aug: The Best of luck! George to wed Mary

1984, 16 March: Angie loses the lot

1984, 1 May: George's home goal

1984, 29 Aug: Tea-crazy George gets a proper tannin

1984, 5 Nov: Arrested Best rushed to hospital after he collapses

1984, 5 Nov: Best: The moment of arrest

1984, 4 Dec: The fall and fall of George Best

1984, 18 Dec: Terrified Best on his way to prison

1984, 19 Dec: 'He's still my Georgie, but I gave him up to save our son'

1989, 15 Feb: Love story that kept United's broken hearts beating strong

1990, 20 Sept: Worst of Best

1990, 21 Sept: Morning after the night before with my friend George

1990, 20 Sept: Best has lost his hold on reality

1994, 19 Aug: Let's face it, George was always best playing away / Genius who lost control

1994, 8 Oct: What's my line, Rod?

1996, 18 May: What does a soccer star do if he never grows up?

1997, 31 Jan: After all these years, Bestie, I thought you'd changed

1998, 28 March: George Best (sense and sexuality)

2000, 17 July: Best thing for George? Don't serve him alcohol

2005: 28 Oct: Don't go Dad before we can make things right

2007, 27 Jan: Best son left just a watch

SUNDAY EXPRESS

1961, 22 Jan: Matt the Magician is forging a new United

1964, 25 Oct: Will this boy become the star of stars?

1966, 13 March: Young Best ranks with the great

1966, 17 April: George Best limps in

1966, 24 April: Poisoned letters do hurt

1967, 22 Oct: Best provides bright spot

1968, 15 Dec: At last – a dream has come true for Matt Busby

1970, 8 Feb: By George – It's 6 of the Best!

1980, 19 Feb: George banks on clinic to beat drink

1981, 6 Sept: Best's wife in £1,000 air robbery mystery

1981, 27 Sept: Why George Best is now happy to settle for a pot of tea

1990, 23 Sept: George Best – Out to Lunch

1993, 26 Sept: United forever: How the Busby family made football history

SUN

1965, 10 Aug: The boy with the world at his priceless feet

1966, 12 March: The return of El Beatle

1966, 12 March: Caramba! It's Best

1968, 28 May: Specially for mother, portrait of a celebrity

1970, 27 Feb: Georgie by Georgie's girls

1970, 22 April: George Best says 'I didn't fight'

1971, 12 Jan: Upset Best heads for home

1971, 14 Jan: Little Boy Lost

1971, 27 Sept: Laughter's a must

1972, 11 Jan: George trains with the boys

1972, 17 Jan: George and Eva, by 'mum'

1972, 22 May: My bottle a day, by Best

1972, 1 Dec: George Best Clobbered!

1972, 6 Dec: Price tag for the body beautiful: £400,000 / So the love affair has ended now the greatest soccer auction begins

1973, 12 Jan: Club Girl was drunk, says George

1973, 29 March: My Best team

1976, 14 Dec: Best's bird is a bunny

1977, 26 Feb: George Best: I had just three drinks all night

1978, 25 Jan: Second Best!

1978, 11 May: Soccer ban on Best as old flame weds

1981, 7 Feb: Boy! He's just like dad, says Angie

1982, 24 March: Best hits the bottle and Angie walks out

1982, 22 July: My new love, by Best's wife Angie

1983, 27 April: Fury over Best's '£750 charity game payout'

1983, 4 June: They're Best of pals again

1984, 6 Nov: Tragic Best's worst day

1984, 4 Dec: The fall and fall of bad boy Best

1984, 20 Dec: Xmas day in the slammer!

1985, 7 Jan: Best's cold porridge

1985, 11 Feb: Jail baron saved me from gay prisoner

1985, 13 Feb: Terrorists try to spring me!

1985, 14 Feb: Our centre forward escaped at half-time!

1985, 15 Feb: I count the days to freedom – and Angie's caresses

1990, 20 Sept: Drunk Best in Wogan show storm

1995, 3 July: George bedded 20 other girls in one year

1999, 18 Sept: I know what it's like to be homeless

2000, 14 April: Best warned: Liver surgery will kill you

2003, 17 July: Drink or two won't hurt George says pal

2003, 12 Aug: Ooh .. me 'ed, son

2004, 21 Feb: Give it your Best shot for the fans

2005, 4 Oct: George in last chance saloon / George doesn't care if he lives or dies . . .

2005, 19 Nov: Bestie's weight falls to 6 stone

2005, 21 Nov: Swear you'll live / Outlook is grim for frail George

2005, 24 Nov: Stricken Best on ventilator

2005, 25 Nov: Bestie's limo rolled up and Bestie rolled out

2005, 25 Nov: 5 years back on the bottle

2005, 25 Nov: George was downing 10 bottles of wine a day; Lover reveals the scale of boozing

2005, 25 Nov: Mates say farewell

2005, Nov 25: He could beat any footballer on earth . . . but not the bottle

2005, 29 Nov: Put on a show to celebrate the Best

2005, 30 Nov: Bestie didn't have a chance

2005, 1 Dec: Many United

2005, 2 Dec: 2 teams for Bestie

2005, 3 Dec: Rest in peace Bestie: funeral tributes to soccer legend

2005, 3 Dec: Return of Belfast's prodigal son

2005, 5 Dec: He carried us for years . . . it was an honour to carry him

2006, 7 Dec: George Best revelations by Tommy Docherty

2009, 15 May: Parky: George was like a son to me

DAILY SKETCH

1967, 25 July: Soccer's Beatle on a serious kick

1968, 15 Jan: Matt

1968, 14 Oct: 'Half the women here would like to mother him. The rest want to marry him'

1969, 17 Nov: He treats girls like hurdles in an obstacle race . . . 'maybe I'm afraid of marriage'

1970, 13 March: George Best faces quiz on punch-up

1970, 25 April: George Best – On booze, boredom and hangers on

1970, 16 Oct: The new Best pad . . .

1970, 12 Dec: Best . . . and the woman who told him about the facts of life

INDEPENDENT

1993, 5 March: Yes, he remembers the Best of times

1996, 18 May: A rare brilliance that will never fade . . .

1996, 20 May: Review of 'Best Night' on BBC2

1998, 29 May: The night Busby met United's destiny

1998, 14 Oct: You ask the questions

2001, 20 Feb: Exclusive (only 29 years late): Best wants a transfer

2001, 26 June: TV review: George Best's Body

2004, 21 May: Team spirit and hot air; George Best and 21 others by Colin Shindler (book review)

2005, 28 Oct: Ken Jones: Best paradox was part of a brilliant talent the world called 'El Beatle'

2005, 19 Nov: Best returns to intensive care with severe infection

2005, 21 Nov: Best faces crucial 24 hours in fight for life

2005, 25 Nov: Best: the end of the road. Blessed with gifts from gods, but cursed by his own nature

2005, 25 Nov (*Independent Extra*): The Player, by Arthur Hopcraft

2005, 26 Nov: Obituary: George Best, Mercurial football genius whose flamboyant lifestyle brought a premature end to his playing career

2005, 1 Dec: Poignant night as United pay tribute to Best

2005, 3 Dec: A final day of grace for George, a beloved and tragic figure who enhanced our lives

2005, 3 Dec: Lone piper greets coffin as Best makes his final return to Belfast

2005, 3 Dec: The enduring myth of the fatally flawed genius should be laid to rest

2009, 24 April: None better than Best

2010, 21 Oct: Best's treasures net €230,000

INDEPENDENT ON SUNDAY

1994, 23 Jan: Hero who rose above the prejudice

1996, 26 May: A thirst for tributes to football at its Best

2000, 12 March: Last chance, George. No more saloons

2001, 24 June: Vision of a genius heartbreakingly washed up

2005, 27 Nov: George Best Special: Remember the football, he said. I do

2005, 27 Nov: Taylor wants lessons learnt from the pain

2005, 27 Nov: Yes, we should have done more to protect him from himself, by Denis Law

2009, 8 March: The new review: George and me

2011, 16 Jan: United came in to buy me and manager said 'we have decided you can't go'

SCOTLAND ON SUNDAY

2001, 23 Sept: Survival of the fittest

GUARDIAN

1969, 15 Jan: The most philosophical footballer

1970, 29 Oct: Chelsea fall to goal by Best

1972, 10 Jan: Best – What does O'Farrell do now?

1972, 6 Dec: George Best must go – United

1977, 10 Sept: Georgie Porgie ran away . . .

1979, 26 Sept: Second Best

1984, 4 Dec: Royal George

1990, 21 Sept: TV companies risk action replay despite foul on Wogan

1990, 22 Sept: Better the Best we knew – Talking Point

1994, 21 Jan: United he stood / Kindness of a true champion

1996, 11 May: BBC's 'Best Fest' recalls 50 years of the good, the bad and the bubbly

1996, 18 May: Best the eternal swinger notches his half-century . . .

1997, 21 March: The princes of Scottish lore

1998, 20 May: Portrait of the world's second-Best footballer

1998, 6 June: George Best: 'I used to go for training pissed as a fart'

2000, 11 March: Soccer legend renounces alcohol

2000, 21 April: Best 'on the wagon for good'

2001, 21 April: George Best: my derby heaven and hell

2005, 21 Nov: Best still critical on life support

2005, 22 Nov: Best desperately ill, says doctor

2005, 25 Nov: El Beatle, the artist who was greater than the team: George Best held a terrible fascination for people who would normally never cross the road to see a match

2005, 25 Nov: George Best: Life and times: His star rose and fell in only six years but the memories are still vivid

2005, 25 Nov (G2): The long goodbye

2005, 30 Nov (G2): Few people in their twenties felt George Best was important to them. So why did the media give his death such attention?

2005, 3 Dec: Best and the Beeb – pure sixties bliss

2005, 5 Dec: George Best's funeral – Hail and farewell: the people of Belfast salute a fallen hero

2010, 20 Feb: 100 years on Old Trafford is the true symbol of United's potency

2012, 18 Aug: Football fans get chance to eat and sleep George Best

OBSERVER

1963, 15 Sept: Now that Busby is right back on top

1967, 24 Sept, Clear Vision of Matt Busby

1968, 17 Nov: Sir Matt Busby: 'There's something in the really gifted player that hits you . . .'

1969, 19 Jan: The magic of Sir Matt

1971, 13 June: The Business: Shirt tale

1972, 9 Jan: What's best for Best?

1972, 12 Dec: Best gets £20,000 disco offer

1977, 9 Jan (*Magazine*): Fulham's firework display

1992, 18 Oct (*Magazine*): The Best years of our lives

1994, 23 Jan: Crying like a babe

1996, 26 May: By George, our hero has done it

1999, 9 May: 'Saint' Busby demonised in BBC biography

2000, 12 March: A legend's fate: facing up to his biggest challenge

2000, 23 April: Death waits in his every glass

2005, 20 Nov: Belfast boy in a life less ordinary

2005, 27 Nov: Football's tribute to Best / Sober lessons about drink / Pewter cast of feet? Just £100 / Top liver specialist treated bankrupt hero free of charge

2005, 27 Nov: Appreciation: George Best 1946–2005: Football's first icon

2005, 27 Nov: Pitch perfect, by Sean O'Hagan

2005, 27 Nov: Remember this – he was that good

2005, 4 Dec: Tens of thousands turn out for the 'special one'

2009, 19 April: How the bottle destroyed not only George Best but his mother as well

2011, 29 May: George Best's women launch legal fight against author's 'totally unfair' memoir

OBSERVER REVIEW

1972, 10 Dec: The Loner – a profile by Arthur Hopcraft

EVENING STANDARD

1970, 16 April: Eva and Best in 'childish games'

1972, 10 Jan: O'Farrell gives George three of the best

1973, 18 Jan: George Best will appeal

1973, 7 Feb: George Best transferred to the shelf!

1976, 2 Sept: Best can play – league relent

1978, 24 Jan: The Best choice for a model bride

1978, 26 Jan: Marriage Language

1979, 15 Nov: Besting George . . .

1980, 20 Feb: JAK cartoon

1993, 14 April: Why did I go to America? Because I saw a sign saying
Drink Canada Dry

1994, 23 Aug: Sex, lies and the worst of Best

2000, 10 March: Was it all worth it for George?

2005, 30 Nov: George Best

THE ECONOMIST

1972, 1 June: Cartoon – Belt up George Best

1978, 4 March: Star-spangled soccer

EVENING NEWS

1972, 7 Jan: George Best Vanishes

1972, 10 Jan: Best must leave home

1973, 11 Jan: George Best 'an arrogant bully'

1976, 14 Dec: Angela walks out on Best 'to stay sane'

EVENING COURIER

1995, 23 Feb: Soccer star Emlyn leads from front

MANCHESTER EVENING NEWS

1965, 13 March: Lawmen gun down treble-shooters

1970, 7 Feb: 6 of the best, George!

1970, 24 March: 'Greatest ever semi,' says Busby

1971, 25 Oct: Police in new guard on Best

1972, 2 June: Best wants to stay, says agent / Best – he will play

1973, 21 April: Our salute to Bobby Charlton

1989, May: Sir Matt Busby 80th Birthday souvenir special

1994, 21 Jan: Matt Busby 1909–1994. Special Memorial Issue

2005, 26 Nov: The Best 1946–2005

2011, 3 Aug: Glory days and hard times – the men who led Manchester United

2011, 19 Dec: The man who saved United

SUNDAY SUN

1971, 24 Oct: 'We'll kill Best' Threat

THE SCOTSMAN

1967, 23 Oct: 4–3–3 pattern is not for Scotland

BELFAST TELEGRAPH

1964, 16 April: Ireland's new 'Hopefuls'

1967, 23 Oct: 'What went wrong?' ask Scots

1970, 22 April: This was Best the genius, not the prima donna

1971, 1 Nov: Best threats: United say no to Ireland / The fixture of Fear

1977, 15 July: 'Bud' McFarlane dies on holiday

2005, 28 Nov: George Best – 1946–2005. A celebration of a football genius

2009, 27 April: George Best drama: an intrusive film that failed to tell the whole story

2010, 20 Oct: Best's Cup medal sold for £156,000

IRELAND'S SATURDAY NIGHT

2005, 3 Dec: The Final Journey – special edition

THE TIMES

1966, 10 March: Inspired football from Manchester United

1970, 24 April: Best's muddy shot splatters the make-up

1970, 15 Oct: The house that George built

1971, 19 Aug: George Best sent off and more than 30 booked as referees clamp down

1972, 22 May: Decision final, says Best

1974: 25 April: George Best is cleared 'without character stain'

1980, 10 Oct: Team that Busby inherited, made and bought

1981, 29 Aug: Bested

1990, 28 Sept: BBC stops £150 Wogan fee to Best

2001, 25 June: Best has fingers crossed for stitch in time

2001, 26 June: TV review 'George Best's Body' (Channel 4)

2005, 7 Oct: Dark days when our national treasure was vilified as a rough diamond

2005, 22 Oct: Best of times, worst of times

2005, 25 Nov: The best, the bravest and the most beautiful footballer that has ever lived

2005, 25 Nov: Sad days of boorish behaviour and booze

2005, 26 Nov: Obituary – George Best

2005, Nov 2006: Tearful memories at Old Trafford shrine

2005, 29 Nov: My very own Best exclusive – from Mavis, aged 68

2005, 30 Nov: United prepare to say their goodbyes

2005, 2 Dec: Why many of us mourned the loss of George Best three decades ago

2005, 3 Dec: Province unites for its tribute to George Best, the Belfast Boy

2005, 3 Dec: Funeral echoes from down the sporting years

2005, 5 Dec: 24-hour guard on Best's grave

2009, 26 May: Man who found holy grail. On the 100th anniversary of the former United manager's birth, Patrick Barclay salutes the pioneer behind the club's European adventures

2011, 18 Jan: Man who created the monster has no regrets

SUNDAY TIMES

1965, 25 April: Mr B of Man U

1967, 22 Oct: Genius of Best beats Scotland

1968, 24 Oct: How Best became better

1970, 8 Feb: United made it look easy

1970, 22 March: The problems of a superstar

1971, 3 Oct: . . . cooled by Best

1972, 9 Jan: George Best: Time for the truth

1976, 10 Oct: Jilly Cooper talks to . . . George Best

1984, 9 Dec: The Best of times, the worst of times

1997, 26 Jan: Best's sporting life to hit screen

1999, 23 May: Best conjures up spirit of '68

2000, 12 March: Sober truths for Best

2005, 20 Nov: Ailing George Best goes back on life support

2005, 26 Nov: Obituaries: George Best

2005, 27 Nov: A nation of two halves

2005, 27 Nov: Thousands set to mourn Best in his home city

2005, 27 Nov: Fans united in applause for George Best

2005, 27 Nov: Pure genius with a taste for trouble

2007, 2 Dec (*Magazine*): Alcohol killed my mother and brother

2009, 12 July: When it comes to Orange mascots, Best is worst

2009, 4 Oct: Best & Worst – John Fitzpatrick

2010, 9 May: Fulham's Rollercoaster: Bestie gave a TV interview to pay the drinks bill

2011, 27 Nov: Best & Worst – Tony Dunne

GLASGOW HERALD

1967, 23 Oct: Best Upsets Scotland's European Title Hopes

THE STANDARD

1972, 25 May: Best forgotten

1984, 2 March: From bad to better to Best
1984, 3 Dec: Best sent to jail

STOCKPORT EXPRESS
2003, 26 Nov: George Best's house is for the young at heart

CHRONICLE & ECHO
1970, 9 Feb: What effect will this thrashing have on the cobblers?

EMPIRE NEWS and *SUNDAY CHRONICLE*
1957, 14 April: Matt Busby tells the secrets of his wonder team –
    Madrid's manager challenged my team to 'identity parade'
1957, 21 April: Matt Busby tells the secrets of his wonder team – I've
    got no 'under the counter' players!
1957, 5 May: Soccer mum was a Star

DAILY RECORD
2005, 26 Nov: George Best 1946–2005. High Life of a Legend

SUNDAY LIFE
2005, 4 Dec: George Best 1946–2005. PEACE – a legend laid to rest

REVEILLE
1969, 1–7 May: I go to United – and walk out
1969, 8–14 May: I keep my hair on
1969, 15–21 May: No marriage yet – but I'm building a dream home
1971, 5–11 June: Sir Matt Busby – Hard Man to follow
1971, 25 Sept: Worst side of Best

TELEGRAPH & ARGUS
1973, 19 April: Reaching for the sports stars

ESQUIRE
1991, Oct: The Afterlife – What the hell happened to George Best?

FOURFOURTWO
1995, Sept: The best of Best

MANCHESTER UNITED MAGAZINE
1993, March: Number one is George Best

HELLO
2002, May: My Home, By George Best
2006, 7 Feb: Alex Best – speaks of her final moments with George and their undying love
2006, 15 Aug: Angie Best and son Calum talk about moving on and why Britain is their home once more
2007, 10 July: Angie Best issues a wake-up call to women drinkers
2007, 16 Oct: Two years after his death George Best's sister Barbara tells how she is determined to keep his memory alive
2008, 11 March: Angie Best talks of past times and new goals
2009, 16 Nov: Son of football legend George Calum Best opens his heart about the painful reality of life with an alcoholic dad

RADIO TIMES
2009, 25 April–1 May: Why the footballing genius was doomed – George Best by Michael Parkinson

WOMAN'S OWN
1980, 3 May: Why the real George makes me cry
1985, 16 Feb: 'If he drinks again, I'll leave him'

WOMAN
1978, 3 June: All except one
1981, 6 June: George and Angie's crazy marriage
1982, 4 Sept: Angie Best: Why I had to kiss-and-tell on Georgie

READER'S DIGEST
2011, June: The letter I wish I'd sent my dad

BLITZ
1990, Nov: George and the dragon

THE ADVERTISER
1975, 13 Nov: George's night
1975, 4 Dec: One of the Best

SHEFFIELD TELEGRAPH
1962, 23 Oct: Salute Santos!

YORKSHIRE POST
1962, 23 Oct: Coutinho Hat-trick for Santos

BIRMINGHAM POST
1963, 16 Sept: Disorder without Law

EVENING NEWS & CHRONICLE
1963, 16 Sept: United miss Law spark

DUNSTABLE GAZETTE
1974, 9 Aug: Town's night of glory

MERCURY NEWS
Talent and Tragedy

IRISH DAILY STAR SUNDAY
Best – Portrait of a legend – A tribute

IRISH NEWS
1977, 16 July: Hugh 'Bud' McFarlane . . .

BELFAST NEWS LETTER
1968, 18 March: Old age? I want to die young
1973, 16 Oct: Best's fans invade pitch – but man who found him
   bows out

2005, 2 Dec: GEORGE BEST Life of a legend 1946– 2005
2005, 2 Dec: George Best Death of a legend

WESTERN MAIL
1964, 16 April: Ireland shock youngsters of Wales

7 DAYS
1972, 19 Jan: Stay on Strike George, you're only human!

MANCHESTER UNITED FOOTBALL CLUB:
UNITED REVIEW
1963, 18 May v Leyton Orient
1963, 14 Sept v West Brom
A celebration of the life and times of Sir Matt Busby 1909–1994
1993, March: The Magazine of Manchester United Football Club

SHOOT
1970, 7 Nov: How good is George Best?
1971, 25 Sept: 'I look forward to wearing the green of Ireland'
1971, 9 Oct: 'United can win the Championship'
1971, 16 Oct: 'It's "Businessman Best" outside football'
1971, 20 Nov: 'You can't beat British keepers'
1972, 26 Feb: 'Don't write off United. . .'
1972, 4 March: 'This is my life . . . in digs'
1972, 11 March: 'Games I'd like to forget. . .'
1972, 1 April: 'I haven't time to be bored. . .'
1972, 8 April: 'Few goals – but plenty of thrills!
1972, 1 July: 'My first-team debut was a secret'
1972, 15 July: 'I win first big honour'
1972, 22 July: 'Foreign fans dub me "El Beatle"'
1973, 15 Sept: Best to play again

GOAL

1971, 30 Jan: Is George Best too big for his golden boots?

INSIDE FOOTBALL!

1971, 9 Jan: Sir Matt – King of United

1971, 18 Sept: Don't waste this chance George!

1973, Oct: Don't be beastly to Best!

SOCCER STAR

1965, 28 May: East or West – George is Best

1966, 11 Feb: One George Best, five Derby players and a ref

1966, 27 May: Lucky Charm Jenni says George is best

1968, 2 May: Slender lead

1968, 14 June: Busby Babes – Just

SPORTS ILLUSTRATED

1972, 27 March: Bubbly, birds and the game of soccer

CITY WEEK

1970, 9 July: I don't even enjoy visiting Belfast now

WEEKEND MAGAZINE

1966: This is fan worship at its most intense

CHARLES BUCHAN'S FOOTBALL MONTHLY

1968, May: Matt Busby, Man and Manager

WHEN SATURDAY COMES

1994, March: Founding Father

JIMMY HILL'S FOOTBALL WEEKLY

1968, 1 Nov: I had no deliberate intention to hit out at anyone – it just happened in a split-second and I regretted it instantly

1969, 30 May: We were playing so brilliantly against AC Milan that we would have gone on to win if that 'goal' had counted

1969, July: The top non-League clubs should be given a chance
1969, 26 Sept: The George Best supplement
1970, 27 March: Best on Football

One-On-One web interview
Ezine article
The legendary George Best
Spiked-online
2005, 1 Dec: Can George Best save the peace process?

MANCHESTERCONFIDENTIAL.COM
2009, 30 April: Best: His mother's son

MAIL Online
The night Aston was Busby's best man as United conquered Europe
2004, 23 April: A view from both ends of George at his best
2006, 8 June: Footballers' wives of 1966 relive the memories
2010, 21 Oct: Best's legacy is sold for £250,000

BBC NEWS Online
2008, 18 Aug: Best's childhood home up for sale

Index

GB indicates George Best.